Design and Implementation of Compiler

Design and Implementation of Compiler

Ravendra Singh
B.E., Ph.D. (C.S. & Engg.)
Professor and Head
Department of Computer Science & Information Technology
MJP Rohilkhand University
Bareilly (UP)

Vivek Sharma
B.Tech.(C.S.), MBA (Operational Research)
Project Manager
HCL Technologies, Noida (UP)

Manish Varshney
M.Tech.
Department of Computer Science & Engineering
SRMS College of Engineering & Technology
Bareilly (UP)

PUBLISHING FOR ONE WORLD

NEW AGE INTERNATIONAL (P) LIMITED, PUBLISHERS

New Delhi • Bangalore • Chennai • Cochin • Guwahati • Hyderabad
Jalandhar • Kolkata • Lucknow • Mumbai • Ranchi
Visit us at **www.newagepublishers.com**

Published by New Age International (P) Ltd., Publishers
First Edition: 2009
Reprint: 2010

Branches:
- 37/10, 8th Cross (Near Hanuman Temple), Azad Nagar, Chamrajpet, **Bangalore**-560 018.
Tel.: (080) 26756823, Telefax: 26756820, E-mail: bangalore@newagepublishers.com
- 26, Damodaran Street, T. Nagar, **Chennai**-600 017. Tel.: (044) 24353401, Telefax: 24351463,
E-mail: chennai@newagepublishers.com
- CC-39/1016, Carrier Station Road, Ernakulam South, **Cochin**-682 016. Tel.: (0484) 2377004, Telefax: 4051303,
E-mail: cochin@newagepublishers.com
- Hemsen Complex, Mohd. Shah Road, Paltan Bazar, Near Starline Hotel, **Guwahati**-781 008.Tel.: (0361) 2513881,
Telefax: 2543669, E-mail: guwahati@newagepublishers.com
- No. 105, 1st Floor, Madhiray Kaveri Tower, 3-2-19, Azam Jahi Road, Nimboliadda, **Hyderabad**-500 027.
Tel.: (040) 24652456, Telefax: 24652457, E-mail:hyderabad@newagepublishers.com
- RDB Chambers (Formerly Lotus Cinema)106A, 1st Floor, S.N. Banerjee Road, **Kolkata**-700 014.
Tel.: (033) 22273773, Telefax: 22275247, E-mail:kolkata@newagepublishers.com
- 16-A, Jopling Road, **Lucknow**-226 001. Tel.: (0522) 2209578, 4045297, Telefax: 2204098,
E-mail: lucknow@newagepublishers.com
- 142C, Victor House, Ground Floor, N.M. Joshi Marg, Lower Parel, **Mumbai**-400 013. Tel.: (022) 24927869,
Telefax: 24915415, E-mail: mumbai@newagepublishers.com
- 22, Golden House, Daryaganj, **New Delhi**-110 002. Tel.: (011) 23262370, 23262368, Telefax: 43551305,
E-mail: sales@newagepublishers.com

ISBN : 978-81-224-2398-3

Rs. 295.00

C-10-02-4325

Printed in India at Ramprintograph, Delhi.
Typeset at Inhouse.

PUBLISHING FOR ONE WORLD
NEW AGE INTERNATIONAL (P) LIMITED, PUBLISHERS
4835/24, Ansari Road, Daryaganj, New Delhi-110002
Visit us at www.newagepublishers.com

Dedicated to

Dear Shantanu

PREFACE

This book attempts to provide a unified overview of the broad field of compiler and their practical implementation. The organization of book reflects an attempt to break this massive subject into comprehensible parts and to build piece by piece, a survey of the state of art. This book emphasizes basic principles and topics of fundamental importance concerning the design issues and architecture of this field and provides detailed discussion leading edge topics.

Although the scope of this book is broad, there are a number of basic principles that appear repeatedly as themes and that unify this field. This book addresses a full spectrum of compiler design. The emphasis is on solving the problems universally encountered in designing a compiler regardless of the source language or target machine. The book examines alternative approaches to meeting specific design requirements of compiler. The concepts of designing and step-by-step practical implementation of compiler in 'C' language are main focus of the book.

The book is intended for students who have completed a programming based two-semester introductory computer sequence in which they have written programs that implemented basic algorithms manipulate discrete structures and apply basic data structures and have studied theory of computation also. An important feature of the book is the collection of problems and exercises. Across all the chapters, the book includes over 200 problems, almost all of the developed and class-tested in homework and exams as part of our teaching of the course. We view the problems as a crucial component of the book, and they are structured in keeping with our overall approach to the material. Basically, the book is divided according to different phases of compilers. Each chapter includes problems and suggestions for further reading. The chapters of the book are sufficiently modular to provide a great deal of flexibility in the design of course. The first and second chapters give a brief introduction of the language and compiler is important to understand the rest of the book. The approach used in different phases of compiler covers the various aspects of designing a language translator in depth.

To facilitate easy understanding, the text book and problems have been put in simpler form. The concepts are supported by programming exercise in 'C' language. This book certainly helps the readers to understand the subject in better way. For many instructors, an important component of compiler course is a project or set of projects by which student gets hands-on experience to reinforce concepts from the text. This book provides an unparalleled degree of support for including a projects component in the course. The two projects on compiler in Chapter 12 will be helpful to students to deep understanding the subject.

The book is intended for both academic and professional audience. For the professional interested in this field, the book serves as a basic reference volume and suitable for self study. The book is primarily designed for use in a first undergraduate course on the compiler; it can also be used as the basis for an introductory graduate course. This book covers the syllabus of U.P. Technical University, Lucknow and other Universities of India. As a textbook it can be used for a one semester course.

It is said, "To err in human, to forgive divine." In this light I wish that the short comings of the book will be forgiven. At the same time the authors are open to any kind of constructive criticism and suggestions for further improvement. Intelligent suggestions are welcome and we will try our best to incorporate such valuable suggestions in the subsequent edition of this book.

AUTHORS

ACKNOWLEDGEMENTS

Once again it is pleasure to acknowledge our gratitude to the many persons involved, directly, or indirectly, in production of this book. First of all, we would like to thank almighty God who gave us the inspiration to take up this task. Prof. S.K. Bajpai of Institute of Engineering and Technology Lucknow and Shantanu student at S.R.M.S., CET Bareilly were key collaborator in the early conceptualization of this text. For the past several years, the development of the book has benefited greatly from the feedback and advice of the colleagues of various institutes who have used prepublication drafts for teaching. The course staffs we've had in teaching the subject have been tremendously helpful in the formulation of this material. We thank our undergraduate and graduate teaching assistants of various institutes who have provided valuable in-sights, suggestions, and comments on the text. We also thank all the students in these classes who have provided comments and feedback on early drafts of the book over the years. Our special thanks to **Shantanu** for producing supplementary material associated with the book, which promises to greatly extend its utility to future instructors. We wish to express our deep sense of gratitude to Mrs. Veena Mathur, Executive Chairperson, Prof. Manish Sharma, Dr. Neeraj Saxena of RBMI Group of Institutions, and Mr. Devmurtee, Chairman, Prof. Prabhakar Gupta, Saket Aggrawal of SRMS CET, Bareilly, Mr. Zuber Khan, Mr. Ajai Indian of IIMS, Bareilly and Dr. S.P. Tripathi, Dr. M H. Khan of IET, Lucknow for their kind co-operation and motivation for writing this book. We would particularly like to thank our friends Dr. Verma S. at Indian Institute of Information Technology, Allahabad and Prof. Anupam Shrivastav at IFTM, Moradabad for numerous illuminating conversations and much stimulating correspondence.

We are grateful to M/s New Age International (P) Limited, Publishers and the staff of editorial department for their encouragement and support throughout this project.

Finally, we thank our parents and families— Dr. Deepali Budhoria, Mrs. Nishi Sharma, Mrs. Pragati Varshney, and kids Ritunjay, Pragunjay and sweet Keya. We appreciate their support, patience and many other contributions more than we can express in any acknowledgements here.

AUTHORS

CONTENTS

CHAPTER 1

INTRODUCTION TO LANGUAGE

CHAPTER HIGHLIGHTS

Avram Noam Chomsky, Ph.D. (born December 7, 1928) is the Institute Professor Emeritus of linguistics at the Massachusetts Institute of Technology. Chomsky is credited with the creation of the theory of generative grammar, considered to be one of the most significant contributions to the field of theoretical linguistics made in the 20th century. He also helped spark the cognitive revolution in psychology through his review of B.F. Skinner's *Verbal Behaviour*, in which he challenged the behaviourist approach to the study of mind and language dominant in the 1950s. His naturalistic approach to the study of language has also affected the philosophy of language and mind (see Harman, Fodor). He is also credited with the establishment of the Chomsky–Schützenberger hierarchy, a classification of formal languages in terms of their generative power.

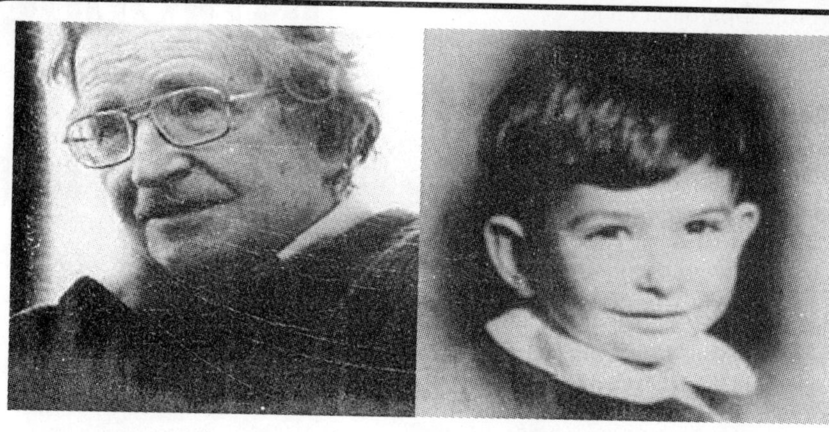

Noam Chomsky *Chomsky as a child*

Born: December 7, 1928 East Oak Lane, Philadelphia, Pennsylvania

Occupation: Linguist

Chomsky was born in the East Oak Lane neighbourhood of Philadelphia, Pennsylvania, the son of Hebrew scholar and IWW member William Chomsky, who was from a town in Ukraine. His mother, Elsie Chomsky (born Simonofsky), came from what is now Belarus, but unlike her husband she grew up in the United States and spoke "ordinary New York English". Their first language was Yiddish, but Chomsky says it was "taboo" in his family to speak it. He describes his family as living in a sort of "Jewish ghetto", split into a "Yiddish side" and "Hebrew side", with his family aligning with the latter and bringing him up "immersed in Hebrew culture and literature". Chomsky also describes tensions he personally experienced with Irish Catholics and anti-Semitism in the mid-1930s, stating, "I don't like to say it but I grew up with a kind of visceral fear of Catholics. I knew it was irrational and got over it but it was just the street experience."

1.1 CHOMSKY HIERARCHY

Chomsky is famous for investigating various kinds of formal languages and whether or not they might be capable of capturing key properties of human language. His Chomsky hierarchy partitions formal grammars into classes, or groups, with increasing expressive power, i.e., each successive class can generate a broader set of formal languages than the one before. Interestingly, Chomsky argues that modelling some aspects of human language requires a more complex formal grammar (as measured by the Chomsky hierarchy) than modelling others. For example, while a regular language is powerful enough to model English morphology, it is not powerful enough to model English syntax. In addition to being relevant in linguistics, the Chomsky hierarchy has also become important in computer science (especially in compiler construction and automata theory).

Table 1.1: Automata theory: Formal languages and formal grammars

Chomsky hierarchy	Grammars	Languages	Minimal automaton
Type 0	Unrestricted	Recursively enumerable	Turing machine
n/a	(no common name)	Recursive	Decider
Type 1	Context-sensitive	Context-sensitive	Linear-bounded
Type 2	Context-free	Context-free	Pushdown
Type 3	Regular	Regular	Finite

Each category of languages or grammar is a proper subset of the category directly above it.

1.2 DEFINITION OF GRAMMAR

A phase structure grammar (or simply grammar) is (V_n, Σ, P, S)

- where V_n is finite nonempty set whose elements are called variables.
- **Σ** is finite nonempty set whose elements are called terminals.
- $V_n \cap \Sigma = \phi$
- S is specific variable (i.e., an element of V_n) called the start symbol.
- P is finite nonempty set whose elements are $\alpha \to \beta$.

1.2.1 Some Other Definitions

String : A string over some alphabet is a finite sequence of symbol and word drawn from that alphabet. Length of string denoted by |S| & ε if empty string.

Language : Language denotes any set of string over some fixed alphabet. Abstract language like ϕ , ε are also part of language. The language may contain a finite or an infinite number of strings. Let L and M be two languages where L = {dog, ba, na} and M = {house, ba} then following operation will performed on language.

- Union: $L \cup M$ = {dog, ba, na, house}
- Concatenation: LM = {doghouse, dogba, bahouse, baba, nahouse, naba}
- Expontentiation: $L^2 = LL$
- By definition: $L^0 = \{\epsilon\}$ and $L^1 = L$

The kleene closure of language L, denoted by L^*, is "zero or more concatenation of" L.

$$L^* = L^0 \cup L^1 \cup L^2 \cup L^3 \ldots \cup L^n \ldots$$

For example, If L = {a, b}, then

$$L^* = \{\in, a, b, aa, ab, ab, ba, bb, aaa, aba, baa, \ldots\}$$

The positive closure of Language L, denoted by L^+, is "one or more concatenation of" L.

$$L^+ = L^1 \cup L^2 \cup L^3 \ldots \cup L^n \ldots$$

For example, If L = {a, b}, then

$$L^+ = \{a, b, aa, ba, bb, aaa, aba, \ldots\}$$

Prefix: A string obtained by removing zero or more trailing symbol of string. Example: RA is prefix of RAM.

Suffix : A string obtained by removing zero or more leading symbol of string. Example: AM is suffix of RAM.

Substring: A string obtained by removing prefix and suffix of a string. Example : A is substring of RAM.

Proper Prefix, Suffix, Substring : Any nonempty string 'X' i.e., proper prefix , suffix, substring of string 'S' if X is not equal to S.

Subsequence: Any string formed by deleting zero or more not important contiguous symbol from string.

In the string of length 'n'

Prefix	=	n
Suffix	=	n
Substring	=	$^nC_r(1 <= r <= n)$
Proper Prefix	=	n–1
Subsequence	=	$^nC_r(1 <= r <= n)$

1.3 REGULAR LANGUAGES

letter (letter|digit)*

Above notation show regular expression. Each regular expression '**r**' denotes a language '**L(r)**'. A language denoted by a regular expression is said to be a '**Regular-Set**'. Regular expressions are useful for representing certain sets of string in an algebraic fashion. The regular expression over alphabet specifies a language according to the following rules:

1. ε is a regular expression that denotes {ε}, that is, the set containing the empty string.
2. If a is a symbol in alphabet, then a is a regular expression that denotes {a}, that is, the set containing the string 'a'.
3. Suppose 'r' and 's' are regular expression denoting the languages L(r) and L(s). Then
   (a) (r)|(s) is a regular expression denoting L(r) ∪ L(s).
   (b) (r)(s) is a regular expression denoting L(r) L(s).
   (c) (r)* is a regular expression denoting (L(r))*.
   (d) (r) is a regular expression denoting L(r), that is, extra pairs of parentheses may be used around regular expressions.

Recursive definition of regular expression over Σ as follow:

4. Any terminal symbol ^, ϕ are regular expression.
5. The union of two regular expressions **R1** and **R2**, written as **R1 + R2**, is also a regular expression.
6. The concatenation of two regular expressions **R1** and **R2**, written as **R1R2**, is also a regular expression.
7. The iteration or closure of a regular expression **R**, written as **R***, is also a regular expression.
8. If **R** is regular expressions then **(R)** is also a regular expression.

1.3.1 Algebraic Operation on RE

Suppose r, s and t are regular expression denoting the languages L(r) L(s) and L(t). Then

(a) $r \mid s$ is a regular expression denoting $L(r) \cup L(s)$. Here | is commutative.

(b) $r \mid (s \mid t) = (r \mid s) \mid t$. Here | is associative.

(c) $(rs)\,t = r\,(st)$. Here concatenation is associative.

(d) $r\,(s \mid t) = rs \mid rt$. Here concatenation is distributive.

(e) $\varepsilon r = r = r\varepsilon$. Here ε is identity element.

(f) $r^* = (r \mid \varepsilon)^*$.

(g) $r^{**} = r^*$. Here * is idempotent element.

Unnecessary parenthesis can be avoided in regular expressions using the following conventions:

- The unary operator * (kleene closure) has the highest precedence and is left associative.
- Concatenation has a second highest precedence and is left associative.
- Union has lowest precedence and is left associative.

1.3.2 Identities for RE

1. $\phi + R = R$
2. $\phi R = R\phi = \phi\lambda$
3. $\lambda R = R\lambda = R$
4. $\lambda^* = \lambda$ OR $\phi^* = \lambda$
5. $R + R = R$
6. $R^*R^* = R^*$
7. $RR^* = R^*R$
8. $(R^*)^* = R^*$
9. $\lambda + RR^* = R^* = \lambda + R^*R$
10. $(PQ)^*P = P(QP)^*$
11. $(P+Q)^* = (P^*Q^*)^* = (P^* + Q^*)^*$
12. $(P+Q)R = PR + QR$

1.3.3 Algorithm 1.1 (Anderson Theorem)

Let P and Q be two regular expression over Σ. If P does not contain λ, then R = Q + RP has a unique solution given by

$$R = QP^*$$

We have

$R = Q + RP$ and now we put the proven value of R to R.H.S. of this, apply rule no. 9 to this and get

$$R = Q + (QP)^*P$$
$$= Q(\lambda + P^*P)$$
$$= QP^*$$

Hence we prove that $R = QP^*$ is the solution of given equation. Now, to prove the uniqueness, we replace R by R.H.S. of given equation and get,

$$Q + RP = Q + (Q + RP)P$$
$$= Q + QP + RPP$$
$$= Q + QP + QP2 + \ldots\ldots\ldots + QPi + RPi+1$$
$$= Q(\lambda + P + P2 + P3 + \ldots\ldots\ldots\ldots + Pi) + RPi+1$$

So, it will be equal to given equation as : $R = Q(\lambda + P + P2 + P3 + \ldots\ldots\ldots\ldots + Pi) + RPi + 1 \quad \text{for } i >= 0$

Now, suppose proven statement is true then R must satisfy above equation. Let 'w' be a string of length i in the set R then w belongs to above equation. As P does not contain λ, RPi+1 has no string of length less then i +1 and so 'w' is not in the set of RPi+1.This mean 'w' belong to set $Q(\lambda + P + P2 + P3 + \ldots\ldots\ldots\ldots + Pi)$ and hence $R = QP^*$.

1.4 REGULAR DEFINITIONS

A regular definition gives names to certain regular expressions and uses those names in other regular expressions.

Example 1.1: Here is a regular definition for the set of Pascal identifiers that is define as the set of strings of letter and digits beginning with a letters.

letter → A | B | . . . | Z | a | b | . . . | z

digit → 0 | 1 | 2 | . . . | 9

id → letter (letter | digit)*

The regular expression id is the pattern for the Pascal identifier token and defines **letter** and **digit**.

Where **letter** is a regular expression for the set of all upper-case and lower-case letters in the alphabet and **digit** is the regular for the set of all decimal digits.

Example 1.2: The pattern for the Pascal unsigned number can be specified as follows:

digit → 0 | 1 | 2 | . . . | 9

digit → digit digit*

Optimal-fraction $\rightarrow$. digits | ε

Optimal-exponent $\rightarrow$ (E (+ | – | ε) digits) | ε

num $\rightarrow$ digits optimal-fraction optimal-exponent:

This regular definition says that:

- An optimal-fraction is either a decimal point followed by one or more digits or it is missing (i.e., an empty string).
- An optimal-exponent is either an empty string or it is the letter E followed by an ' optimal + or – sign, followed by one or more digits.

1.4.1 Notational Shorthand

- The unary postfix operator + means "one of more instances of" $(r)^+ = rr^*$
- The unary postfix operator? means "zero or one instance of" $r? = (r \mid \varepsilon)$

Using this shorthand notation, Pascal unsigned number token can be written as:

digit $\rightarrow$ 0 | 1 | 2 | . . . | 9

digits $\rightarrow$ $digit^+$

optimal-fraction $\rightarrow$ (. digits)?

optimal-exponent $\rightarrow$ (E (+ | –)?digits)?

num $\rightarrow$ digits optimal-fraction optimal-exponent

1.4.2 Closure Properties for Regular Language

"If certain languages are regular and language L is formed than by certain operations then L is also regular." This is often called closure property of regular language, since they show that the class of regular language is closed under the operation mentioned. Here is the summary of the principle closure properties of regular language.

1. The union of two regular languages is regular.
2. The intersection of two regular languages is regular.
3. The complement of regular languages is regular.
4. The difference of regular languages is regular.
5. The reversal of regular languages is regular.
6. The closure of regular languages is regular.
7. The concatenation of regular languages is regular.
8. The homomorphism (substitution of string for symbols) of regular languages is regular.
9. The inverse homomorphism of two regular languages is regular.

1.5 AUTOMATA

1.5.1 Definition of an Automata

An automaton (plural: *automata*) is a **self-operating machine**. The word is sometimes used to describe a robot, more specifically an autonomous robot. ***Automaton*, from the Greek αΰτόματος, *automatos*, "acting of one's own will, self-moving," is more often used to describe non-electronic moving machines, especially those that have been made to resemble human or animal actions.**

"An automaton is defined as a system where energy, materials, and information are transformed, transmitted and used for performing some function without direct participation of man." *EXAMPLES* are automatic tools, automatic packing machines and automatic photo printing machine.

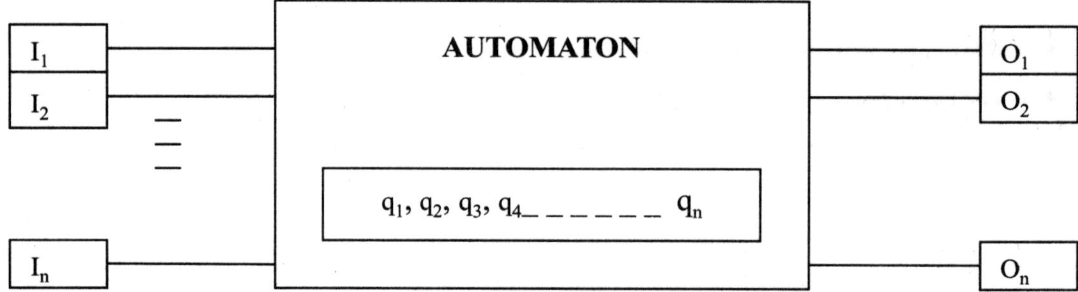

Figure 1.1

1.5.2 Characteristics of an Automata

(i) **INPUT:** At each of the discrete instants of time input values are I_1, I_2, ... are applied to input side of model shown.

(ii) **OUTPUT:** O_1, O_2, ... are the output of model.

(iii) **STATES:** At any time automata is any one of state q_1, q_2 ,q_3, q_4 ....

(iv) **TRANSITION RELATION:** The next state of automata is determined by present state of automata.

(v) **OUTPUT RELATION:** Output of automata is depend only on state or both input and state.

1.5.3 Finite Automata

A recognizer for a language is a program that takes a string 'x' as an input and answers "yes" if 'x' is a sentence of the language and "no" otherwise. A finite state machine (FSM) or finite state automaton (plural: *automata*) is a model of behaviour composed of a finite number of states, transitions between those states, and actions. A state stores information about the past. A transition indicates a state change and is described by a condition that would need to be fulfilled to enable the transition. An action is a description of an activity that is to be performed at a given moment. There are several action types:

- Entry action execute the action *when entering* the state.
- Exit action execute the action *when exiting* the state.

- Input actions execute the action dependent on present state and input conditions.
- Transition action execute the action when performing a certain transition.

The concept of the FSM is at the center of theory of computing. FSM can be represented using a state diagram (or state transition diagram).

"One can compile any regular expression into a recognizer by constructing a generalized transition diagram called a finite automation."

A further distinction is between **deterministic** (DFA) and **non-deterministic** (NDFA, GNFA) automata. In deterministic automata, for each state there is exactly one transition for each possible input. In non-deterministic automata, there can be none or more than one transition from a given state for a given possible input. This distinction is relevant in practice, but not in theory, as there exists an algorithm which can transform any NDFA into an equivalent DFA, although this transformation typically significantly increases the complexity of the automaton.

1.5.4 Mathematical Model

1.5.3.1 Non-deterministic Finite Automata (NFA)

A non-deterministic finite automation is a mathematical model consists of 5 **quintuple** (S, Σ, δ, s_0, F) as

1. A set of states S;
2. A set of input symbol, Σ, called the input symbols alphabet.
3. A transition function, δ, move that maps state-symbol pairs to sets of states as
$$S \times (\Sigma \cup \{\varepsilon\}) \rightarrow 2S$$
4. A state s_0, called the initial or the start state. The start state is usually shown drawn with an arrow "pointing at it from nowhere."
5. A set of states F called the accepting or final state. An **accept state** (sometimes referred to as an **accepting state**) is a state at which the machine has successfully performed its procedure. It is usually represented by a double circle.

An NFA can be described by a **transition graph** (labeled graph) where the nodes are states and the edges shows the transition function. The labeled on each edge is either a symbol in the set of alphabet, Σ, or denoting empty string ε.

Example 1.3: The following example explains a NFA M, with a binary alphabet, which determines if the input contains an even number of 0s or an even number of 1s.

$M = (S, \Sigma, \delta, s_0, F)$

- where $\Sigma = \{0, 1\}$
- $S = \{S_0, S_1, S_2, S_3, S_4\}$
- $s_0 = \{S_0\}$
- $F = \{S_1, S_3\}$

The transition function δ can be defined by this state transition table:

	0	1	ε
S_0	{}	{}	$\{S_1\}$
S_1	$\{S_2\}$	$\{S_1\}$	{}
S_2	$\{S_1\}$	$\{S_2\}$	{}
S_3	$\{S_3\}$	$\{S_4\}$	{}
S_4	$\{S_4\}$	$\{S_3\}$	{}

The state diagram for *M* is the transition is

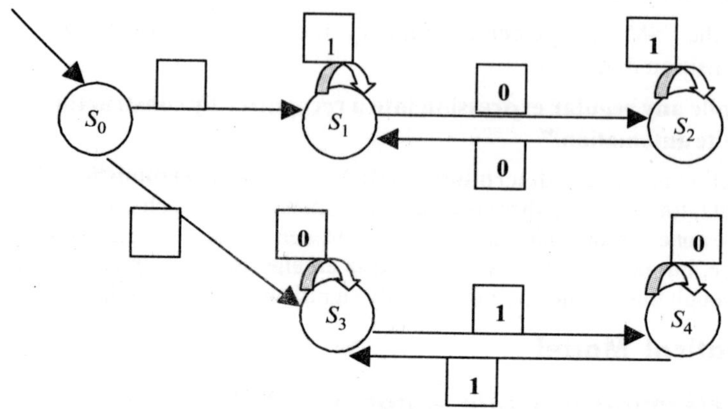

The advantage of transition table is that it provides fast access to the transitions of states and the disadvantage is that it can take up a lot of source.

1.5.3.2 Deterministic Finite Automata (DFA)

A deterministic finite automation is a special case of a non-deterministic finite automation (NFA) in which

(a) no state has an ε-transition.

(b) for each state 's' and input symbol 'a', there is at most one edge labeled a leaving 's'.

A DFA has at most one transition from each state on any input. It means that each entry on any input. It means that each entry in the transition table is a single state (as oppose to set of states in NFA).Because of single transition attached to each state; it is vary to determine whether a DFA accepts a given input string. In general,

A deterministic finite automation is a mathematical model consists of 5 tuples (S, Σ, δ, s_0, F) as

1. A set of states S;
2. A set of input symbol, 'Σ', called the input symbols alphabet.
3. A transition function, δ, move that maps state-symbol pairs to sets of states as

$$S \times \Sigma \rightarrow 2S$$

4. A state, s_0, called the initial or the start state.
5. A set of states F called the accepting or final state.

Example 1.4

$M = (S, \Sigma, \delta, s_0, F)$

where $S = \{S_1, S_2\}$,

$\Sigma = \{0, 1\}$,

$s_0 = S_1$,

$F = \{S_1\}$, and

The transition function δ is defined by the following state transition table:

	0	1
S_1	S_2	S_1
S_2	S_1	S_2

The state diagram for *M* isThe transition is

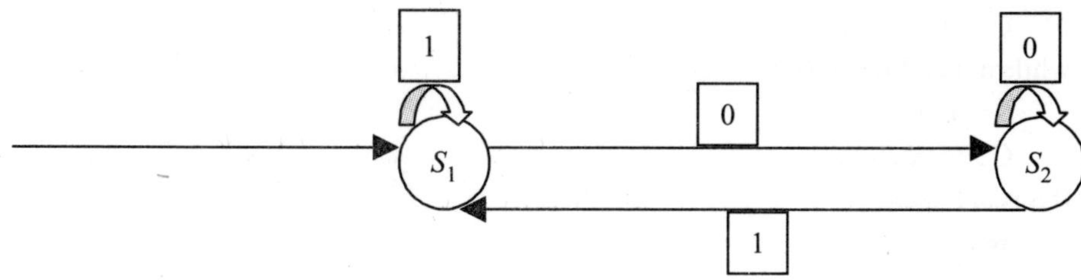

Language of DFA

It have been explained informally that DFA defines a language: The set of all strings that result in a sequence of state from start state to an accepting state. Now we can define the language of a DFA 'M'. This language is denoted by L(M) and defined by L(M) = {w: $\delta(q_0, w)$ is in F}.i.e. the language of M is the set of strings (w) that take the start q_0 to one of the accepting states.

If L is L(M) for some deterministic finite automata, then we say L is a regular language.

Advantage of DFA

DFAs are one of the most practical models of computation, since there is a trivial linear time, constant-space, online algorithm to simulate a DFA on a stream of input. Given two DFAs there are efficient algorithms to find a DFA recognizing the union, intersection, and complements of the languages they recognize. There are also efficient algorithms to determine whether a DFA accepts any strings, whether a DFA accepts all strings, whether two DFAs recognize the same language, and to find the DFA with a minimum number of states for a particular regular language.

Disadvantage of DFA

DFAs are of strictly limited power in the languages they can recognize many simple languages, including any problem that requires more than constant space to solve, cannot be recognized by a DFA. The classical example of a simply described language that no DFA can recognize is the language consisting of strings of the form $a^n b^n$ — some finite number of a's, followed by an equal number of b's. It can be shown that no DFA can have enough states to recognize such a language.

1.5.3.3 Algorithm 1.2 (Simulating a DFA)

INPUT:

- string x
- a DFA with start state, S_0 . . .
- a set of accepting state's F.

OUTPUT:

- The answer 'yes' if D accepts x; 'no' otherwise.

FUNCTION:

- The function move (S, C) gives a new state from state s on input character C.
- The function 'nextchar' returns the next character in the string.

```
Initialization:
    S := S0
    C := nextchar;
while not end-of-file do
    S := move (S, C)
    C := nextchar;
If S is in F then
    return "yes"
else
   return "no".
```

Following figure shows a DFA that recognizes the language (a|b)*abb:

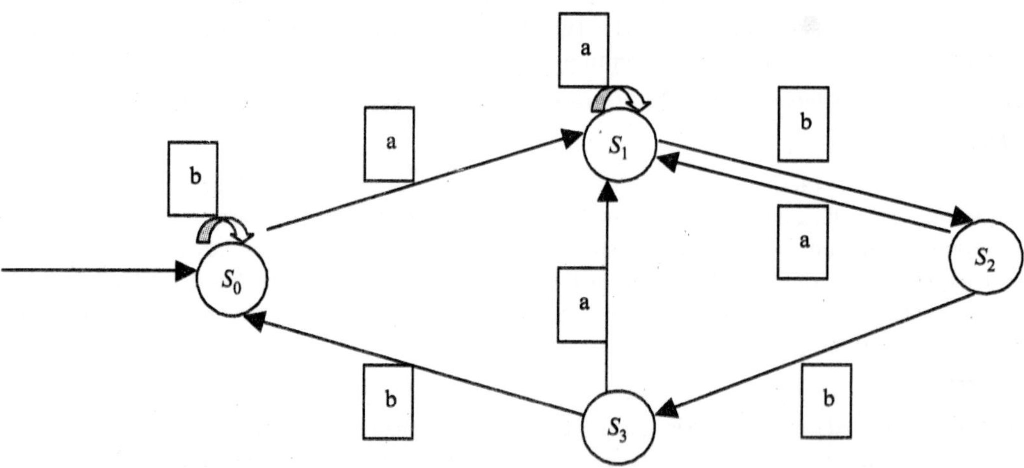

The transition table is

State	a	b
0	1	0
1	1	2
2	1	3
3	1	0

1.5.3.4 Conversion of an NFA into a DFA

It is hard for a computer program to simulate an NFA because the transition function is multivalued. Fortunately, an algorithm, called the **subset construction** will convert an NFA for any language into a DFA that recognizes the same languages. Note that this algorithm is closely related to an algorithm for constructing LR parser.

- In the transition table of an NFA, entry is a set of states.
- In the transition table of a DFA, each entry is a single state.

The general idea behind the NFA-to-DFA construction is that the each DFA state corresponds to a set of NFA states.

For example, let T be the set of all states that an NFA could reach after reading input: $a_1, a_2, \ldots, a_n$ — then the state that the DFA reaches after reading $a_1, a_2, \ldots, a_n$ corresponds to set T.

Theoretically, the number of states of the DFA can be exponential in the number of states of the NFA, i.e., **$\theta(2^n)$,** but in practice this worst case rarely occurs.

1.5.3.5 Algorithm 1.3 (Subset construction)

INPUT: An NFA N

OUTPUT: A DFA D is accepting the same language.

METHOD: Construct a transition table DTrans. Each DFA state is a set of NFA states. DTran simulates in parallel all possible moves N can make on a given string.

Operations to keep track of sets of NFA states:

ε-Closure (S): Set of states reachable from state S via epsilon.

ε-Closure (T): Set of states reachable from any state in set T via epsilon.

move (T, a): Set of states to which there is an NFA transition from states in T on a symbol a.

Algorithm:

```
Initially, ε-Closure (S0) in DTrans
While unmarked state T in DTrans
mark T
for each input symbol 'a'
   do u = ε-Closure (T, a)
      If u is not in DTrans
         then add u to DTrans
      DTrans [T, a] = u
```

Following algorithm shows a computation of ε-Closure function:

```
Push all states in T onto stack.
initialize ε-Closure (T) to T
while stack is not empty
   do pop top element 't'
      for each state u with ε-edge
            t to u
         do If u is not in ε-Closure(T)
```

do add u ε-Closure (T)

push u onto stack

Example 1.5: We apply above algo to construct a DFA that accept (a | b)* abb

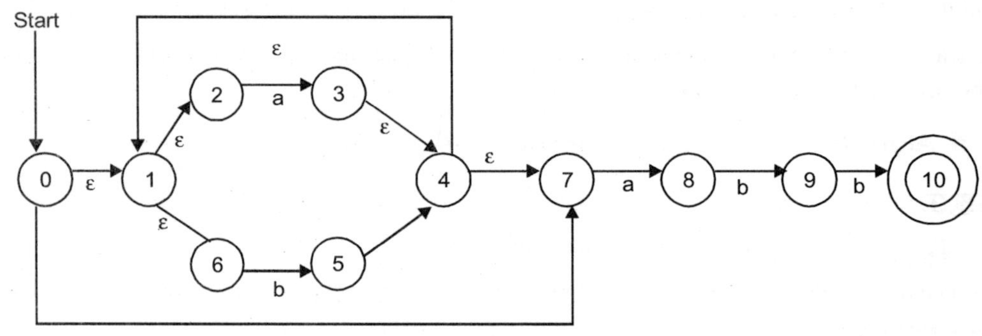

STEP 1: ε-Closure (S_0) = A = {0, 1, 2, 4, 7 }

STEP 2: move (A, a) = B = { set of state of NFA have transition on 'a' from A} = { 0, 1, 2, 4, 7}

STEP 3: ε-Closure (move (B, a)) = ε-Closure (3, 8) = C = { 1, 2, 3, 4, 6, 7, 8 } = DTran[A, a] = C

STEP 4: similarly ε-Closure (move (B, b)) = ε-Closure (5) = D = {1, 2, 4, 5, 6, 7} = DTran[A, b] = D

In next steps we continue this process with state C and D, we reach the point where all sets are of the DFA's state are marked and we have power (2,11) sets but five different sets are as:

A = {0, 1, 2, 4, 7}

B = {1, 2, 3, 4, 6, 7, 8}

C = {1, 2, 4, 5, 6, 7}

D = {1, 2, 4, 5, 6, 7, 9}

E = {1, 2, 4, 5, 6, 7, 10}

Now 'A' is starting state and 'E' is accepting state and DTran is as:

State	Input Symbol 'a'	Input Symbol 'b'
A	B	C
B	B	D
C	B	C
D	B	E
E	B	C

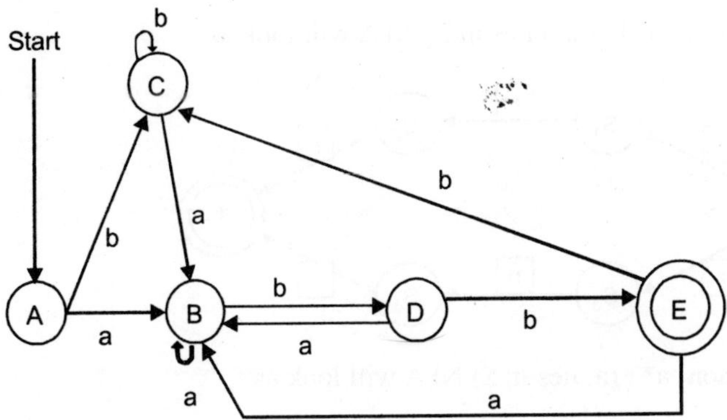

1.5.3.6 Conversion of a Regular Expression into a NFA

Thompson's construction is an NFA from a regular expression. The Thompson's construction is guided by the syntax of the regular expression with cases following the cases in the definition of regular expression. A basic regular expression is of form 'a' , 'ε', 'ϕ' where 'a' represent a match of a single character from the alphabet, 'ε' represent a match of the empty string and 'ϕ' represent a match of no string at all.

1.5.3.7 Algorithm 1.4 (Thompson's construction)

INPUT: A regular expression 'r' over an alphabet Σ_{10}.

OUTPUT: An NDFA N is accepting the regular expression.

METHOD: Firstly, we construct each NFA state and then combine them to produce a NFA.

Algorithm: This algo consist two steps in which first for construction of NFA state and remaining one for combination of these states.

STEP 1

(i) for every ε transition NFA will look as :

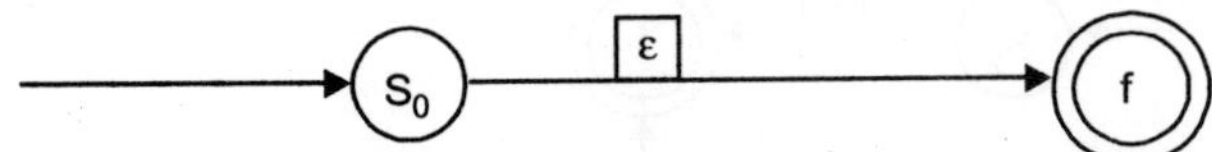

(ii) for every transition 'a' (a lies in Σ) NFA will look as :

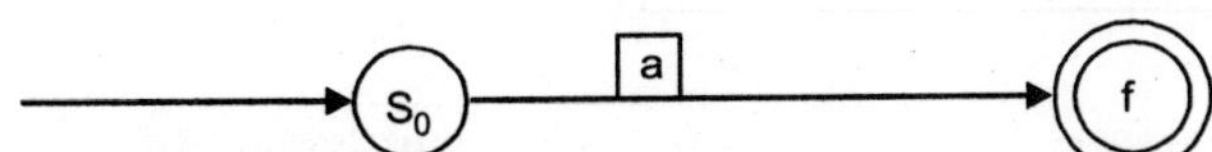

(iii) for every transition 'ab' (a, b lies in Σ) NFA will look as :

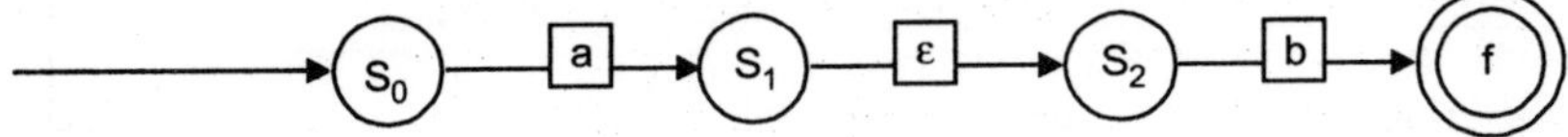

(iv) for every transition 'a | b' (a, b lies in Σ) NFA will look as :

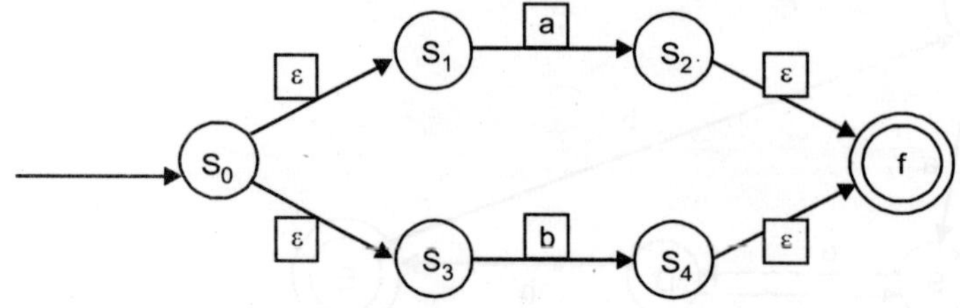

(v) for every transition 'a*' (a, lies in Σ) NFA will look as :

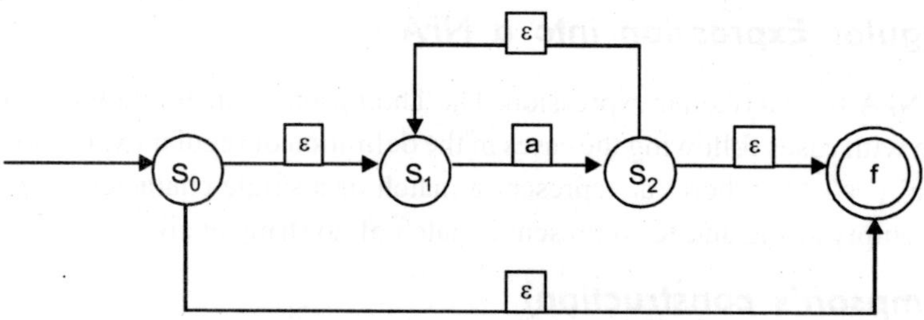

STEP 2: Now we combine these states as per problem

Following example illustrates the method by constructing a NDFA from the Regular Expression.

Example 1.6: We apply above algorithm to construct regular expression (a) * (a | b) aba

STEP 1: for a* (from rule 1 (V))

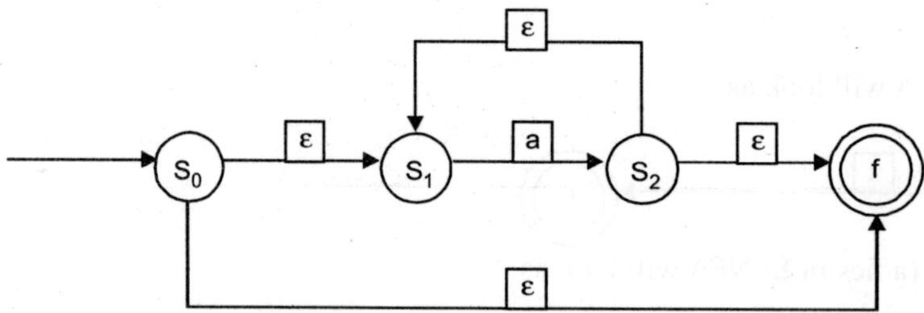

STEP 2: for a | b (from rule 1 (v)

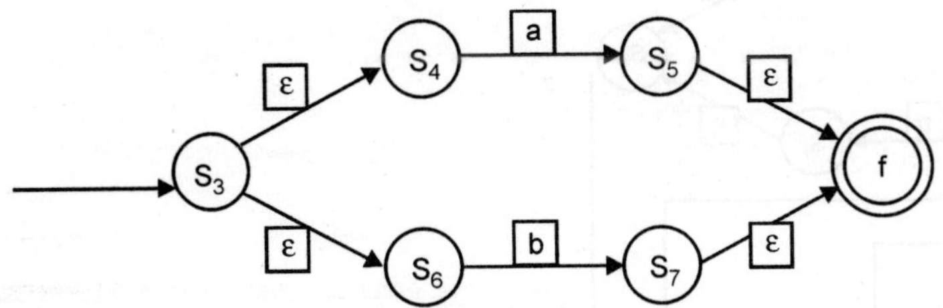

STEP 3: for ab (from rule 1 (III))

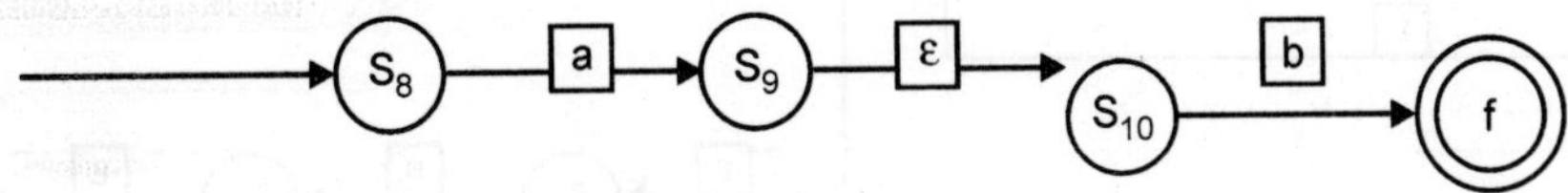

STEP 4: for abb (from rule 1 (III))

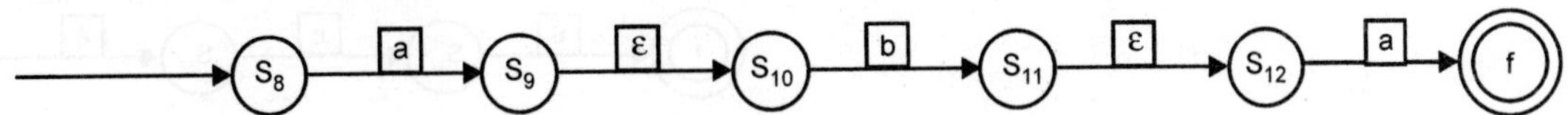

STEP 5: for (a | b) abb (from rule 1 (III))

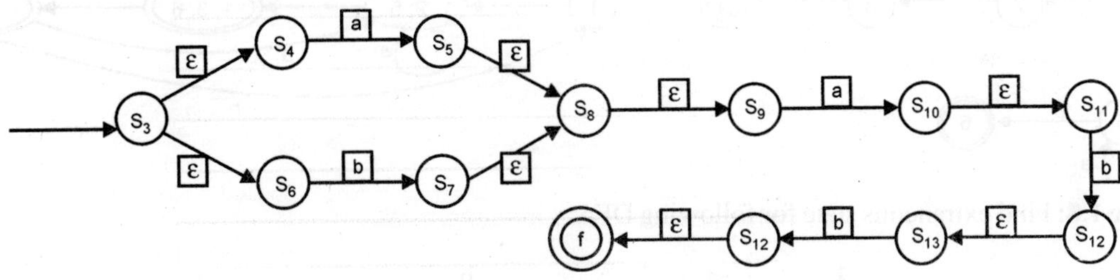

STEP 6: for (a) * (a | b) abb (from rule 1 (III))

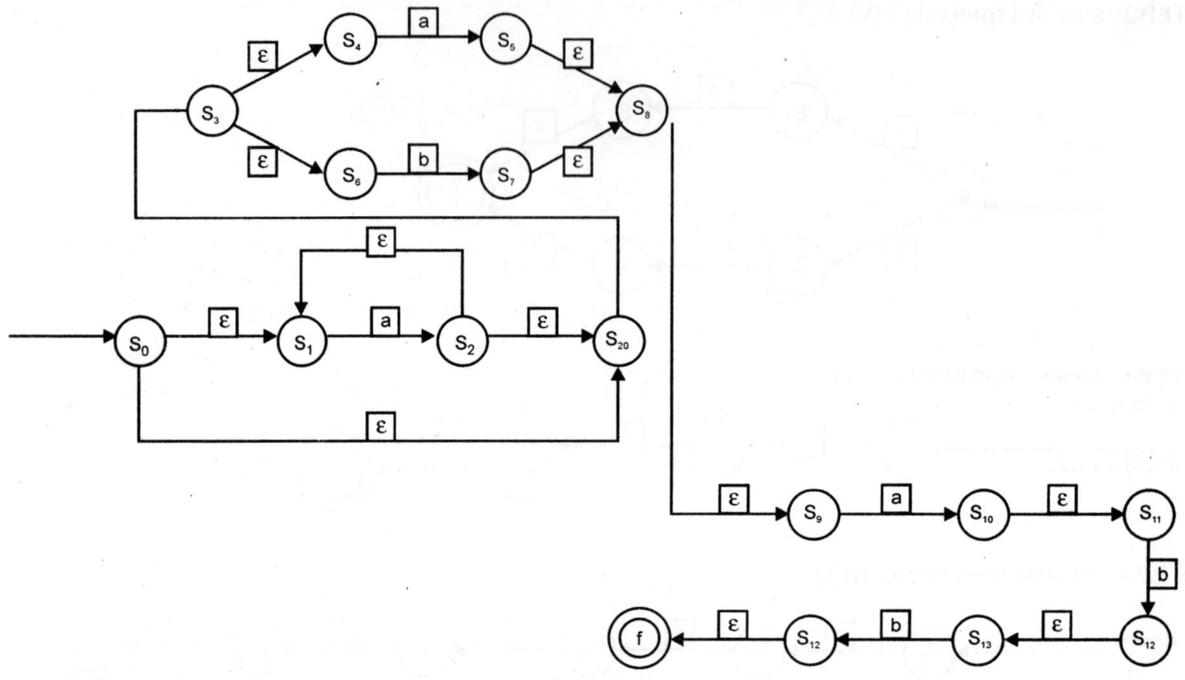

Example 1.7: Construct a NFA and a DFA for $(a|b)^*(abb \mid a^+b)$

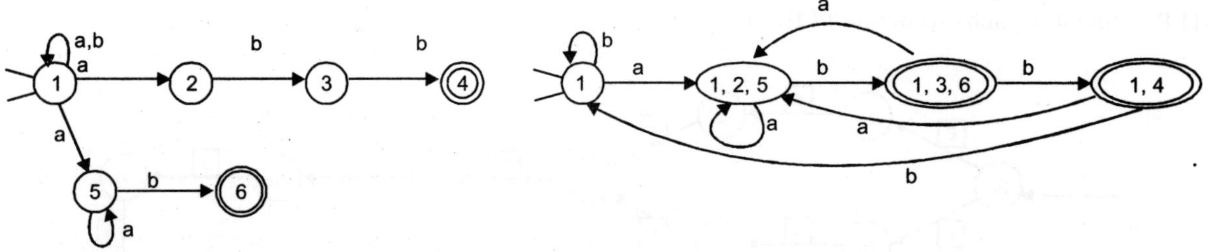

Example 1.8: Find extraneous state for following DFA:

	a	b	c
→ (1)	3	5	7
2	10	5	7
3	10	1	8
4	6	1	7
5	5	7	8
6	4	9	1
7	8	1	10
8	7	8	2
9	4	6	7
10	2	7	8

Answer: From given DFA following state move are possible:

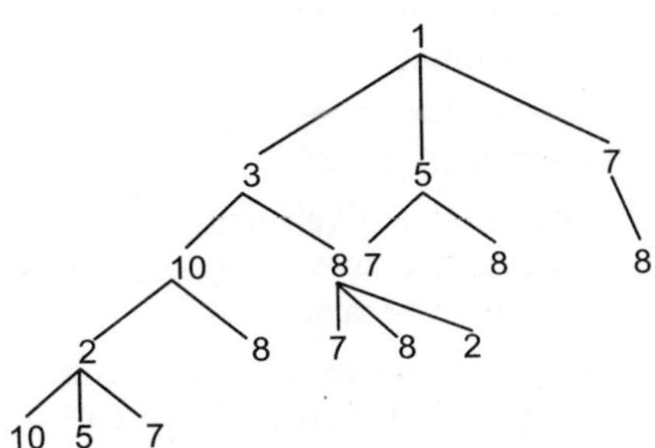

Here repeated state are not shown. So from diagram it is clear that there is no path to 4 and 9 from any node, so extrenious states are 4, 9.

1.6 CONTEXT FREE LANGUAGES

A type -2 production is a production of form $A \rightarrow \alpha$, where A belongs to V_n and α belongs to $(V_n \cup \Sigma)^*$. In other word, the L.H.S has no left context* or right context**. EXAMPLE: $S \rightarrow Aa$, $A \rightarrow \alpha$, $B \rightarrow abc$, $A \rightarrow$ null, $S \rightarrow aSb \mid \varepsilon$, $S \rightarrow x \mid y \mid z \mid S+S \mid S-S \mid S*S \mid S/S \mid (S)$, It is also called context free grammar. BNF **(Backus-Naur Form)** is the most common notation used to express context-free grammar.

Other examples :

(I) $S \rightarrow U \mid V$

$U \rightarrow TaU \mid TaT$

$V \rightarrow TbV \mid TbT$

$T \rightarrow aTbT \mid bTaT \mid \varepsilon$

(II) $S \rightarrow bSbb \mid A$

$A \rightarrow aA \mid \varepsilon$

For every context-free grammar, there exists a pushdown automaton such that the language generated by the grammar is identical with the language generated by the automaton.

1.6.1 Closure Properties

Context-Free Languages are closed under the following operations. That is, if *L* and *P* are Context-Free Languages and *D* is a Regular Language, the following languages are Context-Free as well:

- The Kleene star L^* of *L*
- The homomorphism ϕ (L) of *L*.
- The concatenation of *L* and *P*
- The union of *L* and *P*
- The intersection (with a Regular Language) of *L* and *D*.

Context-Free Languages are not closed under complement, intersection, or difference.

1.6.2 Derivations/Parse Tree

A parse tree over grammar 'g' is a rooted labled tree with the following properties:

1. Each terminal is labeled with a terminal or nonterminal or a ε.

2. Root node is labeled with the start symbol S.
3. Each leaf node is leveled with a terminal or with ε.
4. Each nonleaf is leveled with a nonterminal.
5. If a node with label 'A' belongs to 'N' has 'n' children with labels X_1, X_2, ……X_n, then $A \rightarrow X_1X_2$ ……..X_n belongs to P (a production of grammar).

There are two common ways to describe how a given string can be derived from the start symbol of a given grammar. The simplest way is to list the consecutive strings of symbols, beginning with the start symbol and ending with the string, and the rules that have been applied.

If we introduce a strategy such as "**always replace the left-most nonterminal first**" then for context-free grammar the list of applied grammar rules is by itself sufficient. This is called **the *leftmost derivation*** of a string.

If we introduce a strategy such as "**always replace the right-most nonterminal first**" then for context-free grammar the list of applied grammar rules is by itself sufficient. This is called **the *right most derivation*** of a string. For example, if we take the following grammar:

(1) $S \rightarrow S + S$
(2) $S \rightarrow 1$
(3) $S \rightarrow a$ and the string "1 + 1 + a" is.

Then a left derivation of this string is the list [(1), (1), (2), (2), (3)] i.e:

$S \rightarrow S + S$ (1)
$S \rightarrow S + S + S$ (1)
$S \rightarrow 1 + S + S$ (2)
$S \rightarrow 1 + 1 + S$ (2)
$S \rightarrow 1 + 1 + a$ (3)

And then a left derivation of this string is the list [(1), (3), (1), (2), (2)].i.e.,

$S \rightarrow S + S$ (1)
$S \rightarrow S + S + S$ (3)
$S \rightarrow S + S + a$ (1)
$S \rightarrow S + 1 + a$ (2)
$S \rightarrow 1 + 1 + a$ (2)

"A derivation also imposes in some sense a hierarchical structure on the string that is derived known as derivation tree."

A derivation or parse tree is made up of nodes and branches. The figure below is a linguistic parse tree representing an English sentence. In the figure, the parse tree is the entire structure, starting from S and ending in each of the leaf nodes (John,ball,the,hit).

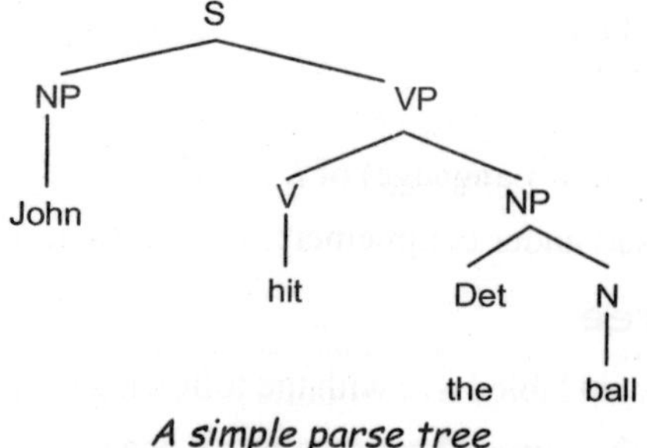

A simple parse tree

In a parse tree, each node is either a **root** node, a **branch** node, or a **leaf** node. In the above example, S is a root node, NP and VP are branch nodes, while John, ball, the, and hit are all leaf nodes. Nodes can also be referred to as parent nodes and child nodes. A **parent** node is one which has at least one other node linked by a branch under it. In the example, S is a parent of both NP and VP. A **child** node is one which has at least one node directly above it to which it is linked by a branch of the tree. Again from our example, hit is a child node of V.

For example, the left most derivation tree of the string "1 + 1 + a" would be:

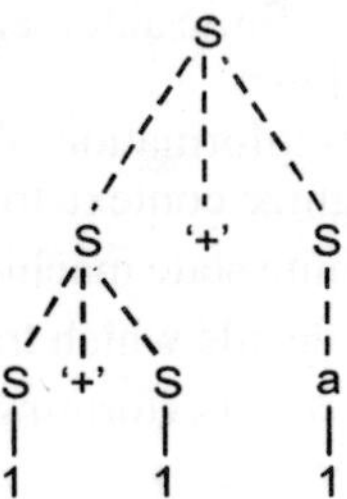

And the right most derivation tree of the string "1 + 1 + a" would be:

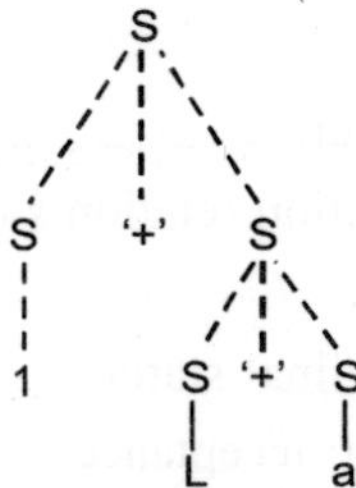

If for certain strings in the language of the grammar there is more than one parsing tree then the grammar is said to be an **ambiguous grammar.** Such grammar are usually hard to parse because the parser cannot always decide which grammar rule it has to apply. DISCUSS IN NEXT CHAPTER.

1.6.3 Properties of Context-free Languages

- An alternative and equivalent definition of context-free languages employs non-deterministic push-down automata: a language is context-free if and only if it can be accepted by such an automaton.
- A language can also be modeled as a set of all sequences of terminals which are accepted by the grammar. This model is helpful in understanding set operations on languages.
- The union and concatenation of two context-free languages is context-free, but the intersection need not be.
- The reverse of a context-free language is context-free, but the complement need not be.
- Every regular language is context-free because it can be described by a regular grammar.
- The intersection of a context-free language and a regular language is always context-free.
- There exist context-sensitive languages which are not context-free.
- To prove that a given language is not context-free, one may employ the pumping lemma for context-free languages.
- Another point worth mentioning is that the problem of determining if a context-sensitive grammar describes a context-free language is undecidable.

1.6.4 Notational Shorthand

1. These are terminals: Lower case letter as 'a', operator symbol as '+', punctuation symbol as ' ;', digit as '1', boldface strings as '**id**'.
2. These are nonterminals : uppercase letter as 'A', letter symbol 'S', lowercase italic symbol as '*expr*'.

1.6.5 Pushdown Automaton

In automata theory, a **pushdown automaton** is a finite automaton that can make use of a stack containing data. The term "pushdown" refers to the "pushing down" action by which the prototypical mechanical automaton would physically contact a punchcard to read its information. The term "pushdown automata" (PDA) currently refers to abstract computing devices that recognize context-free languages.

Pushdown automata differ from normal finite state machines in two ways:

1. They can use the top of the stack to decide which transition to take.
2. They can manipulate the stack as part of performing a transition

A PDA 'P' can be defined as a 7-tuple:

$P = (Q, \Sigma, \phi, \sigma, s, \Omega, F)$

where Q is a finite set of states.

Σ is a finite set of the input alphabet.

Φ is a finite set of the stack alphabet.

σ (or sometimes δ) is a finite transition relation s is an element of Q the start state

Ω is the initial stack symbol

F is subset of Q, consisting of the final states.

There are two possible acceptance criteria: acceptance by *empty stack* and acceptance by *final state*. The two are easily shown to be equivalent: a final state can perform a pop loop to get to an empty stack, and a machine can detect an empty stack and enter a final state by detecting a unique symbol pushed by the initial state. Some use a 6-tuple, dropping the Ω for the initial stack symbol, instead adding a first transition which writes a start symbol to the stack.

Example 1.9: Consider CFG: S→SS + |SS*|*a* and generate '*aa* + *a**' and construct parse tree also:

Ans: S → SS*
→ SS + S*
→ aa + a*

Parse Tree

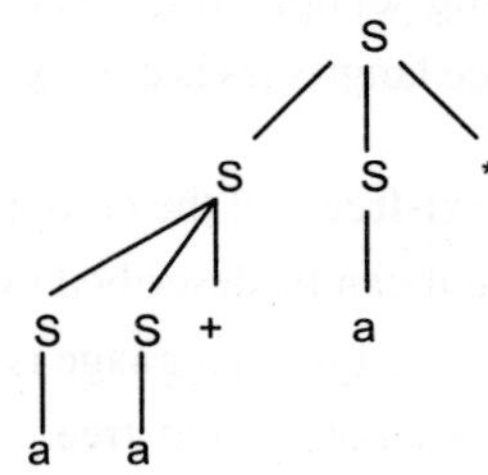

Example 1.10: Find language generated by

(i) S→ 0S1| 01

CASE (I) S → 0S1
S → 0011

CASE (II) S → 0S1
S → 00S11
S → 000111

CASE (III)S → 0S1
S → 00S11
S → 000S111
S → 00001111

L(G)= {$O^n 1^n$|n>0 }

(ii) S → +SS|–SS|a

CASE (I) S → +SS
→ +– SSS
→ +– aaa

CASE (II) S → +SS
→ ++SSS
→ ++– SSSS
→ ++– aaaa

L(G) ={Profix expression for a combination of a}

(iii) S → SS + |SS*|a

CASE (I) S → SS+
→ aa +

CASE (II) S → SS+
→ SSS* +
→ aaa* +

CASE (III) S → SS+
→ SSS* +
→ SSS*S* +
→ aaa* + a**

L(G)= {postfix expression for a combination of a}

(iv) S → S(S)S| ∊

CASE (I) S → S(S)S
S → ε(ε)ε
→ ( )

CASE (II) S → S(S)S

→ S(S(S)S)S

→ ε(ε(ε)ε)ε

→ (( ))

L(G)= {balance set of parenthesis}

(v) **S → aSbS| bSaS| ε**

CASE (I) S → aSbS

→ aεbε

→ ab

CASE (II) S → bSaS

→ bεaε

→ ba

CASE (III) S → aSbS

→ abSaSbS

→ abεaεbε

→ abab

L(G) = {set of equal no. of a's & b's}

(vi) **S → a|S+S|SS|S*|(S)**

CASE (I) S → S+S

→ SS+S

→ SS+S*

→ aa+a*

CASE (II) S → SS

→ (S)S

→ (S+S)S

→ (S+S)S*

→ (a+a)a*

L(G)= {an expressing using combination of 'a' including balance parenthesis}

Example 1.11: Describe in language (English)- language generated by following grammar whose starting symbol is E.

E	→	ET+	|T
T	→	TF*	|F
F	→	FP*	|P
P	→	E|id	

CASE (I)

E	→	ET+
	→	TT+
	→	TF*T +
	→	FF*F +
	→	PF *P +
	→	PFP *P+
	→	PFP *P +
	→	PPP * P+
	→	id id id * id +

CASE (II)

E	→	ET+
	→	TT+
	→	FF+
	→	PP+
	→	id id +
	→	id id+

So it generate postfix notation for any language.

Example 1.12: **Do the following grammar will generate same language.**

X	→	0|0 Y|1Z	A	→	OB|E
Y	→	1|1 Y|OX B		→	OA|IF|ε
Z	→	OZ|2X	C	→	OC|1A
			D	→	OA| 1D|ε
			E	→	OC|1A
			F	→	OA|1B|ε

Answer:

X	→	0Y	A	→	0B
	→	01Y		→	01F
	→	010X		→	010A
	→	0101Z		→	0101E
	→	01010Z		→	01010C
	→	010101X		→	010101A
	→	0101010		→	0101010B
				→	0101010ε
				→	0101010

So, both grammar will not generate the same languages.

1.7 CONTEXT SENSITIVE LANGUAGES

A production of form $\phi A \psi \rightarrow \phi \alpha \psi$ is called type 1 production is α is not equal to null. A grammar is called type-1 or context sensitive or context dependent if all the production is type 1 production. A production of A → null is not allowed in this grammar.

Example 1.13 : aAbcD → a**bcD**bcD, A**B** → a**bBc**, A → abA.

1.7.1 Linear Bounded Automata (LBA)

An LBA is a limited Turing machine; instead of an infinite tape, the tape has an amount of space proportional to the size of the input string. LBAs accept context-sensitive languages

1.8 RECURSIVELY ENUMERABLE LANGUAGES

A type 0 grammar is any phrase structure grammar without any restriction.

1.8.1 Turing Machines

These are the most powerful computational machines and first proposed by Alan Turing in 1936 called the ***Turing Machine***. Similar to finite automata but with an unlimited and unrestricted memory, a Turing Machine is a much more accurate model of general purpose computer. A Turing Machine can do everything that a real computer can do. They possess an infinite tape as its unlimited memory and a head which can read and write symbols and move around on the tape. Initially the tape contains only the input string and blank everywhere else. If the machine needs to store information, it may write this information on the tape. To read the information that it has written, the machine can move its head back over it. The machine continues computing until it decides to produce an output. The outputs accept and *reject* are obtained by entering designated accepting and rejecting states. If it doesn't enter an accepting or a rejecting state, it will go on forever, never handling. Turing machines are equivalent to algorithms, and are the theoretical basis for modern computers. Turing machines decide recursive languages and recognize recursively enumerable languages.

1.9 PROGRAMMING LANGUAGE

A programming language is an artificial language that can be used to control the behaviour of a machine, particularly a computer. Programming languages, like human languages, are defined through the use of syntactic and semantic rules, to determine structure and meaning respectively. Programming languages are used to facilitate communication about the task of organizing and manipulating information, and to express algorithms precisely. Authors disagree on the precise definition, but traits often considered important requirements and objectives of the language to be characterized as a programming language:

- **Function:** A programming language is a language used to write computer programs, which instruct a computer to perform some kind of computation, and/or organize the flow of control between external devices (such as a printer, a robot, or any peripheral).
- **Target:** Programming languages differ from natural languages in that natural languages are only used for interaction between people, while programming languages also allow humans to communicate instructions to machines. In some cases, programming languages are used by one program or machine to program another; PostScript source code, for example, is frequently generated programmatically to control a computer printer or display.
- **Constructs:** Programming languages may contain constructs for defining and manipulating data structures or for controlling the flow of execution.

- **Expressive power:** The theory of computation classifies languages by the computations they can express (see Chomsky hierarchy). All Turing complete languages can implement the same set of algorithms. ANSI/ISO SQL and Charity are examples of languages that are not Turing complete yet often called programming languages.

Language designers need to have a basic vocabulary about language structure, meaning and other pragmatic features that aids in the understanding of how language work with computers to help programmers express algorithmic ideas. The design principle of programming languages can be categorized as: Syntax, Type systems and semantics, Memory management and Exception handling.

1.9.1 History

The first programming languages predate the modern computer. The 19th century had "programmable" looms and player piano scrolls which implemented, what are today recognized as examples of, domain-specific programming languages. By the beginning of the twentieth century, punch cards encoded data and directed mechanical processing. In the 1930s and 1940s, the formalisms of Alonzo Church's lambda calculus and Alan Turing's Turing machines provided mathematical abstractions for expressing algorithms; the lambda calculus remains influential in language design. Basically Programming languages can be grouped in four categories:

- **Imperative programming language:** Imperative programming is a paradigm that emerged alongside the first computers and computing programs in 1940s, and its elements directly mirror the architectural characteristics of most modern computers. The architecture of the so-called von Neumann machine is the basis of imperative programming and imperative languages. The imperative languages have variable declarations, expressions, and commands. These languages are action oriented, so computation is viewed as a sequence of operation and data structure of this language is array.
- **Object oriented programming language:** The object oriented programming programs is as a collection of interacting objects that communicate via message passing. Each object can be thought of separate machine consisting of both data and operations on the data. In this language the data type is bound together with the initializations and other operations on the type. The type is referred to a class, local variable are called instance variable their initialization are accomplished by special methods called constructors and other operations are implemented by methods.
- **Functional programming language:** Functional languages are having properties like pure values, first class functions and implicit storage management and data structure of this language is list. Its creation was motivated by needs of researchers in artificial intelligence and its subfields—symbolic computation, theorem resolving, rule based systems and natural language processing. The original functional language was LISP, developed by John McCarthy in 1960. The LISP language is primarily for symbolic data processing and its computation is viewed as a mathematical function mapping inputs to outputs. Unlike imperative programming, there is no implicit notation of state therefore no need of assignment statement.
- **Declarative (logic) programming language:** Logic programming language deals with relations rather than functions and data structure of this language is relation. It is based on promise that the programming with relation more flexible than functions because relation treats arguments.

Relations have no sense of direction, no prejudice about who is computed from whom. A concrete view of relation is table with $n \geq 0$ columns and possibly infinite set of rows. Applications of Logic programming language falls in two major domains: Database design and Artificial Intelligence. In database area, the SQL has been a dominant declarative language, while in the A. I. area, Prolog has been very influencing. It is used for specifying algorithms, searching database, writing compilers and building expert systems.

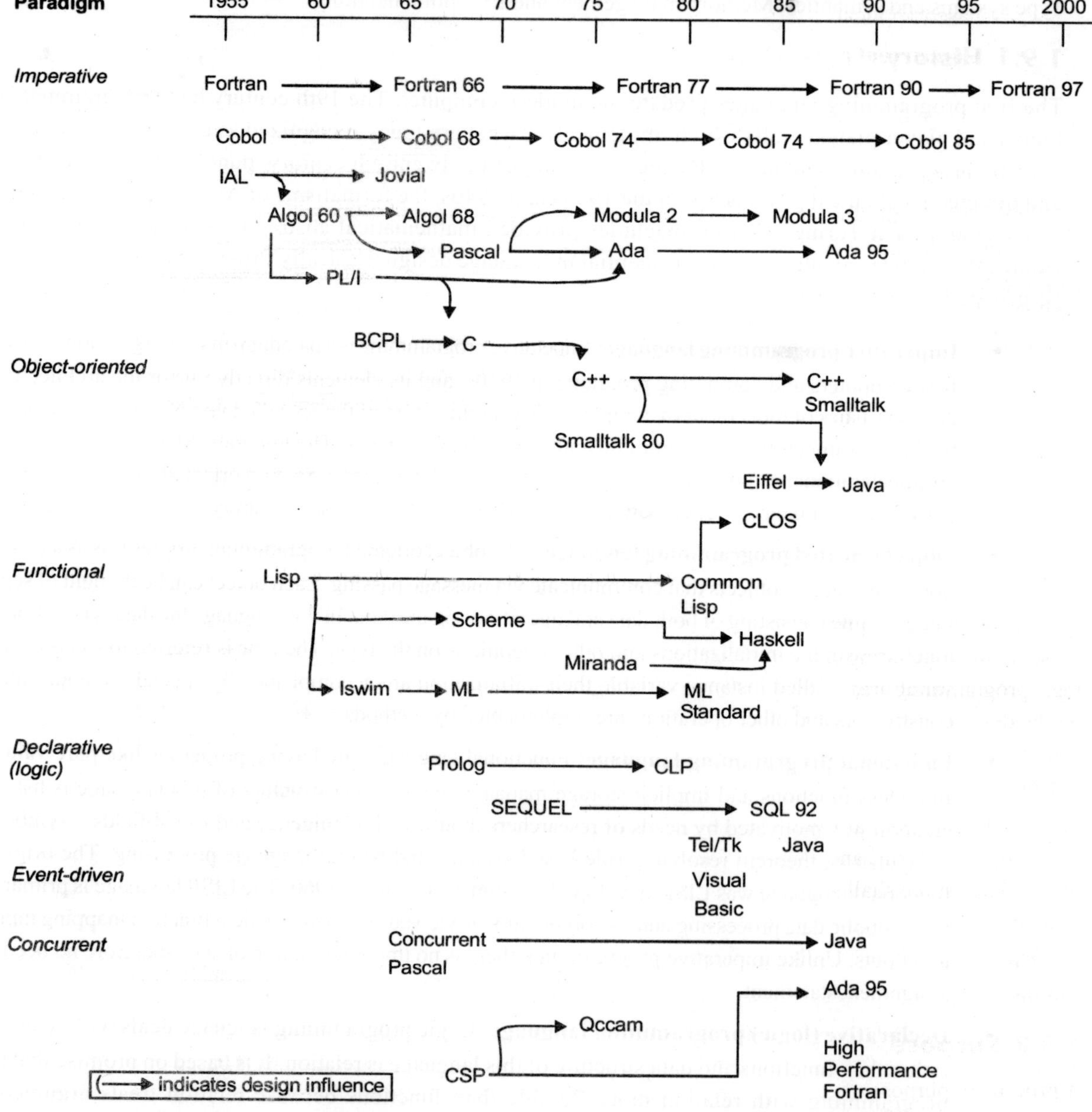

Figure 1.2: A Brief Historical Lineage of Some Key Programming Languages.

- **Event Driven programming language:** The event driven programs do not predict the control sequences that will occur; they are written to react reasonably to any particular sequence of events that may occur once execution begins. In this model, the input data governs the particular sequence of control that is actually carried out by the program. Moreover, execution of event driven program does not typically terminate; such a program is designed to run for a arbitrary period of time, often indefinitely. The most widespread example of an event driven program is the GUI mouse and widows-driven user interface found on most computers in use today. Event driven programs also drive web-based applications.
- **Concurrent programming language:** Concurrent programming provides the parallelism in the underlying hardware using concurrent treads or processes to achieve a significant speedup. Such program is said to be multithreaded, since it has more than one execution sequence. A good example of concurrent program is the modern web browser which begins to render a page, even though it may still be downloading various images or graphics files.

In the 1940s, the first electrically powered digital computers were created. The computers of the early 1950s, notably the UNIVAC I and the IBM 701 used machine language programs. Several hundred programming languages and dialects have been developed since that time. Most have had a limited life span and utility, while a few have enjoyed wide spread success in or more application domains. A general overview of the history of few of the most influential programming languages is summarized in figure 1.2.

No single figure can capture the rich history of programming languages and the evolution of features across language and paradigms. The languages, dates, and paradigms characterized in Figure 1.2 provide only a general overview of this history and most of the major players in the design of programming languages.

Notably, Cobol and Fortran have evolved greatly since their emergence in the late 1950s. These languages built a large following and have remained fairly autonomous in their evolution and influence on the design has had a tremendous influence on the development of several of its successors, including Pascal, Modula, Ada, C++, and Java. Java the experimental language developed for the text, is Algol-like in nature.

In the functional programming area, Lisp was dominant in early years and continues its influence to the present day, motivating the development of more recent languages such as Scheme, ML and Haskell. In the logic programming area, only one language, Prolog, has been the major player, but Prolog enjoys little influence on the design of languages outside that area. The event-driven and concurrent programming areas are much earlier in the their evolution, and lonely a few languages are prominent. Some the these, like High Performance Fortran (HPF), derive their features by extending those of a widely used base language (Fortran, in this case).

Finally, notice that the language Java appears several times in Figure 1.2 once for each of the object-oriented, concurrent, and event-driven paradigms. Java offers strong support for programming in each of these styles, as we shall see in later chapters of this book. That is one o f the reasons why language designers find java such an interesting programming language.

New languages will undoubtedly emerge in the near future as the younger programming paradigms evolve and their demands for computational power and versatility continue to expand.

1.9.2 Purpose

A prominent purpose of programming languages is to provide instructions to a computer. As such, programming languages differ from most other forms of human expression in that they require a greater degree of precision and completeness. When using a natural language to communicate with other people, human, authors and speakers can be ambiguous and make small errors, and still expect their intent to be understood. However, computers do exactly what they are told to do, and cannot understand the code the programmer "intended" to write. The combination of the language definition, the program, and the program's inputs must fully specify the external behaviour that occurs when the program is executed. Many languages have been designed from scratch, altered to meet new needs, combined with other languages, and eventually fallen into disuse. Although there have been attempts to design one "universal" computer language that serves all purposes, all of them have failed to be accepted in this role.The need for diverse computer languages arises from the diversity of contexts in which languages are used:

- Programs range from tiny scripts written by individual hobbyists to huge systems written by hundreds of programmers.
- Programmers range in expertise from novices who need simplicity above all else, to experts who may be comfortable with considerable complexity.
- Programs must balance speed, size, and simplicity on systems ranging from microcontrollers to supercomputers.
- Programs may be written once and not change for generations, or they may undergo nearly constant modification.
- Finally, programmers may simply differ in their tastes: they may be accustomed to discussing problems and expressing them in a particular language.

One common trend in the development of programming languages has been to add more ability to solve problems using a higher level of abstraction. The earliest programming languages were tied very closely to the underlying hardware of the computer.

1.9.3 Specification

The specification of a programming language is intended to provide a definition that language users and implementers can use to interpret the behaviour of programs when reading their source code. A programming language specification can take several forms, including the following:

- An explicit definition of the syntax and semantics of the language. While syntax is commonly specified using a formal grammar, semantic definitions may be written in natural language (e.g., the C language), or a formal semantics (e.g., the Standard ML).
- A description of the behaviour of a translator for the language (e.g., the C++ and Fortran). The syntax and semantics of the language has to be inferred from this description, which may be written in natural or a formal language.
- A *model* implementation, sometimes written in the language being specified (e.g., Prolog). The syntax and semantics of the language are explicit in the behaviour of the model implementation.

1.9.4 Implementation

An implementation of a programming language provides a way to execute that program on one or more configurations of hardware and software. There are, broadly, two approaches to programming language implementation: *compilation* and *interpretation*. It is generally possible to implement a language using both techniques.

Computer languages are generally classed as being "high-level" (like Pascal, Fortran, Ada, Modula-2, Oberon, C or C++) or "low-level" (like ASSEMBLER). High-level languages may further be classified as "imperative" (like all of those just mentioned), or "functional" (like Lisp, Scheme, ML, or Haskell), or "logic" (like Prolog). High-level languages have several advantages over low-level ones:

- **Readability:** A good high-level language will allow programs or coding may be done in a way that is essentially self-documenting, a highly desirable property when one considers that many programs are written once, but possibly studied by humans many times thereafter.
- **Portability:** Portability refers to achieve machine independence. High-level languages may deny access to low-level features, and are sometimes spurn by programmers who have to develop low-level machine dependent systems. JAVA was specifically designed to allow portability.
- **Structure and object orientation:** There is general agreement that the structured programming movement of the 1960's and the object-oriented movement of the 1990's have resulted in a great improvement in the quality and reliability of code. High-level languages can be designed so as to encourage or even subtly enforce these programming paradigms.
- **Generality:** Most high-level languages allow the writing of a wide variety of programs, thus relieving the programmer of the need to become expert in many diverse languages.
- **Brevity:** Programs expressed in high-level languages are often considerably shorter (in terms of their number of source lines) than their low-level equivalents.
- **Error checking:** Programmers make many mistakes in the development of a computer program. Many high-level languages force a great deal of error checking both at compile-time and at run-time. For this they are, of course, often criticized by programmers who have to develop time-critical code, or who want their programs to abort as quickly as possible.
- **Clearly defined:** It must be clearly described, for the benefit of both the user and the compiler writer.
- **Quickly translated:** It should admit quick translation, so that program development time when using the language is not excessive.
- **Modularity:** It is desirable that programs can be developed in the language as a collection of separately compiled modules, with appropriate mechanisms for ensuring self-consistency between these modules.
- **Efficient:** It should permit the generation of efficient object code.
- **Widely available:** It should be possible to provide translators for all the major machines and for all the major operating systems.

Every programming language have syntax and semantic or we can say that every programming language follow some syntax and semantic:

- **Syntax** describe the *form* of the sentences in the language. For example, in English, the sentence "They can fish" is syntactically correct, while the sentence "Can fish they" is incorrect. To take another example, the language of binary numerals uses only the symbols 0 and 1, arranged in strings formed by concatenation, so that the sentence 101 is syntactically correct for this language, while the sentence 1110211 is syntactically incorrect.
- **Semantic** define the *meaning* of syntactically correct sentences in a language. By itself the sentence 101 has no meaning without the addition of semantic rules to the effect that it is to be interpreted as the representation of some number using a positional convention. The sentence "They can fish" is more interesting, for it can have two possible meanings; a set of semantic rules would be even harder to formulate.

EXAMPLES

EX. 1: Write a program to reorganize a D.F.A. for strings like "facetious" and "abstemious" that contain all five vowels, in order, but appearing only once each. (refer to appendix A-1)

EX. 2: Write a program to reorganize a D.F.A. that accept all strings of 0's and 1's that have an odd number of 0's and an even number of 1's. (refer to appendix A-2)

EX. 3: Draw DFA for the following:

(i) DFA for ϕ :

(ii) DFA for ε :

EX. 4: Construct a DFA that contains zeros and ones but odd number of zero must be lie

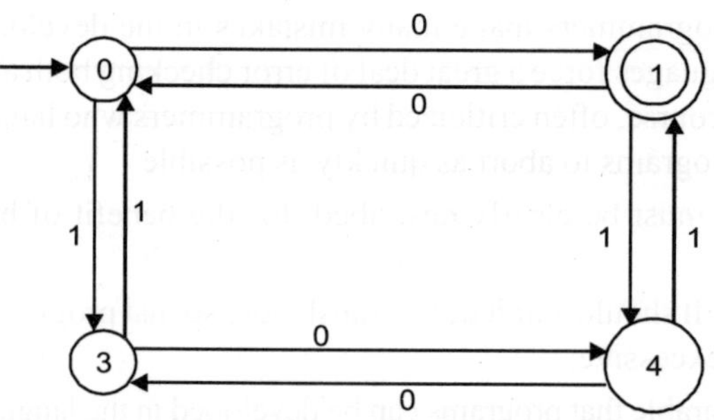

EX. 5: Find NFA for aa*|bb*

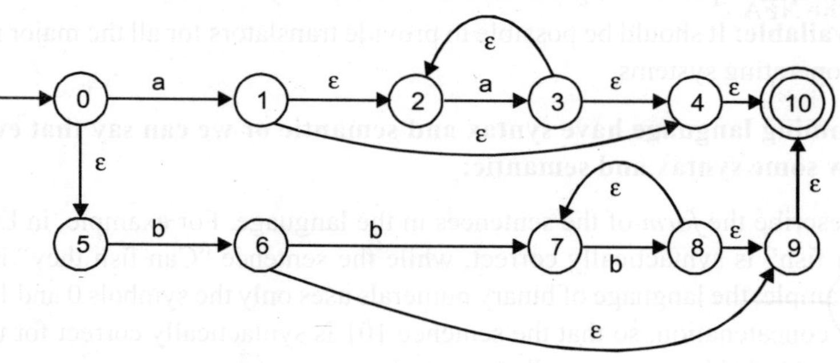

EX. 6: Let R = {(S, C), (a, b), p, F} where P consist
S→ aCa,
C→ aCa | b. Find L(G).

S → aCa

S → aba   using C → b

S → aaCaa using both rule

S → aabaa

S → $a^n b a^n$

So L(G) = { $a^n b a^n$ | n >= 1} belongs to L(G)

EX. 7: Let S→ aS|bS|a|b find L(G)

S→ aS→ aa

S→aS→ ab

S→abS→ aba

S—aas→ aab

So L(G) = $\{a,b\}^+$

EX. 8: Write a grammar for the following String and then generate a leftmost and Rightmost derivation tree for S;.

String is => {S;, S; S;, S; S; S;……………….}

Grammar for the following String is S → S; S|ε

Case I

S→ S; S

→ S; S; S

→ S; S;

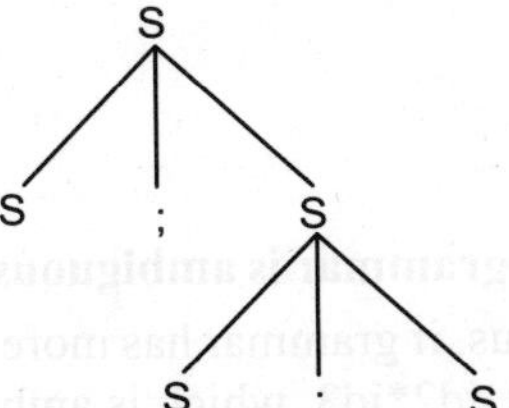

Case II

S→ S; S

→ S; S; S

→ S; S; S

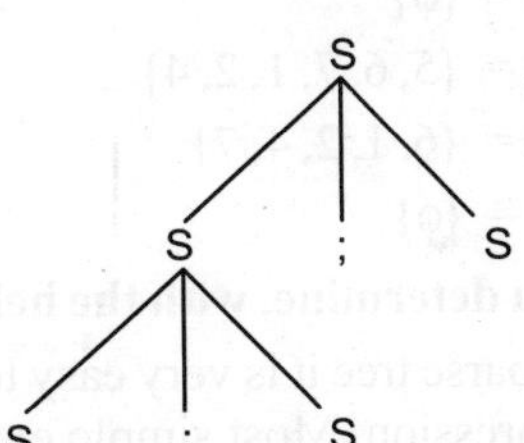

EX. 9: Construct the NFA for the following regular expression – letter|(letter or digit)*

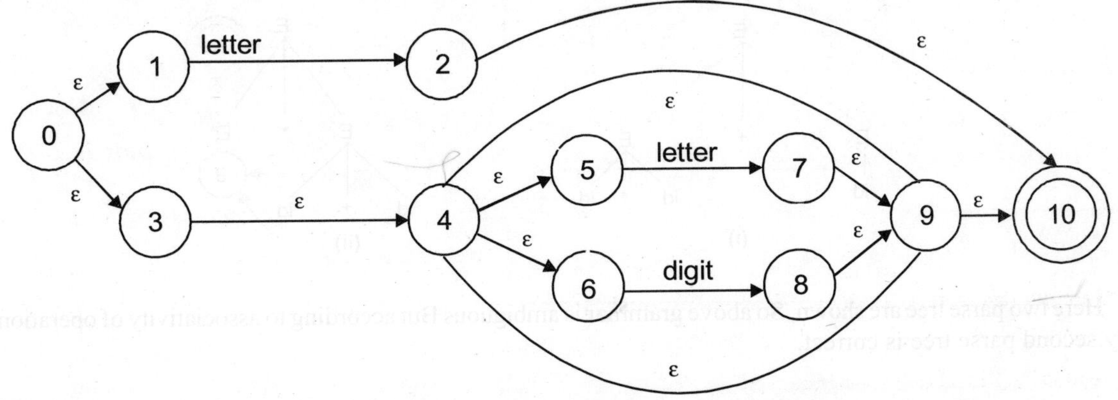

EX. 10: Find the null – closure of the following NFA

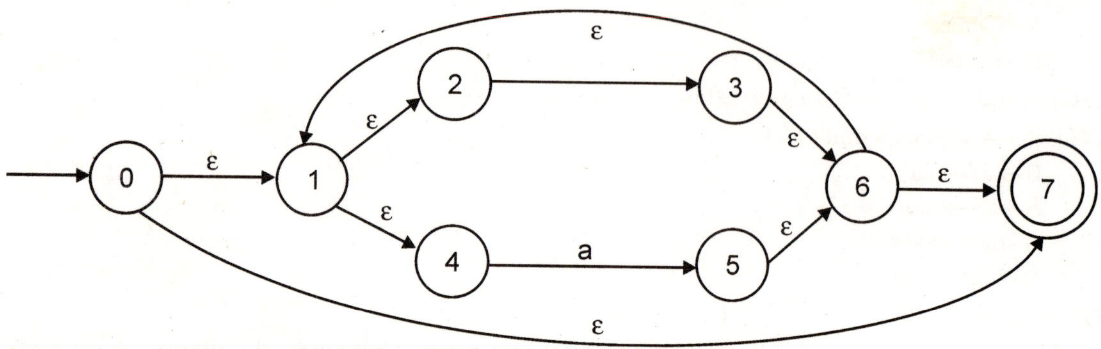

As we now that,

ε Closure (S) = Set of states reachable from state S via epsilon.

ε Closure (T) = Set of states reachable from any state in set T via epsilon.

ε closure (0) = {0, 1, 2, 4, 7}

ε closure (1) = {2, 4, 1}

ε closure (2) = {ϕ}

ε closure (3) = {3, 6, 7, 1, 2, 4}

ε closure (4) = {ϕ}

ε closure (5) = {5, 6, 7, 1, 2, 4}

ε closure (6) = {6, 1, 2, 4, 7}

ε closure (7) = {ϕ}

EX. 11: How can you determine, with the help of parse tree that the given grammar is ambiguous ?

With the help of parse tree it is very easy to say any grammar is ambiguous, if grammar has more than one parse tree for one expression. Most simple example of this category is id1 + id2*id3 which is ambiguous if following grammar is used

E → E + E | E*E | id

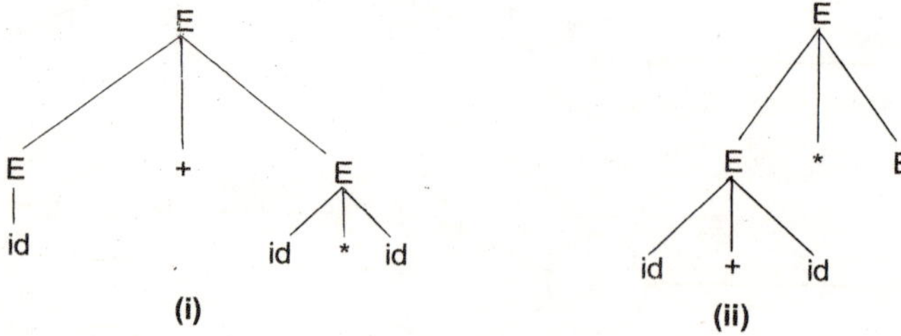

Here two parse tree are shown, So above grammar is ambiguous But according to associativity of operations only second parse tree is correct.

EX. 12: Give the left and right most derivation , parse tree for aabbaa using

S → aAS | a , A→ SbA | SS | ba

(i) Left Most Derivation Tree

S → aAS
→ aSbAS
→ aabAS
→ aabbaS
→ aabbaa

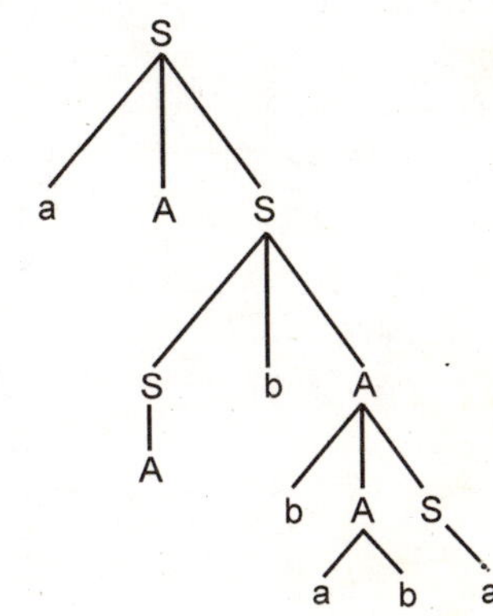

(ii) Right Most Derivation Tree

S → aAS
→ aAa
→ aSbAa
→ aabbaa
→ aabbaa

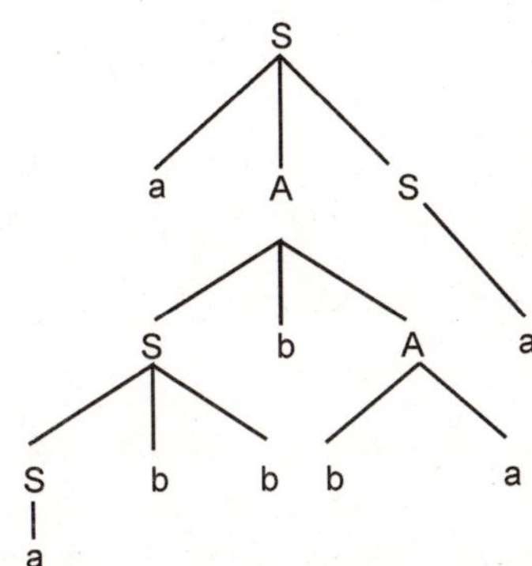

EX. 13: Consider the following grammar and give left most, right most derivation for the (a 23(m x Y)

exp → atom | list

atom → num | id

list → (lexp — seq)

lexp → seq → lexp → seq exp%exp

(i) Left Most Derivation-

exp à list
→ (lexp–seq)
→ (lexp–seq exp)
→ (lexp–seq exp exp)
→ (exp exp exp)
→ (atom exp exp)
→ (id exp exp)
→ (a num exp)

→ (a 23 list)
→ (a 23 (lexp–seq))
→ (a 23 (lexp–seq exp))
→ (a 23 (lexp–seq exp exp))
→ (a 23 (exp exp exp))
→ (a 23(atom exp exp))
→ (a 23 (id exp exp))
→ (a 23 (id atom exp))
→ (a 23 (id id exp)
→ (a 23 (id id atom))
→ (a 23 (id id id))

(ii) Right Most Derivation-
exp → list
→ (lexp–seq)
→ (lexp–seq exp)
→ (lexp–seq list)
→ lexp–seq (lexp–seq))
→ (lexp–seq (lexp–seq exp))
→ (lexp–seq (lexp–seq atom))
→ (lexp–seq (lexp–seq id))
→ (lexp–seq (lexp–seq exp id))
→ (lexp–seq (lexp–seq atom id))
→ (lexp–seq (lexp–seq id id))
→ (lexp–seq (exp id id))
→ (lexp–seq (atom id id))
→ (lexp–seq (id id id))
→ (lexp–seq exp(id id id))
→ (lexp–seq atom(id id id))
→ (lexp–seq num(id id id))
→ (lexp–seq 23 (id id id))
→ (exp 23 (id id id))
→ (atom 23 (id id id))
→ (id 23 (id id id))

TRIBULATIONS

1.1 Consider the following context-free grammar:

P : S.
S : '(' L ')' / 'a'.
L : L ',' S / S.

Using this grammar, write derivations of each of the following sentences. Draw parse trees corresponding to your derivations.

- (a, a)
- (a, (a, a))
- ((a, (a, a)), a)

1.2 Show that the following grammar is ambiguous.

P : S.

S : 'a' S 'b' S / 'b' S 'a' S /.

1.3 Consider the following grammar:

G → S $$

S → A M

M → S

A → a E | b A A

E → a B | b A | /* empty */

B → b E | a B B

Describe in English the language that the grammar generates. Show the parse tree for the string "abaa".

1.4 What is the use of regular expression D.F.A. in lexical analysis.

1.5 Make a list of as many translators as you can think of that can be found on your computer system.

1.6 In some programming languages, identifiers may have embedded underscore characters. However, the first character may not be an underscore, nor may two underscores appear in succession. Write a regular expression that generates such identifiers.

1.7 Find a regular expression that generates the Roman representation of numbers from 1 through 99.

1.8 Develop simple grammar to describe each of the following:

(a) A person's name, with optional title and qualifications (if any), for example,

S.B. Terry, BSc

Master Kenneth David Terry

Helen Margaret Alice Terry

(b) A railway goods train, with one (or more) locomotives, several varieties of trucks, and a guard's van at the rear.

(c) A mixed passenger and goods train, with one (or more) locomotives, then one or more goods trucks, followed either by a guard's van, or by one or more passenger coaches, the last of which should be a passenger brake van. In the interests of safety, try to build in a regulation to the effect that fuel trucks may not be marshalled immediately behind the locomotive, or immediately in front of a passenger coach.

(d) A book, with covers, contents, chapters and an index.

(e) A shopping list, with one or more items, for example

3 Practical assignments

124 bottles Castle Lager

12 cases Rhine Wine

large box aspirins

(f) Input to a postfix (reverse Polish) calculator. In postfix notation, brackets are not used, but instead the operators are placed after the operands.

For example,

infix expression	reverse Polish equivalent
6 + 9 =	6 9 + =
(a + b) * (c + d)	a b + c d + *

(g) A message in Morse code.

(h) Unix or MS-DOS file specifiers.

(i) Numbers expressed in Roman numerals.

(j) Boolean expressions incorporating conjunction (OR), disjunction (AND) and negation (NOT).

1.9 C programmers should be familiar with the use of the standard functions scanf and printf for performing input and output. Typical calls to these functions are

scanf("%d %s %c", &n, string, &ch);

printf("Total = %–10.4d\nProfit = %d\%%\n", total, profit);

in which the first argument is usually a literal string incorporating various specialized format specifiers describing how the remaining arguments are to be processed.

1.10 Develop sets of productions for algebraic expressions that will describe the operations of addition and division as well as subtraction and multiplication according to issues of associativity and precedence.

1.11 Develop sets of productions which describe expressions $a + \sin(b + c) * (- (b - a))$

1.12 Derive the strings using given grammar

$A \rightarrow aABC \mid abC$ (1,2)

$CB \rightarrow BC$ (3)

$bB \rightarrow bb$ (4)

$bC \rightarrow bc$ (5)

$cC \rightarrow cc$ (6)

abc and *aaabbbccc*

1.13 Show that the strings '*abbc* , *aabc* and *abcc*' cannot be derived using above grammar.

1.14 Derive a context-sensitive grammar for strings of 0's and 1's so that the number of 0's and 1's is the same.

1.15 Develop a context-free grammar that specifies the set of REAL decimal literals that may be written in Fortran. Examples of these literals are

–21.5 0.25 3.7E–6 .5E7 6E6 100.0E+3

1.16 Develop a context-free grammar that generates all palindromes constructed of the letters *a* and *b* (palindromes are strings that read the same from either end, like *ababbaba*).

1.17 Can you describe signed integers and Fortran identifiers in terms of regular grammar as well as in terms of context-free grammar?

1.18 Can you develop a regular grammar that specifies the set of float decimal literals that may be written in C++?

1.19 Develop a grammar for describing scanf or printf statements in C. Can this be done in a context-free way, or do you need to introduce context-sensitivity?

1.20 Develop a grammar for describing Fortran FORMAT statements. Can this be done in a context-free way, or do you need to introduce context-sensitivity?

1.21 Give Thompson Construction theorem and apply this algo for given regular expression to convert into NFA .

(i) (a | b) * a (a | b)

(ii) (a | b)*ab*a (a | b)

(iii) (a | b)* ab*a

(iv) (a | b)*ab

1.22 Prove that for any regular expression 'r'

L (r**) = L (r*)

1.23 Draw DFA for ϕ

1.24 Consider the following grammar and give a DFA that accept this

S → 0A | 1B | 0 | 1

A → 0S | 1B | 1

B → 0A | 1S

1.25 What do you mean by regular expression? Write some properties of regular grammar?

1.26 What are the notational conventions for context free grammar?

1.27 Develop an algorithm to simulate an NFA reading an input string. What is time space complexity of your algorithm as function of size and length of input string?

1.28 How the following regular expressions are same by constructing optimized DFA?

(i) (a | b)*

(ii) (a* | b)*

(iii) (a | b*)*

FURTHER READINGS AND REFERENCES

- **About Chomsky**

[1] Chomsky (1951). *Morphophonemics of Modern Hebrew.* Master's thesis, University of Pennsylvania.

[2] Chomsky (1955). *Logical Structure of Linguistic Theory.*

[3] Chomsky (1955). *Transformational Analysis.* Ph.D. dissertation, University of Pennsylvania.

[4] Collier, Peter; and David Horowitz (2004). *The Anti-Chomsky Reader.*

[5] Goertzel, Ted (2003-12). "Noam Chomsky and the Political Psychology Anti-Imperialism". *Clio's Psyche.* Retrieved on 2006-12-28

- **For Taxonomy of Automata**

[6] Bruce W. Watson, *Taxonomies and Toolkits of Regular Language Algorithms*, Ph.D. thesis, Eindhoven University of Technology, the Netherlands, 1995.[bibtex]

[7] Emmanuel Roche and Yves Schabes, *Finite-State Language Processing*, Bradford Book series, MIT Press, Cambridge, Massachusetts, USA, 1997.[bibtex]

[8] Michael A. Arbib and A.J. Kfoury and Robert N. Moll, *Introduction to Formal Language Theory*, Springer Verlag, New York, New York, USA, 1988.[bibtex]

[9] A.V. Aho, J. E. Hopcroft and J. D. Ullman. *The Design and Analysis of Computer Algorithms*, Addison-Wesley Publishing Company, 1974.[bibtex]

[10] John E. Hopcroft and Jefferey D. Ullman. *Introduction to Automata Theory, Languages, and Computation,* Adison-Wesley Publishing Company, Reading, Massachusetts, USA, 1979.[bibtex]

[11] Alfred V. Aho and Ravi Sethi and Jeffrey D. Ullman. *Compilers — Principles, Techniques and Tools*, Addison Wesley, 1986.[bibtex]

[12] Mishra K.L.P. and N. Chandrasekaran. *Theory of Computer Science.*

- **For Finite State Machine**

[13] Wagner, F., "*Modeling Software with Finite State Machines*: *A Practical Approach*", Auerbach Publications, 2006.

[14] Cassandras, C., Lafortune, S., *"Introduction to Discrete Event Systems"*. Kluwer, 1999, ISBN 0-7923-8609-4.

[15] Timothy Kam, *Synthesis of Finite State Machines: Functional Optimization*. Kluwer Academic Publishers, Boston 1997.

[16] Tiziano Villa, *Synthesis of Finite State Machines: Logic Optimization*. Kluwer Academic Publishers, Boston 1997.

- **For Deterministic Finite Automata (DFA)**

[17] Michael Sipser. *Introduction to the Theory of Computation*. PWS, Boston. 1997. Section 1.1: Finite Automata, pp. 31–47. Subsection "Decidable Problems Concerning Regular Languages" of section 4.1: Decidable Languages, pp.152–155. 4.4 DFA can accept only regular language.

- **For Nondeterministic Finite Automata (NDFA)**

[18] NFA Michael Sipser. *Introduction to the Theory of Computation*. PWS, Boston. 1997. Section 1.2: Nondeterminism, pp. 47–63.

- **For Push Down Automata PDA**

[19] Michael Sipser *(1997). Introduction to the Theory of Computation. PWS Publishing.* Section 2.2: Pushdown Automata, pp.101–114.

[20] Michael Sipser *(1997). Introduction to the Theory of Computation. PWS Publishing.* Chapter 2: Context-Free Languages, pp. 91–122.

[21] BalaSundaraRaman; Ishwar. S, Sanjeeth Kumar Ravindranath (2003-08-22). *"Context Free Grammar for Natural Language Constructs — An implementation for Venpa Class of Tamil Poetry"*.

- **For Programming** ***Language***

[22] David Gelernter, Suresh Jagannathan. *Programming Linguistics*, The MIT Press, 1990.

[23] Terry P.D. Compilers and Compiler Generators an introduction with C++O, Rhodes University, 1996.

[24] Samuel N. Kamin. *Programming Languages: An Interpreter-Based Approach,* Addison-Wesley, 1990.

[25] Shriram Krishnamurthi. *Programming Languages: Application and Interpretation,* Online publication.

[26] Burce J. MacLennan. *Principles of Programming Languages*, Harcourt Brace Jovanovich 1987.

[27] John C. Mitchell. *Concepts in Programming Languages*, Cambridge University Press, 2002.

[28] Benjamin C. Pierce. *Types and Programming Languages*, The MIT Press, 2002.

[29] Ravi Sethi: *Programming Languages: Concepts and Constructs*, 2nd ed., Addison-Wesley 1996.

[30] Richard L. Wexelblat (ed.): *History of Programming Languages*, Academic Press, 1981.

CHAPTER 2

INTRODUCTION TO COMPILER

CHAPTER HIGHLIGHTS

2.1 Introduction to Compiler
- 2.1.1 What is the Challenge?

2.2 Types of Compilers
- 2.2.1 One-pass versus Multi-pass compilers
- 2.2.2 Where Does the Code Execute?
- 2.2.3 Hardware Compilation

2.3 Meaning of Compiler Design
- 2.3.1 Front End
- 2.3.2 Back End

2.4 Computational Model: Analysis and Synthesis

2.5 Phases of Compiler and Analysis of Source Code
- 2.5.1 Source Code
- 2.5.2 Lexical Analysis
- 2.5.3 Syntax Analysis
- 2.5.4 Senartic Analysis
- 2.5.5 Intermediate Code Generation
- 2.5.6 Code Optimization
- 2.5.7 Code Generation
- 2.5.8 Out Target Program
- 2.5.9 Symbol Table

2.6 Cousins/Relatives of the Compiler
- 2.6.1 Preprocessor
  - Lexical Pre-processors
  - Syntactic Pre-processors
  - General Purpose Preprocessor
- 2.6.2 Assembler
- 2.6.3 Loader and Linker
  - Dynamic Linking

2.7 Interpreter
- 2.7.1 Byte Code Interpreter
- 2.7.2 Interpreter v/s Compiler

2.8 Abstract Interpreter
- 2.8.1 Incentive Knowle*dge*
- 2.8.2 Abstract Interpretation of Computer Programs
- 2.8.3 Formalization
- 2.8.4 Example of Abstract Domain

2.9 Case Tool: Compiler Construction Tools

2.10 A Simple Compiler Example (C Language)

2.11 Decompilers
- 2.11.1 Phases

2.12 Just-In-Time Compilation

2.13 Cross Compiler
- 2.13.1 Uses of Cross Compilers
- 2.13.2 GCC and Cross Compilation
- 2.13.3 Canadian Cross

2.14 Bootstrapping

2.15 Macro
- 2.15.1 Quoting the Macro Arguments

2.16 X-Macros

Examples

Tribulations

Further Readings and References

Early computers did not use compilers. Compilers had not yet been invented because early computers had very little memory and programs were necessarily quite short. Users often entered the decimal or binary machine code for a program directly by turning or toggling switches on the computer console or entering digits via paper tape.

Programmers soon began to create programs to help with the tedious task of entering machine code. Such a program which would translate an alphabetic letter (which were chosen to be mnemonic) into a corresponding numeric instruction which the machine could execute. In this manner, assembly languages and the primitive compiler, the assembler, emerged.

Towards the end of the 1950s, machine-independent programming languages evolved. Subsequently, several experimental compilers were developed then (see, for example, the seminal work by Grace Hopper on the A-0 programming language), but the FORTRAN team led by John Backus at IBM is generally credited as having introduced the first complete compiler, in 1957.

The idea of compilation quickly caught on, and most of the principles of compiler design were developed during the 1960s.With the evolution of programming languages and the increasing power of computers, compilers are becoming more and more complex to bridge the gap between problem-solving modern programming languages and the various computer systems, aiming at getting the highest performance out of the target machines.

A compiler is itself a complex computer program written in some implementation language. Early compilers were written in assembly language. The first **self-hosting compiler** — capable of compiling its own source code in a high-level language — was created for Lisp by Hart and Levin at MIT in 1962. Building a self-hosting compiler is a **bootstrapping** problem — the first such compiler for a language must be compiled either by a compiler written in a different language, or (as in Hart and Levin's Lisp compiler) compiled by running the compiler in an interpreter.

Compiler construction and compiler optimization are taught at universities as part of the computer science curriculum.

2.1 INTRODUCTION TO COMPILER

The use of computer languages is an essential link in the chain between human and computer. In this text we hope to make the reader more aware of some aspects of

- Imperative programming languages — their syntactic and semantic features; the ways of specifying syntax and semantics; problem areas and ambiguities; the power and usefulness of various features of a language.
- Translators for programming languages — the various classes of translator (assemblers, compilers, interpreters); implementation of translators.
- Compiler generators - tools that are available to help automate the construction of translators for programming languages.

Compiler is a version of translator. As the name, translator is a computer program that convert any language to other one language. Here are various types of translator are given :

- Assembler : Translators that map low-level language instructions into machine code which can then be executed directly.
- Assembler: Macro (macro-assembler) : Simlir to assemble but different in some way i.e. some macro statements map into a sequence of machine level instructions very effeniently providing a text replacement facility.

- Compiler : Discuss in later in this chapter.
- Cross Compiler : Discuss in later in this chapter.
- Emulator : Highly specialized translator one that executes the machine level instructions by fetching, analysing, and then interpreting them one by one.
- Disassembler
- Decompiler : Discuss later in this chapter.
- Half Bootstrap : Part of cross compiler and bootstrapping. Discuss later in this chapter.
- Interpretive compilers : Such translators produce intermediate code as output which is basically simple enough to satisfy the constraints imposed by a practical interpreter, even though it may still be quite a long way from the machine code of the system on which it is desired to execute the original program.
- Linkage editors or linkers : Discuss later in this chapter.
- Load-and-Go
- P-code Assembler : Yet another way in which a portable interpretive compiler kit might be used.
- Pre-processor : Discuss later in this chapter.
- Self-Compiling Compilers : Many compilers for popular languages were first written in another implementation language and then rewritten in their own source language. The rewrite gives source for a compiler that can then be compiled with the compiler written in the original implementation language.
- Self-resident translators : Translators generate code for their host machines.

The name **compiler** is primarily used for programs that translate source code from a high level language to a lower level language (e.g., assembly language or machine language). A program that translates from a low level language to a higher level one is a decompiler. A program that translates between high-level languages is usually called a language translator, source to source translator, or language converter. A language rewriter is usually a program that translates the form of expressions without a change of language. The most common reason for wanting to translate source code is to create an executable program.

"A compiler is a complex computer program (or set of programs) **that translates text written in a computer language** (the source language) **into another computer language** (the target language)".

OR

A compiler is a computer program that translates a computer program written in one computer language (the *source language*) into an equivalent program written in another computer language (the *target language*). The process of translation is called *compilation*.

Compiler program often broken into several distinct chunks, called passes, that communicate with one another via temporary files. The passes themselves are only part of the compilation process, however. The process of creating an executable image from source code file can involve several stages other than compilation. The original sequence is usually called the source code and the output called object code Commonly the output has a form suitable for processing by other programs (e.g., a linker), but it may be a human readable text file.

A compiler is likely to perform many or all of the following operations: **lexing, preprocessing, parsing, semantic analysis, code optimizations, and code generation.**

2.1.1 What is the Challenge?

Many variations:

- many programming languages (eg, FORTRAN, C++, Java)
- many programming paradigms (eg, object-oriented, functional, logic)
- many computer architectures (eg, MIPS, SPARC, Intel, alpha)
- many operating systems (eg, Linux, Solaris, Windows)

Qualities of a compiler (in order of importance):

1. the compiler itself must be bug-free
2. it must generate correct machine code
3. the generated machine code must run fast
4. the compiler itself must run fast (compilation time must be proportional to program size)
5. the compiler must be portable (ie, modular, supporting separate compilation)
6. it must print good diagnostics and error messages
7. the generated code must work well with existing debuggers
8. must have consistent and predictable optimization.

Building a compiler requires knowledge of :

- programming languages (parameter passing, variable scoping, memory allocation, etc)
- theory (automata, context-free languages, etc)
- algorithms and data structures (hash tables, graph algorithms, dynamic programming, etc)
- computer architecture (assembly programming)
- software engineering.

The course project (building a non-trivial compiler for a Pascal-like language) will give you a hands-on experience on system implementation that combines all this knowledge.

2.2 TYPES OF COMPILERS

There are many ways to classify compilers according to the input and output, internal structure, and runtime behaviour. For example,

- A program that translates from a low level language to a higher level one is a **decompiler**.
- A program that translates between high-level languages is usually called a **language translator, source to source translator, language converter, or language rewriter**(this last term is usually applied to translations that do not involve a change of language).

2.2.1 One-pass *vs.* Multi-pass Compilers

Compiling involves performing lots of work and early computers did not have enough memory to contain one program that did all of this work. So compilers were split up into smaller programs which each made a pass over the source (or some representation of it) performing some of the required analysis and translations. The ability to compile in a **single pass** is often seen as a benefit because it simplifies the job of writing a compiler and one pass compilers are generally faster than **multi-pass compilers**. Many languages were designed so that they could be compiled in a single pass. (e.g., Pascal).

In some cases the design of a language feature may require a compiler to perform more than one pass over the source. For instance, consider a declaration appearing on line 20 of the source which affects the translation of a statement appearing on line 10. In this case, the first pass needs to gather information about declarations appearing after statements that they affect, with the actual translation happening during a subsequent pass.

One-pass compiler

A One-pass Compiler is a type of compiler that passes through the source code of each compilation unit only once. In a sense, a one-pass compiler can't 'look back' at code it previously processed. Another term sometimes used is narrow compiler, which emphasizes the limited scope a one-pass compiler is obliged to use. This is in contrast to a multi-pass compiler which traverses the source code and/or the abstract syntax tree several times, building one or more intermediate representations that can be arbitrarily refined. Some programming languages have been designed specifically to be compiled with one-pass compilers.

Example 2.1: An example of such is in Pascal. Normally Pascal requires that procedures be fully defined before use. This helps a one-pass compiler with its type checking: calling a procedure that hasn't been defined is a clear error. However, this requirement makes mutually recursive procedures impossible to implement:

```
function odd(n : integer) : boolean
begin
  if n = 0 then
     odd := true
  else if n < 0 then
     odd := not even(n + 1) { Compiler error: 'even' is not defined }
  else
     odd:= not even(n – 1)
end;

function even(n : integer) : boolean
begin
  if n = 0 then
     even := true
  else if n < 0 then
     even := not odd(n + 1)
  else
     even := not odd(n – 1)
end;
```

By adding a forward declaration for the function 'even', before the function 'odd', the one-pass compiler is told that there will be a definition of 'even' later on in the program.

```
function even(n : integer) : boolean; forward;
  function odd(n : integer) : boolean
{ Et cetera.... }
```

The **disadvantage of compiling in a single pass** is that it is not possible to perform many of the sophisticated optimizations needed to generate high quality code. They are unable to generate as efficient programs, due to the limited scope available. It can be difficult to count exactly how many passes an optimizing compiler makes. For instance, different phases of optimization may analyses one expression many times but only analyses another expression once.

Multi-pass compiler

A multi-pass compiler is a type of compiler that processes the source code or abstract syntax tree of a program several times. This is in contrast to a one-pass compiler, which traverses the program only once. Each pass takes the result of the previous pass as the input, and creates an intermediate output. In this way, the (intermediate) code is improved pass by pass, until the final pass emits the final code.

Multi-pass compilers are sometimes called **wide compilers**, referring to the greater scope of the passes: they can "see" the entire program being compiled, instead of just a small portion of it. The wider scope thus available to these compilers allows better code generation (e.g. smaller code size, faster code) compared to the output of one-pass compilers, at the cost of higher compiler time and memory consumption. In addition, some languages cannot be compiled in a single pass, as a result of their design. While the typical multi-pass compiler outputs machine code from its final pass.

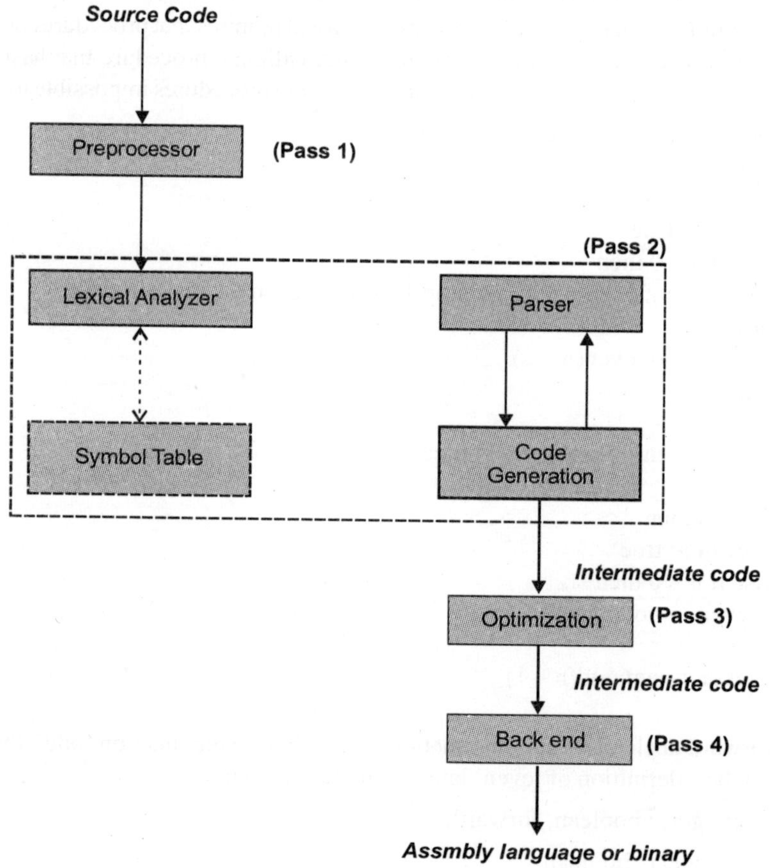

Figure 2.1: Structure of typical four pass compiler

- A "**source-to-source compiler**" is a type of compiler that takes a high level language as its input and outputs a high level language. For example, an automatic parallelizing compiler will frequently take in a high level language program as an input and then transform the code and annotate it with parallel code annotations(e.g., OpenMP) or language constructs (e.g. Fortran's DOALL statements).It is also known as **software simulation**.

- **Stage compiler** that compiles to assembly language of a theoretical machine, like some Prolog implementations.
  - This Prolog machine is also known as the Warren Abstract Machine (or WAM). Bytecode compilers for Java, Python, and many more are also a subtype of this.

The structure of a typical four pass compiler is shown in figure 2.1. The preprocessor is the first pass. Preprocessor do typically macro sub situation, strip comments from the source code, and handle various housekeeping tasks with which you don't want to burden the compiler proper. The second pass is heart of compiler. It made up of a lexical analyzer, parse and code generator, and it translate source code into intermediate language code that is much like assembly language. The third pass is the optimizer, which improves the quality of intermediate code, and fourth pass, that translate the optimized code to real assembly language or some form of binary executable code. The detailed description of each block is given in section 2.5.

2.2.2 Where Does the Code Execute?

One method used to classify compilers is by the platform on which the generated code they produce and executes

- A **native or hosted compiler** is one whose output is intended to directly run on the same type of computer and operating system as the compiler itself runs on.
- **Cross compiler** is designed to run on a different platform. Cross compilers are often used when developing software for embedded systems that are not intended to support an environment intended for software development.

The output of a compiler that produces code for a Virtual machine (VM) may or may not be executed on the same platform as the compiler that produced it. For this reason such compilers are not usually classified as native or cross compilers.

2.2.3 Hardware Compilation

The output of some compilers may target hardware at a very low level, such compilers are said to be **hardware compilers** because the programs they compile effectively control the final configuration of the hardware.

2.3 MEANING OF COMPILER DESIGN

A compiler for a relatively simple language written by one person might be a single, monolithic, piece of software. When the source language is large and complex, and high quality output is required the design may be split into a number of relatively independent phases, or passes. Having separate phases means development can be parceled up into small parts and given to different people. The division of the compilation processes in phases (or passes), terms **front end, middle end** (rarely heard today), and **back end**.

The **front end** is generally considered to be where syntactic and semantic processing takes place, along with translation to a lower level of representation (than source code). In general, the front end includes all analysis phases end the intermediate code generator.

The **middle end** is usually designed to perform optimizations on a form other than the source code or machine code. This source code/machine code independence is intended to enable generic optimizations to be shared between versions of the compiler supporting different languages and target processors. This end includes:

- Interprocedural analysis
- Alias analysis
- Loop nest optimisation
- SSA optimisation
- Automatic parallelisation

The **back end** takes the output from the middle. It may perform more analysis, transformations and optimizations that are for a particular computer. Then, it generates code for a particular processor and OS. In general, the back end includes the code optimization phase and final code generation phase.

This front end/middle/back end approach makes it possible to combine front ends for different languages with back ends for different CPUs.

2.3.1 Front End

The front end analyses the source code to build an internal representation of the program, called the intermediate representation or *IR*. It also manages the symbol table, a data structure mapping each symbol in the source code to associated information such as location, type and scope. This is done over several phases:

- Preprocessing some languages, e.g., C, require a preprocessing phase to do things such as conditional compilation and macro substitution. In the case of C the preprocessing phase includes lexical analysis.
- Lexical analysis breaks the source code text into small pieces called *tokens*. Each token is a single atomic unit of the language, for instance a keyword, identifier or symbol name. It also strop their keywords, require a phase before parsing, which is to take the input source and convert it to a canonical form ready for the parser.
- Syntax analysis involves parsing the token sequence to identify the syntactic structure of the program.
- Semantic analysis is the phase that checks the *meaning* of the program to ensure it obeys the rules of the language. One example is type checking. The compiler emits most diagnostics during semantic analysis, and frequently combines it with syntax analysis.

So, the front end is largely independent of the target machine.

2.3.2 Back End

The term of Back end is sometime confused with code generator for the overlapped functionality of generating assembly code. Some literature use Middle end to distinguish the generic analysis and optimization phases in the back end from the machine dependent code generators. The work in the back end is done in multiple steps:

- Compiler analysis - This is the process to gather program information from the intermediate representation of the input source files. Typical analyses are variable define-use and use-define chain, dependence analysis, alias analysis, pointer analysis, escape analysis etc. Accurate analysis is the base for any compiler optimization. The call graph and control flow graph are usually also built during the analysis phase.
- Optimization - The intermediate language representation is transformed into functionally equivalent but faster (or smaller) forms. Popular optimizations are inline expansion, dead code elimination, constant propagation, loop transformation, register allocation or even automatic parallelization.
- Code generation - The transformed intermediate language is translated into the output language, usually the native machine language of the system. This involves resource and storage decisions, such as deciding which variables to fit into registers and memory and the selection and scheduling of appropriate machine instructions.

So, the back end depends very heavily on the target machine.

2.4 COMPUTATIONAL MODEL: ANALYSIS AND SYNTHESIS

Any translator work on analysis and synthesis model. As we know that translator convert any text written in any language to other language so it will must follow two phases according to analysis and synthesis model i.e. ANALYSIS and SYNTHESIS.

Analysis phase in which the source program is analyzed to determine whether it meets the syntactic and static semantic constraints imposed by the language.Analysis phase take input string or source program as input and break it into atomic entity. Theses atomic entities are converted into low level language or in other intermediate form which lies between source program language and target language. In this phase, other operations are also performed as remove errors, store data type in storage as per type. If we compare it to compiler then get three phase of compile belongs to analysis phase in which lexical analysis, syntax analysis, semantic analysis and intermediate code generation occur. Lex convet source program into atomic entity as token and remaining two phases remove errors and store dataobjects and finally intermediate codes are generated as low level language or in intermediate form.

Synthesis part constructs desired program from low level language or other intermediate. This phase also employ various operation that will generate efficient low level language or other intermediate form to construct target program efficiently. In case of compiler code optimization and code generation phase belong to this phase in which efficient, small intermediate code is generated and target program is produced respectively.

2.5 PHASES OF COMPILER AND ANALYSIS OF SOURCE CODE

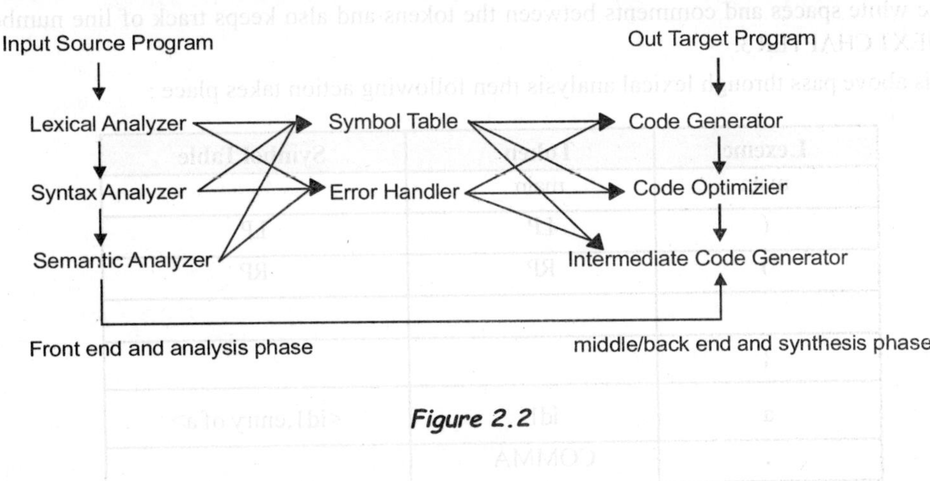

Figure 2.2

The cousins/relatives of the compiler are

1. Preprocessor
2. Assembler
3. Loader and Link-editor.

2.5.1 Source Code

Source code (commonly just **source** or **code**) is any series of statements written in some human-readable computer programming language. In modern programming languages, the source code which constitutes a program is usually in several text files, but the same source code may be printed in a book or recorded on tape (usually without a filesystem). The term is typically used in the context of a particular piece of computer software. A computer program's source code is the collection of files that can be converted from human-readable form to an equivalent computer-executable form. The source code is either converted into an executable file by a compiler for a particular computer architecture, or executed on the fly from the human readable form with the aid of an interpreter.The **code base** of a programming project is the larger collection of all the source code of all the computer programs which make up the project.

Example 2.2: If we write a code in C language as

```
main()
{
        int a ,b,c;
        float z;
        a=10, b=25;
        if(b>a)
                z = a + b * 3.14 ;
}
```

2.5.2 Lexical Analysis

In case of compile, lexical analysis is also known as liner analysis or scanning and works as interface between source program and syntax analyzer. The main task of Lexical Analyzer is to read a stream of characters as an input and produce a sequence of tokens such as names, keywords, punctuation marks etc.. for syntax analyzer. It discards the white spaces and comments between the tokens and also keeps track of line numbers. DISCUSSED in NEXT CHAPTER 3.

When this above pass through lexical analysis then following action takes place :

Lexeme	Token	Symbol Table
main	main	-
(	LP	LP
)	RP	RP
{		
a	id1	<id1,entry of a>
,	COMMA	-
b	id2	<id2,entry of b>
c	id3	<id3,entry of c>
;	SEMI	-
z	id4	<id4,entry of z>
=	RELOP	<assign_op, >

if	IF	-
>	RELOP	<GT,>
+		
*		
3.14		
}		

2.5.3 Syntax Analysis

Syntax analysis is also known as hieratical analysis or parsing analysis. In computer science, **parsing** is the process of analyzing a sequence of tokens in order to determine its grammatical structure with respect to a given formal grammar. So, the **syntax analyser or parser groups the tokens produced by the scanner into syntactic structures - which it does by parsing expressions and statements.** In general, output of the syntax analyzer is abstract syntax tree, a tree with a finite, labeled, directed tree, where the internal nodes are labeled by operators, and the leaf nodes represent the operands of the operators. It is formally named syntax analysis. A **parser** is a computer program that carries out this task.

Parsing transforms input text into a data structure, usually a tree, which is suitable for later processing and which captures the implied hierarchy of the input. Generally, parsers operate in two stages, first identifying the meaningful tokens in the input, and then building a parse tree from those tokens.

The task of the parser is essentially to determine if and how the input can be derived from the start symbol within the rules of the formal grammar. This can be done in essentially two ways:

- Top-down parsing
  - Recursive descent parser
  - LL parser
  - Packrat parser
  - Unger parser
  - Tail Recursive Parser
- Bottom-up parsing
  - Precedence parsing
  - BC (bounded context) parsing
  - LR parser
    - SLR parser
    - LALR parser
    - Canonical LR parser
    - GLR parser
  - Earley parser
  - CYK parser

DISCUSSED in NEXT CHAPTER 4.

PARSE TREE

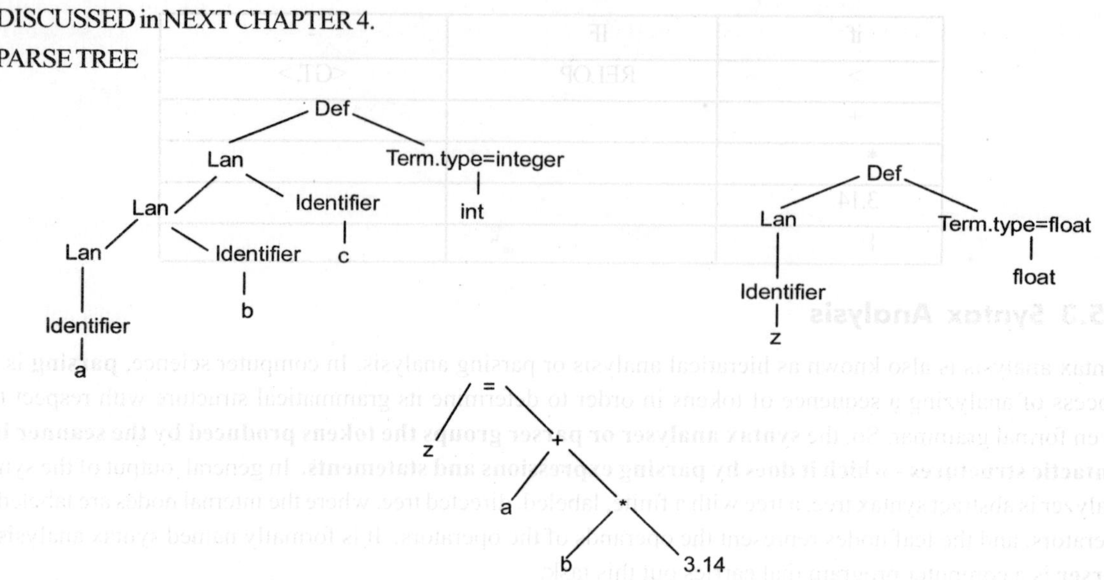

2.5.4 Semantic Analysis

Semantic is a term used to describe meaning so this analyzer is called SEMANATIC ANALYZER. Semantic analysis is a pass by a compiler that adds semantical information to the parse tree and performs certain checks based on this information. It logically follows the parsing phase or hierarchical phase, in which the parse tree is generated. Typical examples of semantical information that is added and checked is typing information (**type checking**) and the binding of variables and function names to their definitions (**object binding**). Sometimes also some early code optimization is done in this phase. For this phase the compiler usually use *symbol tables* in which each symbol are stored (variable names, function names, etc.) DISCUSSED in NEXT CHAPTER 5.

Example 2.3: In above code 'a', 'b', 'c' are defined as integer variable while 'z' is defined as float variable. So expression "z = a + b * 3.14" show error (type mismatch error) and can solve automatically or show error message.

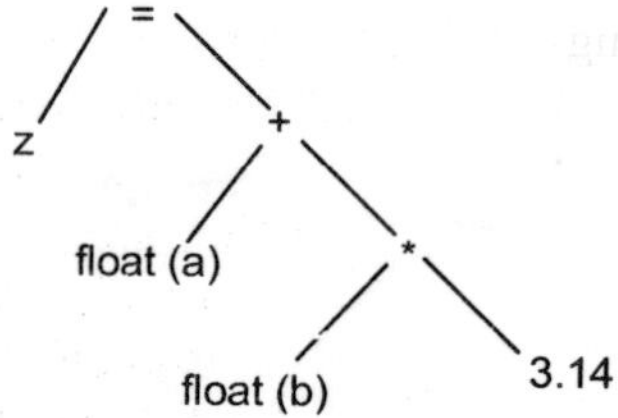

2.5.5 Intermediate Code Generation

In computer science, **three address code** (TAC) is a form of representing intermediate code used by compilers to aid in the implementation of code-improving transformations. Each TAC can be described as a quadruple (operator, operand1, operand2, result), triples (operator, operand1, operand2) and indirect triple. DISCUSSED in NEXT CHAPTER 6.

Each statement has the general form of:

z = x op y

where *x*, *y* and *z* are variables, constants or temporary variables generated by the compiler. '*op*' represents any operator, *e.g.* an arithmetic operator.

The term **three address code** is still used even if some instructions use more or less than two operands. The key features of three address code are that every instruction implements exactly one fundamental operation, and that the source and destination may refer to any available register.

Example 2.4: For above code intermediate code will be as

```
100)   a = 10
101)   b = 25
102)   if b > a then goto 104
103)   goto next
104)   temp1 = float (b)
105)   temp2 = float (a)
106)   temp3 = temp1 * 3.14
107)   temp4 = temp2 + temp3
108)   z = temp4
```

2.5.6 Code Optimization

Compiler optimization is the process of tuning the output of a compiler to minimize some attribute (or maximize the efficiency) of an executable program. The most common requirement is to minimize the time taken to execute a program; a less common one is to minimize the amount of memory occupied. This phase will use various optimization techniques as **Common themes renovation, Avoid redundancy, Less code, Straight line code, fewer jumps, Code locality, Extract more information from code, Avoid memory accesses and loop optimization.** Optimizations fall into three categories:

- **Speed**; improving the runtime performance of the generated object code. This is the most common optimisation .
- **Space**; reducing the size of the generated object code.
- **Safety**; reducing the possibility of data structures becoming corrupted (for example, ensuring that an illegal array element is not written to).

Unfortunately, many "speed" optimizations make the code larger, and many "space" optimizations make the code slower — this is known as the space-time tradeoff.DISCUSSED in NEXT CHAPTER 7.

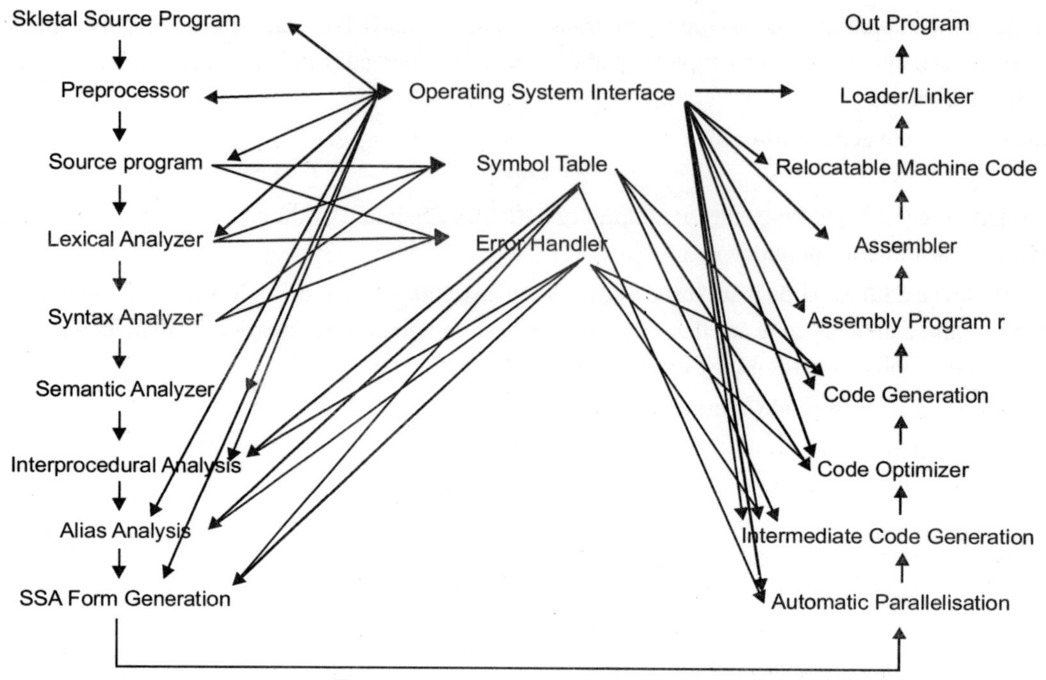

Figure 2.3: A wide compiler model

2.5.7 Code Generation

In computer science, **code generation** is the process by which a compiler's code generator converts a syntactically-correct program into a series of instructions that could be executed by a machine. Sophisticated compilers may use several cascaded code generation stages to fully compile code; this is due to the fact that algorithms for code optimization are more readily applicable in an intermediate code form, and also facilitates a single compiler that can target multiple architectures called **target machines** as only the final code generation stage (the back end) would need to change from target to target.

The input to the code generator stage typically consists of a parse tree, abstract syntax tree, or intermediate language code (often in three address code form). Since the target machine may be a physical machine such as a microprocessor, or an abstract machine such as a virtual machine or an intermediate language, (human-readable code), the output of code generator could be machine code, assembly code, code for an abstract machine (like JVM), or anything between. Major tasks in code generation **are instruction selection, instruction scheduling, register allocation.** DISCUSSED in NEXT CHAPTER 8.

Example 2.5: For above code code generation will do work as

R0 = a
R1 = b
R2 = c
R3 = z
R0 = 10
R1 = 25
R4 = 3.14

```
R5  =  R1 * R4
R6  =  R0+R5
R3  =  R6
a   =  R0
b   =  R1
```

A code generation class might take the form below.

```
enum CGEN_operators {
    CGEN_opadd, CGEN_opsub, CGEN_opmul, CGEN_opdvd, CGEN_opeql,
    CGEN_opneq, CGEN_oplss, CGEN_opgeq, CGEN_opgtr, CGEN_opleq
};

typedef short CGEN_labels;
class CGEN {
  public:
   CGEN_labels undefined;   // for forward references
   CGEN(REPORT *R);
   // Initializes code generator
   void negateinteger(void);
   // Generates code to negate integer value on top of evaluation stack
   void binaryintegerop(CGEN_operators op);
   // Generates code to pop two values A,B from stack and push value A op B
   void comparison(CGEN_operators op);
   // Generates code to pop two values A,B from stack; push Boolean value A op B
   void readvalue(void);
   // Generates code to read an integer; store on address found on top-of-stack
   void writevalue(void);
   // Generates code to pop and then output the value at top-of-stack
   void newline(void);
   // Generates code to output line mark
   void writestring(CGEN_labels location);
   // Generates code to output string stored from known location
   void stackstring(char *str, CGEN_labels &location);
   // Stores str in literal pool in memory and returns its location
   void stackconstant(int number);
   // Generates code to push number onto evaluation stack
   void stackaddress(int offset);
   // Generates code to push address for known offset onto evaluation stack
   void subscript(void);
   // Generates code to index an array and check that bounds are not exceeded
   void dereference(void);
   // Generates code to replace top-of-stack by the value stored at the
```

```
// address currently stored at top-of-stack
void assign(void);
// Generates code to store value currently on top-of-stack on the
// address stored at next-to-top, popping these two elements
void openstackframe(int size);
// Generates code to reserve space for size variables
void leaveprogram(void);
// Generates code needed as a program terminates (halt)
void storelabel(CGEN_labels &location);
// Stores address of next instruction in location for use in backpatching
void jump(CGEN_labels &here, CGEN_labels destination);
// Generates unconditional branch from here to destination
void jumponfalse(CGEN_labels &here, CGEN_labels destination);
// Generates branch from here to destination, conditional on the Boolean
// value currently on top of the evaluation stack, popping this value
void backpatch(CGEN_labels location);
// Stores the current location counter as the address field of the branch
// instruction assumed to be held in an incomplete form at location
void dump(void);
// Generates code to dump the current state of the evaluation stack
void getsize(int &codelength, int &initsp);
// Returns length of generated code and initial stack pointer
int gettop(void);
// Returns the current location counter
};
```

2.5.8 Out Target Program

Out target program also known as **object code**, or an **object file**, is the representation of code that a compiler generates by processing a source code file. Object files contain compact code, often called "binaries". A linker is used to generate an executable or library by linking object files together. An object file consists of machine code (code directly executed by a computer's CPU), together with relocation information, program symbols (names of variables and functions), and possibly debugging information. DISCUSSED in NEXT CHAPTER 8.

2.5.9 Symbol Table

In computer science, a **symbol table** is a data structure used by a language translator such as a compiler or interpreter, where each symbol in a program's source code is associated with information such as location, type and scope level. DISCUSSED in NEXT CHAPTER 9.

A hash table implementation of a symbol table is common and the table is usually maintained throughout all phases of translation. A compiler can use one large symbol table for all symbols or use separated, hierachical symbol tables for different scopes. A symbol table can be a transient structure used only during a language translation process and then discarded, or it can be embedded in the output of that process for later exploitation, for example, during an interactive debugging session, or as a resource for formatting a diagnostic report during or after execution of a program.

"Symbol" in Symbol table can refer to a variable, a function, or a data type in the source code. This symbol table is part of every object file. During the linking of different object files, it is the linker's responsibility to handle any unresolved references.

2.6 COUSINS/RELATIVES OF THE COMPILER

2.6.1 Preprocessor

Preprocessor is a program that processes its input data to produce output that is used as input to another program. The output is said to be a preprocessed form of the input data, which is often used by some subsequent programs like compilers. The amount and kind of processing done depends on the nature of the preprocessor; some preprocessors are only capable of performing relatively simple textual substitutions and macro expansions, while others have the power of fully-fledged programming languages.

2.6.1.1 Lexical Pre-processors

Lexical preprocessors are the lowest-level of preprocessors, insofar as they only require lexical analysis, that is, they operate on the source text, prior to any parsing, by performing simple substitution of tokens to user-defined rules. They typically perform macro substitution, textual inclusion of other files, and conditional compilation or inclusion.

(i) Pre-processing in C/C++

The most common use of the C preprocessor is the

#include "..."

or

#include <...>

directive, which copies the full content of a file into the current file, at the point at which the directive occurs. These files usually (almost always) contain interface definitions for various library functions and data types, which must be included before they can be used; thus, the #include directive usually appears at the head of the file. The files so included are called "header files" for this reason. Some examples include <math.h> and <stdio.h> from the standard C library, providing mathematical and input/output functions, respectively.

(ii) Macros

Macros are commonly used in C to define small snippets of code. During the preprocessing phase, each macro call is replaced, in-line, by the corresponding macro definition. If the macro has parameters, they are substituted into the macro body during expansion; thus, a C macro can mimic a C function. The usual reason for doing this is to avoid the overhead of a function call in simple cases, where the code is lightweight enough that function call overhead has a significant impact on performance.

For instance,

#define max(a, b).a>b?a:b

defines the macro max, taking two arguments 'a' and 'b'. This macro may be called like any C function, using identical syntax. Therefore, after preprocessing,

```
z = max(x, y);
becomes z = x>y?x:y;
```

C macros are capable of mimicking functions, creating new syntax within some limitations, as well as expanding into arbitrary text (although the C compiler will require that text to be valid C source code, or else comments), but they have some limitations as a programming construct. Macros which mimic functions, for instance, can be called like real functions, but a macro cannot be passed to another function using a function pointer, since the macro itself has no address.

2.6.1.2 Syntactic pre-processors

Syntactic preprocessors were introduced with the Lisp family of languages. Their role is to transform syntax trees according to a number of user-defined rules. For some programming languages, the rules are written in the same language as the program (compile-time reflection). This is the case with Lisp and OCaml. Some other languages rely on a fully external language to define the transformations, such as the XSLT preprocessor for XML, or its statically typed counterpart CDuce.

Syntactic preprocessors are typically used to customize the syntax of a language, extend a language by adding new primitives, or embed a Domain-Specific Programming Language inside a general purpose language.

2.6.1.3 General purpose preprocessor

- using C preprocessor for Javascript preprocessing.
- using M4 or C preprocessor as a template engine, to HTML generation.

2.6.2 Assembler

Typically a modern **assembler** creates object code by translating assembly instruction mnemonics into opcodes, and by resolving symbolic names for memory locations and other entities. The use of symbolic references is a key feature of assemblers, saving tedious calculations and manual address updates after program modifications. Most assemblers also include macro facilities for performing textual substitution — e.g., to generate common short sequences of instructions to run inline, instead of in a subroutine.
Assemblers are generally simpler to write than compilers for high-level languages, and have been available since the 1950s. Modern assemblers, especially for RISC based architectures, such as MIPS, Sun SPARC and HP PA-RISC, optimize instruction scheduling to exploit the CPU pipeline efficiently.

More sophisticated high-level assemblers provide language abstractions such as:

- Advanced control structures
- High-level procedure/function declarations and invocations
- High-level abstract data types, including structures/records, unions, classes, and sets
- Sophisticated macro processing.

2.6.3 Loader and Linker

A **linker** or **link editor** is a program that takes one or more objects generated by compilers and assembles them into a single executable program.

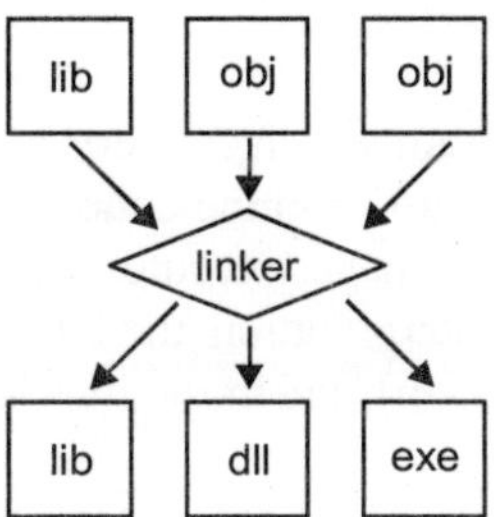

Figure 2.4: The linking process, where object files and static libraries are assembled into a new library or executable.

Examples 2.6:

(i) In IBM mainframe environments such as OS/360 this program is known as a linkage editor.

(ii) On Unix variants the term **loader** is often used as a synonym for **linker**. Because this usage blurs the distinction between the compile-time process and the run-time process, this article will use linking for the former and loading for the latter.

The objects are program modules containing machine code and information for the linker. This information comes mainly in the form of symbol definitions, which come in two varieties:

- Defined or exported symbols are functions or variables that are present in the module represented by the object, and which should be available for use by other modules.
- Undefined or imported symbols are functions or variables that are called or referenced by this object, but not internally defined.

In short, the linker's job is to resolve references to undefined symbols by finding out which other object defines a symbol in question, and replacing placeholders with the symbol's address. Linkers can take objects from a collection called a library. Some linkers do not include the whole library in the output; they only include its symbols that are referenced from other object files or libraries.

The linker also takes care of arranging the objects in a program's address space. This may involve relocating code that assumes a specific base address to another base. Since a compiler seldom knows where an object will reside, it often assumes a fixed base location (for example, zero). Relocating machine code may involve re-targeting of absolute jumps, loads and stores.

2.6.3.1 Dynamic linking

Modern operating system environments allow dynamic linking, that is the postponing of the resolving of some undefined symbols until a program is run. That means that the executable still contains undefined symbols, plus a list of objects or libraries that will provide definitions for these. Loading the program will load these objects/libraries as well, and perform a final linking.

Advantages

- Often-used libraries (for example, the standard system libraries) need to be stored in only one location, not duplicated in every single binary.
- If an error in a library function is corrected by replacing the library, all programs using it dynamically will immediately benefit from the correction. Programs that included this function by static linking would have to be re-linked first.

2.7 INTERPRETER

An **interpreter** is a type of translating program which converts high level language into machine code. It translates one statement of high level language into machine code, then executes the resulting machine code, then translates the next instruction of high level language, executes it, and so on. It never translates the whole program of high level language at one time. During interpretation, the HLL (high level language) program remains in the source form itself (or in some intermediate form), and the actions implied by it are performed by the interpreter.

2.7.1 Byte Code Interpreter

Emacs Lisp is compiled to bytecode which is a highly compressed and optimized representation of the Lisp source but is not machine code (and therefore not tied to any particular hardware). This "compiled" code is then interpreted by a bytecode interpreter (itself written in C). **Just-in-time compilation or JIT** refers to a technique where bytecode is compiled to native machine code at runtime; giving the high execution speed of running native code at the cost of increased startup-time as the bytecode is compiled.

2.7.2 Interpreter vs. Compiler

Here are various distinctions between interpreter and compiler as given:

1. If a translator accept a program and transformed it into simplified language (intermediate code) which are executed by interpreter while if a translator accept a HLL program and translate it into machine language, known as compiler.
2. Interpreting code is slower (in sense of there time complexity)than running the compiled code because the interpreter must analyze each statement in the program each time it is executed and then perform the desired action whereas the compiled code just performs the action.
3. Execution time of interpreter is larger than compiler.
4. Size of interpreter is small (in sense of there space complexity) while size of compiler is large.
5. Due to slower execution, except small in space complexity interpreter is not more efficient while compiler is more efficient due to fast execution, except large in space complexity.
6. Interpreter execute program line by line while compiler execute whole program at a time.

2.8 ABSTRACT INTERPRETER

Abstract interpretation was formalized by Patrick Cousot and Radhia Cousot.Abstract interpretation is a theory of sound approximation of the semantics of computer programs, based on monotonic functions over ordered sets, especially lattices. It can be viewed as a partial execution of a computer program which gains information about its semantics (e.g., control structure, flow of information) without performing all the calculations.

2.8.1 Incentive Knowledge

We shall now illustrate what abstract interpretation would mean on real-world, non-computing examples. Let us consider the people in a conference room. If we wish to prove that some persons were not present, one concrete method is to look up a list of the names of all participants. Since no two persons have the same number, it is possible to prove or disprove the presence of a participant simply by looking up his or her number in the list. If the name of a person is not found in the list, we may safely conclude that that person was not present; but if it is, we cannot conclude definitely without further enquiries, due to the possibility of homonyms (people with two same names). Let us note that this imprecise information will still be adequate for most purposes, because homonyms are rare in practice. However, in all hardly, we cannot say for sure that somebody was present in the room; all we can say is that he or she was *possibly* here. If the person we are looking up is a criminal, we will issue an *alarm*; but there is of course the possibility of issuing a *false alarm*. Similar phenomena will occur in the analysis of programs.

2.8.2 Abstract Interpretation of Computer Programs

Given a programming or specification language, abstract interpretation consists in giving several semantics linked by relations of abstraction. A semantics is a mathematical characterization of the possible behaviours of the program. The most precise semantics, describing very closely the actual execution of the program, is called the **concrete semantics**. For instance, the concrete semantics of an imperative programming language may associate to each program the set of execution traces it may produce – an execution trace being a sequence of possible consecutive states of the execution of the program; a state typically consists of the value of the program counter and the memory locations (globals, stack and heap).

2.8.3 Formalization

Let L be an ordered set, called a **concrete set** and let L' be another ordered set, called an **abstract set**. These two sets are related to each other by defining total functions that map elements from one to the other.
A function á is called an **abstraction function** if it maps an element x in the concrete set L to an element á(x) in the abstract set L'. That is, element á(x) in L' is the **abstraction** of x in L.

A function γ is called a **concretization function** if it maps an element x' in the abstract set L' to an element $\gamma(x')$ in the concrete set L. That is, element $\gamma(x')$ in L is a **concretization** of x' in L'.

Let L_1, L_2, L_1' and L_2' be ordered sets. The concrete semantics f is a monotonic function from L_1 to L_2. A function f' from L_1' to L_2' is said to be a **valid abstraction** of f if for all x' in L_1', $(f\,\gamma)(x') \leq (\gamma\, f')(x')$.

Program semantics are generally described using fixed points in the presence of loops or recursive procedures. Let us suppose that L is a complete lattice and let f be a monotonic function from L into L. Then, any x' such that $f'\,(x') \leq x'$ is an abstraction of the least fixed-point of f, which exists, according to the ***Knaster-Tarski theorem***. The difficulty is now to obtain such an x'. If L' is of finite height, or at least verifies the "ascending chain condition" (all ascending sequences are ultimately stationary), then such an x' may be obtained as the stationary limit of the ascending sequence x_n' defined by induction as follows: x_0' (the least element of L') and $x_{n+1}' = f'\,(x_n')$.

In other cases, it is still possible to obtain such an $x2$ through a **widening operator** : "for all x and y, x" y should be greater or equal than both x and y, and for all sequence y_n', the sequence defined by x_0' and $x_{n+1}' = x_n'$, y_n' is ultimately stationary. We can then take $y_n' = f(x_n')$.

In some cases, it is possible to define abstractions using **Galois connections** (α, γ) where α is from L to L' and γ is from L' to L. This supposes the existence of best abstractions, which is not necessarily the case. For instance, if we abstract sets of couples (x, y) of real numbers by enclosing convex polyhedra, there is no optimal abstraction to the disc defined by $x^2 + y^2 \leq 1$.

2.8.4 Example of Abstract Domain

One can assign to each variable x available at a given program point an interval $[l_x, h_x]$. A state assigning the value $v(x)$ to variable x will be a concretization of these intervals if for all x, then $v(x)$ is in $[l_x, h_x]$. From the intervals $[l_x, h_x]$ and $[l_y, h_y]$ for variables x and y, one can easily obtain intervals for $x+y$ $([l_x + l_y, h_x + h_y])$ and for x-y $([l_x - h_y, h_x - l_y])$; note that these are *exact* abstractions, since the set of possible outcomes for, say, $x + y$, is precisely the interval $([l_x + l_y, h_x + h_y])$. More complex formulas can be derived for multiplication, division, etc., yielding so-called **interval arithmetics.**

Let us now consider the following very simple program:

```
y = x;
z = x – y;
```

With reasonable arithmetic types, the result for z should be zero. But if we do interval arithmetics starting from 'x' in [0,1], one gets z in [–1,1]. While each of the operations taken individually was exactly abstracted, their composition isn't. The problem is evident: we did not keep track of the equality relationship between x y; actually, this domain of intervals does not take into account any relationships between variables, and is thus a **non-relational domain**. Non-relational domains tend to be fast and simple to implement, but imprecise.

2.9 CASE TOOL: COMPILER CONSTRUCTION TOOLS

If you are thinking of creating your own programming language, writing a compiler or interpreter, or a scripting facility for your application, or even creating documentation parsing facility, the tools on this page are designed to (hopefully) ease your task. These compiler construction kits, parser generators, lexical analyzer (analyser) (lexers) generators, code optimizers (optimizer generators), provide the facility where you define your language and allow the compiler creation tools to generate the source code for your software.

A compiler-compiler or compiler generator is a program that generates the source code of a parser, interpreter, or compiler from a programming language description. In the most general case, it takes a full machine-independent syntactic and semantic description of a programming language, along with a full language-independent description of a target instruction set architecture, and generates a compiler. In practice, most compiler generators are more or less elaborate parser generators which handle neither semantics nor target architecture. The first compiler-compiler to use that name was written by **Tony Brooker** in 1960 and was used to create compilers for the **Atlas computer at the University of Manchester**, including the **Atlas Autocode compiler.**

The earliest and still most common form of compiler-compiler is a parser generator, whose input is a grammar (usually in BNF) of the language. A typical parser generator associates executable code with each of the rules of the grammar that should be executed when these rules are applied by the parser. These pieces of code are sometimes referred to as semantic action routines since they define the semantics of the syntactic structure that is analyzed by the parser. Depending upon the type of parser that should be generated, these routines may construct a parse tree (or AST), or generate executable code directly.

Some experimental compiler-compilers take as input a formal description of programming language semantics, typically using denotation semantics. This approach is often called 'semantics-based compiling', and was pioneered by Peter Mosses' Semantic Implementation System (SIS) in 1979. However, both the generated compiler and the code it produced were inefficient in time and space. No production compilers are currently built in this way, but research continues.

Now here are list of some important CASE tool for compiler construction.

Elex Scanner Generator: Elex is a lexical scanner (lexer) generator that supports multiple programming languages. It is released under the GNU GPL, and has been tested on Linux.

Flex: Discussed in next chapter 3.

Lex: Discussed in next chapter 3.

JAVACC (Lexer): Discussed in next chapter 3.

SableCC (Lexer): This is an object-oriented framework that generates DFA based lexer, LALR (1) parsers, strictly typed syntax trees, and tree walker classes from an extended BNF grammar (in other words, it is a compiler generator). The program was written in Java itself, runs on any JDK system and generates Java sources.

Aflex and Ayacc (Lexer and Parser Generators) : This combination of a lexer and parser generator was written in Ada and generates Ada source code. It is modelled after lex and yacc.

ANTLR (Recursive Descent Parser Generator) : ANTLR generates a recursive descent parser in C, C++ or Java from predicated-LL(k>1) grammars. It is able to build ASTs automatically. If you are using C, you may have to get the PCCTS 1.XX series (the precursor to ANTLR), also available at the site. The latest version may be used for C++ and Java.

Bison (parser generator) : Bison generates a parser when presented with a LALR (1) context-free grammar that is yacc compatible. The generated parser is in C. It includes extensions to the yacc features that actually make it easier to use if you want multiple parsers in your program. Bison works on Win32, MSDOS, Linux and numerous other operating systems. The link points to the source code which should compile with many compilers.

Byacc/Java (Parser Generator) : This is a version of Berkeley yacc modified so that it can generate Java source code. You simply supply a "-j" option on the command line and it'll produce the Java code instead of the usual C output.

COCO/R (Lexer and Parser Generators) : This tool generates recursive descent LL(1) parsers and their associated lexical scanners from attributed grammars. It comes with source code, and there are versions to generate Oberon, Modula-2, Pascal, C, C++, Java. A version for Delphi is (at the time of this writing) "on the way". Platforms supported appear to vary (Unix systems, Apple Macintosh, Atari, MSDOS, Oberon, etc) depending on the language you want generated.

GOLD Parser (Parser Generator) : The GOLD Parser is a parser generator that generates parsers that use a Deterministic Finite Automaton (DFA) for the tokenizer and a LALR(1) for the state machine. Unlike other parser generators, GOLD does not require you to embed your grammar into your source code. It saves the parse tables into a separate file which is loaded by the parser engine when run.

JACCIE (Java-based Compiler Compiler) (Parser Generator) : Jaccie includes a scanner generator and a variety of parser generators that can generate LL(1), SLR(1), LALR(1) grammar. It has a debugging mode where you can operate it non-deterministically.

LEMON Parser Generator (Parser Generator) : This LALR(1) parser generator claims to generate faster parsers than Yacc or Bison. The generated parsers are also re-entrant and thread-safe. The program is written in C, and only the source code is provided, so you will need a C compiler to compile LEMON before you can use it.

Sid (Parser Generator) : Sid is an LL(1) parser generator that produces C code. It comes with the TenDRA C compiler.

TP Lex/Yacc (Lexical Analyzer and Parser Generators) : This is a version of Lex and Yacc designed for Borland Delphi, Borland Turbo Pascal and the Free Pascal Compiler. Like its lex and yacc predecessors, this version generates lexers and parsers, although in its case, the generated code is in the Pascal language.

YaYacc (Generates Parsers) : YaYacc, or Yet Another Yacc, generates C++ parsers using an LALR(1) algorithm. YaYacc itself runs on FreeBSD, but the resulting parser is not tied to any particular platform (it depends on your code, of course).

Grammatica : Grammatica is a parser generator for C# and Java. It uses LL(k) grammar with unlimited number of look-ahead tokens. It purportedly creates commented and readable source code, has automatic error recovery and detailed error messages. The generator creates the parser at runtime thus also allowing you to test and debug the parser before you even write your source code.

Eli (Semantic Analyzer): Eli handles structural analysis, analysis of names, types, values; stores translation structures and produces the target text. It generates C code. The program is available in source form and has been tested under Linux, IRIX, HP-UX, OSF, and SunOS. Eli itself is distributed under the GNU GPL.

Optimix Optimizer Generator (Optimizer): This optimizer generator allows you "to generate program analysis and transformations". It may be used in a CoSy compiler framework, with the Cocktail tool, or with Java.

Very Portable Optimizer (Code Generator): Very portable optimizer (Vpo) is a global optimizer that is language and compiler independent. It can be retargeted and supports a number of architectures. It is useful if you need a back end for the compiler you're constructing that handles optimized code generation.

Cocktail (compiler construction kit): This is a set of tools that generates programs for almost every phase of a compiler. Rex generates either a C or Modula-2 scanner. Lalr generates table-driven C or Modula-2 LALR parsers from grammar written in extended BNF notation, while Ell does the same for LL(1) parsers. The parsers generated have automatic error recovery, error messages and error repair. Ast generates abstract syntax trees, Ag generates an attribute evaluator, and Puma is a transformation tool based on pattern matching. The scanners and parsers generated are supposed to be faster than those generated by lex and yacc.

2.10 A SIMPLE COMPILER EXAMPLE(C LANGUAGE)

Example is given in **Appendix –A (Ex A.1 & A.2).**

2.11 DECOMPILERS

A **decompiler** is the name given to a computer program that performs the reverse operation to that of a compiler. That is, it translates a file containing information at a relatively low level of abstraction (usually designed to be computer readable rather than human readable) into a form having a higher level of abstraction (usually designed to be human readable).

"Decompiler is most commonly applied to a program which translates executable programs (the output from a compiler) into source code in a (relatively) high level language (which when compiled will produce an executable whose behaviour is the same as the original executable program)." Decompilation is the act of using a decompiler, although the term can also refer to the decompiled output. It can be used for the recovery of lost source code, and is also useful in some cases for computer security, interoperability, error correction, and more (see "Why Decompilation"). The success of decompilation depends on the amount of information present in the code being decompiled and the sophistication of the analysis performed on it.

2.11.1 Phases

Decompilers can be thought of as composed of a series of phases each of which contributes specific aspects of the overall decompilation process.

(i) ***Loader:*** The first decompilation phase is the loader, which parses the input machine code program's binary file format. The loader should be able to discover basic facts about the input program, such as the architecture and the entry point. In many cases, it should be able to find the equivalent of the main function of a C program, which is the start of the user written code. This excludes the runtime initialization code, which should not be decompiled if possible.

(ii) ***Disassembly:*** The next logical phase is the disassembly of machine code instructions into a machine independent intermediate representation (IR). For example, the Pentium machine instruction

```
mov    eax, [ebx+0x04]
```

might be translated to the IR

```
eax := m[ebx+4];
```

(iii) ***Idioms:*** Idiomatic machine code sequences are sequences of code whose combined semantics is not immediately apparent from the instructions' individual semantics. Either as part of the disassembly phase, or as part of later analyses, these idiomatic sequences need to be translated into known equivalent IR. For example:

```
cdq    eax
xor    eax,edx
sub    eax,edx
```

could be translated to

```
eax := abs(eax);
```

Some idiomatic sequences are machine independent; some involve only one instruction. For example, xor eax, eax clears the eax register (sets it to zero). This can be implemented with a machine independent simplification rule, such as a xor a = 0.

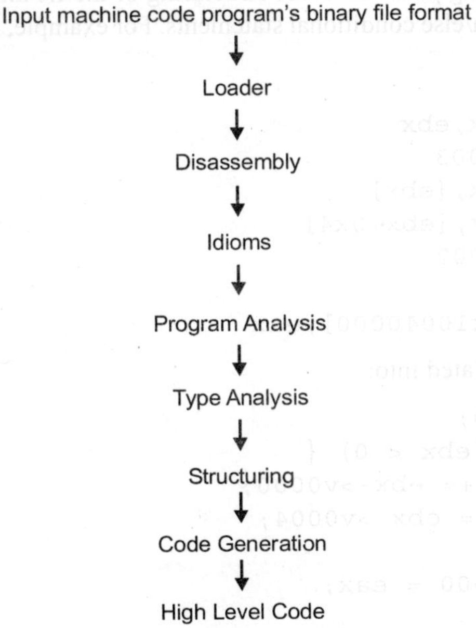

Input machine code program's binary file format
↓
Loader
↓
Disassembly
↓
Idioms
↓
Program Analysis
↓
Type Analysis
↓
Structuring
↓
Code Generation
↓
High Level Code

Figure 2.5: Decompiler's Phases

(iv) ***Program Analysis:*** Various program analyses can be applied to the IR. In particular, expression propagation combines the semantics of several instructions into more complex expressions. For example,

```
mov    eax,[ebx+0x04]
add    eax,[ebx+0x08]
sub    [ebx+0x0C],eax
```

could result in the following IR after expression propagation:

m[ebx+12]:=m[ebx+12] - (m[ebx+4] + m[ebx+8]);

The resulting expression is more like high level language, and has also eliminated the use of the machine register eax. Later analyses may eliminate the ebx register.

(v) ***Type Analysis:*** A good machine code decompiler will perform type analysis. Here, the way registers or memory locations are used result in constraints on the possible type of the location. For example, an 'add' instruction results in three constraints, since the operands may be both integer, or one integer and one pointer (with integer and pointer results respectively; the third constraint comes from the ordering of the two operands when the types are different). The example from the previous section could result in the following high level code:

```
struct T1* ebx;
        struct T1 {
                int v0004;
                int v0008;
                int v000C;
        };
ebx->v000C -= ebx->v0004 + ebx->v0008;
```

(vi) ***Structuring:*** Structuring phase involves structuring of the IR into higher level constructs such as while loops and if/then/else conditional statements. For example, the machine code

```
xor eax,eax
10002:
        or   ebx,ebx
        jge  10003
        add  eax, [ebx]
        mov  ebx, [ebx+0x4]
        jmp  10002
10003:
        mov  [0x10040000],eax
```

could be translated into:

```
eax = 0;
while (ebx < 0) {
   eax += ebx->v0000;
   ebx = ebx->v0004;
}
v10040000 = eax;
```

(vii) ***Code Generation:*** The final phase is the generation of the high level code in the back end of the decompiler. Just as a compiler may have several back ends for generating machine code for different architectures, a decompiler may have several back ends for generating high level code in different high level languages.

2.12 JUST-IN-TIME COMPILATION

Just-in-time compilation (**JIT**), also known as **dynamic translation**, is a technique for improving the performance of bytecode-compiled programming systems, by translating bytecode into native machine code at runtime. The performance improvement originates from pre-translating the entire file and not each line separately. JIT builds upon two earlier ideas in run-time environments: bytecode compilation and dynamic compilation.

Dynamic translation was pioneered by the commercial Smalltalk implementation currently known as VisualWorks, in the early 1980s; various Lisp implementations like Emacs picked the technique up quickly. Sun's Self language used these techniques extensively and was at one point the fastest Smalltalk system in the world; achieving approximately half the speed of optimised C but with a fully object-oriented language. Self was abandoned by Sun but the research went into the Java language, and currently it is used by most implementations of the Java virtual machine. The Microsoft .NET Framework also precompiles code into a portable executable (PE) and then JIT compiles it to machine code at runtime. This is achieved by the installation and/or existence of the .NET Framework (currently, version 3.0) on the target machine, which compiles a .NET application (in MSIL (Microsoft Intermediate Language) form) into machine code.

Overview

In a bytecode-compiled system, source code is translated to an intermediate representation known as bytecode. Bytecode is not the machine code for any particular computer, and may be portable among computer architectures. The bytecode is then interpreted, or run on a virtual machine.

A dynamic compilation environment is one in which the compiler can be used during execution. For instance, most Lisp systems have a compile function which can compile new functions created during the run. While advantageous in interactive debugging, dynamic compilation is less useful in a hands-off deployed system.

In a JIT environment, bytecode compilation is the first step, reducing source code to a portable and optimizable intermediate representation. The bytecode is deployed onto the target system. When the code is executed, the runtime environment's compiler translates it into native machine code. This can be done on a per-file or per-function basis: functions can be compiled only when they are about to be executed (hence the name "just-in-time").

Advantages

"Heavy Lifting" of parsing the original source code and performing basic optimization is handled at compile time, prior to deployment: compilation from bytecode to machine code is much faster than from source. The deployed bytecode is portable, unlike machine code for any given architecture. Compilers from bytecode to machine code are easier to write, because the portable bytecode compiler has already done much of the work. This also offers a better performance as the compiled code is stored in memory cache at runtime, such that subsequent recompilation of compiled code is skipped.

Disadvantages

JIT may have a minor drawback by causing a slight delay in initial execution of an application, because certain optimization processes, such as optimizations for target CPU and operating system model are first performed before pre-compilation into bytecode.

2.13 CROSS COMPILER

A cross compiler is a compiler capable of creating executable code for a platform other than the one on which the cross compiler is run. Such a tool is handy when you want to compile code for a platform that you don't have access to, or because it is inconvenient or impossible to compile on that platform. Cross-compilation is typically more involved and prone to errors than with native compilation. Due to this, cross-compiling is normally only utilized if the target is not yet self-hosting (i.e. able to compile programs on its own), unstable, or the build system is simply much faster. For many embedded systems, cross-compilation is simply the only possible way to build programs as the target hardware does not have the resources or capabilities to compile code on its own. Cross-compilation is also applicable when only the operating system environment differs, as when compiling a FreeBSD program under Linux, or even just the system library, as when compiling programs with uClibc on a glibc host.

Example 2.7: Following example shows multi-pass compiler and cross compiler.

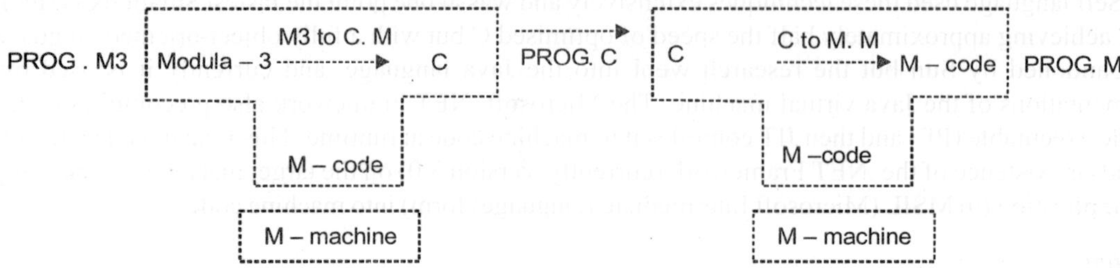

Compiling Modula-3 by using C as an intermediate language

In implementing a cross compiler, care must be taken to ensure that the behaviour of the arithmetic operations on the host architecture matches that on the target architecture, as otherwise enabling constant folding will change the behaviour of the program. This is of particular importance in the case of floating point operations, whose precise implementation may vary widely.

2.13.1 Uses of Cross Compilers

The fundamental use of a cross compiler is to separate the build environment from the target environment. This is useful in a number of situations:

- Embedded computers where a device has extremely limited resources. EXAMPLE : Microwave oven will have an extremely small computer to read its touchpad and door sensor, provide output to a digital display and speaker, and to control the machinery for cooking food. This computer will not be powerful enough to run a compiler, a file system, or a development environment.
- Compiling for multiple machines.

Example 2.8: Company may wish to support several different versions of an operating system or to support several different operating systems. By using a cross compiler, a single build environment can be maintained that would build for each of these targets.

- Compiling on a server farm.
- Bootstrapping to a new platform. When developing software for a new platform, or the emulator of a future platform, one uses a cross compiler to compile necessary tools such as the operating system and a native compiler.

2.13.2 GCC and Cross Compilation

GCC, a free software collection of compilers, can be set up to cross compile; it supports dozens of platforms and a handful of languages. However, due to limited volunteer time and the huge amount of work it takes to maintain working cross compilers, in many releases some of the cross compilers are broken.

Cross compiling gcc's requires that a portion of the C standard library is available for the targeted platform on the host platform. At least the crt0, ... components of the library has to be available in some way. You can choose to compile the full C library, but that can be too large for many platforms.

The GNU auto tools packages (i.e., autoconf, automake, and libtool) use the notion of a build platform, a host platform, and a target platform. The build platform is where the code is actually compiled. The host platform is where the compiled code will execute. The target platform usually only applies to compilers as it represents what type of object code the package itself will produce.

2.13.3 Canadian Cross

The Canadian Cross is a technique for building cross compilers for other machines. Given three machines A, B, and C, one uses machine A to build a cross compiler that runs on machine B to create executables for machine C. When using the Canadian Cross with gcc's, there may be four compilers involved:

- The proprietary native Compiler for machine A (1) is used to build the gcc's native compiler for machine A (2).
- The gcc's native compiler for machine A (2) is used to build the gcc's cross compiler from machine A to machine B (3)
- The gcc's cross compiler from machine A to machine B (3) is used to build the gcc's cross compiler from machine B to machine C (4)

The end-result cross compiler (4) will not be able to execute the resulting compiler on your build machine A; instead you would use it on machine B to compile an application into executable code that would then be copied to machine C and executed on machine C.

Example 2.9: NetBSD provides a POSIX Unix shell script named "build.sh" which will first build its own tool chain with the host's compiler; this, in turn, will be used to build the cross-compiler which will be used to build the whole system.

2.14 BOOTSTRAPPING

Now you think that compiler creation is a vary complicated task, but bootstrapping is an important concept for building new compilers. A simple language is used to translate a more complicated program, which in turn may handle an even more complicated program is known as **bootstrapping** For constructing a new compiler three languages are required.

(i) Source language (S) — that is compiled by new compiler.

(ii) Implementation language (I) — which is used for writing any new compiler.

(iii) Target language (T) — that is generated by new compiler.

These languages can be represented by 'T'- digram as shown below and represented as SI^T or CI^{ST}.

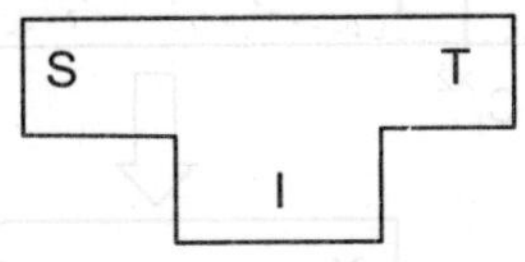

T-diagrams is a useful notation for describing a computer translator or compiler. T-diagrams were first introduced by Bratman (1961). They were further refined by Earley and Sturgis (1970).

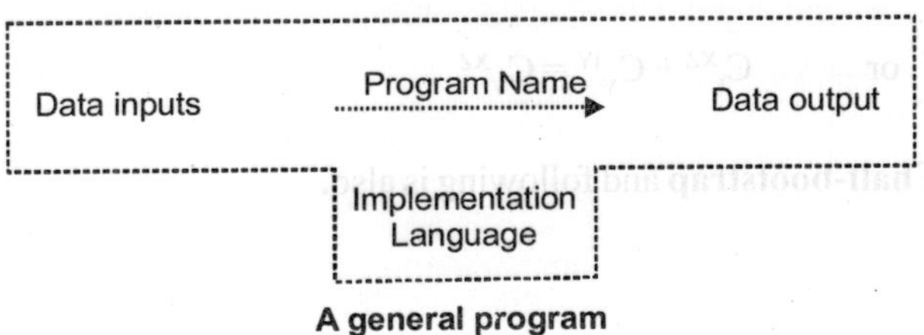

A general program

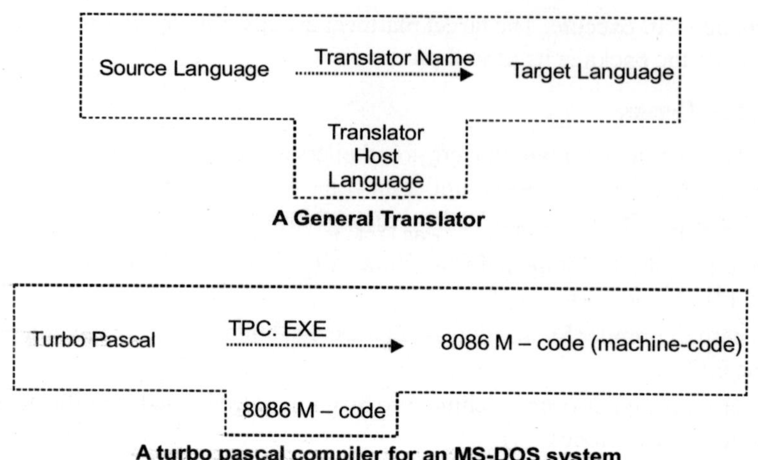

A General Translator

A turbo pascal compiler for an MS-DOS system

Example 2.10: We created a new compiler in new language 'X' which use implementation language 'I' as source language and produce code for 'Y' using same implementation language 'Y' In this case, both compilers are represented as:

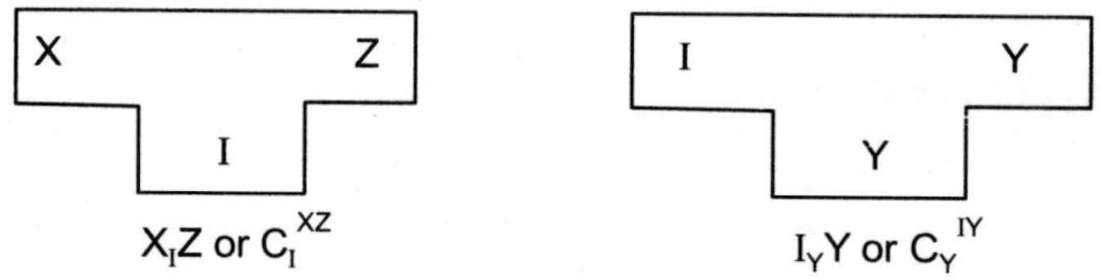

X_IZ or C_I^{XZ} I_YY or C_Y^{IY}

Now if we want to create a new compiler XYZ then we use bootstrapping as:

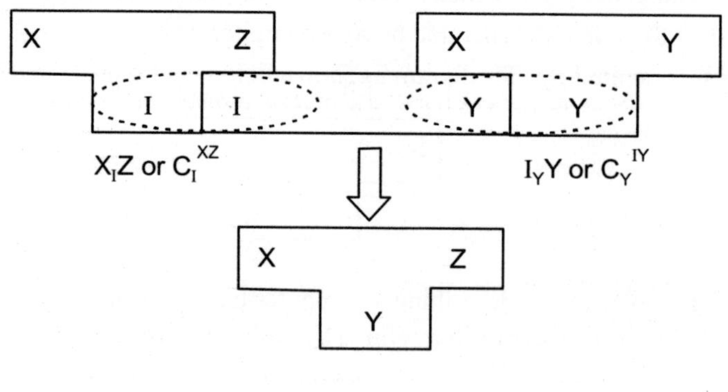

X_IZ or C_I^{XZ} I_YY or C_Y^{IY}

$X_IZ + I_YY = X_YZ$ or $C_I^{XZ} + C_Y^{IY} = C_Y^{XZ}$

This is the example of **half-bootstrap** and following is also.

Example 2.11: In this example we want to create new compiler XYA then

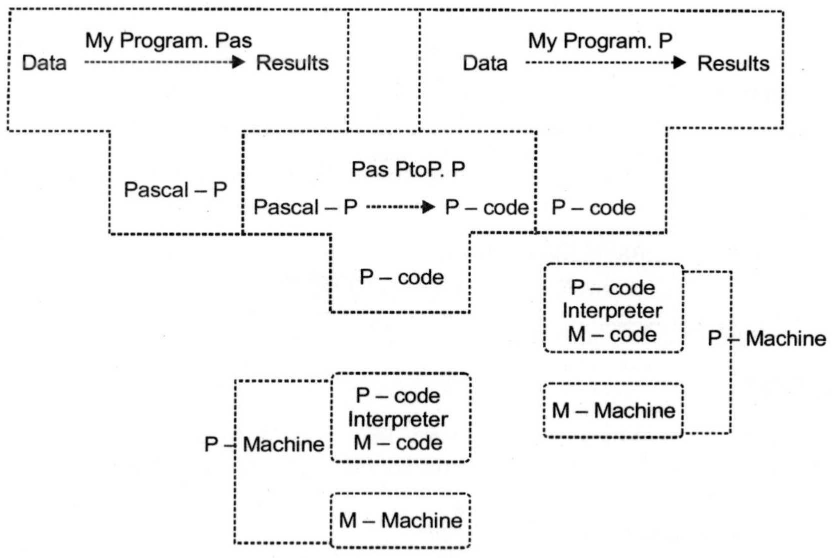

Compiling and executing a program with the P-compiler

2.15 MACRO

"Macros are commonly used in C to define small snippets of code. During the preprocessing phase, each macro call is replaced, in-line, by the corresponding macro definition."

There are two types of macros ***object-like*** **and** ***function-like.*** Function-like macros take parameters; object-like macros don't. The generic syntax for declaring an identifier as a macro of each type is, respectively,

```
#define <identifier> <replacement token list>
#define <identifier>(<parameter list>) <replacement token list>
```

Note that there must **not** be any whitespace between the macro identifier and the left parenthesis.

Wherever the identifier appears in the source code it is replaced with the replacement token list, which can be empty. For an identifier declared to be a function-like macro, it is only replaced when the following token is also a left parenthesis that begins the argument list of the macro invocation. The exact procedure followed for expansion of function-like macros with arguments is subtle.

Object-like macros are conventionally used as part of good programming practice to create symbolic names for constants, e.g.

#define PI 3.14159

instead of hard-coding those numbers throughout one's code.

An example of a function-like macro is:

#define RADIEN(x) ((x) * 57.29578)

This defines a radians to degrees conversion which can be written subsequently, e.g. RADIEN(34).

2.15.1 Quoting the Macro Arguments

Although macro expansion does not occur within a quoted string, the text of the macro arguments can be quoted and treated as a string literal by using the "#" directive. For example, with the macro

```
#define QUOTEME(x) #x
```
the code
```
printf("%s\n", QUOTEME(1+2));
```
will expand to
```
printf("%s\n", "1+2");
```
This capability can be used with automatic string concatenation to make debugging macros.

- Note that the macro uses parentheses both around the argument and around the entire expression. Omitting either of these can lead to unexpected results. For example:
- Without parentheses around the argument:
  - Macro defined as #define RADIEN(x) (x * 57.29578)
  - RADIEN(a + b) expands to (a + b * 57.29578)

2.16 X-MACROS

One little-known usage-pattern of the C preprocessor is known as "X-Macros". X-Macros are the practice of using the #include directive multiple times on the same source header file, each time in a different environment of defined macros.

```
File: commands.def

COMMAND(ADD, "Addition command")
COMMAND(SUB, "Subtraction command")
COMMAND(XOR, "Exclusive-or command")
enum command_indices {
#define COMMAND(name, description)      COMMAND_##name ,
#include "commands.def"
#undef COMMAND
    COMMAND_COUNT /* The number of existing commands */
};

char *command descriptions[] = {
#define COMMAND(name, description)      description ,
#include "commands.def"
#undef COMMAND
    NULL
};

result_t handler_AND (state_t *)
{
   /* code for AND here */
}

result_t handler_SUB (state_t *)
{
   /* code for SUB here */
}
```

```
result_t handler_XOR (state_t *)
{
  /* code for XOR here */
}
typedef result_t (*command_handler_t)(state_t *);
command_handler_t command_handlers[] = {
#define COMMAND(name, description)                &handler_##name
#include "commands.def"
#undef COMMAND
    NULL
};
```

The above allows for definition of new commands to consist of changing the command list in the X-Macro header file (often named with a .def extension), and defining a new command handler of the proper name. The command descriptions list, handler list, and enumeration are updated automatically by the preprocessor. In many cases however full automation is not possible, as is the case with the definitions of the handler functions.

EXAMPLES

EX. 1: Discuss the action taken by every phase of compiler on following string:

A = B*C + D/E

(i) First Phase-Lexical Analysis

Lexeme	Token	Symbol Table
A	id 1	<id 1,entry of A in ST>
=	RELOP	<Assign,>
B	id 2	<id 2,entry of B in ST>
*	MUL	<MUL,>
C	Id 3	<id 3, entyr of C in ST>
+	PLUS	<PLUS ,>
D	id 4	<id 4,entry of D in ST>
/	DIV	<DIV ,>
E		<id 5, entry of E in ST>

(ii) Second Phase-Syntax Analysis

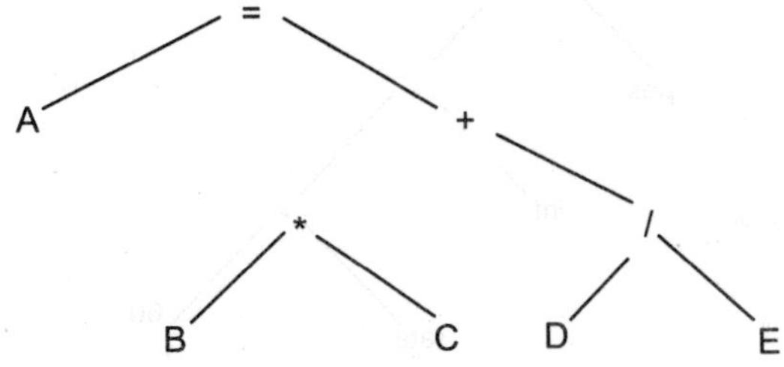

(iii) Third Phase : Semantic Analysis: No action performed because all variables are in same case or type.

(iv) Fourth Phase : Intermediate Code Generation

(1) t1 = B * C

(2) t2 = D / E

(3) t3 = t1 + t2

(4) A = t3

(v) Fifth Phase - Code Optimization

t1 = B * C
t2 = D / E
A = t1 +t2

(vi) Sixth Phase - Code Generation

R1 ← B
R2 ← C
R3 ← B * C
R1 ← D
R2 ← E
R4 ← D / E
R1 ← R3 + R4
A ← R1

EX. 2: Discuss the actions taken by compiler on " pos = int + rate * 60"

(i) First phase-Lexical Analysis

Lexeme	Token	Symbol Table
pos	id 1	< id 1, entry of pos in ST>
=	Assign	< Assign , >
int	id 2	< id 2,entry of int in ST>
+	plus	< plus , >
rate	id 3	< id 3,entry of rate in ST>
*	Mul	< Mul ,>
60	Num1	< Num1,entry of 60 inST>

(ii) Second Phase

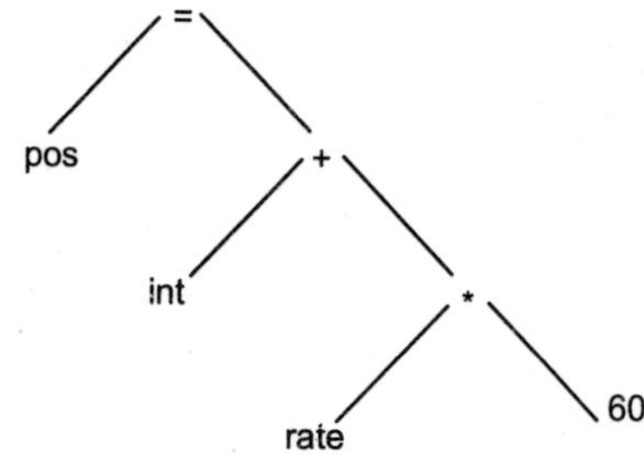

(iii) Third Phase

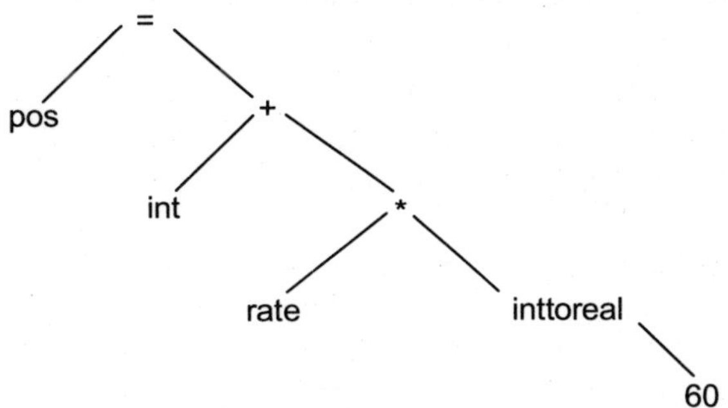

(iv) Fourth Phase - Intermediate Code Generation

t1 = intooreal (60)

t2 = t1 * rate

t3 = int + t2

pos = t3

(v) Fifth Phase - Code Optimization

t1 = inttoreal (60)

t2 = t1 * rate

pos = int + t2

(vi) Sixth Phase - Code Generation

R1 ← int
R2 ← rate
R2 ← rate * 60
R3 ← R2 + R1
Pos ← R3

TRIBULATIONS

2.1 An excellent compiler that translates Pascal to C is called p2c, and is widely available for Unix systems from several ftp sites. If you are a Pascal programmer, obtain a copy, and experiment with it.

2.2 Draw the T-diagram representations for the development of a P-code to M-code assembler, assuming that you have a C++ compiler available on the target system.

2.3 Try to find out which of the translators you have used are interpreters, rather than full compilers.

2.4 If you have access to both a native-code compiler and an interpreter for a programming language known to you, attempt to measure the loss in efficiency when the interpreter is used to run a large program (perhaps one that does substantial number-crunching).

2.5 Explain various phases of compilers.

2.6 What is cross compiler? How is the bootstrapping of compiler done to a second machine?

2.7 How source program is interpreted? What are the similarities and differences between compiler and interpreter?

2.8 Differences between macro processor and preprocessor.

2.9 What are the types of translation. Describe in detail the structure of C-compiler.

2.10 Justify your answer for the following:

(i) Time complexity of multipass compiler is large.

(ii) Parse can always generate the parse tree.

2.11 Write input alphabet of the following languages:

(i) Pascal

(ii) C

(iii) Fortran 77

(iv) Ada

(v) Lisp

2.12 Discuss the role of compiler writing tools . Describe various compiler writing tools.

2.13 Describe the technique used for reducing number of passes.

2.14 Describe role of Macro in programming language.

FURTHER READINGS AND REFERENCES

- **About Compiler**

[1] Alfred V. Aho, Ravi Sethi, and Jeffrey D. Ullman. *Compilers: Principles, Techniques and Tools.*

[2] Holub, Allen, *Compiler Design in C,* Extensive examples in "C".

[3] Appel, Andrew, *Modern Compiler Implementation in C/Java/ML* (It is a set of cleanly written texts on compiler design, studied from various different methodological perspectives).

[4] Brown, P.J. *Writing Interactive Compilers and Interpreters*, Useful Practical Advice, not much theory.

[5] Fischer, Charles & LeBlanc, Richard. *Crafting A Compiler*, Uses an ADA like pseudo-code.

[6] Weinberg, G.M. *The Psychology of Computer Programming: Silver Anniversary Edition,* Interesting insights and anecdotes.

[7] Wirth, Niklaus *Compiler Construction,* From the inventor of Pascal, Modula-2 and Oberon-2, examples in Oberon.

[8] *Compiler Textbook References,* A Collection of References to Mainstream Compiler Construction.

[9] Niklaus Wirth, *Compiler Construction*, Addison-Wesley 1996, 176 pages.

[10] C. Cifuentes. *Reverse Compilation Techniques*. Ph.D thesis, Queensland University of Technology, 1994. (available as compressed postscript).

[11] B. Czarnota and R.J. Hart, *Legal Protection of Computer Programs in Europe:* A guide to the EC directive. 1991, London: Butterworths.

[12] P.D. Terry, *Compilers and Compiler—Generators—An Introduction with C++*. Rhodes University, 1996.

- **About Bootstraping**

[13] Alfred V. Aho, Ravi Sethi, and Jeffrey D. Ullman, *Compilers: Principles, Techniques and Tools*

[14] P.D. Terry, *Compilers and Compiler Generators an introduction with C++*. Rhodes University, 1996.

[15] Holub, Allen, *Compiler Design in C,* Extensive examples in "C".

- **About Preprocessor and Macros**

[16] F.E. Allen, *"A History of Language Processor Technology in IBM"*. IBM Journal of Research and Development, V. 25, No. 5, September 1981.

[17] Randall Hyde, *The Art of Assembly Language Programming,* [2].

[18] T. Snyder, Show how to use *C-preprocessor* on JavaScript files. *"JavaScript is Not Industrial Strength"*.

[19] J. Korpela, Show how to use *C-preprocessor as template engine. "Using a C preprocessor as an HTML authoring tool"*, 2000.

- **About Assembler**

[20] Robert Britton: *MIPS Assembly Language Programming.* Prentice Hall.

[21] John Waldron: *Introduction to RISC Assembly Language Programming,* Addison Wesley.

[22] Jeff Duntemann, *Assembly Language Step-by-Step.*

CHAPTER 

INTRODUCTION TO SOURCE CODE AND LEXICAL ANALYSIS

CHAPTER HIGHLIGHTS

3.1 SOURCE CODE

Source code (commonly just **source** or **code**) is any series of statements written in some human-readable computer programming language. In modern programming languages, the source code which constitutes a program is usually in several text files, but the same source code may be printed in a book or recorded on tape (usually without a filesystem). The term is typically used in the context of a particular piece of computer software. A computer program's source code is the collection of files that can be converted from human-readable form to an equivalent computer-executable form. The source code is either converted into an executable file by a compiler for a particular computer architecture, or executed on the file from the human readable form with the aid of an interpreter.The code base of a programming project is the larger collection of all the source code of all the computer programs which make up the project.

Example 3.1: We write a code in C language as

```
main()
{
        int a ,b,c;
        float z;
        a=10, b=25;
        if (b>a)
                z = a + b * 3.14 ;
}
```

3.1.1 Purposes

Source code is primarily either used to produce object code (which can be executed by a computer directly), or to be run by an interpreter. Source code has a number of other uses as: It can be used for the description of software, as a tool of learning; beginning programmers often find it helpful to review existing source code to learn about programming techniques and methodology, as a communication tool between experienced programmers, due to its (ideally) concise and unambiguous nature. The sharing of source code between developers is frequently cited as a contributing factor to the maturation of their programming skills.

Source code is a vital component in the activity of porting software to alternative computer platforms. Without the source code for a particular piece of software, portability is generally so difficult as to be impractical and even impossible. Binary translation can be used to run a program without source code, but not to maintain it, as the machine code output of a compiler is extremely difficult to read directly. Decompilation can be used to generate source code where none exists, and with some manual effort, maintainable source code can be produced. Programmers frequently borrow source code from one piece of software to use in other projects, a concept which is known as Software reusability.

3.1.2 Organization

The source code for a particular piece of software may be contained in a single file or many files. A program's source code is not necessarily all written in the same programming language; for example, it is common for a program to be written primarily in the C programming language, with some portions written in assembly language for optimization purposes. It is also possible for some components of a piece of software to be written and compiled separately, in an arbitrary programming language, and later integrated into the software using a technique called **library linking**. Yet another method is to make the main program an interpreter for a programming language, either designed specifically for the application in question or general-purpose, and then write the bulk of the actual user functionality as macros or other forms of add-ins in this language, an approach taken for example by the GNU Emacs text editor. Moderately complex software customarily requires the compilation or assembly of several, sometimes dozens or even hundreds, of different source code files. The revision control system is another tool frequently used by developers for source code maintenance.

3.1.3 Licensing

Software, and its accompanying source code, typically falls within one of two licensing paradigms: Free software and Proprietary software. Generally speaking, software is ***free*** if the source code is free to use, distribute, modify and study, and ***proprietary*** if the source code is kept secret, or is privately owned and restricted. The provisions of the various copyright laws are often used for this purpose, though trade secrecy is also relied upon. Frequently source code of commercial software products additionally to licensing requires some protection from decompilation, reverse engineering, analysis and modifications to prevent illegal use integrating in an application a copy protection. There are different types of source code protection as code encryption, code obfuscation or code morphing.

3.1.4 Quality

The way a program is written can have important consequences for its maintainers. Many source code programming style guides, which stress readability and some language-specific conventions, are aimed at the maintenance of the software source code, which involves debugging and updating. Other issues also come into considering whether code is well written, such as the logical structuring of the code into manageable sections. For more quality code languages provide **general syntactic criteria** and **syntactic elements.**

3.1.4.1 General syntactic criteria

The primary purpose of syntax is to provide a notation for communication between the programmer and programming language translator. Now, we discuss some aspects of language that can create a code more effective.

- ***Readability:*** If underlying structure of source code and data represented by source code is apparent from an inspection of source code text then source code is said to be readable. A readable source code is said to be self documenting i.e. it is understandable without any separate documentation. Readability can be enhanced by using language's element as structured statement, use of library keywords, embedded comments, noise word, operator symbol, free field format.
- ***Writeability:*** Syntactic features that make a source code easy to write are often in conflict with those features that make it easy to read. Writeability can be enhanced by use of concise and regular expression while readability is enhanced by more verbose construct. A source code is said to be redundant if it communicate the same data object in more than one way. Main disadvantage of redundant source code is that it will be very hard to write.
- ***Ambiguity:*** Ambiguity is main problem of any language i.e. any statement can show different meanings of one thing by this way unique meaning of source code is impossible. The most common example of this case is "if – else statement" as

```
if exprl then
        if expr2 then
                statement1
        else
                statement2
```

```
if exprl then
        if expr2 then
                statement1
else
                statement2
```

- ***Verifiability:*** Verifiability is also related to source code. Working on any language up to long time make easy to understand the language construct while it will also difficult to know the working behind them, so we can only say that source code is verifiable.

3.1.4.2 Syntactic elements of source code

If we use syntactic elements in source code then readability, writeability and verifiability is enhanced. All syntactic elements of source code are predefined in respective language as 'character-set', 'operator-symbols', 'keywords', 'noise-words', 'comments', 'identifier-definitions', 'delimeters (which show end or beginning of new line or new structures as tab, space and brackets)', 'free / fixed format size of source code'.

3.1.5 Phrase Structure and Lexical Structure

It should not take much to see that a set of productions for a real programming language grammar will usually divide into two distinct groups. In such languages we can distinguish between the productions that specify the phrase structure - the way in which the words or tokens of the language are combined to form components of programs - and the productions that specify the lexical structure or lexicon - the way in which individual characters are combined to form such words or tokens. Some tokens are easily specified as simple constant strings standing for themselves. Others are more generic - lexical tokens such as identifiers, literal constants, and strings are themselves specified by means of productions (or, in many cases, by regular expressions).

3.1.6 The Structure of the Program

We can analyze a computer program on four levels:

1. Lexical structure level
2. Syntactic structure level
3. Contextual structure level
4. Semantic structure level

3.1.6.1 Lexical structure

The lexical level of any program is lowest level. At this level computer programs are viewed as simple sequence of lexical items called tokens. In fact at this level programs are considered as different groups of strings that make sense. Such a group is called a token. A token may be composed of a single character or a sequence of characters. We can classify tokens as being either:

- ***Identifier:*** In a particular language names chosen to represent data items, functions and procedures etc. are called identifiers. Considerations for the identifier may differ from language for example, some computer language may support case sensitivity and others may not. Number of characters in identifiers is also dependent on the design of the computer language.
- ***Keywords:*** Keywords are the names chosen by the language designer to represent facts of particular language constructs which can not be used as identifiers. Let us see example of language C.

```
int id;                    // Here id is identifier.
Struct id1
{                   // Here id is identifier.
int a;
char b;
}
```

- ***Operators:*** In some languages special "keywords" used to identify operations to be performed on operands that is math operators. For example in language C;
  - Arithmathematical operators (+,–,*, /, %)
  - Logical operator (>, =>, <, = =,!,!=)
- ***Separators:*** These are punctuation marks used to group together sequences of tokens that have a unit meaning. When outputting text it is often desirable to include punctuation, where these are also used as separators.
- ***Literals:*** Some languages support literals which denote direct value, can be
  - Number that is 1–123, 3.14, 6.02.
  - Characters that is 'a'
  - String that is 'some text'
- ***Comments:*** we know that a good program is one that is understandable. We can increase understandability by including meaningful comments into our code.

3.1.6.2 Syntactic structure

The syntactic level describes the way that program statements are constructed from tokens. This is always very precisely defined in terms of content-free grammar. The best known examples are BNF (Backus Naur Form) or EBNF (Extended Backus Naur Form).

Let us see an EBNF example:

```
<Sum> =  <operand>
         <Operator>
         <Operand>
<Operand> = <number> / (<sum>)
<Operator> = + / –
```

3.1.6.3 Contextual structure

The contextual level of analysis is concerned with the 'context' in which program statements usually contain identifier whose value is dictated by earlier statements. Consequently the meaning of statement is dependent on "what has gone before" context.

Let us see an example of language C,

```
int c = a + b;  //not valid because a, b, c are not defined.
int  a;         //valid
int  b;
int  c;
int  c = a + b; //valid because a, b, c are defined.
```

3.2 LEXICAL ANALYZER

Lexical analyzer is the first phase of compiler. Lexical analyzer takes the source program as an input and produces a long string of tokens. It discards the white spaces and comments between the tokens and also keep track of line numbers. It can be define as :

"Lexical analysis is the processing of an input sequence of characters (such as the source code of a computer program) to produce a sequence of symbols called "lexical tokens", or just tokens as output"

For example, lexers for many programming languages convert the character sequence '123 abc' into two tokens: 123 and abc (whitespace is not a token in most languages). The purpose of producing these tokens is usually to forward them as input to another program parser.

3.2.1 Implementation and Role

A lexical analyzer, or lexer for short, can be thought of having two stages, namely a **scanner** and an **evaluator/ lex analysis**. (These are often integrated, for efficiency reasons, so they operate in parallel.)

The first stage, **the scanner**, is usually based on a finite state machine. It has encoded within it information on the possible sequences of characters that can be contained within any of the tokens it handles (individual instances of these character sequences are known as **lexemes**). For instance, an integer token may contain any sequence of numerical digit characters. In many cases the first non-whitespace character can be used to result out the kind of token that follows the input characters are then processed one at a time until reaching a character that is not in the set of characters acceptable for that token.

The second stage of lexical analyzer is **evaluator / lex analysis** to construct a token, which goes over the characters of the lexeme to produce a value. The lexeme's type combined with its value is what properly constitutes a token, which can be given to a parser. The evaluators for integers, identifiers, and strings can be considerably more complex. Sometimes evaluators can hide a lexeme entirely, hiding it from the parser, which is useful for whitespace and comments.

Example 3.1: In the source code of a computer program the string

this_book_by_vivek_sharma = (project - manager)

might be converted (with whitespace hiding) into the token as:

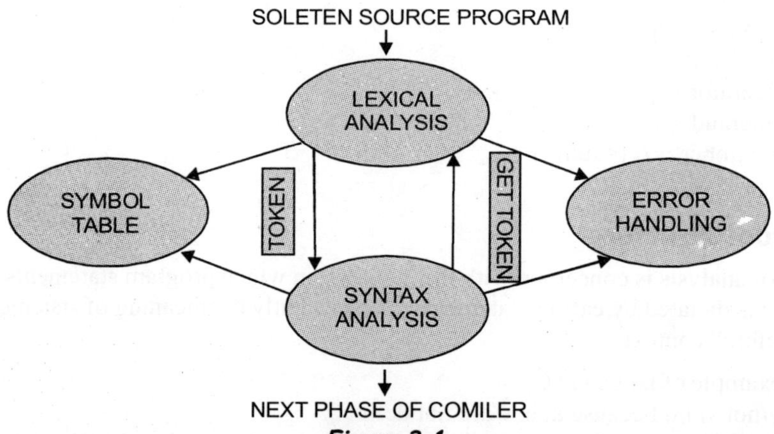

Figure 3.1

Lexeme	Token	Symbol Table
this_book_by_vivek_sharma	id1	<id1,entry of this_book_by_vivek_sharma >
=	RELOP	<assign_op, >
(	LP	LP
project	id2	<id2,entry of project >
-	_	_
manager	id3	<id3,entry of manager>
)	RP	RP

It is possible and sometimes necessary to write a lexer by hand, lexers are often generated by automated tools(Lex)*. These tools generally accept regular expressions+ that describe the tokens allowed in the input stream. Each regular expression is associated with a production in the lexical grammar of the programming language that evaluates the lexemes matching the regular expression.

So , the main work of lexical analyzer is :

1. Produce a sequence of atomic unit called token.
2. Remove white spaces and comments form skeleton source program.
3. Keep track of line numbers.

Advantages:

(i) Compiler efficiency is improved due to removation of white spaces and comments form skeleton source program.

(ii) Compiler portability is improved due to use of symbol table.

Disadvantages

Requires enormous amount of space to store tokens and trees.

3.3 TOKEN

"A lexical tokens / tokens are a sequence of characters that can be treated as a unit in the grammar of the programming languages."

Example of tokens:

- Type token ("id" {a-z, A-Z, 0-9}, "num" {0-9}, "real", . . .)
- Punctuation tokens ("if", "void", "return", "begin", "call", "const", "do", "end", "if", "odd", "procedure", "then", "var", "while". . .)
- Alphabetic tokens ("keywords")
- Symbol tokens ('+', '–', '*', '/', '=', '(', ')', ',', ';', '.', ':=', '<', '<=', '<>', '>', '>='.......)

Example of non-tokens:

- Comments, preprocessor directive, macros, blanks, tabs, newline, . . .

3.3.1 Attributes of Token

A token has only a single attribute— a pointer to the symbol table. This entry will consist all information related to a token .

Example 3.2: If we pass following expression from lexical analyzer then following token will produced and these are with there attribute.

(i) this_book_by_vivek_sharma = (project - manager)

TOKENS are 'this_book_by_vivek_sharma', '=', '(', 'project', '-' , 'manager'

TOKENS with there attributes as

<id , pointer to symbol table entry for this_book_by_vivek_sharma>

<assign_op , >

<LP ,>

<id pointer to symbol table entry for project>

<MINUS , >

<id pointer to symbol table entry for manager>

<RP , >

(ii) c = a + b
TOKENS are 'c', '=', 'a', '+', 'b'
TOKENS with there attributes as
<id , pointer to symbol table entry for c>
<EQ,>
<id , pointer to symbol table entry for a>
<PLUS,>
<id , pointer to symbol table entry for b>

3.3.2 Specification of Token

This section contains definition of grammar, string, language, regular expression and regular language. Please refer to Chapter 1.

3.3.3 Recognition of Token

It will be difficult to lexical analyzer to get tokens as first time when source code is encountered to lexical analyzer. It can be clarify with the example of simple identifier definition in C language as "int a; 2*a;". When this statement is encountered to lexical analyzer at first time it recognize int as predefined symbol and then create entry for 'a' in symbol table but in next line when lex get '2*a' then problem arise i.e., 2*a is a token or is a statement used for multiply 'a' to '2'. We can also take another example for this purpose that is related to 'if' statement of C language as "if a=2.5 or if a=25 (without any statement and else part)". In this case when first 'if' statement is encounter lex read statement up to found '.' in statement and then say 'if a=2' (after remove of whitespace) is not an identifier but in second 'if' statement lex is totally confused due there is no '.' and no statement that should follow if or any else part.

Exmaple 3.3: If we pass '10 DO 20 I = 1 . 30' then following two case arises:

CASE (i):

Lexeme	Tokens
10	label
DO	keyword
20	statement label
I	INTEGER identifier
=	assignment operator
1	INTEGER constant
.	separator
30	INTEGER constant

CASE (ii):

Lexeme	Tokens
10	label
DO20I	REAL identifier
=	assignment operator
1.30	REAL constant

3.3.4 Scanning/Lexical Analysis via a Tool-JavaCC

In JavaCC's terminology the scanner/lexical analyzer is called the **token manager** and the generated class that contains the token manager is called **ParserNameTokenManager**. Of course, following the usual Java file name requirements, the class is stored in a file called **ParserNameTokenManager.java**. The ParserName part is taken from the input file. In addition, JavaCC creates a second class, called **ParserNameConstants.** That second class, as the name implies, contains definitions of constants, especially token constants. JavaCC also generates a boilerplate class called Token. That one is always the same, and contains the class used to represent tokens. One also gets a class called ParseError. This is an exception which is thrown if something went wrong.

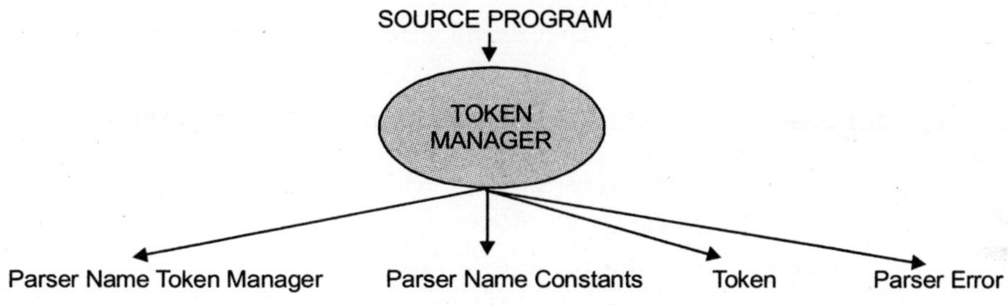

Figure 3.2

is possible to instruct JavaCC not to generate the Parser Name Token Manager, and instead provide your own, hand-written, token manager.

3.3.4.1 Terminology the JavaCC Grammar File

- ***TOKEN:*** Regular expressions which specify the tokens the token manager should be able to recognize.
- ***SPECIAL TOKEN:*** Special token are similar to tokens. Only, that the parser ignores them. This is useful to e.g. specify comments, which are supposed to be understood, but have no significance to the parser.

  SKIP: Tokens which is supposed to be completely ignored by the token manager. This is commonly used to ignore whitespace.
- ***MORE :*** This is used for an advanced technique, where a token is gradually built. More tokens are put in a buffer until the next token or special token matches. Then all data, the accumulated token in the buffer, as well as the last token or special token is returned.

Each of the above mentioned keywords can be used as often as desired. This makes it possible to group the tokens, e.g. in a list for operators and another list for keywords. All sections of the same kind are merged together as if just one section had been specified.Every specification of a token consists of the token's symbolic name, and a regular expression. If the regular expression matches, the symbol is returned by the token manager.

Example:

```
//
// Skip whitespace in input
// if the input matches space, carriage return, new line or a tab,
```

```
// it is just ignored
//
SKIP: { " " | "\r" | "\n" | "\t" }
// Define the tokens representing our operators
//
TOKEN: {
    < PLUS:   "+" >
  | < MINUS:  "-" >
  | < MUL:    "*" >
  | < DIV:    "/" >
}
//
// Define the tokens representing our keywords
//
TOKEN: {
    < IF:     "if" >
  | < THEN:   "then" >
  | < ELSE:   "else" >
}
```

All the above token definitions use simple regular expressions,

3.3.4.2 Defining Tokens in the JavaCC Grammar File

A JavaCC grammar file usually starts with code which is relevant for the parser, and not the scanner. For simple grammar files it looks similar to:

```
options { LOOKAHEAD=1; }

PARSER_BEGIN(ParserName)
public class ParserName {
    // code to enter the parser goes here
}
PARSER_END(ParserName)
```

This is usually followed by the definitions for tokens. Four different kinds described above indicated by four different keywords are understood by JavaCC.

3.4 LEXEME

A lexeme is an abstract unit of morphological analysis in linguistics, that roughly corresponds to a set of words that are different forms of the same word. For example, English 'run, runs, ran and running' are forms of the same lexeme. A related concept is the lemma (or citation form), which is a particular form of a lexeme that is chosen by convention to represent a canonical form of a lexeme. Lemmas are used in dictionaries as the headwords, and other forms of a lexeme are often listed later in the entry if they are unusual in some way. In the same way lexeme is define for compilers as:

"A lexeme is a sequence of character in program that is matched by pattern for a token."

3.5 PATTERN

A pattern is a form, template, or model (or, more abstractly, a set of rules) which can be used to make or to generate things or parts of a thing, especially if the things that are generated have enough in common for the underlying pattern to be inferred or perceived, in which case the things are said to exhibit the pattern. Pattern matching is the act of checking for the presence of the constituents of a pattern. The detection of underlying patterns is called pattern recognition. In the same way lexeme is define for compilers as:

"There is a set of a string in input for which the same token is produced as output .These set of string is described by a rule called pattern."

Or

"A pattern is a rule describing the set of lexeme that represent particular token."

3.6 FUNCTION WORD

Function words (or grammatical words) are words that have little lexical meaning or have ambiguous meaning, but instead serve to express grammatical relationships with other words within a sentence, or specify the attitude or mood of the speaker. Words which are not function words are called **content words or lexical words**: these include nouns, verbs, adjectives, and most adverbs, though some adverbs are function words (e.g. then, why). Dictionaries define the specific meanings of content words, but can only describe the general usages of function words. By contrast, grammar describe the use of function words in detail, but have little interest in lexical words.

Example 3.4: Identify tokens & lexemes & give reasonable value for tokens.

```
Function Max (i,j: integer): integer;
{
        Return max : integer
        Begin
                if i>j then
                        max:=i
                else
                        max:=j
        End;
    }
```

Lexeme	Token	Symbol Table Entry
Function	Function	
Max	Max	
(	Left Parenthesis	<LP,>
i	int, id1	<id1, entry of i>
,	**comma**	-
j	id2	<id2, entry of j>
:	**colon**	**<Col,>**
integer		int -
)	Right Parenthesis	<RP,>

Contd...

;	**SCOL**	**<SCOL,>**
{	**Left Braces**	**<LSB,>**
Return	return	<return,>
max	id3	<id3, entry of max>
:		
integer		
if	if	-
>	id4	<, entry of >
Begin	BGN	<Begin,>
then	THEN	<then>
Max		
=	RELOP	<assign-op,>
else	ELSE	-
End	END	-
}	**Right Braces**	**<RSB,>**

Example 3.5: Identify lexeme & give reasonable attributes value for token.

```
int max (i,j)
{
        return i>j ? i: j;
}
```

Lexeme	Token	Symbol Table
int	int	-
max	id1	<id1, entry of max
(		
{	**Left Braces**	**<LSB,>**
i	id2	id2, entry of i>
,	**comma**	-
j	id3	<id3, entry of j>
return	return	<return,>
>	RELOP	<GP,>
:	**Colen**	**<Col,>**
;	**SCOL**	**<SCOL,>**
}	**Right Braces**	**<RSB,>**

NOTE : Here may be difference between entry of ',', ';', '?', '{', '}', ':' in symbol table according to various books. This will be clear by following example.

Example 3.6: Identify lexeme & give reasonable attributes value for tokens.

```
Function max (i,j)
//Return max of integer I &j
        if (i GTj ) Then
            max=i
        else
```

```
            max=j
        end if
Return (max)
```

Lexeme	Token	Symbol table
int	int	-
max	id1	<id1, entry of max
Function	Function	-
max	max	-
(	LP	LP
i	id1	<id1, entry of i>
,	**Comma**	-
j	id2	<id2, entry of j>
)	RP	RP
if	IF	-
GT	RELOP	<GT,>
Then	THEN	-
=	RELOP	<assign-op,>
else	ELSE	-
End if	ENDIF	-
Return	Return	-

3.7 LEX PROGRAMMING TOOL

Lex is a program that generates lexical analyzers /scanners/ lexer. This tool also known as Lex-Compiler.Lex is commonly used with the yacc parser generator. Lex, originally written by **Eric Schmidt and Mike Lesk**, is the standard lexical analyzer generator on Unix systems, and is included in the POSIX standard. Lex reads an input stream specifying the lexical analyzer and outputs source code implementing the lexer in the C programming language.

Though traditionally proprietary software, versions of Lex based on the original AT&T code are available as open source, as part of systems such as Open Solaris and Plan 9 from Bell Labs. Another popular open source version of Lex is **Flex, the "fast lexical analyzer"**.

For lex analyzer, firstly we prepared all the specification of lex analyzer in lex language as lex.l. Then lex.l is run via lex compiler to produce a 'C' compiler program as lex.yy.c which is the tabular representation of a translation diagram contructed from regular expression of lex.l which will finally run via 'C' compiler to produce an object file as a.out.

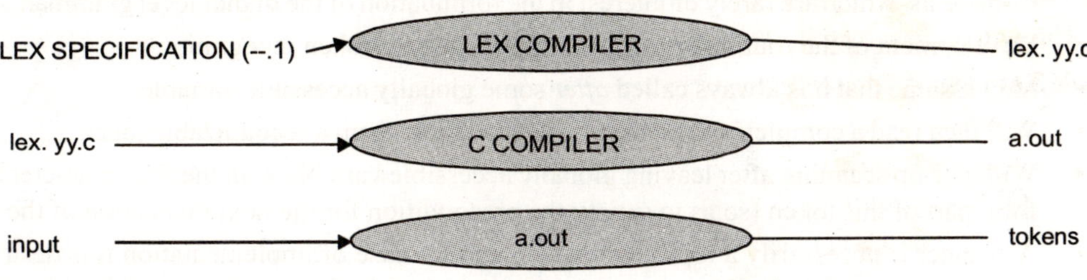

Figure 3.3

Structure of a Lex File

The structure of a lex file are divided up into three sections, separated by lines that contain only two percent signs, as follows:

Definition section
%%
Rules section
%%
C code section

The **definition section** is the place to define macros and to import header files written in C. It is also possible to write any C code here, which will be copied literally into the generated source file.

The **rules** section is the most important section; it associates patterns with C statements. Patterns are simply regular expressions. When the lexer sees some text in the input matching a given pattern, it executes the associated C code. This is the basis of how lex operates.

The **C code** section contains C statements and functions that are copied literally to the generated source file. These statements presumably contain code called by the rules in the rules section. In large programs it is more convenient to place this code in a separate file and link it in at compile time.

3.7.1 Construction of Simple Scanners (*some part may be related to chapter 4)

A scanner or lexical analyzer may be thought of as just another syntax analyzer. It handles a grammar with productions relating non-terminals such as identifier number and Relop to terminals supplied as single characters of the source text. Each spell of the scanner is very much bottom-up rather than top-down; its task ends when it has reduced a string of characters to a token, without predetermined ideas of what that should be. These tokens or non-terminals are then regarded as terminals by the higher level recursive descent parser that analyses the phrase structure of Block, Statement, and Expression and so on.

There are at least five reasons for wishing to decouple the scanner from the main parser:

- The productions involved are usually very simple. Very often they amount to regular expressions, and then a scanner may be programmed without recourse to methods like recursive descent.
- A symbol like an identifier is lexically equivalent to a "reserved word"; the distinction may sensibly be made as soon as the basic token has been synthesized.
- The character set may vary from machine to machine, a variation easily isolated in this phase.
- The semantic analysis of a numeric literal constant (deriving the internal representation of its value from the characters) is easily performed in parallel with lexical analysis.
- The scanner can be made responsible for screening out superfluous separators, like blanks and Comments, which are rarely of interest in the formulation of the higher level grammar.
- Development of the routine or function responsible for token recognition
- May assume that it is always called *after* some globally accessible variable.
- Will then read a complete sequence of characters that form a recognizable token.
- Will give up scanning after leaving globally accessible variable with the first character that does not form part of this token (so as to satisfy the precondition for the next invocation of the scanner).
- A scanner is necessarily a top-down parser, and for ease of implementation it is desirable that the productions defining the token grammar also obey the LL(1) rules. However, checking these is much

simpler, as token grammar are almost frequently regular, and do not display self-embedding and thus can be almost always easily be transformed into LL(1) grammar.

- There are two main strategies that are employed in scanner construction:
- Rather than being decomposed into a set of recursive routines, simple scanners are often written in an adhoc manner, controlled by a large CASE or switch statement, since the essential task is one of choosing between a number of tokens, which are sometimes distinguishable on the basis of their initial characters.
- Alternatively, since they usually have to read a number of characters, scanners are often written in the form of a **finite state automaton** (FSA) controlled by a loop, on each iteration of which a single character is absorbed, the machine moving between a number of "states", determined by the character just read. This approach has the advantage that the construction can be official in terms of a widely developed automata theory, leading to algorithms from which scanner generators can be constructed automatically.

3.7.2 The Generated Lexical Analyzer Module

There are some special circumstances in which it is necessary to change the interactions between the lexical analyzer and its environment. For example, there is a mismatch between the lexical analyzer and the source code input module of a FORTRAN 90 compiler: The unit of input text dealt with by the source code module is the line, the unit dealt with by the lexical analyzer is the statement and there is no relationship between lines and statements. One line may contain many statements, or one statement may be spread over many lines. This mismatch problem is solved by requiring the two modules to interact via a buffer, and managing that buffer so that it contains both an integral number of lines and an integral number of statements. Because the lexical analyzer normally works directly in the source module's buffer, that solution requires a change in the relationship between the lexical analyzer and its environment.

The interaction between the lexical analyzer and its environment is governed by the following interface:

```
#include "gla.h"
/* Entities exported by the lexical analyzer module
* NORETURN   (constant)     Classification of a comment
* ResetScan  (variable)     Flag causing scan pointer reset
* TokenStart (variable)     Address of first classified character
* TokenEnd   (variable)     Address of first unclassified character
* StartLine  (variable)     Column index = (TokenEnd - StartLine)
* glalex     (operation)    Classify the next character sequence
***/
```

There are three distinct aspects of the relationship between the lexical analyzer and its environment

1. First we consider how the lexical analyzer selects the character sequence to be scanned i.e. interaction between the lexical analyzer and the text.
2. Second we see how the lexical analyzer's attention can be switched i.e. **resetting the scan pointer.**
3. Finally how the classification results are reported i.e. t**he classification operation.**

3.7.2.1 Interaction between the lexical analyzer and the text

There is no internal storage for text in the lexical analyzer module. Instead, 'TokenEnd' is set to point to arbitrary text storage. The text pointed to must be an arbitrary sequence of characters, the last of which is an ASCII NUL. At the beginning of a scan, 'TokenEnd' points to the beginning of the string on which a sequence is to be classified. The lexical analyzer tests that string against its set of regular expressions, finding the longest sequence that begins with the first character and matches one of the regular expressions.

If the regular expression matched is associated with an auxiliary scanner then that auxiliary scanner is invoked with the matched sequence .The auxiliary scanner returns a pointer to the first character that should not be considered part of the character sequence being matched, and that pointer becomes the value of 'TokenEnd'. 'TokenStart' is set to point to the first character of the string.

When no initial character sequence matches any of the regular expressions an error report is issued, 'TokenEnd' is advanced by one position (thus discarding the first character of the string), and the process is restarted. If the string is initially empty, no attempt is made to match any regular expressions. Instead, the auxiliary scanner 'auxNUL' is invoked immediately. If this auxiliary scanner returns a pointer to an empty string then the auxiliary scanner 'auxEOF' is invoked immediately. Finally, if 'auxEOF' returns a pointer to an empty string then the Token processor 'EndOfText' is invoked immediately. (If either 'auxNUL' or 'auxEOF' returns a pointer to a non-empty string, scanning begins on this string as though TokenEnd had pointed to it initially.)

TokenStart addresses a sequence of length 'TokenEnd-TokenStart' when a token processor is invoked. Because TokenStart and TokenEnd are exported variables, the token processor may change them if that is appropriate. All memory locations below the location pointed to by 'TokenStart' are undefined in the fullest sense of the word: Their contents are unknown, and they may not even exist. Memory locations beginning with the one pointed to by 'TokenStart', up to but not including the one pointed to by 'TokenEnd', are known to contain a sequence of non-NUL characters. 'TokenEnd' points to a sequence of characters, the last of which is an ASCII NUL. If the token processor modifies the contents of 'TokenStart' or 'TokenEnd', it must ensure that these conditions hold after the modification.

3.7.2.2 Resetting the scan pointer

If the exported variable ResetScan is non-zero when the operation glalex is invoked, the lexical analyzer's first action is to execute the macro SCANPTR. SCANPTR guarantees that TokenEnd addresses the string to be scanned. If ResetScan is zero when glalex is invoked, TokenEnd is assumed to address that string already. ResetScan is statically initialized to 1, meaning that SCANPTR will be executed on the first invocation of glalex.

In the distributed system, SCANPTR sets TokenEnd to point to the first character of the source module's text buffer. Since this is also the first character of a line, StartLine must also be set.

```
#define SCANPTR { TokenEnd = TEXTSTART; StartLine = TokenEnd – 1; }
```

This implementation can be changed by supplying a file 'scanops.h', containing a new definition of SCANPTR, as one of your specification files.

ResetScan is set to zero after SCANPTR has been executed. Normally, it will never again have the value 1. Thus SCANPTR will not be executed on any subsequent invocation of glalex. Periodic refilling of the source module's text buffer and associated re-setting of TokenEnd is handled by auxNUL when the lexical analyzer detects that the string is exhausted. More complex behaviour, using ResetScan to force resets at arbitrary points, is always possible via token processors or other clients.

3.7.2.3 The classification operation

The classification operation glalex is invoked with a pointer to an integer variable that may be set to the value representing the classified sequence. An integer result specifying the classification is returned by glalex, and the coordinates of the first character of the sequence are stored in the error module's exported variable curpos. There are three points at which these interactions can be altered:

1. Setting coordinate values
2. Deciding on a continuation after a classification
3. Returning a classification

All of these alterations are made by supplying macro definitions in a specification file called 'scanops.h'.

3.7.2.3.1 Setting coordinate values

The coordinates of the first character of a sequence are set by the macro SETCOORD. Its default implementation uses the standard coordinate invariant.

```
/* Set the coordinates of the current token
 * On entry-
 *  LineNum=index of the current line in the entire source text
 *  p=index of the current column in the entire source line
 * On exit-
 *   curpos has been updated to contain the current position as its
 *   left coordinate
 */
#define SETCOORD(p) { LineOf(curpos)=LineNum; ColOf(curpos)=(p); }
```

When execution monitoring is in effect, more care must be taken. In addition to the above, SETCOORD must also set the cumulative column position, which is the column position within the overall input stream (as opposed to just the current input file). Ordinarily the two column positions will be the same, so the default implementation of SETCOORD for monitoring is:

```
#define SETCOORD(p) { LineOf(curpos)=LineNum;
                      ColOf(curpos)=CumColOf(curpos)=(p); }
```

When monitoring, it is also necessary to set the coordinates of the first character beyond the sequence. This is handled by the macro SETENDCOORD:

```
/* Set the coordinates of the end of the current token
 * On entry-
 *  LineNum=index of the current line in the entire source text
 *  p=index of the current column in the entire source line
 * On exit-
 *   curpos has been updated to contain the current position as its
 *   right coordinate
 */
#ifndef SETENDCOORD
#define SETENDCOORD(p) { RLineOf(curpos)=LineNum;
              RColOf(curpos)=RCumColOf(curpos)=(p); }
#endif
```

3.7.2.3.2 Deciding on a continuation after a classification

Classification is complete after the regular expression has been matched, any specified auxiliary scanner invoked, and any specified token processor invoked. At this point, one of three distinct actions is possible:

RETURN v

Terminate the invocation of glalex, returning the value v as the classification.

goto rescan

Start a new scan at the character addressed by TokenEnd, without changing the coordinate value.

continue

Start a new scan at the character addressed by TokenEnd, resetting the coordinates to the coordinates of that character.

WRAPUP is the macro responsible for deciding among these possibilities. When it is executed, TokenEnd addresses the first character beyond the classified sequence and extcode holds the classification code. Here is the default implementation:

```
#define WRAPUP { if(extcode != NORETURN) RETURN extcode; }
```

If WRAPUP does not transfer control, the result is the continue action. Thus the default implementation of WRAPUP terminates the invocation of glalex if the current character sequence is not classified as a comment (extcode != NORETURN), and starts a new scan at the next character if the current character sequence is classified as a comment.

If execution monitoring is in effect, the classification event must be reported in addition to selecting a continuation:

```
#define WRAPUPMONITOR {
 if(extcode != NORETURN) {
  char save = *TokenEnd;
  *TokenEnd = '\0';
  generate_token("token", LineOf(curpos), ColOf(curpos),
                 CumColOf(curpos), RLineOf(curpos), RColOf(curpos),
                 RCumColOf(curpos), TokenStart, TokenEnd - TokenStart,
                 *v, extcode);
  *TokenEnd = save;
 }
}
```

WRAPUPMONITOR is invoked instead of WRAPUP if execution monitoring is in effect.

3.7.2.3.3 Returning a classification

Once the decision has been made to terminate the glalex operation and report the classification, it is possible to carry out arbitrary operations in addition to returning the classification code. For example, execution monitoring requires that this event be reported. Here is the default implementation:

```
#ifdef MONITOR
#define RETURN(v) { generate_leave("lexical"); return v; }
#else
#define RETURN(v) { return v; }
#endif
```

3.8 COMPLETE C PROGRAM FOR LEX

Program in 'C Language is given in appendix-**A (A.4)**

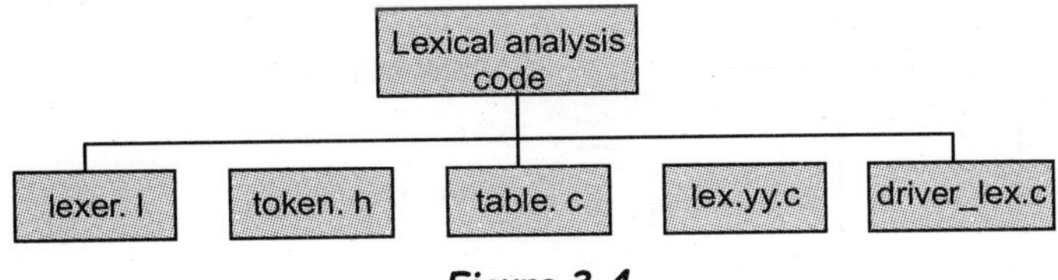

Figure 3.4

3.9 FLEX LEXICAL ANALYZER

FLEX generates a lexical analyzer in C or C++ given an input program. Flex (fast lexical analyzer generator) is an alternative to Lex. It is frequently used with the free Bison parser generator. Flex was originally written in C by Vern Paxson around 1987.It is compatible with the original lex, although it has numerous features that make it more useful if you are writing your own scanner. It is designed so that it can be used together with yacc. It is highly compatible with the Unix lex program. It can be described as :

"Flex is a tool for generating scanners: programs which recognize lexical patterns in text. Flex reads the given input files, or its standard input if no file names are given, for a description of a scanner to generate. The description is in the form of pairs of regular expressions and C code, called rules. Flex generates as output a C source file, `lex.yy.c', which defines a routine `yylex()'. This file is compiled and linked with the `-lfl' library to produce an executable. When the executable is run, it analyzes its input for occurrences of the regular expressions. Whenever it finds one, it executes the corresponding C code..."

A similar lexical scanner for C++ is flex++.

Flex is a non-GNU project, but the GNU project developed the manual for Flex.

EXAMPLES

EX. 1: Discuss Lexical Analysis with at least two examples.

Ans. In compiler, linear analysis is lex analysis. Lex analysis is an interface between source program & compiler. In this phase, source program's characters are read by lex analyzer one at a time & break-out into a sequence of character called token. Token is a sequence of characters that represent a single logical entity. Tokens are identifier, keywords, etc.

e.g. (i) If (5>4) then goto

Tokens – If, (, 5, >, 4,), then, goto

(ii) For (i=0; i< 10; i++)

Tokens - for, (, I,=0,; <, 10, +,0)

EX. 2: What do you mean by translation diagram? Draw a translation diagram for relational operators, identifiers, keywords, and all token of any general program.

Ans. An intermediate step in the construction of a lexical analyzer, we draw a pictorial representation of token know as translation diagram which show all the action taken by a lexical analyzer or parser. A translation diagram is a set of nodes and edges in which nodes represent states and edges show the action taken if corresponding token is received.

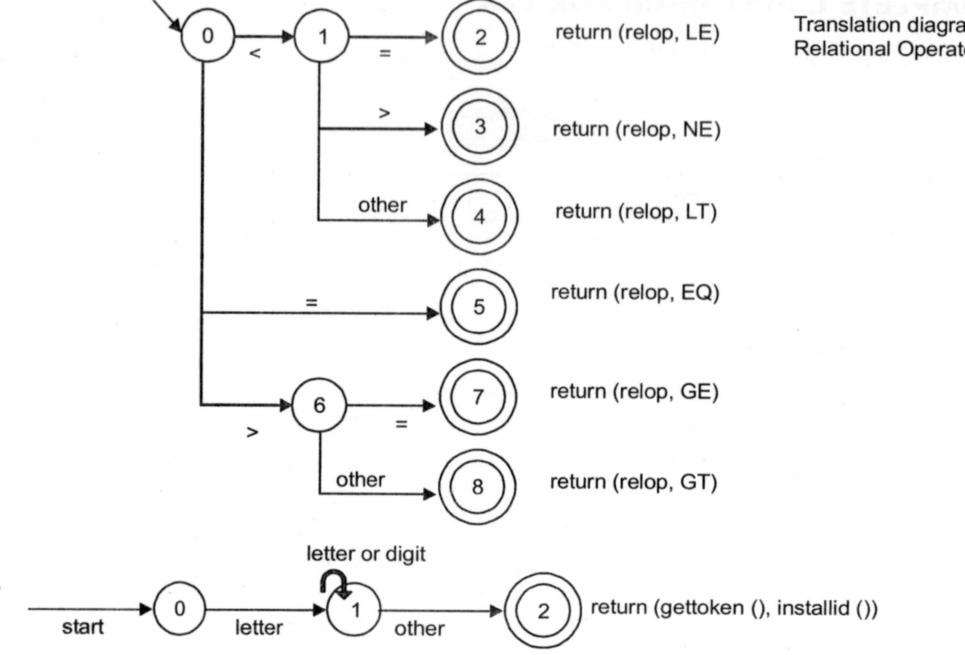

Translation Diagram for Identifiers and Keywords

Figure 3.5

Here installid() returns a pointer to the symbol table entry and gettoken() look for the lexeme in the symbol table.

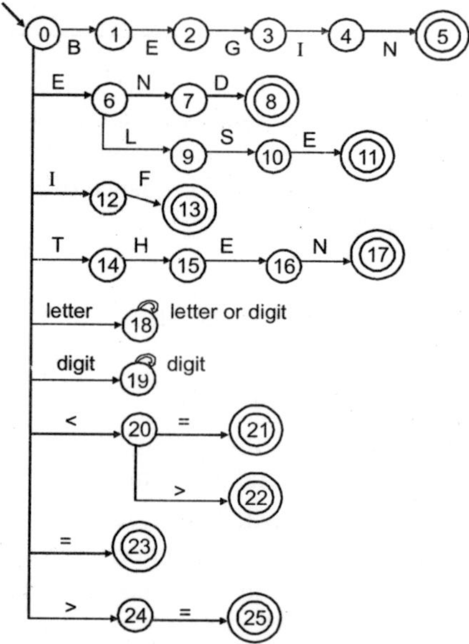

Figure 3.6

TRIBULATIONS

3.1 Assume that you are writing a lexical analyzer for a language with the following classes of basic symbols:

- identifiers that must start with a letter or an underscore and can continue with letters, underscores, or digits
- integers that contain one or more digits
- real numbers that contain zero or more digits followed by a decimal point followed by one or more digits
- comments that are delimited by curly braces; comments cannot be nested

3.2 Write regular expressions and draw syntax diagrams that define each of these classes of basic symbol.

3.3 What is the use of regular expression D.F.A. in lexical analysis.

3.4 What do you understand by automatic lexical generator.

3.5 Specify the lexical form of numeric constant in the language of C.

3.6 Give the translation diagram for all reserve keywords?

3.7 Write a simple approach to design of Lexical analyzer for the digits 0,1,2...........9 and rational operation?

3.8 Define RE and Tokens in detail?

3.9 How Lexical analyzer removes white spaces from a source file?

FURTHER READINGS AND REFERENCES

- **About Source Code**

[1] Terrence Pratt & Marvin Zelkowitz, Programming Languages Design and Implementation.

- **About Lexical Analysis**

[2] Aho, Alfred & Sethi, Ravi & Ullman, Jeffrey. Compilers: Principles, Techniques, and Tools.

[3] Appel, Andrew, *Modern Compiler Implementation in C/Java/ML* (It is a set of cleanly written texts on compiler design, studied from various different methodological perspectives).

[4] Brown, P.J. *Writing Interactive Compilers and Interpreters*. Useful Practical Advice, not much theory.

[5] Fischer, Charles & LeBlanc, Richard. *Crafting A Compiler*. Uses an ADA like pseudo-code.

[6] Holub, Allen, *Compiler Design in C*. Extensive examples in "C".

[7] Hunter, R. *The Design and Construction of Compilers*. Several chapters on theory of syntax analysis, plus discussion of parsing difficulties caused by features of various source languages.

[8] Pemberton, S. & Daniels, M.C. *Pascal Implementation—The P4 Compiler*. (Discussion) and (Compiler listing) Complete listing and readable commentary for a Pascal compiler written in Pascal.

[9] Weinberg, G.M. *The Psychology of Computer Programming*: Silver Anniversary Edition. Interesting insights and anecdotes.

[10] Wirth, Niklaus, *Compiler Construction*. From the inventor of Pascal, Modula-2 and Oberon-2, examples in Oberon.

CHAPTER 4

SYNTAX ANALYSIS AND DIRECTED TRANSLATION

CHAPTER HIGHLIGHTS

The **syntactic analysis** of source code entails the transformation of a linear sequence of tokens into a hierarchical syntax tree or abstract syntax trees. Syntax analysis, also known as parsing, is one of the first actions performed by a compiler. There are a tool that automatically generates parsers from a specification of a language grammar written in Backus-Naur form, e.g., Yacc (yet another compiler compiler). In general, syntax analysis is equivalent of checking that some ordinary text written in a natural language (e.g. English) is grammatically correct (without worrying about meaning). But in case of compiler, purpose of syntax analysis or parsing is to check that we have a valid sequence of tokens. Note that this sequence need not be meaningful; as far as syntax goes, a phrase such as "**true** + 3" is valid but it doesn't make any sense in most programming languages. Now in this chapter we discuss about syntax definitions, problems of syntax analysis, syntax directed translation schema and parsing techniques. Now we are standing at second phase of compiler. Input to this phase is sequence of tokens from lexical analysis as:

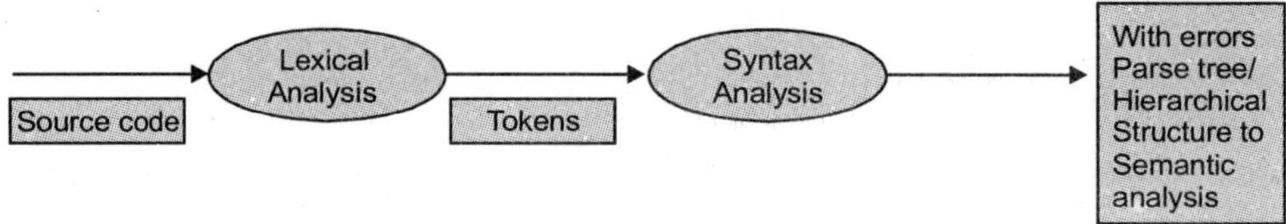

Figure 4.1

4.1 SYNTAX DEFINITION

A contex free grammar, CFG, (synonyms: Backus-Naur Form of BNF) is a common notation for specifying the syntax of a languages. For example, an "IF-ELSE" statement in C-language has the form

IF (Expr) stmt ELSE stmt

In other words, it is the concatenation of:

- the keyword IF ;
- an opening parenthesis (;
- an expression Expr ;
- a closing parenthesis) ;
- a statement stmt ;
- a keyword ELSE ;
- Finally, another statement stmt.

The syntax of an 'IF-ELSE' statement can be specified by the following 'production rule' in the CFG.

stmt → IF (Expr) stmt ELSE stmt

The arrow (→) is read as "can have the form".

Multiple production with the same nonterminal on the left like:

list → + digit

list → – digit

list → digit

may be grouped together separated by vertical bars, like:

list → + digit | – digit | digit

4.2 PROBLEMS OF SYNTAX ANALYSIS OR PARSING

4.2.1 Ambiguity

A grammar is ambiguous if two or more different parse trees can be desire the same token string.

Or

A grammar 'G' is ambiguous if there exists a string 'w' belongs to L(G) such that 'w' has two distinct parse tree. Equivalently, an ambiguous grammar allows two different derivations for a token string.

Grammar for compiler should be unambiguous since different parse trees will give a token string different meaning.

Example 4.1:

(i) string → string + string | string - string | string * string | string / string | 0 | 2 | . . . | 9

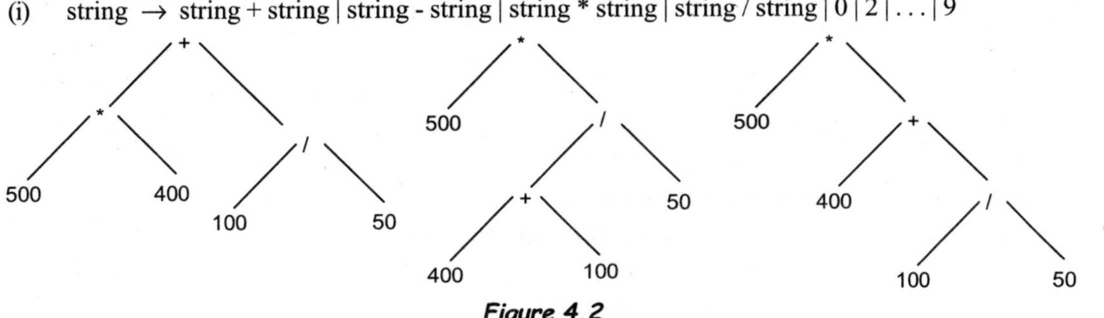

Figure 4.2

To show that a grammar is ambiguous all we need to find a "single" string that has more than one parse tree.

Above figure show three different parse trees for the string '500 * 400 + 100 / 50' that corresponds to two different way of parenthesizing the expression:

(500 * 400) + (100 / 50) or 500 * (400 + 100) / 50 or 500 * (400 + (100 / 50))

The first parenthesization evaluates to 200002, 40,201000. The reason that the above grammar is ambiguous.

(ii) S → IF b THEN S ELSE S | IF b THEN S | a

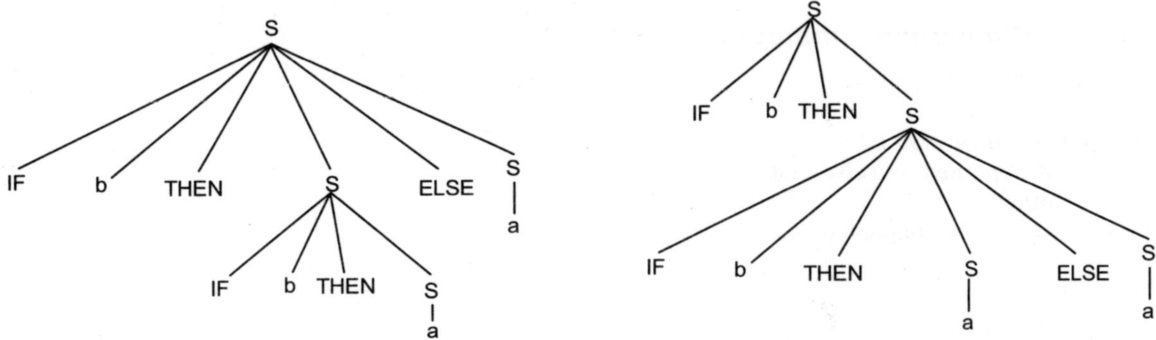

Figure 4.3

Above figure show three different parse trees for the string 'IF b THEN IF b THEN a ELSE a' that corresponds to two different way of parenthesizing the expression:

IF b THEN (IF b THEN a) ELSE a or
IF b THEN (IF b THEN a ELSE a) .
The reason that the above grammar is ambiguous.

Example 4.2: Prove that given grammar is ambiguous.

E → S + S | S * S | a | b for a+a*b

This can be prove if we can generate the two parse tree for a+a*b.

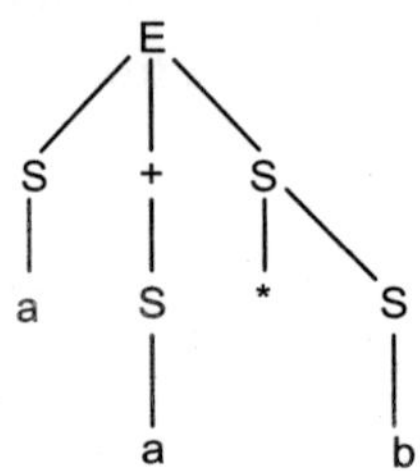

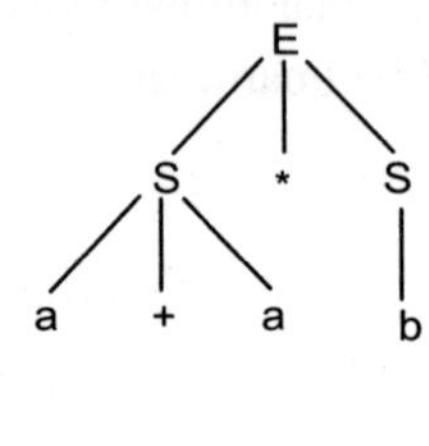

so ,it is proved that above grammar is ambiguous.

Example 4.3: Can following grammar is ambiguous or not

S → 0B | 1A ,A → 0 | 0S | 1AA , B → 1 | 1S | 0BB for 00110101.

S → 0B	S → 0B
→ 00BB	→ 00BB
→ 001B	→ 00B1S
→ 0011S	→ 00B10B
→ 00110B	→ 00B101S
→ 001101S	→ 00B1010B
→ 0011010B	→ 00B10101
→ 00110101	→ 00110101

because above expression '00110101' can be generated by the two ways i.e. leftmost or rightmost derivation. So it is ambiguous.

4.2.1.1 Eliminating ambiguity

If we have following grammar

stmt → **if** expr **then** stmt
  | **if** expr **then** stmt **else** stmt
  | **other**

Then we can eliminate ambiguity as:

stmt → match_stmt
  | unmatch_stmt
match_stmt → **if** expr **then** match_stmt **else** match_stmt
  | **other**
unmatch_stmt → **if** expr **then** stmt
  | **if** expr **then** match_stmt **else** unmatch_stmt

4.2.2 Left Recursion

Left recursion is a special case of recursion. A formal grammar that contains left recursion cannot be parsed by a recursive descent parser. In contrast, left recursion is preferred for LALR parsers because it results in lower stack usage than right recursion.

"A grammar is left-recursive if we can find some non-terminal 'A' which will eventually derive a sentential form with itself as the left-symbol."

4.2.2.1 Immediate left recursion

Immediate left recursion in its simplest form could be defined as

$A \rightarrow A\alpha \mid \beta$

Where α and β are sequences of nonterminals and terminals, and β doesn't start with A.

Example 4.4 :

$Expr \rightarrow Expr + Term$

is immediately left-recursive. The recursive descent parser for this rule might look like

```
function Expr() {
Expr(); match('+'); Term();
}
```

4.2.2.2 Indirect left recursion

Indirect left recursion in its simplest form could be defined as

$A \rightarrow B\alpha \mid C$

$B \rightarrow A\beta \mid D$

Possibly giving the derivation $A \Rightarrow B\alpha \Rightarrow A\beta \Rightarrow A \Rightarrow ....$

More generally, for the non-terminals $A_0, A_1, ..., A_n$, indirect left recursion can be defined as being of the form :

$A_0 \rightarrow A_1\alpha_1 \mid ....$

$A_1 \rightarrow A_2\alpha_2 \mid ....$

....

$A_n \rightarrow A_0\alpha_{(n+1)} \mid ....$

Where $\alpha_1, \alpha_2, ..., \alpha_n$ are sequences of nonterminals and terminals.

4.2.2.3 Removing left recursion

Removing Immediate Left Recursion

The general algorithm to remove immediate left recursion follows. For each rule of the form

$A \rightarrow A\alpha_1 \mid .... \mid A\alpha_n \mid \beta_1 \mid \beta_m$

Where

- A is a left-recursive nonterminal
- α is a sequence of nonterminals and terminals that is not null ( )
- β is a sequence of nonterminals and terminals that does not start with A.

Replace the A-production by the production

$A \rightarrow \beta_1 A' | .... | \beta_m A'$

And create a new nonterminal

$A' \rightarrow \varepsilon | \alpha_1 A' | .... | \alpha_n A'$

This newly created symbol is often called the "tail", or the "rest".

Example 4.5: Consider following grammar and show that given grammar is LL(1) or not. If not then make it.

A→Ba | Aa | c
B→Bb | Ab | d

This grammer is not LL(1) because it contain immediate left recursion. So we remove it and then grammar will become as :

A→ Ba | Aa | c
A→ cA' ———— 1
A'→ baA' | aA' | ε ———— 2
B→ Bb | d
B→dB' | Ab ———— 3
B'→ bB' | ε

Example 4.6: Remove left recursion from the following grammar

S→(L) | a
L→L, S | S

Here, L→L, S contain left recursion. Now we remove left recursion as using given rules,

L→S L1
L1→,SL1 | ε

So after removing:-
S→(L) | a
L→SL1
L1→,SL1 | ε

Removing Indirect Left Recursion

If the grammar has no ε-productions (no productions of the form $A \rightarrow .... | \varepsilon | ....$) and is not cyclic (no derivations of the form $A \Rightarrow .... \Rightarrow A$ for any nonterminal A), this general algorithm may be applied to remove indirect left recursion:

Arrange the nonterminals in some (any) fixed order $A_1, ... A_n$.

for i = 1 to n {
for j = 1 to i – 1 {

- let the current A_j productions be

  $A_j \rightarrow \delta_1 | .... | \delta_k$

- replace each production $A_i \rightarrow A_j \gamma$ by

  $A_i \rightarrow \delta_1 \gamma | .... | \delta_k \gamma$

- remove direct left recursion for A_i

  }

  }

Example 4.7:

$Expr \rightarrow Expr + Term \mid Term$

$Term \rightarrow Term * Factor \mid Factor$

$Factor \rightarrow (Expr) \mid Int$

After having applied standard transformations to remove left-recursion, we have the following grammar :

$Expr \rightarrow TermExpr'$

$Expr' \rightarrow +TermExpr' \mid \varepsilon$

$Term \rightarrow FactorTerm'$

$Term' \rightarrow *FactorTerm' \mid \varepsilon$

$Factor \rightarrow (Expr) \mid Int$

Parsing the string 'a + a + a' with the first grammar in an LALR parser (which can recognize left-recursive grammar) would have resulted in the parse tree

```
        Expr
        /  \
   Expr  + Term
    / \\      \
 Expr + Term   Factor
  |      |       |
 Term  Factor   Int
  |      |
 Factor  Int
  |
 Int
```

This parse tree grows to the left, indicating that the '+' operator is left associative, representing (a + a) + a. But now that we've changed the grammar, our parse tree looks like this :

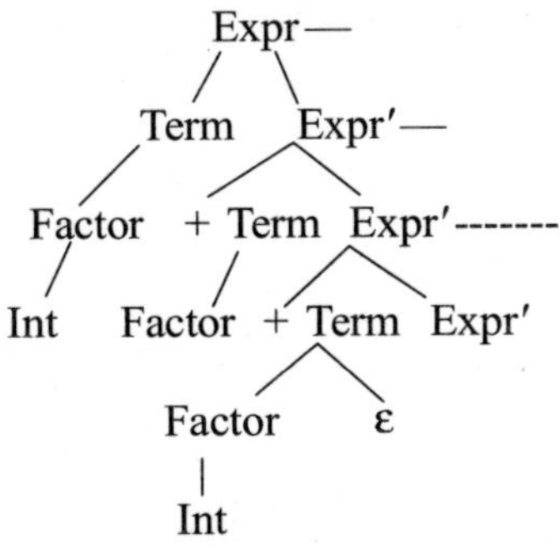

We can see that the tree grows to the right, representing a + (a + a). We have changed the associativity of our operator '+', it is now right-associative. While this isn't a problem for the associativity of addition with addition it would have a signifcantly different value if this were subtraction.

The problem is that normal arithmetic requires left associativity. Several solutions are:

(a) Rewrite the grammar to be left recursive, or

(b) Rewrite the grammar with more nonterminals to force the correct precedence/associativity, or

(c) If using YACC or Bison, there are operator declarations, %left, %right and %nonassoc, which tell the parser generator which associativity to force.

Algorithm:

$\leftarrow$ for i 1 to m

$\leftarrow$ for j 1 to i – 1

replace each grammar rule choice of form $A_i \rightarrow A_j \beta$ by the $Ai \rightarrow \alpha_1\beta \mid \alpha_2\beta \mid \ldots\ldots \alpha_k\beta$

where

$A_j \rightarrow \alpha_1 \mid \alpha_2 \mid \ldots\ldots \alpha_k$ is current rule for A_j

Example 4.8: Remove left recursion from given grammar

$S \rightarrow aBDh$

$B \rightarrow Bb|c$

$D \rightarrow EF$

$E \rightarrow g|\varepsilon$

$F \rightarrow F|\varepsilon$

In given grammar only one production exist in form of $A \rightarrow A\alpha \mid \alpha$ i.e. $B \rightarrow Bb \mid c$. So we remove left recursion from $B \rightarrow Bd|c$ as

$B \rightarrow cB$

$B' \rightarrow bB' \mid \in$

So now above grammar is not left recursive.

Example 4.9: Is the grammar is in left recursion or not

$S \rightarrow A$

$A \rightarrow Ad|Ae|aB|aC$

$B \rightarrow bBC|f$

$C \rightarrow g$

Yes, above grammar is in left recursion. Second production violate condition of left recursion. So after removing left recursion above grammar look like:

$S \rightarrow A$

$A \rightarrow aBA' \mid aCA'$

$A' \rightarrow dA' \mid eA' \mid \varepsilon$

$B \rightarrow bBC \mid f$

$C \rightarrow g$

4.2.3 Left-Factoring

Even if a context-free grammar is unambiguous and non-left-recursion, it still may not be LL(1). The problem is that there is only look-ahead buffer. After the addition of a new rule in the grammar, it may take of the form:

$$A \rightarrow \alpha\beta_1 \mid \alpha\beta_2 \mid \alpha\beta_3 \ldots$$

The parser generated from this kind of grammar is not efficient as it requires backtracking. To avoid this problem we left factor the grammar. To left factor a grammar, we collect all productions that have the same left hand side and begin with the same symbols on the right hand side. We combine the common strings into a single production and then append a new nonterminal symbol to the end of this new production. Finally, we create a new set of productions using this new nonterminal for each of the suffixes to the common production.

After left factoring the above grammar is transformed into:

$$A \rightarrow \alpha A_1$$

$$A_1 \rightarrow \alpha\beta_1 \mid \alpha\beta_2 \mid \alpha\beta_3 \ldots$$

The above grammar is correct and is free from conflicts.

Algorithm:

while there are changes to grammar

for each nonterminal A

let α be a prefix of maximal length that is shared by two or more production choices for A

if $\alpha != \varepsilon$ then

$\rightarrow$ let A $\alpha_1 \mid \alpha_2 \mid \ldots\ldots \alpha_n$ by all production choices for A and $\alpha_1 \ldots\ldots \alpha_k$ share αso

$\rightarrow$ that A $\alpha\beta_1 \mid \alpha\beta_2 \mid \ldots \alpha\beta_k \mid \alpha\beta_{(k+1)} \mid \ldots\ldots \alpha_n$, the β_j's share no common prefix and

$\rightarrow$ the A $\alpha_1 \mid \alpha_2 \mid \ldots \alpha_n$ by

$\rightarrow$ A $\alpha A' \mid \alpha_{(k+1)} \ldots \mid \alpha_n$

$\rightarrow$ A' $\beta_1 \mid \ldots\ldots \beta_k$

Example 4.10: Consider following grammar then make it compatible grammar to LL(1) parser

if-stmt → **if**(exp) statement
| **if** (exp) statement **else** statement.

Above grammar should be left factored as because it will non-left-recursive but still left factor grammar. So we apply above rules to remove left factoring as:

if-stmp → **if** (exp) statement Else
Else → **else** statement | ε

Now this grammar is correct and free from conflits.

Example 4.11: Perform left factoring on the following grammar if exist:

S → iCtS | iCtSeS | a
C → b

Here, S → iCtS | iCtSeS | a comparing with A → αA1 | αA2 then A = S, α= iCtS, A1 = ε, A2 = eS, and now the solution will be in the form of

A → αA′
A′ → A1 | A2

So S → iCtSS′ | a
S′ → eS | ε
C → b

4.3 SYNTAX-DIRECTED TRANSLATION

Modern compilers use syntax-directed translation to interleaves the actions of the compiler phases. The syntax analyzer directs the whole process during the parsing of the source code.

- Calls the lexical analyzer whenever syntax analyzer wants another token.
- Perform the actions of semantic analyzer.
- Perform the actions of the intermediate code generator.

The actions of the semantic analyzer and the intermediate code generator require the passage of information up and/or down the parse tree. We think of this information as attributes attached to the nodes of the parse tree and the parser moving this information between parent nodes and children nodes as it performs the productions of the grammar.

4.3.1 Semantic Rules

Value for the attribute in any grammar are computed by semantic rule associated with grammar production. Here are two notation for associating semantic rule with productions are (I) Syntax – Directed Translation (II) Translation Schema

- Syntax directed translation definition is high level specification for translation and generalization of a context free grammar in which grammar symbol has an associated set of attribute, partitioned into two subsets called **Synthesized and Inherited** attribute. An attribute can represent anything we choose as a string, a number, a type, a memory location, etc. Value for the attribute in any parse tree's node is defined by a semantic rule associated with the production at node as synthesized and inherited attribute. They also hide many implementation details and free from having to specifying explicitly the order in which translation take place. A syntax directed translation definition is said to be **circular** if the dependency graph for some parse tree generated by its grammar has a cycle. So, syntax-directed translation.
- A syntax-directed definition uses a CFG to specify the syntactic structure of the input.
- A syntax-directed definition associates a set of attributes with each grammar symbol.
- A syntax-directed definition associates a set of semantic rules with each production rule.
- Translation schema indicates order in which semantic rules are to be evaluated. They allow some implementation details. Both syntax directed translation and translation take input token stream and build the parse tree and then traverse the tree as needed to evaluate the semantic rule at parse tree's node.

4.3.2 Annotated Parse Tree

A parse tree showing the value of attribute at each node known as annotated parse tree. Process of computing value at any node known as annotating.

4.4 SYNTAX TREE

Syntax tree is condensed form of parse useful for representing language constructs. In syntax tree operator and reserve keywords don't appear at leaves.

OR

A syntax tree is a finite, labeled, directed tree, where the internal nodes are labeled by operators, and the leaf nodes represent the operands of the operators. Thus, the leaves are NULL operators and only represent variables or constants.

In computing, it is used in a parser as an intermediate between a parse tree and a data structure, the latter which is often used as a compiler or interpreter's internal representation of a computer program while it is being optimized and from which code generation is performed. The range of all possible such structures is described by the abstract syntax. An syntax tree differs from a parse tree by omitting nodes and edges for syntax rules that do not affect the semantics of the program. Creating an syntax tree in a parser for a language described by a context free grammar, as nearly all programming languages are, is straightforward. Most rules in the grammar create a new node with the nodes edges being the symbols in the rule.

Examples 4.12:

(I) For string ' while ((A<B) && (B< C)) syntax tree look like as

A=B+C

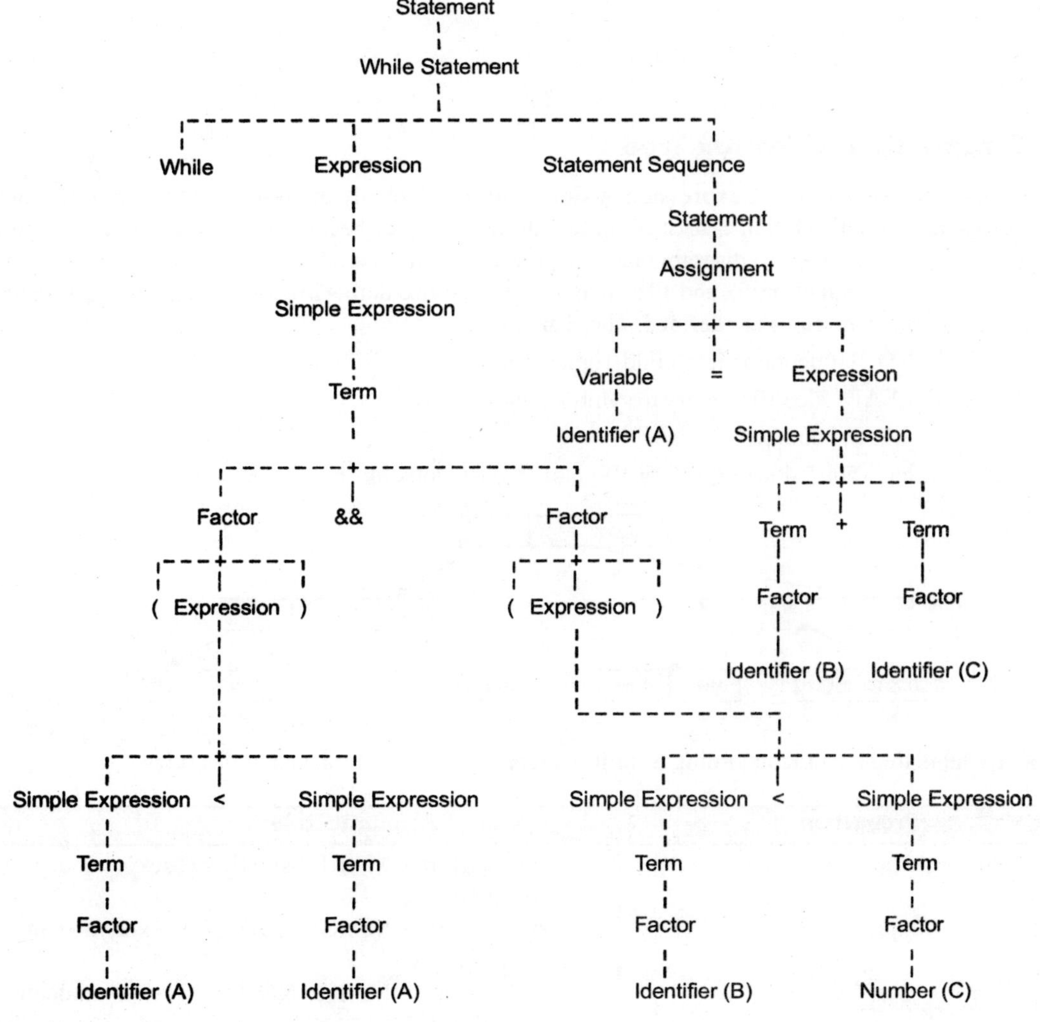

(II) Give the syntax tree for the following:

If (a=b) then

a = c * d
else
b= c * d

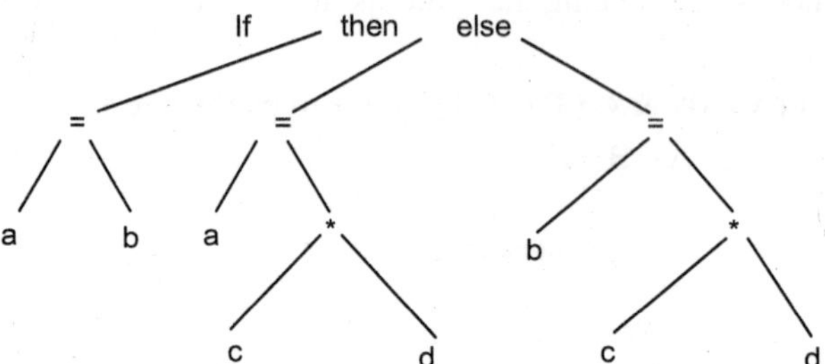

4.4.1 Construction of Syntax Tree

Construction of syntax tree for an expression is similar to translate any expression into its **postfix form or reverse polish notation or RPN** in case of compiler internal structure because there is only one interpretation and we do not need parenthesis to disambiguate the grammar or in case of representation it will be similar to translate any expression into its prefix and all semantics rules are aiso define in prefix form. For constructing any syntax tree here three main rules are defined. These are as:

1. MAKE_NODE (operator, left_child, right_child)
2. MAKE_LEAF (identifier ,entry to symbol table)
3. MAKE_LEAF (number , value)

So, now for string '(500 * 400) + (100 / 50)' syntax tree will look like as

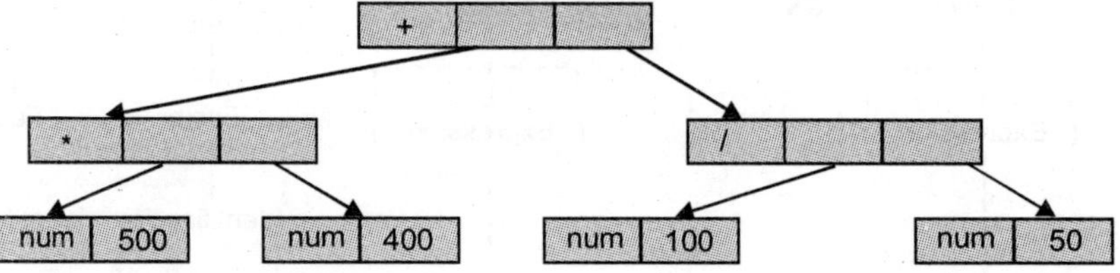

Above syntax tree is build according to following production rule and semantics rules.

Production	Semantic Rule
expr $\rightarrow$ $expr_1 + expr_2$	expr.nodeptr : = MAKE_NODE('+' , $expr_1$.nodeptr ,$expr_2$.nodeptr)
expr $\rightarrow$ $expr_1 - expr_2$	expr.nodeptr : = MAKE_NODE('–' , $expr_1$.nodeptr ,$expr_2$.nodeptr)
expr $\rightarrow$ $expr_1 * expr_2$	expr.nodeptr : = MAKE_NODE('*' , $expr_1$.nodeptr ,$expr_2$.nodeptr)
expr $\rightarrow$ $expr_1 / expr_2$	expr.nodeptr : = MAKE_NODE('/' , $expr_1$.nodeptr ,$expr_2$.nodeptr)
expr $\rightarrow$ term	expr.nodeptr : = term.nodeptr

Contd....

term → fact fact → num fact → identifier symbol table)	term.nodeptr := fact.nodeptr fact.nodeptr : = MAKE_ LEAF(num, num.value) fact.nodeptr : = MAKE_ LEAF(identifier ,entry to

So, now for string '(500 * 400) + (100 / 50)' annotated parse tree and syntax tree will look like as:

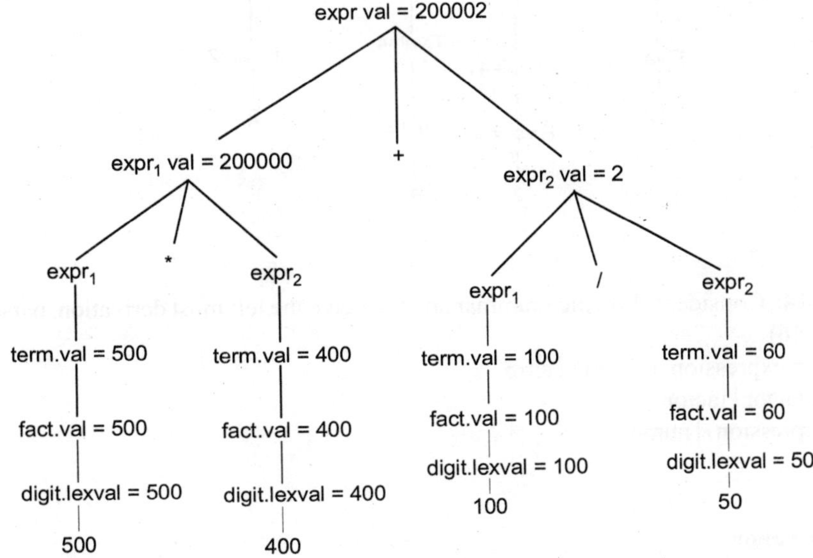

Example 4.13: Consider following translation schema

E → E* T	{E. val = E. val * T.val}
E → T	{E.val = T.val}
T → T - E	{T. val = T. val - E.val}
T → F	{T.val = F.val}
F → 2	{F.val = 2}
F → 4	{F.val = 4}

Construct annonated parse tree for ' 4-2 - 4*2'

Answer: Order of production in which they are applied as:

E→T	{E.val = T.val}
T→T-E	{T. val = T. val - E.val}
T→T–E	{T. val = T. val - E.val}
E→ E* T	{E, val = E. val * T.val}
E→T	{E.val = T.val}
F→2	{F.val = 2}
F→4	{F.val = 4}

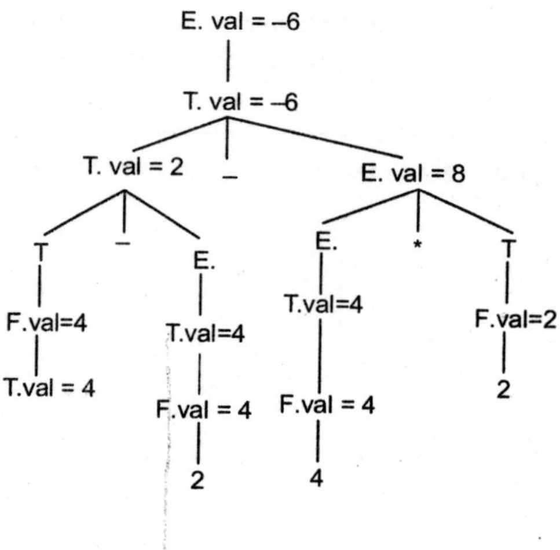

Example 4.14: Consider following grammar and then give the left most derivation, parse tree, syntax tree for 33*(10 – 11 + 16)

→ expression expression op1 term | term

→ term op2 factor | factor

→ factor (expression) | number

op1 → + | –

op2 → * | /

(i) Left Most Derivation

Expression → term
→ term op2 factor
→ factor op2 factor
→ number op2 factor
→ 33 op2 factor
→ 33 * factor
→ 33 * (expression)
→ 33 * (expression op1 term)
→ 33 * (expression op1 term op1 term)
→ 33 * (term op1 term op1 term)
→ 33 * (factor op1 term op1 term)
→ 33 * (number op1 term op1 term)
→ 33 * (10 op1 term op1 term)
→ 33 * (10 – term op1 term)
→ 33 * (10 – factor op1 term)
→ 33 * (10 – number op1 term)
→ 33 * (10 – 16 op1 term)
→ 33 * (10 – 16 + term)
→ 33 * (10 – 16 + factor)
→ 33 * (10 – 16 + number)
→ 33 * (10 – 16 + 11)

(ii) Parse tree

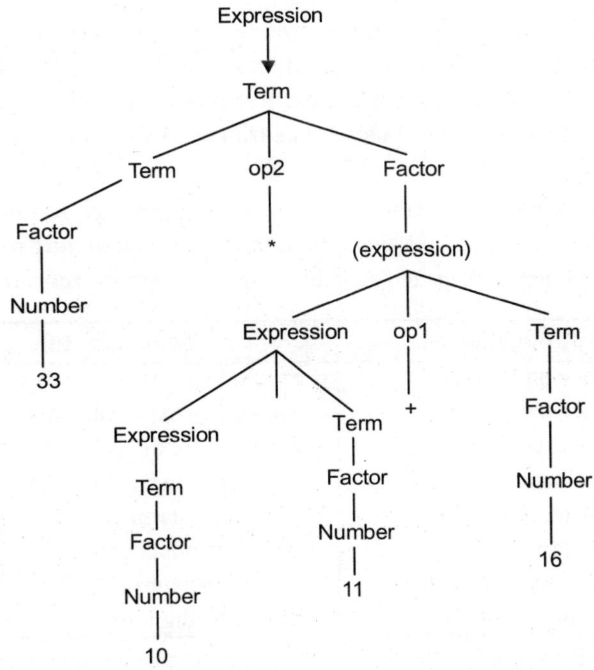

(iii) Syntax tree

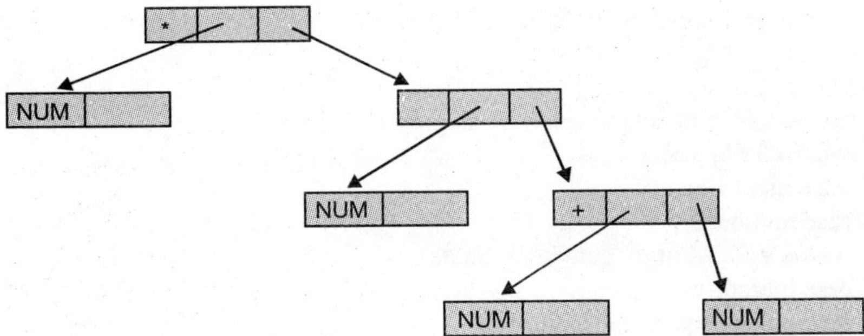

4.5 ATTRIBUTE GRAMMAR

An Attribute grammar is a formal way to define attributes for the productions of a formal grammar, associating these attributes to values. The evaluation occurs in the nodes of the abstract syntax tree, when the language is processed by some parser or compiler. Attribute grammar can also be used to translate the syntax tree directly into code for some specific machine, or into some intermediate language and strength of attribute grammar is that they can transport information from anywhere in the abstract syntax tree to anywhere else, in a controlled and formal way.

The attributes are divided into two groups: synthesized attributes and inherited attributes.

Synthesized Attributes

The synthesized attributes are the result of the attribute evaluation rules, and may also use the values of the inherited attributes. **An attribute is synthesized if its value at a parent node can be determined from attributes of its children**. In general, given a context-free production rule of the form 'A = a B g 'then an associated semantic rule of the form "A.attribute$_i$ = f(a.attribute$_j$, B.attribute$_k$, g.attribute$_l$)" is said to specify a **synthesized attribute** of A.

In some approaches, synthesized attributes are used to pass semantic information up the parse tree. Synthesized attributes can be evaluated by a single bottom-up traversal of the parse tree. Production rules and semantic rules are also define for synthesized attribute with 'val' synthesized attribute as :

Production	Semantic Rule
expr → expr1 + expr_2	expr.val : = expr_1 .val + expr_2.val
expr → expr_1 – expr_2	expr.val : = expr_1 .val + expr_2.val
expr → expr_1 * expr_2	expr.val : = expr_1 .val + expr_2.val
expr → expr_1 / expr_2	expr.val : = expr_1 .val + expr_2.val
expr → term	expr.val : = term.val
term → fact	term.val : = fact.val
fact → (expr)	fact.val := expr.val
fact → digit	fact.val := digit.lexval

Example 4.15: Now for string '(500 * 400) + (100 / 50)' parse tree with synthesized attribute with 'val' will look like as

Example 4.16: we have a situation in which the attributes of any particular node depend only on the attributes of nodes in the subtrees of the node as:

```
void Factor(int &value)
 // Factor = identifier | number | "(" Expression" )" .
 { switch (SYM.sym)
   { case identifier:
    case number:
     value = SYM.num; getsym(); break;
    case lparen:
     getsym(); Expression(value);
     accept(rparen, " Error - ')' expected"); break;
    default:
     printf("Unexpected symbol\n"); exit(1);
   }
 }

 void Term(int &value)
 // Term = Factor { "*" Factor | "/" Factor } .
 { int factorvalue;
  Factor(value);
  while (SYM.sym == times || SYM.sym == slash)
  { switch (SYM.sym)
```

```
    { case times:
       getsym(); Factor(factorvalue); value *= factorvalue; break;
      case slash:
       getsym(); Factor(factorvalue); value /= factorvalue; break;
    }
  }
}

void Expression(int &value)
// Expression = Term { "+" Term | "-" Term } .
{ int termvalue;
 Term(value);
 while (SYM.sym == plus || SYM.sym == minus)
 { switch (SYM.sym)
   { case plus:
      getsym(); Term(termvalue); value += termvalue; break;
     case minus:
      getsym(); Term(termvalue); value -= termvalue; break;
   }
 }
}
```

Inherited Attribute

An inherited attribute is one whose value at a node in parse tree is defined by in term of there sibling/ brother or parents. Generally, given a context-free production rule of the form 'A = a B g' an associated semantic rule of the form "B.attribute$_i$ = f(a.attribute$_j$, A.attribute$_k$, g.attribute$_l$)" is said to specify an **inherited attribute** of B. The inherited attributes are passed down from parent nodes to children nodes of the abstract syntax tree during the semantic analysis of the parsing process, are a problem for bottom-up parsing because in bottom-up parsing, the parent nodes of the abstract syntax tree are created after creation of all of their children.. Inherited attributes help pass semantic information down it. For instance, when constructing a language translation tool, such as a compiler, it may be used to assign semantic values to syntax constructions. For examples 'int a, b, c, d;'. Production rules and semantic rules are also define for inherited attribute with 'enter' inherited attribute as:

Production	Semantic Rule
Def → Term, Lan	Term.type:=Lan.enter
Lan → Lan1 , identifier	Lan1.enter := L.enter addtype(identifier.entry to st , L.enter)
Lan → identifier	addtype(identifier.entry to st , L.enter)
Term → int	Term.type := integer
Term → float	Term.type := float
Term → char	Term.type := character
Term → double	Term.type := double

Here 'addtype' is a function that inserts entry to symbol table and 'type' is also a function that shows the type of construct.

Example 4.17: Now for string 'int a, b, c, d, e, f, g' parse tree with inherited attribute with 'enter' will look like as

Example:

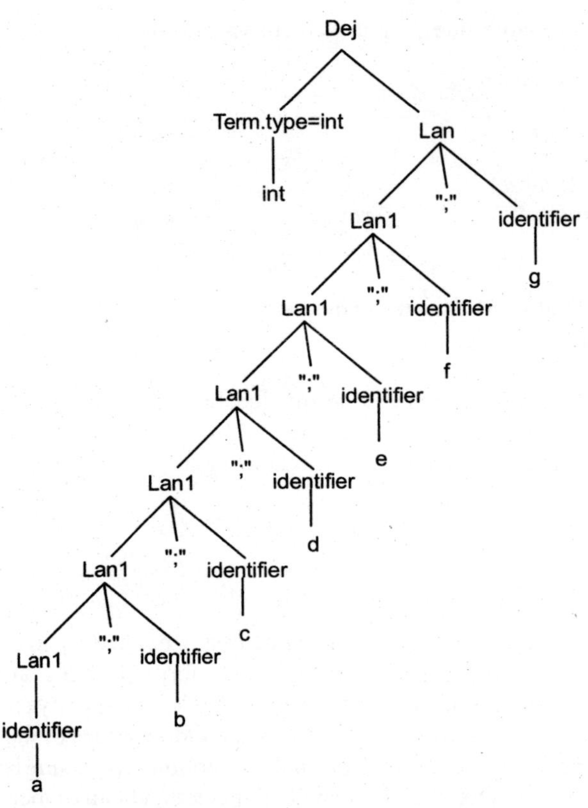


```
PROGRAM PAYMENT;
  CONST
    Bonus = 4;
  VAR
    Pay;
  BEGIN
    WRITE(Pay + Bonus)
  END.
```

which has the parse tree shown as:

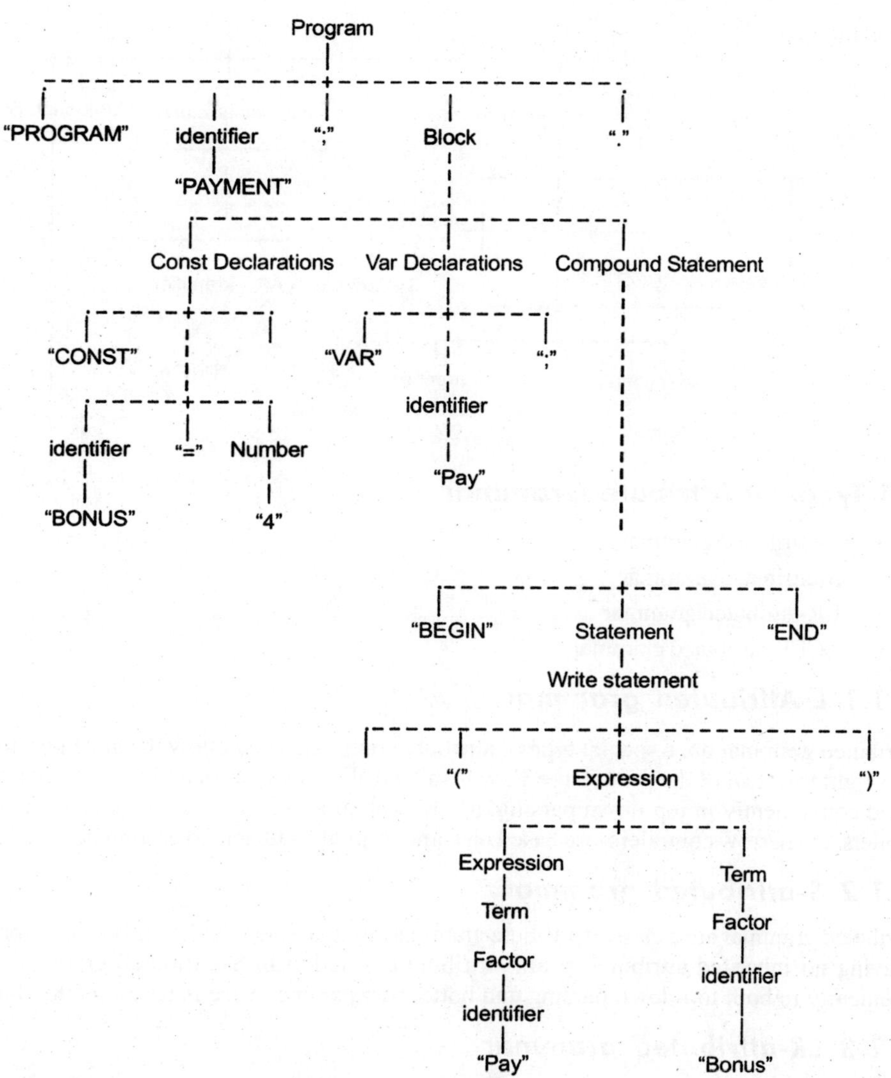

In this case we can think of the Boolean IsConstant and IsVariable attributes of the nodes CONST and VAR as being passed up the tree (synthesized), and then later passed back down and inherited by other nodes like Bonus and Pay as given below:

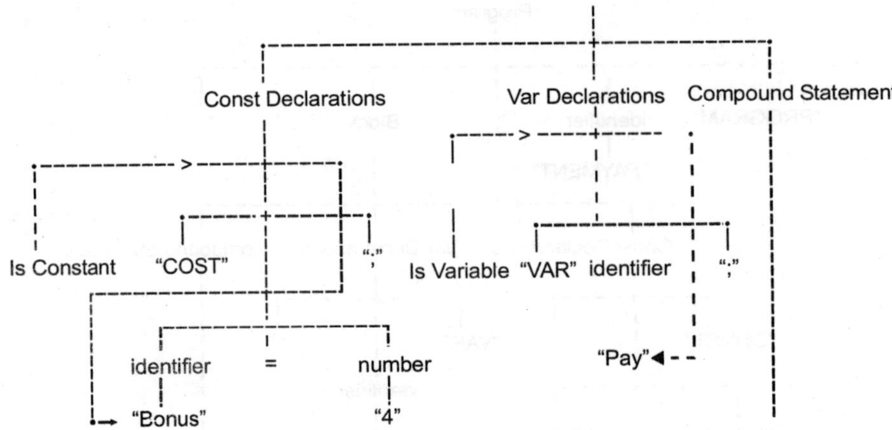

4.5.1 Types of Attribute Grammar

- L-attributed grammar
- S-attributed grammar
- LR-attributed grammar
- ECLR-attributed grammar

4.5.1.1 L-Attributed grammar

L-attributed grammar are a special type of attribute grammar. They allow the attributes to be evaluated in one left-to-right traversal of the syntax tree. As a result, attribute evaluation in L-attributed grammar can be incorporated conveniently in top-down parsing. Many programming languages are L-attributed. Special types of compilers, the narrow compilers, are based on some form of L-attributed grammar.

4.5.1.2 S-attributed grammar

S-attributed grammar are a class of attribute grammar, comparable with L-attributed grammar but characterized by having no inherited attributes at all. Attribute evaluation in S-attributed grammar can be incorporated conveniently in both top-down parsing and bottom-up parsing. Yacc is based on the S-attributed approach.

4.5.1.3 LR-attributed grammar

LR-attributed grammar are a special type of attribute grammar. They allow the attributes to be evaluated on LR parsing. As a result, attribute evaluation in LR-attributed grammar can be incorporated conveniently in bottom-up parsing. YACC is based on LR-attributed grammar. They are a subset of the L-attributed grammar, where the attributes can be evaluated in one left-to-right traversal of the abstract syntax tree. **They are a superset of the S-attributed grammar**, which allow only synthesized attributes.

4.5.1.4 ECLR-attributed grammar

ECLR-attributed grammar are a special type of attribute grammar. They are a variant of LR-attributed grammar where an equivalence relation on inherited attributes is used to optimize attribute evaluation. EC stands for equivalence class. They are a superset of LR-attributed grammar.

EXAMPLE : Consider the following grammar:

1. num → num dig | dig
2. dig → 0 | 1 | 2 | 3 | 4 | 5 | 6 | 7 | 8 | 9

(i) Give the attributed grammar with synthesized attribute 'val'.

PRODUCTION	SEMANTIC RULE
num → num1 dig	num.val = num1.val * 10 + dig.val
num → dig	num.val = dig.val
dig → 0	dig.val = 0
dig → 1	dig.val = 1
dig → 2	dig.val = 2
dig → 3	dig.val = 3
dig → 4	dig.val = 4
dig → 5	dig.val = 5
dig → 6	dig.val = 6
dig → 7	dig.val = 7
dig → 8	dig.val = 8
dig → 9	dig.val = 9

(ii) Draw the syntax tree for 456

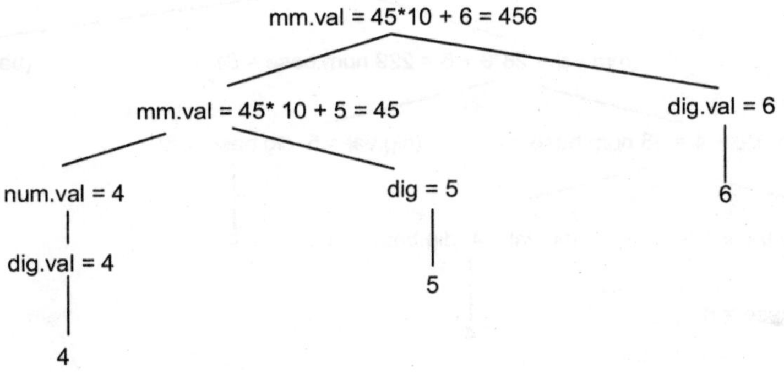

Example 4.18: Consider the following grammar:

1. base _num → num basechar
2. basechar → octal | decimal
3. num → num dig | dig
4. dig → 0 | 1 | 2 | 3 | 4 | 5 | 6 | 7 | 8 | 9

(i) Give the attributed grammar with synthesized attribute 'val' and 'base'.

PRODUCTION	SEMANTIC RULE
base_num → num basechar	base_num.val = num.val num.base = basechar.base
basechar → octal	basechar.base = 8
basechar → decimal	basechar.base = 10
num → num1 dig	num.val = { if dig.val = error or num1.val =error Then error Else num1.val * num.base + dig.val num1.base = num.base dig.base = num.base

num → dig	num.val = dig.val
	dig.base = num.base
dig → 0	dig.val = 0
dig → 1	dig.val = 1
dig → 2	dig.val = 2
dig → 3	dig.val = 3
dig → 4	dig.val = 4
dig → 5	dig.val = 5
dig → 6	dig.val = 6
dig → 7	dig.val = 7
dig → 8	dig.val = { if dig.base = 8 then error else 8 }
dig → 9	dig.val = { if dig.base = 8 then error else 9 }

(ii) Draw the syntax tree for octal number 345 and convert it into decimal

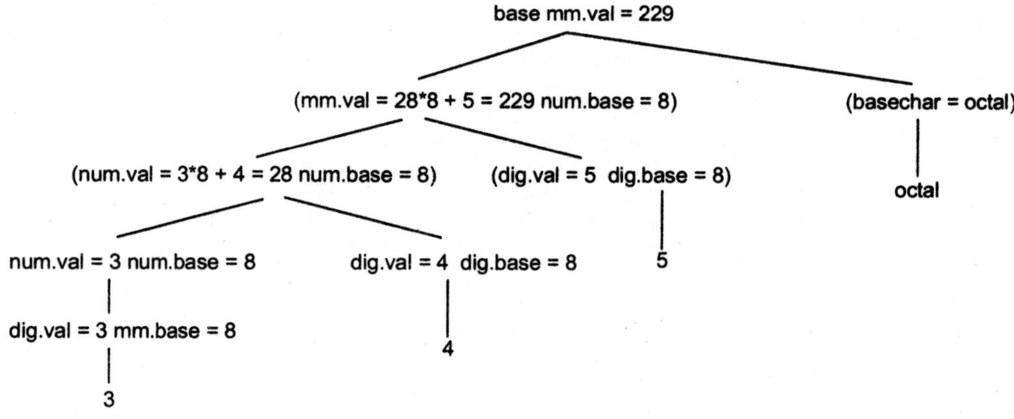

4.6 DEPENDENCY GRAPH

If an attribute 'y' is evaluated after the evolution of 'z' then we say that y is dependent on z this dependency can be shown by parse tree with some other relation known as dependency graph. Dependency graph exist in both synthesized and inherit attribute as :

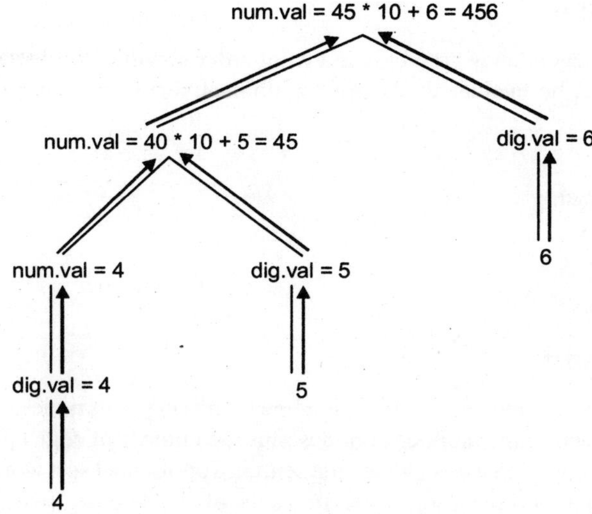

Figure 4.4: Dependency graph for synthesized attribute

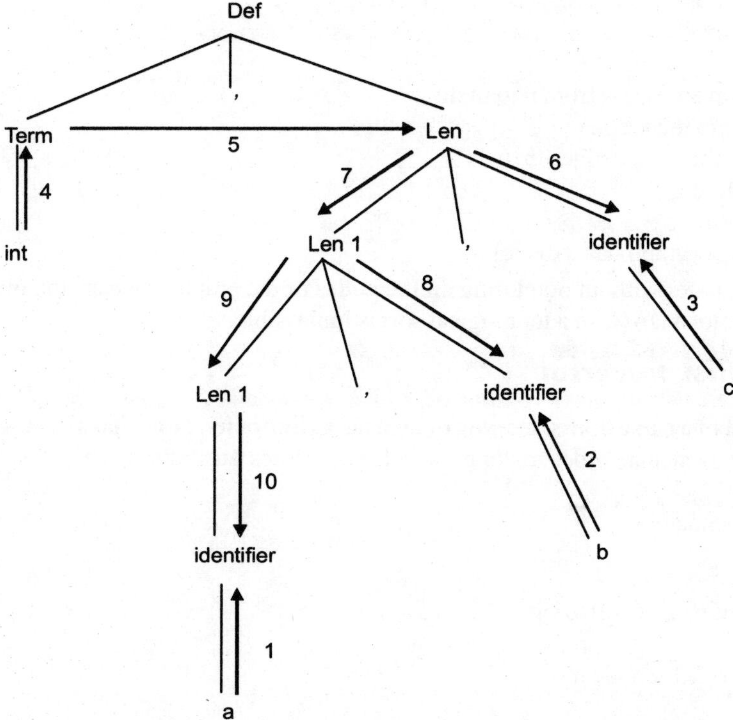

Figure 4.5: Dependency graph for inherit attribute

4.6.1 Evaluation Order

Any topological sort of any dependency graph gives a valid order in which the semantic rules associated with the nodes in a parse tree can be evaluated. Except topological sort some other mehod are also evaluates semantic rules as:

- Topological Sort
- Depth First Traversal
- Parse Tree Method
- Rule base Method
- Oblivious Method

4.6.1.1 Topological sort

A topological sort of a directed acyclic graph (DAG) is a linear ordering of its nodes. Algorithms for topological sorting have running time linear in the number of nodes plus the number of edges ($\theta(|V|+|E|)$). An alternative algorithm for topological sorting is based on depth first search. Topological sort works by choosing vertices in the same order as the eventual topological sort. First, find a list of "start nodes" which have no incoming edges and insert them into a queue Q. Then,

```
Q ← Set of all nodes with no incoming edges
while Q is non-empty do
  remove a node n from Q
   output n
  for each node m with an edge e from n to m do
    remove edge e from the graph
    if m has no other incoming edges then
      insert m into Q
if graph has edges then
   output error message (graph has a cycle)
```

If this algorithm terminates without outputting all the nodes of the graph, it means the graph has at least one cycle and therefore is not a DAG, so a topological sort is impossible.

4.6.1.2 Depth-first traversal

A depth-first traversal of a parse tree is one way of evaluating attributes. Note that a syntax-directed definition does not impose any particular order as long as order computes attribute of parent after all its children's attributes.

```
PROCEDURE visit (n: node)

BEGIN
   FOR each child m of n, from left to right
      Do visit (m);
   Evaluate semantic rules at node n
END
```

4.6.1.3 Parse tree method

These methods obtain an evolution order from a topological sort of dependency graph constructed from the parse tree for each input. This method will fail if parse tree have a cycle.

4.6.1.4 Rule based method

At compiler construction time semantic rules associated with production are analysized. For each production, order in which the attributes with that production are evaluated is predetermined at compiler construction time.

4.6.1.5 Oblivious method

Evolution order is chosen without considering any semantic rule. For example – If translation takes place during parsing then order of evolution is forced by the parsing method.

4.7 PARSING

Parsing is the process of analyzing a sequence of tokens in order to determine its grammatical structure with respect to a given formal grammar. It is formally named syntax analysis. A parser is a computer program that carries out this task. The term parseable is generally applied to text or data which can be parsed. Parsing transforms input text into a data structure, usually a tree, which is suitable for later processing and which captures the implied hierarchy of the input. Generally, parsers operate in two stages, first identifying the meaningful tokens in the input, and then building a parse tree from those tokens. So, most common use of parsers is to parse computer programming languages.

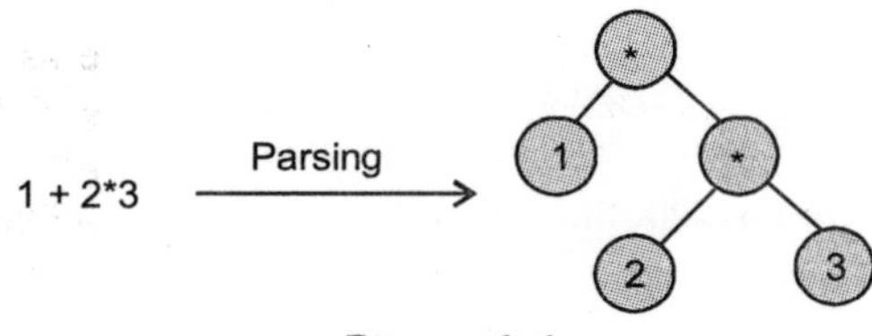

Figure 4.6

Overview of process

The following example demonstrates the common case of parsing a computer language with two levels of grammar: lexical and syntactic.

The first stage is the token generation, or lexical analysis, by which the input character stream is split into meaningful symbols defined by a grammar of regular expressions as described in chapter 3. For example, a calculator program would look at an input such as "12*(3+4)^2" and split it into the tokens 12, *, (, 3, +, 4,), ^ and 2, each of which is a meaningful symbol in the context of an arithmetic expression. The parser would contain rules to tell it that the characters *, +, ^, (and) mark the start of a new token, so meaningless tokens like "12*" or "(3" will not be generated.

The next stage is syntactic parsing or syntax analysis, which is checking that the tokens form an allowable expression. This is usually done with reference to a context-free grammar which recursively defines components that can make up an expression and the order in which they must appear. However, not all rules defining programming languages can be expressed by context-free grammar alone, for example type validity and proper declaration of identifiers. These rules can be formally expressed with attribute grammar.

The final phase is semantic parsing or analysis, which is working out the implications of the expression just validated and taking the appropriate action. DISCUSSED IN NEXT CHAPTER.

Types of parsers

The task of the parser is essentially to determine if and how the input can be derived from the start symbol within the rules of the formal grammar. This can be done in essentially two ways:

- *Top-down parsing:* A parser can start with the start symbol and try to transform it to the input. Intuitively, the parser starts from the largest elements and breaks them down into incrementally smaller parts. LL parsers are examples of top-down parsers.
- *Bottom-up parsing:* A parser can start with the input and attempt to rewrite it to the start symbol. Intuitively, the parser attempts to locate the most basic elements, then the elements containing these, and so on. LR parsers are examples of bottom-up parsers. Another term used for this type of parser is Shift-Reduce parsing.

Another important distinction is whether the parser generates a leftmost derivation or a rightmost derivation. LL parsers will generate a leftmost derivation and LR parsers will generate a rightmost derivation (although usually in reverse).

- Top-down parsers
  - Recursive descent parser
  - LL parser
  - Packrat parser
  - Unger parser
  - Tail Recursive Parser
- Bottom-up parsers
  - Precedence parsing
  - BC (bounded context) parsing
  - LR parser
    - SLR parser
    - LALR parser
    - Canonical LR parser
    - GLR parser
  - Earley parser
  - CYK parser
- Top-down vs Bottom-up
  - Bottom-up more powerful than top-down;
  - Can process more powerful grammar than LL, will explain later.
  - Bottom-up parsers too hard to write by hand, but JavaCUP (and yacc) generates parser from spec;
  - Bottom up parser uses right most derivation; Top down uses left most derivation;
  - Less grammar translation is required, hence the grammar looks more natural;
  - Intuition: bottom-up parse postpones decisions about which production rule to apply until it has more data than was available to top-down.

4.7.1 Parsing Table

A parsing table is a table describing what action its parser should take when a given input comes while it is in a given state. It is a tabular representation of a pushdown automaton that is generated from the context-free grammar of the language to be parsed. This is possible because the set of viable prefixes (that is, the sequence of input that can be set aside before a parser needs to either perform a reduction or return an error) of a context-free language is a regular language, so the parser can use a simple parse state table to recognize each viable prefix and determine what needs to be done next. A parsing table is used with a stack and an input buffer. The stack starts out empty, and symbols are shifted onto it one by one from the input buffer with associated states; in each step, the parsing table is consulted to decide what action to take.

The parsing table consists of two parts, the **action table** and the goto table. The action table takes the state at the top of the stack and the next symbol in the input buffer (called the "lookahead" symbol) and returns the action to take, and the next state to push onto the stack. The goto table returns the next state for the parser to enter when a reduction exposes a new state on the top of the stack. The goto table is needed to convert the operation of the deterministic finite automaton of the Action table to a pushdown automaton.

Action table consist three operations Reduction, a Shift, or Accept or None.

- ***Reduction :*** When the parser recognizes a sequence of symbols to represent a single nonterminal, and substitutes that nonterminal for the sequence then reduction take place. For example, in an LR parser, this means that the parser will pop 2*N entries from the stack (N being the length of the sequence recognized - this number is doubled because with each token pushed to the stack, a state is pushed on top, and removing the token requires that the parser also remove the state) and push the recognized nonterminal in its place. This nonterminal will not have an associated state, so to determine the next parse state, the parser will use the goto table.
- ***Shift :*** In this case, the parser makes the choice to shift the next symbol onto the stack. The token is moved from the input buffer to the stack along with an associated state, also specified in the action table entry, which will be the next parser state. The parser then advances to the next token.
- ***Accept :*** When a parse is complete and the sequence of tokens in question can be matched to an accept state in the parse table.

4.7.2 Top-Down Parsing

Top-down parsing is a strategy of analyzing unknown data relationships by hypothesizing general parse tree structures and then considering whether the known fundamental structures are compatible with the hypothesis. It occurs in the analysis of both natural languages and computer languages. **The main idea behind the top down parsing is to contruct an efficient non backtracking form of top down parser called a predictive parser or LL parser.**

Topdown parsing with backtracking

- S → cAd
- A → ab|a
- w = cad

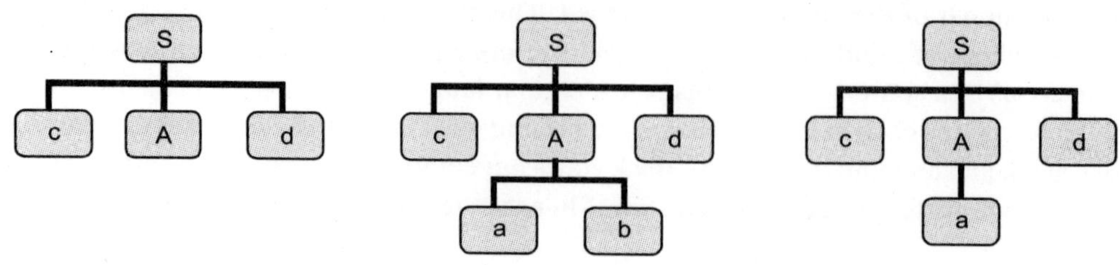

Figure 4.5

Parsing trace:

Expansion	Remaining Input	Action
S	cad	Try S → cAd
cAd	cad	Match c
Ad	ad	Try A → ab
abd	ad	Match a
bd	d	Dead end, backtrack
ad	ad	Try A → a
ad	ad	Match a
d	d	Match d
Success		

4.7.2.1 Recursive descent parser

Recursive descent parser is a top-down parser built from a set of mutually-recursive procedures (or a non-recursive equivalent) where each such procedure usually implements one of the production rules of the grammar. Thus the structure of the resulting program closely mirrors that of the grammar it recognizes.

Recursive descent with backup or backtracking is a technique that determines which production to use by trying each production in turn. Although predictive parsers are widely used, programmers often prefer to create LR or LALR parsers via parser generators without transforming the grammar into LL(k)* form. Recursive descent parsers are particularly easy to implement in functional languages such as Haskell or ML.

Example 4.19: here is a grammar for recursive descent parser

- program → statement program | statement
- statement → assignment
- assignment → ID EQUAL expr

Example 4.20: Consider following grammar as

expression → expression op term | term
term → term op1 factor | factor
factor → expression | number
Op → + | -
Op1 → *

Now we present a procedure that recognizes a factor. In this procedure there is a 'token' variable that keeps the current next token in the input and 'match' is an another procedure that match current next token with its parameter.

```
Procedure factor
        Begin
                Case token
                        (match) ( ) ;
                                expression;
                                match ( ) );
                number : match (number);
                Else error
        End case
End
```

```
Procedure match (expected token );
Begin
        If token = expected token then
                Gettoken
        Else
                Error
        End if
End
```

Example 4.21: Recursive descent calculator for simple integer arithmetic.For this purpose we consider the following grammar as :

```
#include<stdio.h>
#include<conio.h>
char token;
int exp(void);
int term(void);
void factor(void);
void error void
{
    fprintf(stderr, "error");
    exit(1);
}
void match (void)
{
    if(token = = expectedToken)
            token = getchar( );
    else error( );
}
int exp (void)
{
    int temp = term ( );
    while ((token = = '+' || token = = '–' ));
switch(token)
    {
            case '+'   : match('+');
```

```
                                        temp += term( );
                                        break;
                        case '-'   : match('–');
                                        temp  – = term();
                                        break;
      }
return temp;
}
int term(void)
{
      int temp = factor ( );
while (token == '*')
      {
            match('*');
            temp *= factor();
      }
      return temp;
}
int factor(void)
{
      int temp;
      if (token = = '(')
      {
            match( '(')
            temp = exp( );
            match ( ')' );
      }
      else if( is digit (token))
      {
            ungetc( token, stdin );
            scanf(" %d " , &temp);
            token = getchar( );
      }
      else error
      return temp;
}
void main()
{
      int result;
      token = getchar( );
      result = exp ( );
      if(token  = = '\n')
            printf("result  = %d",result);
      else
            error ( );
      return 0;
}
```

4.7.2.2 LL parser

An LL parser is a top-down parser for a subset of the context-free grammar. It parses the input from left to right, and constructs a leftmost derivation of the sentence. The class of grammar which are parsable in this way is known as the LL grammar. An LL parser is called An LL(k) parser if it uses k tokens of look-ahead when parsing a sentence. If such a parser exists for a certain grammar and it can parse sentences of this grammar without backtracking then it is called an LL(k) grammar. Of these grammar, LL(1) grammar, although fairly restrictive, are very popular because the corresponding LL parsers only need to look at the next token to make their parsing decisions.

A predictive parser is a recursive descent parser with no backup or backtracking. Predictive parsing is possible only for the class of LL(k) grammar, which are the context-free grammar for which there exists some positive integer k that allows a recursive descent parser to decide which production to use by examining only the next k tokens of input. (The LL(k) grammar therefore exclude all ambiguous grammar, as well as all grammar that contain left recursion. Any context-free grammar can be transformed into an equivalent grammar that has no left recursion, but removal of left recursion does not always yield an LL(k) grammar.) A predictive parser runs in linear time.

This parser has an **input buffer**, a **stack** on which it keeps symbols from the grammar, a parsing table which tells it what grammar rule to use given the symbols on top of its stack and its input tape. To explain its workings we will use the following small grammar:

(1) $S \rightarrow F$

(2) $S \rightarrow (S + F)$

(3) $F \rightarrow 1$

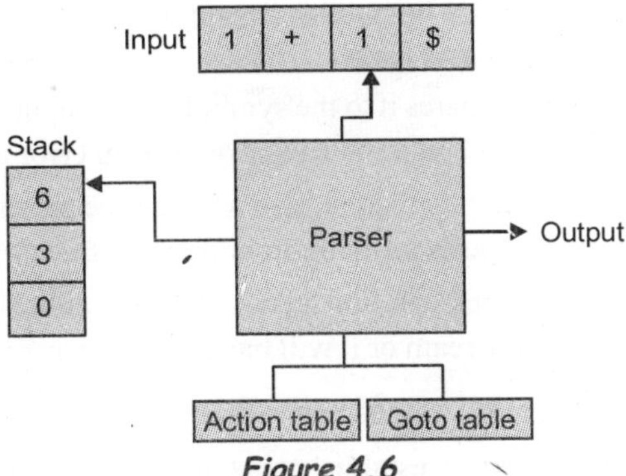

Figure 4.6

The parsing table for this grammar looks as follows:

	(	)	1	+	$
S	2	–	1	–	–
F	–	–	3	–	–

(Note that there is special terminal, represented here as $, that is used to indicate the end of the input stream and bottom of the stack.)

Depending on the top-most symbol on the stack and the current symbol in the input stream, the parser applies the rule stated in the matching row and column of the parsing table (e.g., if there is an 'S' on the top of the parser stack and a '1' in the front-most position of the input stream, the parser executes rule number 1, i.e., it replaces the 'S' on its stack by 'F').

When the parser starts it always starts on its stack with [S, $] where S is the start symbol of the grammar. The parser will attempt to rewrite the contents of this stack to what it sees on the input stream. However, it only keeps on the stack what still needs to be rewritten. For example, let's assume that the input is "(1 + 1)".

When the parser reads the first "(" it knows that it has to rewrite S to "(S + F)" and writes the number of this rule to the output. The stack then becomes as [(, S, +, F,), $].

In the next step it removes the '(' from its input stream and from its stack as [S, +, F,), $]. Now the parser sees a '1' on its input stream so it knows that it has to apply rule (1) and then rule (3) from the grammar and write their number to the output stream. This results in the following stacks as [F, +, F,), $] and [1, +, F,), $].

In the next two steps the parser reads the '1' and '+' from the input stream and also removes them from the stack, resulting in [F,), $]. In the next three steps the 'F' will be replaced on the stack with '1', the number 3 will be written to the output stream and then the '1' and ')' will be removed from the stack and the input stream.

So the parser ends with both '$' on its stack and on its input steam. In this case it will report that it has accepted the input string and on the output stream it has written the list of numbers [2, 1, 3, 3] which is indeed a leftmost derivation of the input string (therefore, the derivation goes like this: $S \rightarrow (S + F) \rightarrow (F + F) \rightarrow (1 + F) \rightarrow (1 + 1)$).

As can be seen from the example the parser performs three types of steps depending on whether the top of the stack is a nonterminal, a terminal or the special symbol $:

- If the top is a nonterminal then it looks up in the parsing table on the basis of this nonterminal and the symbol on the input stream which rule of the grammar it should use to replace it with on the stack. The number of the rule is written to the output stream. If the parsing table indicates that there is no such rule then it reports an error and stops.
- If the top is a terminal then it compares it to the symbol on the input stream and if they are equal they are both removed. If they are not equal the parser reports an error and stops.
- If the top is $ and on the input stream there is also a $ then the parser reports that it has successfully parsed the input, otherwise it reports an error. In both cases the parser will stop.

These steps are repeated until the parser stops, and then it will have either completely parsed the input and written a leftmost derivation to the output stream or it will have reported an error.

Constructing an LL(1) parsing table

In order to fill the parsing table, we have to establish what grammar rule the parser should choose if it sees a nonterminal A on the top of its stack and a symbol a on its input stream. It is easy to see that such a rule should be of the form $A \rightarrow w$ and that the language corresponding to w should have at least one string starting with a.• For this purpose we define the **First-set** and **Follow-set** of w.

FIRST{w}:

written as FIRST{w}, as the set of terminals that can be found at the start of any string in w, plus ε if the empty string also belongs to w. Given a grammar with the rules $A_1 \rightarrow w_1, \ldots, A_n \rightarrow w_n$, we can compute the FIRST{w_i} and FIRST{A_i} for every rule as follows:

1. initialize every FIRST{w_i} and FIRST{A_i} with the empty set { }.
2. add FIRST{w_i} to FIRST{A_i} for every rule $A_i \rightarrow w_i$, where FIRST is defined as follows:
   - If w_i is terminal then add FIRST{A_i} = { a }.
   - If w_i is ε then add FIRST{A_i} = { ε }.
   - If w_i is nonterminal and $w_i \rightarrow z_1\ z_2\ z_3\ z_4$ -------- $z_{i-1}\ z_i$ ---------- z_k then add FIRST{A_i} =

{z_1} if z_1 is not derive ε else discard z_i up-to ε is derived and add FIRST{A_i} = {z_{i+1}, ε }

3. add FIRST{w_i} to FIRST{A_i} for every rule $A_i \rightarrow w_i$
4. do steps 2 and 3 until all First sets stay the same.

Algorithm

```
FIRST (A)
for all non terminal A do First(A) = { }
while there are changes to any FIRST(A)
for each production choice A → X1X2 . ........Xn do
    K=1;
    continue = true
    while continue = true and k<=n do
            add FIRST(Xk) ={ε} to FIRST (A)
            If ε is not in first (Xk) then
continue = false
K=K+1
If continue = true then
add ε to FIRST(A);
```

Example 4.22 : a simple grammar is as:

1. S → Aa | b
2. A → bdZ | eZ
3. Z → cZ | adZ | ε
   - FIRST(S) = {FIRST(A), FIRST(b)} (by rule 3) = {b, e}
   - FIRST(A) = {FIRST(b), FIRST(e)}= {b, e} (by rule 2, rule 1)
   - FIRST(Z) = {a, c, ε } (by rule 2, rule 1)

Eample 4.23: Find the FIRST and FOLLOW for the following grammar:

S → ACB | CbB | Ba
A → da | BC
B → g | ε
C → h | ε

First Sets

FIRST (S) = FIRST (ACB) ∪ FIRST (CbB) ∪ FIRST (Ba) ——(1)
FIRST(A) = FIRST(da) ∪ FIRST(BC) ——(2)
FIRST(B) = FIRST(g) ∪ FIRST(ε) ——(3)
FIRST(C) = FIRST (h) ∪ FIRST (ε) ——(4)
So FIRST(B) = {g , ε} ——(5) (from 3)
FIRST(C) = { h , ε} ——(6)(from 4)
FIRST(BC) = [FIRST (B) – { ε }] ∪ FIRST(C)
= [{g, ε } – {ε}] ∪ {h , ε}
= {g} ∪ {h, ε }
= {g, ε } ——(7)
So FIRST (A) = {d, g, ε} ——(8)(from 2&7)
FIRST(ACB) = [FIRST (A) – {ε}] ∪ [FIRST(C) – {ε}] ∪ FIRST(B)
= {d, g} ∪ {h} ∪ {g, ε}
= {d, g, h, ε} ——(8)

FIRST(CbB) = [FIRST(C) – {ε}] ∪ [FIRST(b)] ∪ [FIRST(B)]
= {b, g, h, ε} ———(9)
FIRST (Ba) = [FIRST(B) – {ε}] ∪ FIRST(a)
= {g, a} ———(10)
So FIRST(S) = {a, b, d, g, h, ε} (from 1,8,9, & 10)

Follow{w}:

written as FOLLOW{w} here, which is defined as the set of terminals a such that there is a string of symbols αAaβ that can be derived from the start symbol. Computing the Follow-sets for the nonterminals in a grammar can be done as follows:

1. initialize every FOLLOW{A_i} with the empty set and a entry of $ at the end of this set.
2. if there is a rule of the form $A_j \rightarrow wA_iw'$, then
    - if the terminal a is in FIRST{w′}, then add a to FOLLOW{A_i}
    - if ε is in FIRST {w′}, then add FOLLOW{A_j} to Fo{A_i} or any production of form occur like $A_j \rightarrow wA_i$
3. repeat step 2 until all FOLLOW sets stay the same.

Algorithm

FOLLOW (A)
FOLLOW(start_symbol) = {$}
for all non terminal ≠ start-symbol do
    FOLLOW(A) = {}
while there are changes to any FOLLOW set do
    for each production $A \rightarrow X_1X_2X_3$........Xn do
        for each X_i that is a nonterminal do
            add first(X_{i+1} X_{i+2} .... X_n)- {ε} to FOLLOW (X_i)
            If ε is in FIRST(X_{i+1} X_{i+2} .... X_n) then
                Add FOLLOW(A) to FOLLOW(X_i)

Example 4.24: another simple grammar is as:

- S → Aa | b
- A → bdZ |eZ
- Z → cZ | adZ | ε

Follow(S) = {$} Follow(A) = {a} Follow(Z) = {Follow(A)} = {a}

The use of First () and Follow ()

if we want to expand S in this grammar:

- S → A ... |B ...
- A → a...
- B → b ... | a...
- If the next input character is b, we should rewrite S with A... or B ....?
    - since First(B) = {a, b}, and First(A)= {a}, we know to rewrite S with B;
    - First and FOLLOW gives us information about the next characters expected in the grammar.
- If the next input character is a, how to rewrite S?
    - a is in both First(A) and First(B);
    - The grammar is not suitable for predicative parsing.

Constructing an LL{1} parsing table

Now we can define exactly which rules will be contained where in the parsing table. If P[A, a] denotes the entry in the table for nonterminal A and terminal a, then

1. For each production A → w do step 2.
2. P[A,a] contains the rule A → w if and only if
   - a is in FIRST{w} or
   - ε is in FIRST{w} and a is in FOLLOW{A}.

If the table contains at most one rule in every one of its cells, then the parser will always know which rule it has to use and can therefore parse strings without backtracking. It is in precisely this case that the grammar is called an LL(1) grammar.

Example 4.25: (i) (1) S → F
(2) S → (S + F)
(3) F → 1

FIRST – SET of 'S' and ' F'

- FIRST {S} = FIRST {F} = {1}
- FIRST {S} = FIRST { (} = { (}
- FIRST {F} = FIRST { 1 } = {1}

So, FIRST {S} = { 1 ,(} AND FIRST {F} = {1}

FOLLOW – SET of 'S' and ' F'

- FOLLOW { S } = FOLLOW { F ,$}
- FOLLOW { S } = FOLLOW { +F) ,$ }
- FOLLOW { S+} = FOLLOW { F) , $}
- FOLLOW { S+F } = FOLLOW {) , $}
- FOLLOW { S } = FOLLOW { S+F) , $ }
- FOLLOW {F} = FOLLOW {1}

So, FOLLOW {S} = { ,$ } AND FOLLOW {F} = { ,$ }

LL{1} Table

Nonterminals	Input Symbols				
	(	)	1	+	$
S	S → (S + F)		S → F		
F			F → 1		

(ii) Consider following grammar and give predictive parser

S → stmt S′
S′ → ; S | ε
stmt → s

Now FIRST SETs for given grammar are as

FIRST (S) = {s}
FIRST(S′) = {; , ε}
FIRST (stmt) = {$}

& FOLLOW SETS

FOLLOW (S) = { $}
FOLLOW (S′) = { $ }
FOLLOW (stmt } = { ; , $ }

Now construction of parsering table take place as

Parsing table :

	s	;	$
S	S → stmt S′		
S′		S′ → ;S	S′ → ε
stmt	stmt → s		

Example 4.26:

1. S→P $
2. P→ { D; C}
3. D→ d,D | d
4. C→ c, C| c

- The above grammar corresponds loosely to the structure of programs. Need to left factor the grammar first.

1. S→P $
2. P → { D; C}
3. D → d D2
4. D2 → , D | ε
5. C → c C2
6. C2 → , C | ε

- Now we find the FIRST & FOLLOW sets as:

	First	Follow
S	{	$
P	{	$
D	d	;
D2	, ε	;
C	c	}
C2	, ε	}

- Now, constructing LL parser table

	{	}	;	,	c	d	$
S	S → P$						
P	P → {D;C}						
D						D → dD2	
D2			D2 → ε	D2 →, D			
C					C → cC2		
C2		C2 → ε		C2 → , C			

Example 4.27 : Find the FIRST and FOLLOW of the following grammar and then parse it via LL(1) parser.

exp → term exp1

exp1 → op1 term exp1 | ε

term → factor term1

term1 → op2 factor term1 | ε

factor → (exp) | **num**

op1 → + | –

op2 → *

We find the FIRST & FOLLOW sets as:

First Sets	Follow Sets
FIRST(exp) = {(,num} FIRST(exp1) = {+,–,ε} FIRST(term) = {(,num} FIRST(term1) = {*,ε} FIRST(factor) = { (,num} FIRST(op1) = {+,–} FIRST(op2) = {*}	FOLLOW(exp) = {),$} FOLLOW(exp1) = {),$} FOLLOW(term) = {),+,–,$} FOLLOW(term1) = {),+,–,$} FOLLOW(factor) = {),+,–,*,$} FOLLOW(op) = { (,num}

Now, we parse given grammar and design LL(1) parser

	(	number	)	+	–	*	$
exp	exp →term exp1	exp→term exp1					
exp1			exp→ε	exp1→ op1 term exp1	exp1→ op1 term exp1		exp1→ε
term	term→factor term1	term→factor term1					
term1			term1→ε	term1→ε	term1→ε	term1→ε op2 factor term1	term1→ε
factor	factor→(exp)	factor →num					
op1				op1→ +	op1 → –		
op2						op2→ *	

Example 4.28: Find the FOLLOW for the following grammar, if possible otherwise parse it using LL(1).

S → A

A → aB

B → bBC | f

C → g

In above grammar no ε production ,so there is no need for calculating FOLLOW SETS. We can parse it directly with the help of

FIRST SET.

So, FIRST(S) = {a}

FIRST (A) = {a}

FIRST(B) = {b,f}

FIRST(C) = {g}

And parse table:

	a	b	f	g	d	$
S	S → A					
A	A → aB					
B		B → bBC	B → f			
C				C → g		

Example 4.29: Construct the LL(1) parsing table for the following grammar:

S → aBDh
B → cC
C → bC | ε
D → EF
E → g | ε
F → f | ε

We find the FIRST & FOLLOW sets as:

First Sets	Follow Sets
FIRST(S) = {a}	FOLLOW(C) = {g,f,h,$}
FIRST(B) = {c}	FOLLOW(E) = {f,h,$}
FIRST(C) = {b,ε}	FOLLOW(F) = {h,$}
FIRST(D) = {g,f,ε}	FOLLOW(D) = {h,$},
FIRST(E) = {g,ε}	
FIRST(F) = {f,ε}	

And now, Parse table:

	Q	A	B	C	$
S′	S′ → S				
S	S → qABC				
A		A → a	A → bbD		
B		B → a	B →		B → ε
C			C → b		C → ε
D		D → ε	D → ε	D → c	D → ε

Confliction in LL(1) Grammar

- No ambiguous grammar can be LL(1)
- No left recursive grammar can be LL(1)
- Grammar is LL(1) if $A \rightarrow | \alpha | \beta$ are two distinct production of grammar the following condition hold :
- For no terminal a do both α and β derive strings beginning with a.
- At most one of α and β can derive the empty string,
- If $\beta \rightarrow \varepsilon$, then α does not derive any string beginning with a terminal in FOLLOW (A).

In general, no two grammar rule will alive in same row.

Example 4.30: non-LL(1) grammar with a conflict is:

1. $S \rightarrow iEtSS1 \mid a$
2. $S1 \rightarrow eS \mid \varepsilon$
3. $E \rightarrow b$

FIRST (S) = { i ,a }
FOLLOW (S) = { ,$ }

FIRST (S1) = { e , ε }
FOLLOW(S1) = { e , $ }

FIRST (E) = { b }
FOLLOW(E) = { , $ }

Non-terminals	Input Symbols					
	a	b	e	i	t	$
S	$S \rightarrow a$			$S \rightarrow iEtSS1$		
S1			**$S1 \rightarrow eS \mid \varepsilon$**			$S1 \rightarrow \varepsilon$
E		$E \rightarrow b$				

Example 4.31: consider the following grammar (ambiguous)

$S \rightarrow I \mid$ **other**
$I \rightarrow$ **if (exp)** S E
$E \rightarrow$ **else** S | **ε**
Exp $\rightarrow$ **0** | **1**

Now FIRST SETs

FIRST(S) = {if , other }
FIRST(I) = {if}
FIRST(E) = {else, ε}
FIRST(Exp) = { 0,1 }

& FOLLOW sets

1. FOLLOW (S) = FOLLOW (I) = { $ }
2. FOLLOW (Exp) = FIRST ( )) = {),$ }
   FOLLOW (S) = FIRST (E) = {else,$}
3. FOLLOW (E) = FOLLOW (S)
   FOLLOW (E) = FOLLOW (I)

so ;

FOLLOW (S) = { else , $}
FOLLOW (I) = { else , $}
FOLLOW (E) = {else , $}
FOLLOW (Exp) = {), $ }

& now constructing parsing table –

	if	other	else	0	1	$
S	S → I	S → **other**				
I	I → **if** (Exp) S E					
E			E → **else** S | ε			E → ε
Exp				Exp → **0**	Exp → **1**	

LL(k) parser generators

Modern parser generators that generate LL parsers with multi-token lookahead include:

ANTLR, Coco/R, JavaCC, PCCTS is now ANTLR, SLK : Strong LL(k) parsing, Spirit Parser Framework : is a flexible a LL(∞) parser generation framework in which the grammar themselves are written in pure C++, JetPAG: Jet Parser Auto-Generator. An optimizing LL(k) parser generator, Parsec : is a monadic parser combinator library for Haskell, which can parse LL(∞), context-sensitive grammar, but performs best when the grammar is LL(1), Ocaml Genlex Module, JFLAP : an educational tool to learn LL(1) parsing.

Example in C Language is given in **Appendix–A (A.5)**

Restrictions on grammar so as to allow LL(1) parsing

The top-down approach to parsing looks so promising that we should consider what restrictions have to be placed on a grammar so as to allow us to use the LL(1) approach. Once these have been established we shall pause to consider the effects they might have on the design or specification of "real" languages. A little reflection on the examples will show that the problems arise when we have alternative productions for the next (left-most) non-terminal in a sentential form, and should lead to the insight that the initial symbols that can be derived from the alternative right sides of the production for a given non-terminal must be distinct.

The effect of the LL(1) conditions on language design

We should note that we cannot hope to transform every non-LL(1) grammar into an equivalent LL(1) grammar. To take an extreme example, an ambiguous grammar must have two parse trees for at least one input sentence. If we *really* want to allow this we shall not be able to use a parsing method that is capable of finding only one parse tree, as deterministic parsers must do. We can argue that an ambiguous grammar is of little interest, but the reader should not go away with the impression that it is just a matter of trial and error before an equivalent LL(1) grammar is found for an arbitrary grammar. Often a combination of substitution and refactorization will resolve problems.

4.7.2.3 *Packrat parse*

A packrat parser is a form of top down parser similar to a recursive descent parser in construction, except that during the parsing process it memorizes the intermediate results of all invocations of the mutually recursive parsing functions. Because of this memorization, a packrat parser has the ability to parse many context-free grammar and any parsing expression grammar (including some that do not represent context-free languages) in linear time.

4.7.2.4 *Tail recursive parser*

Tail recursive parsers are derived from the more common Recursive descent parsers. Tail recursive parsers are commonly used to parse left recursive grammar. They use a smaller amount of stack space than regular recursive descent parsers. They are also easy to write. Typical recursive descent parsers make parsing left recursive grammar impossible (because of an infinite loop problem). Tail recursive parsers use a node reparenting technique that makes this allowable. A simple tail recursive parser can be written much like a recursive descent parser. The typical algorithm for parsing a grammar like this using an Abstract syntax tree is:

1. Parse the next level of the grammar and get its output tree, designate it the first tree, F
2. While there is terminating token, T, that can be put as the parent of this node:
   - Allocate a new node, N
   - Set N's current operator as the current input token
   - Advance the input one token
   - Set N's left subtree as F
   - Parse another level down again and store this as the next tree, X
   - Set N's right subtree as X
   - Set F to N
3. Return N

Example in C Language is given in **Appendix–A (A.6)**

4.7.3 Bottom-up Parsing

Bottom-up parsing is a strategy for analyzing unknown data relationships that attempts to identify the most fundamental units first, and then to infer higher-order structures from them. It occurs in the analysis of both natural languages and computer languages. It is common for bottom-up parsers to take the form of general parsing engines, that can either parse or generate a parser for a specific programming language given a specification of its grammar.

Bottom-up parsing is a parsing method that works by identifying terminal symbols first, and combines them successively to produce nonterminals. The productions of the parser can be used to build a parse tree of a program written in human-readable source code that can be compiled to assembly language or pseudocode. This parser also performs one of three actions. These are 'shift', 'reduce', and 'accept'.

- Shift means moving a symbol from the input to the stack.
- Reduce means matching a set of symbols in the stack for a more general symbol.
- Accept.

Type of Bottom-up Parsers

- LR parser
  - LR (0): No look ahead symbol.
  - SLR(1): Simple with one look ahead symbol
  - LALR(1): Look ahead bottom up, not as powerful as full LR(1) but simpler to implement.
  - LR(1): Most general language, but most complex to implement.
  - LR(n) - where n is an integer>=0, indicates an LR parser with n look ahead symbols; while languages can be designed that require more than 1 look ahead practical languages try to avoid this because increasing n can theoretically require exponentially more code and data space (in practice, this may not be as bad).
- Precedence parser
  - Simple precedence parser
  - Operator-precedence parser
  - Extended precedence parser

Examples of shift-reduce parsing

```
Take the grammar:
 S —> AB
 A —> a
 B —> b
And the input : ab
 Then the bottom up parsing is:

    Stack              Input
 ─────+      +-+-+───
      |      |a|b|
 ─────+      +-+-+───
          Shift a
 ────+-+      +-+───
     |a|      |b|
 ────+-+      +-+───
       Reduce a (A —> a)
 ────+-+      +-+───
     |A|      |b|
 ────+-+      +-+───
          Shift b
 ───+-+-+      +───
    |A|b|      |
 ───+-+-+      +───
      Reduce b (B —> b)
 ───+-+-+      +───
    |A|B|      |
 ───+-+-+      +───
```

```
        Reduce AB (S -> AB)
    ------+-+      +------
          |S|      |
    ------+-+      +------
         Accept
```

Example 4.32:

1. $S \to aABe$
2. $A \to Abc \mid b$
3. $B \to d$

Reduce abbcde to S by four steps

→ abbcde
→ aAbcde
→ aAde
→ aABe
→ S

– Notice the d should not be reduced into B in step 2.

$$S \overset{rm}{\Rightarrow} aABe \overset{rm}{\Rightarrow} aAde \overset{rm}{\Rightarrow} aAbcde \overset{rm}{\Rightarrow} abbcde$$

– How to get the right reduction steps?

Handles

$$S \overset{rm}{\Rightarrow} aABe \overset{rm}{\Rightarrow} aAde \overset{rm}{\Rightarrow} aAbcde \overset{rm}{\Rightarrow} abbcde$$

$S \to aABe$

$A \to Abc \mid b$
$B \to d$

- Informally, a handle of a sentential form is a substring that "can" be reduced.
  - Abc is a handle of the right sentential form aAbcde, because
    - A→Abc, and
    - after Abc is replaced by A, the resulting string aAde is still a right sentential form.
  - Is d a handle of aAbcde?
  - No. this is because aAbcBe is not a right sentential form.
- Formally, a handle of a right sentential form γ is a production $A \to \beta$ and a position in γ where the string β may be found and replaced by A.
  - If $S \overset{rm*}{\Rightarrow} \alpha Aw \overset{rm*}{\Rightarrow} \alpha\beta w$, then $A \to \beta$ in the position after $\alpha$is a handle of $\alpha\beta$w.
  - When the production $A \to \beta$ and the position are clear, we simply say "the substring β is a handle".

4.7.3.1 LR parser

An LR parser is a method of parsing for context-free grammar . **LR parsers read their input from left to right and produce a rightmost derivation.** An LR parser is said to perform bottom-up parsing because it attempts to deduce the top level grammar productions by building up from the leaves. The term "LR (*k*) parser" is also used; here the *k* refers to the number of unconsumed "look ahead" input symbols that are used in making parsing decisions. Usually *k* is 1 and is often omitted. A context-free grammar is called LR (*k*) if there exists an LR (*k*) parser for it. In typical use when we refer to An LR parser we mean a particular parser capable of recognizing a particular language specified by a context free grammar. LR parsers are difficult to produce by hand; they are usually constructed by a parser generator or a compiler-compiler.

LR parsing has many benefits:

- Many programming languages can be parsed using some variation of an LR parser. Notable exceptions are C++.
- LR parsers can be implemented very efficiently.
- Of all parsers that scan their input left to right, LR parsers detect syntactic errors as soon as possible.

Organization of LR parsers

The parser has an **input buffer**, a **stack** on which it keeps a list of states it has been in, an **action table** and a **goto table** that tell it to what new state it should move or which grammar rule it should use given the state it is currently in and the terminal or nonterminal it has just read on the input stream similar to LL(1) .

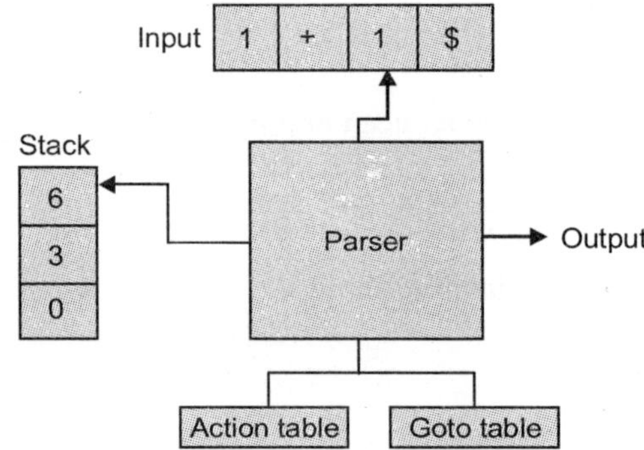

To explain the working of this parse we take the following grammar :

1. E → E * B
2. E → E + B
3. E → B
4. B → 0
5. B → 1

The LR (0) parsing tables for this grammar look as follows:

State	Action						Goto	
	*	+	0	1	$		E	B
0			s1	s2			3	4
1	r4	r4	r4	r4	r4			
2	r5	r5	r5	r5	r5			
3	s5	s6			acc			
4	r3	r3	r3	r3	r3			
5			s1	s2				7
6			s1	s2				8
7	rl	rl	rl	rl	rl			
8	r2	r2	r2	r2	r2			

The action table is indexed by a state of the parser and a terminal (including a special terminal $ that indicates the end of the input stream and bottom of stack) and contains three types of actions:

- *shift*, which is written as 's*n*' and indicates that the next state is *n*.
- *reduce*, which is written as 'r*m*' and indicates that a reduction with grammar rule *m* should be performed.
- *accept*, which is written as 'acc' and indicates that the parser accepts the string in the input stream.

The goto table is indexed by a state of the parser and a nonterminal and simply indicates what the next state of the parser will be if it has recognized a certain nonterminal.

Stack implementation of LR parser

The LR parsing algorithm now works as follows:

1. The stack is initialized with [$]. The current state will always be the state that is on top of the stack.
2. Given the current state and the current terminal on the input stream an action is looked up in the action table. There are four cases:
   - a shift sn:
     - the current terminal is removed from the input stream
     - the state n is pushed onto the stack and becomes the current state,
   - a reduce rm:
     - the number m is written to the output stream,
     - for every symbol in the right-hand side of rule m a state is removed from the stack and
     - given the state that is then on top of the stack and the left-hand side of rule m a new state is looked up in the goto table and made the new current state by pushing it onto the stack.
   - an accept: the string is accepted
   - no action: a syntax error is reported
3. The previous step is repeated until the string is accepted or a syntax error is reported.

To explain why this algorithm working we now proceed with a string like "1 + 1" would be parsed by LR parser. The table below illustrates each step in the process, here the state refers to the element at the top of the stack (the right-most element), and the next action is determined by referring to the action table above. Also note that a $ is appended to the input string to denote the end of it.

State	Input Stream	Output Stream	Stack	Next Action
0	1+1$		[$]	Shift 2
2	+1$		[$,2]	Reduce 5
4	+1$	5	[$,4]	Reduce 3
3	+1$	5,3	[$,3]	Shift 6
6	1$	5,3	[$,3,6]	Shift 2
2	$	5,3	[$,3,6,2]	Reduce 5
8	$	5,3,5	[$,3,6,8]	Reduce 2
3	$	5,3,5,2	[$ 3]	Accept

1. When the parser starts it always starts with the initial state 0 and the stack [$].
2. The first terminal that the parser sees is the '1' and according to the action table it should then go to state 2 resulting in the stack as [$ '1' 2]
3. In state 2 the action table says that whatever terminal we see on the input stream we should do a reduction with grammar rule 5. If the table is correct then this means that the parser has just recognized the right-hand side of rule 5, which is indeed the case. So in this case we write 5 to the output stream, pop one state from the stack, and push on the stack the state from the cell in the goto table for state 0 and B, i.e., state 4, onto the stack. The resulting stack as [$ B 4].
4. However, in state 4 the action table says we should now do a reduction with rule 3. So we write 3 to the output stream, pop one state from the stack, and find the new state in the goto table for state 0 and E, which is state 3. The resulting stack as [$ E 3] .
5. The next terminal that the parser sees is a '+' and according to the action table it should then go to state 6 as [$ E 3 '+' 6] .
6. The next terminal is now '1' and this means that we perform a shift and go to state 2 as [$ E 3 '+' 6 '1' 2] and just as the previous '1' this one is reduced to B giving the stack as [$ E 3 '+' 6 B 8].
7. In state 8 we always perform a reduce with rule 2. Note that the top 3 states on the stack correspond with the 3 symbols in the right-hand side of rule 2 and stack is [$ E 3].
8. Finally, we read a '$' from the input stream which means that according to the action table (the current state is 3) the parser accepts the input string. The rule numbers that will then have been written to the output stream will be [5, 3, 5, 2] which is indeed a rightmost derivation of the string "1 + 1" in reverse.

Algorithm for LR(0) parser

```
BEGIN
  GetSYM(InputSymbol); (* first Sym in sentence *)
  State := 1; Push(State); Parsing := TRUE;
  REPEAT
   Entry := Table[State, InputSymbol];
   CASE Entry.Action OF
    shift:
     State := Entry.NextState; Push(State);
    IF IsTerminal(InputSymbol) THEN
      GetSYM(InputSymbol) (* accept *)
     END
    reduce:
    FOR I := 1 TO Length(Rule[Entry].RightSide) DO Pop END;
     State := Top(Stack);
    InputSymbol := Rule[Entry].LeftSide;
   reject:
    Report(Failure); Parsing := FALSE
    accept:
```

```
        Report(Success); Parsing := FALSE
      END
    UNTIL NOT Parsing
              END
```

Constructing LR(0) parsing tables

The augmented grammar

Before we start, the grammar is always augmented with an extra rule

(0) S → E

where S is a new start symbol and E the old start symbol. The parser will use this rule for reduction exactly when it has accepted the input string.

For our example we will take the same grammar as before and augment it:

(0) S → E
(1) E → E * B
(2) E → E + B
(3) E → B
(4) B → 0
(5) B → 1

Items

The construction of these parsing tables is based on the notion of LR(0) items (simply called items here) which are grammar rules with a special dot added somewhere in the right-hand side. For example the rule E → E + B has the following four corresponding items:

E → • E + B
E → E • + B
E → E + • B
E → E + B •

Rules of the form $A \rightarrow \varepsilon$ have only a single item $A \rightarrow \bullet$. These rules will be used to denote that state of the parser.

Item sets

It is usually not possible to characterize the state of the parser with a single item because it may not know in advance which rule it is going to use for reduction. For example if there is also a rule E → E*B then the items E → E • + B and E → E • * B will both apply after a string corresponding with E has been read. Therefore we will characterize the state of the parser by a set of items.

Closure of item sets

An item with a dot in front of a nonterminal, such as E → E + • B, indicates that the parser expects to parse the nonterminal B next. To ensure the item set contains all possible rules the parser may be in the midst of parsing, it must include all items describing how B itself will be parsed. This means that if there are rules such as B → 1 and B → 0 then the item set must also include the items B → • 1 and B → • 0. In general this can be formulated as follows:

If there is an item of the form $A \rightarrow v \bullet Bw$ in an item set and in the grammar there is a rule of the form $B \rightarrow w'$ then the item $B \rightarrow \bullet\, w'$ should also be in the item set.

Any set of items can be extended such that it satisfies this rule. The minimal extension is called the **closure** of an item set and written as **closure**(I) where I is an item set.

Finding the reachable item sets and the transitions between them:

The first step of constructing the tables consists of determining the transitions between the closed item sets. These transitions will be determined as if we are considering a finite automaton that can read terminals as well as nonterminals. The begin state of this automaton is always the closure of the first item of the added rule: S → • E:

Item set 0

S → • E
+E → • E * B
+E → • E + B
+E → • B
+B → • 0
+B → • 1

The '+' in front of an item indicates the items that were added for the closure. The original items without a '+' are called the **kernel of the item set.**

To find the item set that a symbol x leads to we follow the following procedure:

1. Take the set, S, of all items in the current item set where there is a dot in front of some symbol x.
2. For each item in S, move the dot to the right of x.
3. Close the resulting set of items.
4. We continue this process until no more new item sets are found

Note that in all cases the closure does not add any new items:

1. For the terminal '0' this results in: **Item set 1** : B → 0 •
2. and for the terminal '1' in: **Item set 2** : B → 1 •
3. and for the nonterminal E in: **Item set 3 :** S → E • and E → E • * B and E → E • + B
4. and for the nonterminal B in: **Item set 4** : E → B •
5. Note that. For the item sets 1, 2, and 4 there will be no transitions since the dot is not in front of any symbol. For item set 3 we see that the dot is in front of the terminals '*' and '+'. For '*' the transition goes to: **Item set 5** : E → E * • B and + B → • 0 and + B → • 1
6. and for '+' the transition goes to: **Item set 6** : E → E + • B and + B → • 0 and + B → • 1
7. For item set 5 we have to consider the terminals '0' and '1' and the nonterminal B. For the terminals we see that the resulting closed item sets are equal to the already found item sets 1 and 2, respectively. For the nonterminal B the transition goes to: **Item set 7** : E → E * B •
8. For item set 6 we also have to consider the terminal '0' and '1' and the nonterminal B. As before, the resulting item sets for the terminals are equal to the already found item sets 1 and 2. For the nonterminal B the transition goes to: **Item set 8** : E → E + B •

These final item sets have no symbols behind their dots so no more new item sets are added and we are finished. The transition table for the automaton now looks as follows:

Item Set	*	+	0	1	E	B
0			1	2	3	4
1						
2						
3	5	6				
4						
5			1	2		7
6			1	2		8
7						
8						

Constructing the action and goto table/parse table

From above table, we construct the parse table as follows:

1. the columns for nonterminals are copied to the goto table
2. the columns for the terminals are copied to the action table as shift actions
3. an extra column for '$' (end of input) is added to the action table that contains acc for every item set that contains $S \rightarrow E \bullet$.
4. if an item set i contains an item of the form $A \rightarrow w \bullet$ and $A \rightarrow w$ is rule m with $m > 0$ then the row for state i in the action table is completely filled with the reduce action rm.

State	Action					Goto	
	*	+	0	1	$	E	B
0			s1	s2		3	4
1	r4	r4	r4	r4	r4		
2	r5	r5	r5	r5	r5		
3	s5	s6			acc		
4	r3	r3	r3	r3	r3		
5			s1	s2			7
6			s1	s2			8
7	r1	r1	r1	r1	r1		
8	r2	r2	r2	r2	r2		

Conflicts in the constructed tables

However, when reduce actions are added to the action table it can happen that the same cell is filled with a reduce action and a shift action (a **shift-reduce** conflict) or with two different reduce actions (**a reduce-reduce conflict**). However, it can be shown that when this happens the grammar is not an LR(0) grammar.

Example 4.33: of a non-LR(0) grammar with a shift-reduce conflict is:

1. E → 1 E
2. E → 1

One of the item sets we then find is:

Item set 1 : E → 1 • E
E → 1 •
+E → • 1 E
+E → • 1

There is a shift-reduce conflict in this item set because in the cell in the action table for this item set and the terminal '1' there will be both a shift action to state 1 and a reduce action with rule 2.

Example 4.34: of a non-LR(0) grammar with a reduce-reduce conflict is:

1. E → A 1
2. E → B 2
3. A → 1
4. B → 1

In this case we obtain the following item set:

Item set 1 : A → 1 •
B → 1 •

There is a reduce-reduce conflict in this item set because in the cells in the action table for this item set there will be both a reduce action for rule 3 and one for rule 4.

Both examples above can be solved by letting the parser use the FOLLOW set (see LL parser) of a nonterminal A to decide if it is going to use one of As rules for a reduction; it will only use the rule A → w for a reduction if the next symbol on the input stream is in the FOLLOW set of A. This solution results in so-called Simple LR parsers. This is the best way to prove a parser is LL or LR.

Example 4.35:

1. S ::= E $
2. E ::= E + T | T
3. T ::= T * F | F
4. F ::= id | (E)

State1. I has a **shift-reduce** conflict.

Example 4.36:

S ::= X

1. X ::= Y | id
2. Y ::= id

which includes the following two item sets:

I0: S ::= . X $
X ::= . Y
X ::= . id
Y ::= . id

I1: X ::= id .
Y ::= id .

State `I1` has a **reduce-reduce** conflict.

Example 4.37:

1. S ::= E $
2. E ::= L = R | R
3. L ::= * R | id
4. R ::= L

for C-style variable assignments. Consider the two states:

I0: S ::= . E $
E ::= . L = R
E ::= . R
L ::= . * R
L ::= . id
R ::= . L

I1: E ::= L . = R
R ::= L .

we have a **shift-reduce** conflict in `I1`.

Example 4.38:

S → AaAb
S → BbBa
A → ε
B → ε

This grammar is reduce-reduce conflict grammar example.

(i) Augmented grammar:
S′ → S
S → AaAb
S → BbBa
A → ε
B → ε

(ii) Set of items:

I0 => S′ → .S′
S → .AaAb
S → .BbBa
A →.ε   B →.ε
I1 => S′ → S.
I2 => S → A.aAb
I3 => S → B.bBa
I4 => S → Aa.Ab
A → .

I5 => S → Bb.Ba
I6 => S → AaA.b
I7 => S → BbB.a
I8 => S → AaAb.
I9 => S → BbBa.

(iii) Parsing table:

	Input/Action table			Goto table		
	a	b	$	S	A	B
I0	R3/R4	R3/R4				
I1			Accept			
I2	S4					
I3		S5				
I4	R3	R3			6	
I5	R4	R4				7
I6		S8				
I7	S9					
I8						
I9						

LR(0) versus SLR and LALR parsing

An LR parser is a method of parsing for context-free grammars . LR parsers read their input from left to right and produce a rightmost derivation, hence LR can be compared with LL parser.

Some more examples on LR(0)

Example 4.39

1. *S ::= E $*
2. *E ::= E + T*
3. *| T*
4. *T ::= id*
5. *| (E)*

has the following Item Sets:

I0: S ::= . E $
E ::= . E + T
E ::= . T
T ::= . id
T ::= . (E)

I1: S ::= E . $
E ::= E . + T

I4: E ::= E + T .

I5: T ::= id .

I6: T ::= (. E)
E ::= . E + T
E ::= . T
T ::= . id
T ::= . (E)

I2: S ::= E $.

I3: E ::= E + . T
T ::= . id
T ::= . (E)

I9: E ::= T .

I7: T ::= (E .)
E ::= E . + T

I8: T ::= (E) .

and DFA corresponding to grammar and item sets as

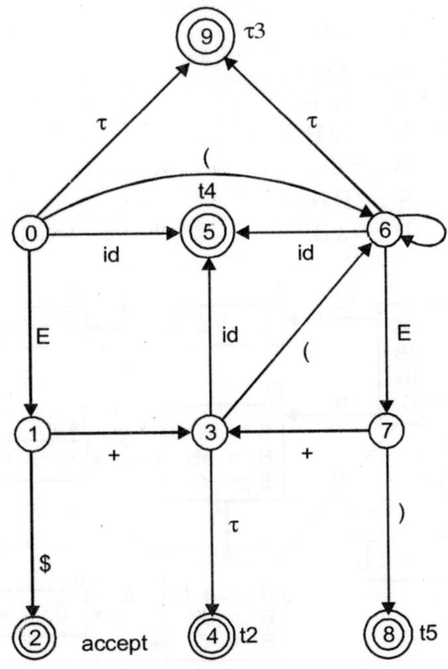

- ACTION & goto TABLE / PARSE TABLE

State	Action					Goto		
	id	(	)	+	$	S	E	T
0	s5	s6					1	9
1				s3	s2			
2	a	a	a	a	a			
3	s5	s6						4
4	r2	r2	r2	r2	r2			
5	r4	r4	r4	r4	r4			
6	s5	s6					7	9
7			s8	s3				
8	r5	r5	r5	r5	r5			
9	r3	r3	r3	r3	r3			

Example 4.40:

(0) S' ::= S $
(1) S ::= B B
(2) B ::= a B
(3) B ::= c

has the following item sets:

I0: S′::=.S$
S ::=.B B
B ::=.a B
B ::=.C

I1: S′::=S.$

I2: S′::=S$.

I3: S ::=B. B
B ::=.a B
B ::=.C

I4: S ::=B B.

I5: B ::=a. B
B ::=.a B
B ::=.C

I6: B ::=a B.

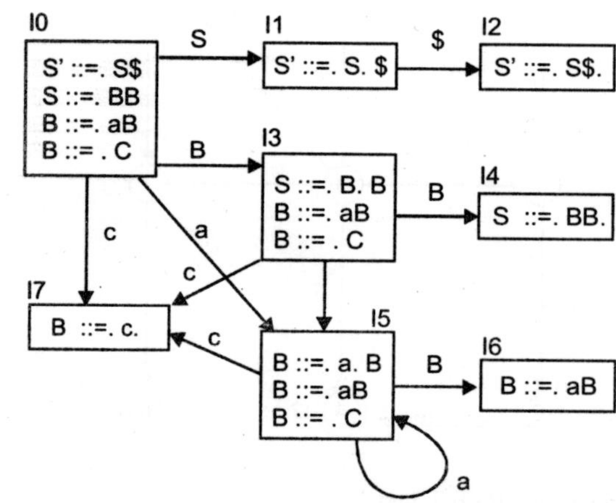

and action and goto table correspond to above DFA is

State	Action			Goto		
	a	c	$	S′	S	B
0	s5	s7			1	3
1			s2			
2	a	a	a			
3	s5	s7				4
4	rl	rl	rl			
5	s5	s7				6
6	r2	r2	r2			
7	r3	r3	r3			

Example 4.41:

1. S ::= R $
2. R ::= R b
3. R ::= a

has the following item sets:

I0 :	S ::= .R $	I1 :	S ::= R. $
	R ::= .R b		R ::= R. b
	R ::= .a	I2	S ::= R $.
I3 :	R ::= a .	I4 :	R ::=Rb.

DFA

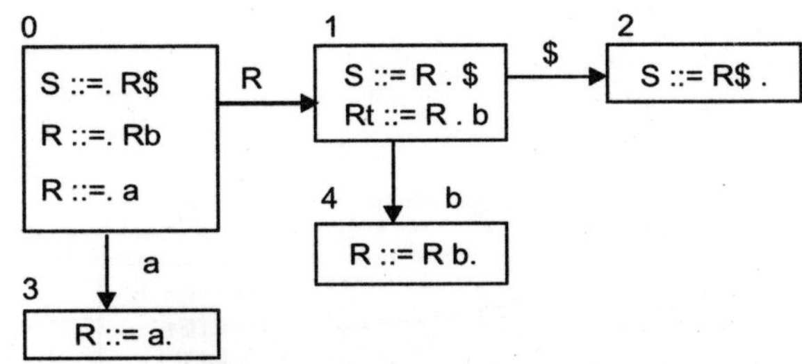

ACTION & TABLE/
PARSE TABLE

State	Action			Goto	
	a	B	$	S	R
0	s3				1
1		S4	s2		
2	a	a	a		
3	r2	r2	r2		
4	r3	r3	r3		

Example 4.42:

(0) E' → E
(1) E → E + T
(2) E → T
(3) T → (E)
(4) T → id

- ITEM SETS:

I0: E′→ •E
E → •E+T
E → •T
T → •(E)
T → •id

I1: E' → E•
E → E•+T

I2: E → T•

I3: T → (•E)
E → •E+T
E → •T
T → •(E)
T → •id

I4: T → id•

I5: E → E+•T
T → •(E)
T → •id

I6: T → (E•)
E → E•+T

I7: T → (E)•

I8: E → E+T•

DFA

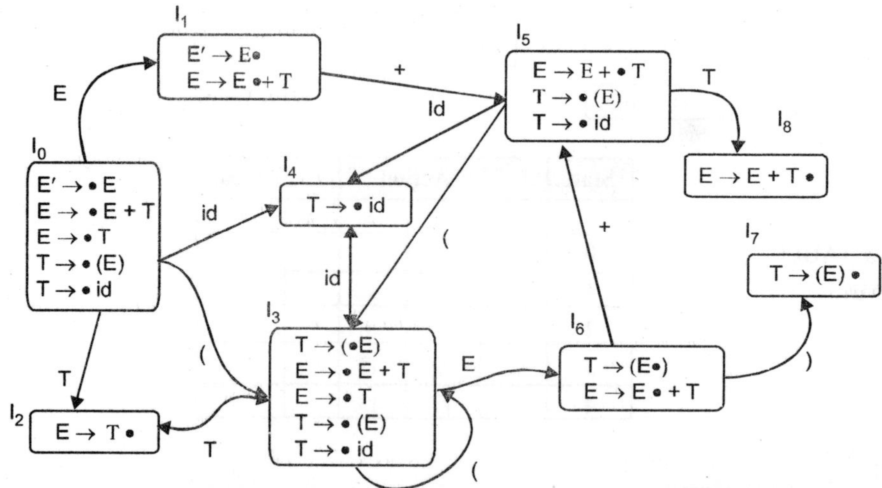

State on TOS	Action					Goto	
	id	+	(	)	$	E	T
0	S4		S3			1	2
1		S5			accept		
2	R2	R2	R2	R2	R2		
3	S4		S3			6	2
4	R4	R4	R4	R4	R4		
5	S4		S3				8
6		S5		S7			
7	R3	R3	R3	R3	R3		
8	R1	R1	R1	R1	R1		

Example 4.43: Find only set of items and DFA

1 . S' → E

2. E → E+T | T

3. T → id | (E) | id[E]

- ITEM SETS:

I0 : E' → •E
E → • E + T
E → • T
T → •(E)
T → • id
T → • id[E]

I1 : E' → E •
E → E • + T

I2 : E → T •

I3 : T → (• E)
E → • E + T
E → • T
T → • (E)
T → • id
T → • id[E]

I4 : T → id •
T → id • [E]

I5 : E → E + • T
T → • (E)
T → • id
T → • id[E]

I6 : T → (E •)
E → E • + T

I7 : T → (E) •

I8 : E → E + T •

I9 : T → id[• E]
E → • E + T
E → • T
T → •(E)
T → • id
T → • id[E]

I10 : T → id[E •]
E -> E • + T

I11: T → id[E] •

& DFA is

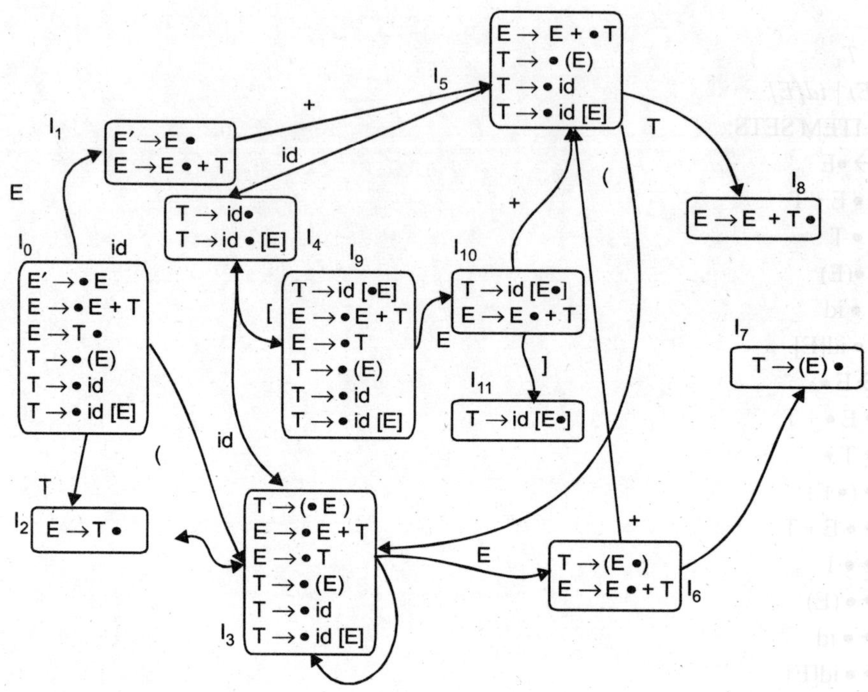

Example 4.44: Find only set of items and DFA

1. *S'→S*
2. *S→Sa*
3. *S→a*

has the following item sets

I0: S′→•S
S′→ • Sa
S → • a

I1: S′→S •
S→ S•a

I2: S → a •

I3: S→ Sa•

DFA

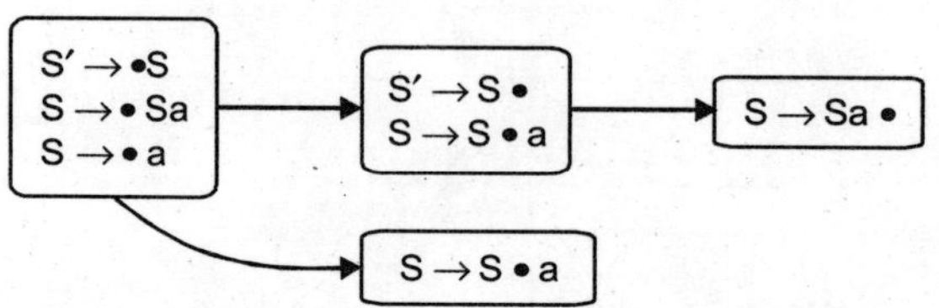

Example 4.45:

1. *S′→S*

2. $S \rightarrow Sa$
3. $S \rightarrow a$

ITEM SETS:

I0: S' → •S
S → • Sa
S → • a

I1: S' → S •
S → S•a

I2: S → a •

I3: S → Sa•

- ACTION & goto TABLE / PARSE TABLE

State	Action		Goto	
	a	$	S′	S
0	s2			1
1	s3	a		
2	a	a		
3	r2	r2		

Example 4.46: Find only set of items and DFA

1. *S ::= E $*
2. *E ::= (L)*
3. *E ::= ()*
4. *E ::= id*
5. *L ::= L , E*
6. *L ::= E*

- ITEM SETS:

I0: S ::= .E $
E ::= .(L)
E ::= .()
E ::= .id
L ::= L , E
L ::= E

I1: S ::= E .$
I2: S ::= E$.

- DFA

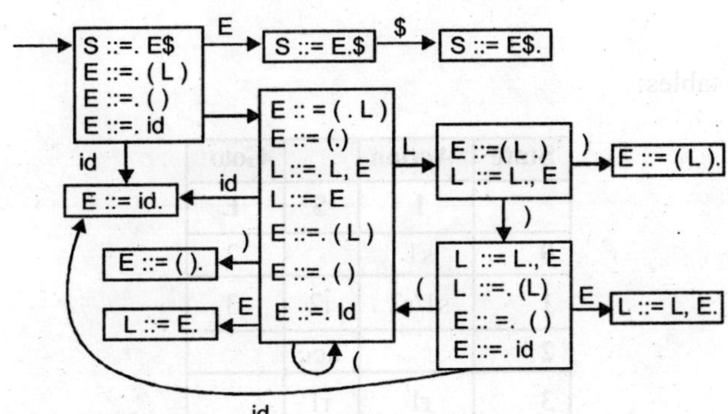

4.7.3.2 Simple LR parser

LR(0) ⊂ SLR(1) – A Simple LR parser or SLR parser is a LR parser for which the parsing tables are generated as for a LR(0) parser. Such a parser can prevent certain shift-reduce and reduce-reduce conflicts that occur in LR (0) parsers and it can therefore deal with more grammar. However, it still cannot parse all grammar that can be parsed by α LR (1) parser. A grammar that can be parsed by a SLR parser is called a **SLR grammar**. A grammar is SLR (1) if the following two conditions hold:

I: For any item A → α• a β in the set, with terminal a, there is no complete item B → γ• in that set with a in FOLLOW(B).

- No shift-reduce conflict on any state. This means the successor function for x from that set either shifts to a new state or reduces, but not both.

II: For any two complete items A → α• and B → β• in the set, the FOLLOW sets must be disjoint. (FOLLOW(A) ⊄ FOLLOW(B) is empty.)

- No reduce-reduce conflict on any state. If more than one non-terminal could be reduced from this set, it must be possible to uniquely determine which using only one token of lookahead.

Example 4.47: A grammar that can be parsed by a SLR parser but not by a LR(0) parser is the following:

1. E →1 E
2. E → 1

Constructing the action and goto table as is done for LR(0) parsers would give the following item sets and tables:

Item set 0

S → • E

+ E → • 1 E

+ E → • 1

Item set 1

E → 1 • E

E → 1 •

+ E → • 1 E

+ E → • 1

Item set 2

S → E •

Item set 3

E → 1 E •

The action and goto tables:

State	Action		Goto
	1	$	E
0	s1		2
1	s1/r2	r2	3
2		acc	
3	rl	rl	

As can be observed there is a shift-reduce conflict for state 1 and terminal '1'. However, the FOLLOW set of E is { $ } so the reduce actions r1 and r2 are only valid in the column for $. The result are the following conflict-less action and goto table:

State	Action		Goto
	1	$	E
0	s1		2
1	s1	r2	3
2		acc	
3		rl	

Example 4.48: consider the grammar " *S→ (S)S* | ε " and construct the SLR parser for the given grammar. In first step, we augment the grammar as:

Agumenting grammar

S' →S

S→ (S)S

S→ε

and now find set of items as:

I0 ⇒ S'→.S
S →.S
S →.

I1 ⇒ S'→ S.

I2 ⇒ S→ (.S)S
S →.(S)S
S →.

I3 ⇒ S→ (S.)S

I4 ⇒ S→ (S).S
S→ .(S)S
S→.

I5 ⇒ S→ (S)S.

And now finally construct the parsing table as:

State	Input/Action			Goto
	(	)	$	S
0	S2	R3	R3	1
1			Accept	
2	S2	R3	R3	3
3		S4		
4	S2	R3	R3	5
5		R2	R2	

Example 4.49: Consider the grammar *E→ E+n* | *n* and construct the SLR parse
similarly as previous grammar S→ (S)S | ε we augment this given grammar after that find set of items and then construct the parsing table. So,

Augmentating grammar

E' → E
E → E+n
E → n

Set of Items

I0 ⇒ E' → .E
E → .E+n
E → .n

I1 ⇒ E' → E.
E → E.+n

I2 ⇒ E → n.

I3 ⇒ E → E+.n

I4 ⇒ E → E+n.

Parsing Table

Set of Items	Input/Action			Goto
	N	+	$	E
0	S2			1
1		S3	Accept	
2		R3	R3	
3	S4			
4		R2	R2	

Example 4.50: Consider the following grammar and construct the SLR parser for this

E→E+T
E→T
*T→T*F*
T→F
F→(E)
F→id

First of all we augment the grammar as:

Augmented Grammar ⇒

E'→E
E→E+T
E→T
T→T*F
T→ F
F→id
F→(E)
F→id.

And now find the set of items as

Set of Items ⇒

I0 ⇒ E'→.E
E→.E+T
E→.T

I5 ⇒ F→id.

I6 ⇒ E→E+.T
T→.T*F

T→.T *F
T→.F
F→.(E)
F→.id
I1 ⇒ E'→E.
E→E.+T
I2 ⇒ F→F.
T→T.*F
I3 ⇒ T→F.
I4 ⇒ F→(.E)
E→.E+T
E→.T
T→.T*F
T→.F
F→.(E)
F→.id

T→.F
F→.(E)
F→.ID
I7 ⇒ T→T*.F
F→.(E)
F→.id
I8 ⇒ F→(E.)
E→E.+T
I9 ⇒ E→E+T.
T→T.*F
10 ⇒ T→T*F.
11 ⇒ F→(E).

Parsing Table:

State	Action/Input						Goto		
	id	+	*	(	)	$	E	T	F
0	S5			S4			1	2	3
1		S6				Accept			
2		R2	S7		R2	R2			
3		R4	R4		R4	R4			
4	S5			S4			8	2	3
5		R6	R6		R6	R6			
6	S5			S4				9	3
7	S5			S4					10
8		S6			S11				
9		R1	S7		R1	R1			
10		R3	R3		R3	R3			
11		R5	R5		R5	R5			

Example 4.51: For the given grammar give the SLR parser

$S \rightarrow aABb$
$A \rightarrow c \mid \varepsilon$
$B \rightarrow d \mid \varepsilon$

First Set	Follow Set
FIRST(S) = {a} FIRST(A) = {c,ε} FIRST(B) = {d,ε}	FOLLOW(S) = {$} FOLLOW(B) = {b,$} FOLLOW(B) = {d,b,$}

Parser Table:

	A	b	c	d	$
S	S → aABb				
A		A → ε		A → ε	A → ε
B		B→ε		B → d	B → ε

The SLR parsing algorithm

1. Initialize the stack with S
2. Read input symbol
3. While true, do:

3.1 if Action(top(stack), input) = S
 NS ← Goto(top(stack),input)
 push NS
 Read next symbol

3.2 else if Action(top(stack), input) = Rk
 output k
 pop |RHS| of production k from stack
 NS ← Goto(top(stack), LHS_k)
 push NS

3.3 else if Action(top(stack),input) = A
 output valid, return
 else
 output invalid, return

Note:

- SLR grammar constitute a small Subset of context free grammar, So an SLR parser can only succeed on a small number of context free grammar.
- By comparing the SLR(1) parser with CLR parser, we find that the CLR parser is more powerful. But the CLR(1) has a greater number of states than the SLR(1) parser, so its storage requirement is also greater than SLR(1) parser.

4.7.3.3 Canonical LR parser

A canonical LR parser or LR(1) parser is a LR parser whose parsing tables are constructed in a similar way as with LR(0) parsers except that the items in the item sets also contain a follow, i.e., a terminal that is expected by the parser after the right-hand side of the rule. For example, such an item for a rule A → B C might be

$$A \rightarrow B \cdot C, a$$

which would mean that the parser has read a string corresponding to B and expects next a string corresponding to C followed by the terminal 'a'. LR(1) parsers can deal with a very large class of grammar but their parsing tables are often very big.

Constructing LR(1) parsing tables

An **LR(1) item** is a production with a marker together with a terminal, e.g., [S → a A · B e, c]. Intuitively, such an item indicates how much of a certain production we have seen already (a A), what we could expect next (B e), and a lookahead that agrees with what should follow in the input if we ever reduce by the production S → a A B e. By incorporating such lookahead information into the item concept, we can make more wise reduce decisions. The lookahead of an LR(1) item is used directly only when considering reduce actions (i.e., when the marker is at the right end).

The **core** of a LR(1) item [S → a A · B e, c] is the LR(0) item S → a A · B e. Different LR(1) items may share the same core. For example, if we have two LR(1) items of the form

- [A → α·, a] and
- [B → α·, b],

we take advantage of the lookahead to decide which reduction to use. (The same setting would perhaps produce a reduce/reduce conflict in the SLR approach.)

Initial item

To get the parsing started, we begin with the initial item of

[S′ → · S, $]. →

Here $ is a special character denoting the end of the string.

Closure

If [A → α· B β, a] belongs to the set of items, and B → γ is a production of the grammar, then we add the item [B → · γ, b] for all b in FIRST(β a). Every state is closed according to Closure.

Goto

A state containing [A → α· X β, a] will move to a state containing [A → αX · β, a] with label X. Every state has transitions according to Goto.

Shift actions

The shift actions are the same. If [A → α· b β, a] is in state I_k and I_k moves to state I_m with label b, then we add the action action[k, b] = "shift m"

Reduce actions

If [A→α., a] is in state I_k, then we add the action: "Reduce A → α" to action[I_k, a]. Observe that we don't use information from FOLLOW(A) anymore. The goto part of the table is as before.

An Algorithm for finding the Canonical Collection of Sets of LR(1) Items:-

/* Let C be the canonical collection of sets of LR (1) items.*/

Input: augmented grammar

Output: Canonical collection of sets of LR (1) items (i.e., set)

1. $C_{old}=\phi$
2. add closure({S1→S,$}) to C
3. while $C_{old} \neq C_{new}$ do

Temp=C_{new}-C_{old}

C_{old}=C_{new}

For every I in temp do

For every X in V ∪ T(i.e. for every grammar symbol X) do

If goto(I,X) is not empty and not in C_{new} then

goto(I,X) to C_{new}

}

4. C=C_{new}

Example 4.52: Consider the following grammar:

S→ AaAb

S→ BbBa

A→ε

B→ε

(i) The augmented grammar will be

S1→S

S→ AaAb

S→ BbBa

A→ ε

B→ ε

(ii) The canonical collection of sets of LR(1) items are computed as follows:

I0=closure({S1→ .S$})={ S1→ .S$

S→ .AaAb,$

S→ .BbBa,$

A→ .,a

B→ .,b

}

goto({I_0,S})=closure({S1→ S.,$})={S1→S.,$}=I_1

goto({I_0,A})=closure({S→ A.aAb,$})={S→A.aAb,$}=I_2

goto({I_0,B})=closure({S→ B.bBa,$})={S→B.bBa.,$}=I_3

goto({I2,a})=closure({S→ Aa.Ab,$})={S→ Aa.Ab,$

A→ .,b

}=I_4

goto({I3,b})=closure({S→ Bb.Ba,$})={ S→ Bb.Ba,$

B→ .,a

}=I_5

goto({I_4,A})=closure({S→ AaA.b,$})={S→AaA.b,$}=I_6

goto({I_5,B})=closure({S→ BbB.a,$})={S→BbB.a,$}=I_7

goto({I_6,b})=closure({S→ AaAb.,$})={S→AaAb.,$}=I_8

goto({I_7,a})=closure({S→ bbBa.,$})={S→ BbBa.,$}=I_9

(iii) The transition diagram of the DFA is shown in the following figure:

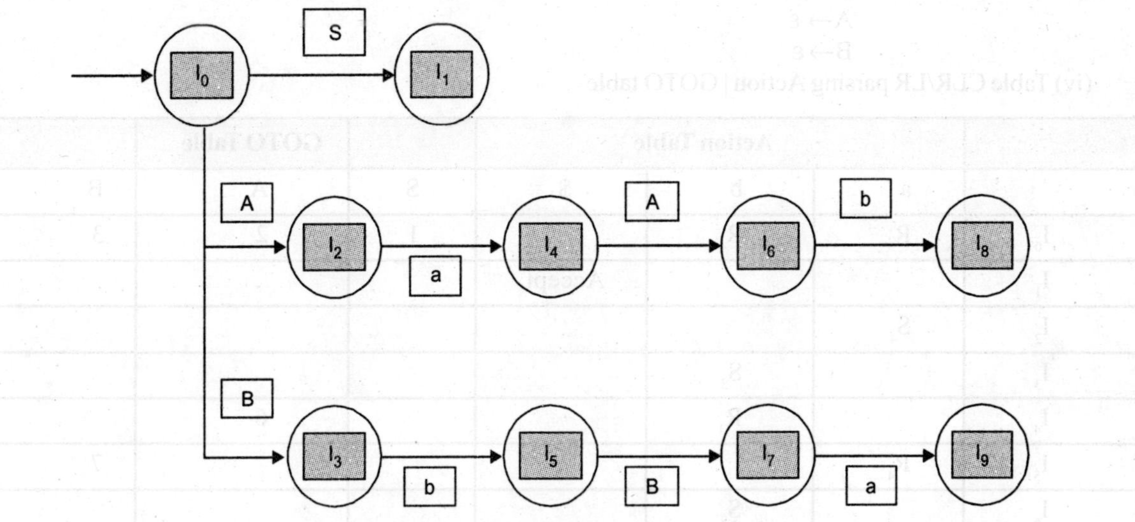

Figure 4.7: Transition diagram for the canonical collection of sets of LR(1) items

Construction of the action and GOTO Table for the LR(1) or CLR Parser

The following steps will construct the parsing action table for the LR(1) parser:-

1. for every state I_i in C do
   for every terminal symbol a do
   if goto(I_i,a)=I_j then
   make action[I_i,a]=S_j/* for shift and enter into the state J*/

2. for every state I_i in C whose underlying set of LR(1) items contains an item of the form A→ α., a do make action[I_i,a]=R_k/* where k is the number of the production A→α, standing for reduce by A→α.*/

3. make[I_i,$]=accept if I_i contains an item S_1→ S.,$

The goto table is simply a mapping of transition in the DFA on nonterminals. Therefore it is constructed as follows:-

for every I_i in C do
for every nonterminal A do
If goto(I_i,A)=I_j then
make goto[I_i,A]=j

This method is called as CLR(1) or LR(1), and is more powerful than SLR (1). Therefore, the CLR or LR parsing table for the grammar having the following productions is as follows:

S1 → S
S→ AaAb
S→ BbBa
A→ ε
B→ ε

(iv) Table CLR/LR parsing Action | GOTO table

	Action Table			GOTO Table		
	a	b	$	S	A	B
I_0	R_3	R_4		1	2	3
I_1			Accept			
I_2	S_4					
I_3		S_5				
I_4		R_3			6	
I_5	R_4					7
I_6		S_8				
I_7	S_9					
I_8			R_1			
I_9			R_2			

where productions are numbered as follows:-

S → AaAb
S → BbBa
A → ε
B → ε

By comparing the SLR(1) parser with the CLR(1) parser, we find that the CLR(1) parser is more powerful. But the CLR(1) has a greater number of states than the SLR(1) parser; hence, its storage requirement is also greater than the SLR(1) parser. Therefore, we can devise a parser that is an intermediate between the two; that is , the parser's power will be in between that of SLR(1) and CLR(1), and its storage requirement will be the same as SLR(1)'s . such a parser,LALR(1) will be much more useful:since each of its states corresponds to the set of LR(1) items, the information about the lookaheads is available in the state itself, making it more powerful than the SLR parser. But a state of the LALR(1) parser is obtained by combining those states of the CLR parser that have identical LR(0) (core) items, but which differ in the lookaheads in their item set representations. Therefore, even if there is no reduce-reduce conflict in the states of the CLR parser that has been combined to form an LALR parser, a conflict may get generated in the state of LALR parser. We may be able to obtain a CLR parsing table without multiple entries for a grammar, but when we construct the LALR parsing table for the same grammar, it might have multiple entries.

4.7.3.4 LALR parser

Constructing LALR parsing tables

The steps in constructing an LALR parsing table are as follows:-

1. Obtain the canonical collection of sets of LR(1) items.
2. If more than one set of LR(1) items exists in the canonical collection obtained that have identical cores or LR(0)s, but which have different lookaheads, then combine these sets of LR(1) items to obtain a reduced collection, c1, of sets of LR(1) items.
3. Construct the parsing table by using this reduced collection, as follows:-

Construction of the Action Table

1. for every state I_i in C_1 do
   for every terminal symbol a do
   if goto (I_i,a)=I_j then
   make action [I_i,a]=S_j/* for shift and enter into the state J*/
2. for every state I_i in C_1 whose underlying set of LR(1) items contains an item of the form A→α. , a, do make action[I_i,a]=R_k/* where k is the number of production A'!Ü standing for reduce by A→α*/
3. make[I_i,$]=accept if I_i contains an item S1→S.,$

Construction of the GOTO Table

The goto table simply maps transitions on nonterminals in the DFA. Therefore, the table is constructed as follows:-

for every I_i in C_1 do
for every nonterminal A do
if goto(I_i,A)=I_j then
make goto(I_i,A)=j

Example 4.53: Consider the following grammar:-

S → AA
A → aA
A → b

(i) The augmented grammar is as follows:-

S_1 → S
S → AA
A → aA
A → b

(ii) The canonical collection of sets of LR(1) items are computed as follows:-

I_0=closure({S_1 → .S,$})={$S_1$ → .S,$
S → AA,$
A → .aA,a/b
A → .b,a/b
}

→goto(I_0,S)=closure({S_1→S.,$})={$S_1$→S.,$}=I_1

goto(I_0,A) =closure({S→A.A,$})={S→ A.A,$
A→.aA,$
A→.b,$
}=I_2

goto(I_0,a) =closure({A→a.A,a/b})={A→ a.A,a/b
A→.aA,a/b
A→.b, a/b
}=I_3

goto(I_0,b) =closure({A→b., a/b})={A→ b., a/b
}=I_4

goto(I_2,A) =closure({S→ AA., $})={S→AA., $
}=I_5

goto(I_2,a) =closure({A→ a.A., $})={A→a.A,$
A→ .aA,$
A→.b,$
}=I_6

goto(I_2,b) =closure({A→ b., $})={A→ b.,$
}=I_7

goto(I_3,A) =closure({A→ aA.,a/b})={A→aA., a/b
}=I_8

goto(I_3,a) =closure({A→ a.A., a/b})={A→a.A,a/b
A→ .aA,a/b
A→ .b,a/b
}=same as I_3

goto(I_3,b) =closure({A→b., a/b})={A→ b., a/b
}=Same as I_4

goto(I_6,A) =closure({A→aA., $})={A→aA,$
}=I_9

goto(I_6,a) =closure({A→ a.A., $})={A→a.A,$
A→ .aA,$
A→ .b,$
}=same as I_6

goto(I_6,b) =closure({A→ b., $})={A→ b.,$
}=same as I_7

We see that the states I_3 and I_6 have identical LR(0) set items that differ only in their lookaheads. The same goes for the pair of states I_4, I_7 and the pair of the states I_8, I_9. hence, we can combine I_3 with I_6, I_4 with I_7, and I_8 with I_9 to obtain the reduced collection shown below:-

I_0=closure({S_1→ .S,$})={$S_1$→ .S,$
S→ .AA,$
A→ .aA,a/b
A→ .b,a/b
}

I_1={S_1→ S.,$}

I_2={ S→ A.A,$
A→ .aA,$
A→.b,$
}

I_{36}={A→a.A, a/b/$
A→ .aA, a/b/$
A→ .b,a/b/$
}
I_{47}={A→b.,a/b/$
}
I_5={S→AA.,$
}
I_{89}={A→ aA.,a/b/$
}

Where I_{36} stands for combination of I_3 and I_6, I_{47} stands for the combination of I_4 and I_7, and I_{89} stands for the combination of I_8 and I_9.

The transition diagram of the DFA using the reduced collection is shown below:-

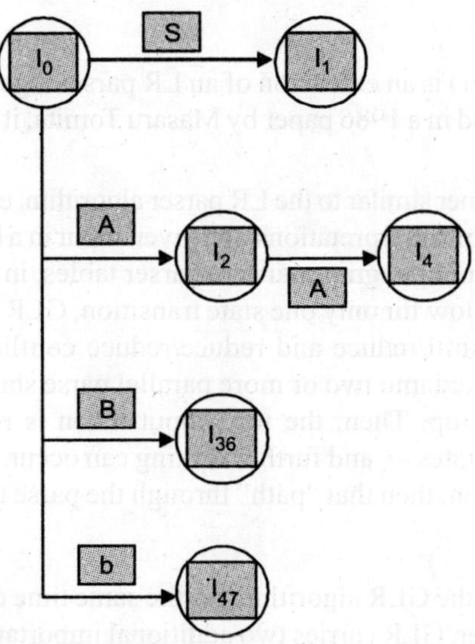

Figure 4.8: Transition diagram for a DFA using a reduced collection.

Therefore the following table shows the LALR parsing table for the grammar having the following productions:-

S_1→S
S→ AA
A→ aA
A→b

Which are numbered as

A→AA——(1)
A→aA ——(2)
A→b——(3)

Now the LALR parsing table for a DFA using a reduced collection is as follows:-

	Action Table			Goto Table	
	a	b	$	S	A
I_0	S_{36}	S_{47}		1	2
I_1			Accept		
I_2	S_{36}	S_{47}			5
I_{36}	S_{36}	S_{47}			89
I_{47}	R_3	R_3	R_3		
I_5	R_4		R_1		
I_{89}	R_2	R_2	R_2		

4.7.3.5 GLR parser

GLR parser (Generalized LR parser) is an extension of an LR parser algorithm to handle nondeterministic and ambiguous grammar. First described in a 1986 paper by Masaru Tomita, it has also been referred to as a "parallel parser".

GLR algorithm works in a manner similar to the LR parser algorithm, except that, given a particular grammar, a GLR parser will process all possible interpretations of a given input in a breadth-first search. On the front-end, a GLR parser generator converts an input grammar into parser tables, in a manner similar to an LR generator. However, where LR parse tables allow for only one state transition, GLR parse tables allow for multiple transitions. In effect, GLR allows for shift/reduce and reduce/reduce conflicts. When a conflicting transition is encountered, the parse stack is forked into two or more parallel parse stacks, where the state corresponding to each possible transition is at the top. Then, the next input token is read and used to determine the next transition(s) for each of the "top" states — and further forking can occur. If any given top state and input token do not result in at least one transition, then that "path" through the parse tables is invalid and can be discarded.

Advantages

When implemented carefully, the GLR algorithm has the same time complexity as the CYK algorithm and Earley algorithm — $O(n^3)$. However, GLR carries two additional important advantages:

- The time required to run the algorithm is proportional to the degree of nondeterminism in the grammar on deterministic grammar the GLR algorithm runs in $O(n)$ time (this is not true of the Earley and CYK algorithms)
- The GLR algorithm is "on-line" that is, it consumes the input tokens in a specific order and performs as much work as possible after consuming each token.

Since most programming languages are deterministic or "almost deterministic", in practice the GLR algorithm often performs markedly better than others.

4.7.3.6 Earley parser

The **Earley parser** named after its inventor, Jay Earley. **Earley parser** uses dynamic programming. Earley parsers are appealing because they can parse all context-free languages. The Earley parser executes in cubic time in the general case, and quadratic time for unambiguous grammar. It performs particularly well when the rules are written left-recursively.

Earley parser uses dot notation similar to LR parser. Given a production A '! BCD (where B, C, and D are symbols in the grammar, terminals or nonterminals), the notation A → B • C D represents a condition in which B has already been parsed and the sequence C D is expected.

For every input, the parser generates a *state set*. Each state is a tuple containing:

- A dot condition for a particular production.
- The position at which the matching of this production began: the *origin position*.

The state set at input position k is called S(k). The parser is seeded with S(0) being the top-level rule. The parser then iteratively operates in three stages: *prediction*, *scanning*, and *completion* (see Aycock and Horspool, Section 2). In the following descriptions, α, β, and γ represent any sequence of terminals/nonterminals (including the null sequence), X, Y, and Z represent single nonterminals, and a represents a terminal symbol.

- **Prediction**: For every state in S(k) of the form (X → α• Y β, j) (where j is the origin position as above), add (Y → • γ, k) to S(k) for every production with Y on the left-hand side.
- **Scanning**: If a is the next symbol in the input stream, for every state in S(k) of the form (X → α• a β, j), add (X → αa • β, j) to S(k+1).
- **Completion**: For every state in S(k) of the form (X → γ•, j), find states in S(j) of the form (Y → α• X β, i) and add (Y → αX • β, i) to S(k).

These steps are repeated until no more states can be added to the set. This is generally realized by making a queue of states to process, and performing the corresponding operation depending on what kind of state it is.

Example 4.54:

P → S # the start rule
S → S + M | M
M → M * T | T
T → number And you have the input: 2 + 3 * 4

Here are the generated state sets:

(state no.) Production (Origin) # Comment

== S(0): • 2 + 3 * 4 ==
(1) P → • S (0) # start rule
(2) S → • S + M (0) # predict from (1)
(3) S → • M (0) # predict from (1)
(4) M → • M * T (0) # predict from (3)
(5) M → • T (0) # predict from (3)
(6) T → • number (0) # predict from (5)

== S(1): 2 • + 3 * 4 ==
(1) T → number • (0) # scan from S(0)(6)
(2) M → T • (0) # complete from S(0)(5)
(3) M → M • * T (0) # complete from S(0)(4)
(4) S→ M • (0) # complete from S(0)(3)
(5) S → S • + M (0) # complete from S(0)(2)
(6) P → S • (0) # complete from S(0)(1)

== S(2): 2 + • 3 * 4 ==
(1) S → S + • M (0) # scan from S(1)(5)
(2) M → • M * T (2) # predict from (1)

(3) M → • T (2) # predict from (1)
(4) T → • number (2) # predict from (3)

== S(3): 2 + 3 • * 4 ==
(1) T → number • (2) # scan from S(2)(4)
(2) M → T • (2) # complete from S(2)(3)
(3) M → M • * T (2) # complete from S(2)(2)
(4) S → S + M • (0) # complete from S(2)(1)
(5) S → S • + M (0) # complete from S(0)(2)
(6) P → S • (0) # complete from S(0)(1)

== S(4): 2 + 3 * • 4 ==
(1) M → M * • T (2) # scan from S(3)(3)
(2) T → • number (4) # predict from (1)

== S(5): 2 + 3 * 4 • ==
(1) T → number • (4) # scan from S(4)(2)
(2) M → M * T • (2) # complete from S(4)(1)
(3) M → M • * T (2) # complete from S(2)(2)
(4) S → S + M • (0) # complete from S(2)(1)
(5) S → S • + M (0) # complete from S(0)(2)
(6) P → S • (0) # complete from S(0)(1)

And now the input is parsed, since we have the state (P → S •, 0)

4.7.3.7 CYK parser

The Cocke-Younger-Kasami (CYK) algorithm (alternatively called CKY) determines whether a string can be generated by a given context-free grammar and, if so, how it can be generated. This is known as parsing the string. The algorithm is an example of dynamic programming.

The standard version of CYK recognizes languages defined by context-free grammar written in Chomsky normal form (CNF). The worst case asymptotic time complexity of CYK is È(n³), where *n* is the length of the parsed string.

The CYK algorithm is a bottom up algorithm and is important theoretically, since it can be used to constructively prove that the membership problem for context-free languages is decidable.

The CYK algorithm for the membership problem is as follows:

Let the input string consist of *n* letters, $a_1 \ldots a_n$.
Let the grammar contain *r* terminal and nonterminal symbols $R_1 \ldots R_r$.
This grammar contains the subset R_s which is the set of start symbols.
Let P[n,n,r] be an array of booleans. Initialize all elements of P to false.
For each i = 1 to n
For each unit production $R_j \rightarrow a_i$, set P[i,1,j] = true.
For each i = 2 to n (Length of span)
For each j = 1 to n–i+1 (Start of span)
For each k = 1 to i–1 (Partition of span)
For each production $R_A \rightarrow R_B R_C$
If P[j, k, B] and P[j + k, i–k, C] then set P[j, i, A] = true
If any of P[1, n, x] is true (x is iterated over the set s, where s are all the indices for R_s)

Then string is member of language
Else string is not member of language

In informal terms, this algorithm considers every possible substring of the string of letters and sets P[i,j,k] to be true if the substring of letters starting from i of length j can be generated from R_k. Once it has considered substrings of length 1, it goes on to substrings of length 2, and so on. For substrings of length 2 and greater, it considers every possible partition of the substring into two halves, and checks to see if there is some production P → Q R such that Q matches the first half and R matches the second half. If so, it records P as matching the whole substring. Once this process is completed, the sentence is recognized by the grammar if the substring containing the entire string is matched by the start symbol.

CYK table						
S						
	VP					
S						
	VP			PP		
S		NP			NP	
NP	V.VP	Det.	N	P	Det	N
she	eats	a	fish	with	a	fork

4.7.3.8 Operator precedence parsing

An **operator precedence parser** is a computer program that interprets an operator-precedence grammar. For example, most calculators use operator precedence parsers to convert from infix notation with order of operations (the usual format humans use for mathematical expressions) into a different format they use internally to compute the result .Operator precedence parsing is based on bottom-up shift-reduce parsing. As an expression is parsed, tokens are shifted to a stack. At the appropriate time, the stack is reduced, applying the operator to the top of the stack. This is best illustrated by example.

step	opr	val	input	action
1	$	$	4 * 2 + 1 $	shift
2	$	$ 4	* 2 + 1 $	shift
3	$ *	$ 4	2 + 1 $	shift
4	$ *	$ 4 2	+ 1 $	reduce
5	$	$ 8	+ 1 $	shift
6	$ +	$ 8	1 $	shift
7	$ +	$ 8 1	$	reduce
8	$	$ 9	$	accept

We define two stacks: `opr`, for operators, and `val`, for values. A "$" designates the end of input or end of stack. Initially the stacks are empty, and the input contains an expression to parse. Each value, as it is encountered, is shifted to the `val` stack. When the first operator is encountered (step 2), we shift it to the `opr` stack. The second value is shifted to the `val` stack in step 3. In step 4, we have a "*" in `opr`, and a "+" input symbol. Since we want to multiply before we add (giving multiplication precedence), we'll reduce the contents of the `val`, applying the "*" operator to the top of the `val`. After reducing, the "+" operator will be shifted to `opr` in step 5.

This process continues until the input and `opr` are empty. If all went well, we should be left with the answer in the `val`. The following table summarizes the action taken as a function of input and the top of `opr`:

	Input		
opr	+	*	$
+	reduce	shift	reduce
*	reduce	reduce	reduce
$	shift	shift	accept

Let's extend the above example to include additional operators.

	Input												
stack	+	-	*	/	^	M	f	p	c	,	(	)	$
+	r	r	s	s	s	s	s	s	s	r	s	r	r
-	r	r	s	s	s	s	s	s	s	r	s	r	r
*	r	r	r	r	s	s	s	s	s	r	s	r	r
/	r	r	r	r	s	s	s	s	s	r	s	r	r
^	r	r	r	r	s	s	s	s	s	r	s	r	r
M	r	r	r	r	r	s	s	s	s	r	s	r	r
f	r	r	r	r	r	r	r	r	r	r	s	r	r
p	r	r	r	r	r	r	r	r	r	r	s	r	r
c	r	r	r	r	r	r	r	r	r	r	s	r	r
,	r	r	r	r	r	r	r	r	r	r	r	r	e4
(	s	s	s	s	s	s	s	s	s	s	s	s	e1
)	r	r	r	r	r	r	e3	e3	e3	r	e2	r	r
$	s	s	s	s	s	s	s	s	s	e4	s	e3	a

The above table incorporates the following operators:

- "M", for unary minus.
- "^", for exponentiation. 5 ^ 2 yields 25.
- "f", for factorial `f (x)` returns the factorial of x.

- "p", for permutations. `p(n,r)` returns the number of permutations for n objects taken r at a time.
- "c", for combinations. `c(n,r)` returns the number of combinations for n objects taken r at a time.

The following operator precedence is implied, starting at the highest precedence:

- unary minus
- exponentiation, right-associative
- multiplication/division, left-associative
- addition/subtraction, left-associative

The following errors are detected:

- error e1: missing right parenthesis
- error e2: missing operator
- error e3: unbalanced right parenthesis
- error e4: invalid function argument

Parentheses are often used to override precedence. On encountering a left parenthesis, we shift it to the `opr` stack. When we input a right parenthesis, the stack is popped until the matching left parenthesis is found. Then we shift the right parenthesis, and reduce by popping both parentheses off the stack.

4.7.3.8.1 Associativity of operators

If operand has operators on both side then by connection, operand should be associated with the operator on the left. In most programming languages arithmetic operators like addition, subtraction, multiplication, and division are left associative.

- Token string: 9 – 5 + 2
- Production rules

list → list-digit | digit
digit → 0 | 1 | 2 | . . . | 9

- Parse tree for left-associative operator is

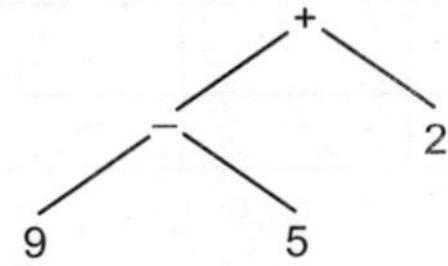

In the C programming language the assignment operator, =, is right associative. That is, token string a = b = c should be treated as a = (b = c).

- Token string: a = b =c.
- Production rules:

right → letter = right | letter
letter → a | b | . . . | z

4.7.3.8.2 Precedence of operators

An expression 9 + 5 * 2 has two possible interpretation: (9 + 5) * 2 and 9 + (5 * 2). Here '+' and '*' give birth to ambiguity. For this reason, we need to know the relative precedence of operators. The convention is to give multiplication and division higher precedence than addition and subtraction. Only when we have the operations of equal precedence, we apply the rules of associative.So, in the example expression: 9 + 5 * 2. We perform operation of higher precedence i.e., * before operations of lower precedence i.e., +. Therefore, the correct interpretation is 9 + (5 *).

4.7.3.8.3 Precedence relations

Bottom-up parsers for a large class of context-free grammar can be easily developed using operator grammar. Operator grammar have the property that no production right side is empty or has two adjacent nonterminals. This property enables the implementation of efficient operator-precedence parsers. This parser rely on the following three precedence relations:

Relation	Meaning
a <· *b*	*a* yields precedence to *b*
a =· *b*	*a* has the same precedence as *b*
a ·> *b*	*a* takes precedence over *b*

These operator precedence relations allow to delimit the handles in the right sentential forms: <· marks the left end, =· appears in the interior of the handle, and ·> marks the right end.

Let assume that between the symbols a_i and a_i+1 there is exactly one precedence relation. Suppose that $ is the end of the string. Then for all terminals we can write: $ <· b and b ·> $. If we remove all nonterminals and place the correct precedence relation:<·, =·, ·> between the remaining terminals, there remain strings that can be analyzed by easily developed parser.

For example, the following operator precedence relations can be introduced for simple expressions: id_1 + id_2 * id_3 after inserting precedence relations becomes **$ <· id_1 ·> + <· id_2 ·> * <· id_3 ·> $**

	id	+	*	$
id		·>	·>	·>
+	<·	·>	<·	·>
*	<·	·>	·>	·>
$	<·	<·	<·	·>

4.7.3.8.4 Identification of handles

Identification of handles as follows:

- scan the string from left until seeing ·>
- scan backwards the string from right to left until seeing <·
- everything between the two relations <· and ·> forms the handle

4.7.3.8.5 Operator precedence parsing algorithm

```
Initialize: Set ip to point to the first symbol of w$
     Repeat:        Let X be the top stack symbol, and a the symbol pointed to by ip
                         if $ is on the top of the stack and ip points to $ then return
                         else
                              Let a be the top terminal on the stack, and b the symbol pointed to by ip
                              if a <· b or a =· b then
                                   push b onto the stack
                                   advance ip to the next input symbol
```

```
else if        a ·> b then
               repeat
                     pop the stack
               until the top stack terminal is related by <·
                     to the terminal most recently popped
          else error()
end
```

4.7.3.8.6 Making operator precedence relations

The operator precedence parsers usually do not store the precedence table with the relations, rather they are implemented in a special way. Operator precedence parsers use precedence functions that map terminal symbols to integers, and so the precedence relations between the symbols are implemented by numerical comparison, but not every table of precedence relations has precedence functions but in practice for most grammar such functions can be designed.

Algorithm

1. Create functions f_a for each grammar terminal a and for the end of string symbol;
2. Partition the symbols in groups so that f_a and g_b are in the same group if $a =\cdot b$ (there can be symbols in the same group even if they are not connected by this relation);
3. Create a directed graph whose nodes are in the groups, next for each symbols a and b do: place an edge from the group of g_b to the group of f_a if $a <\cdot b$, otherwise if $a \cdot> b$ place an edge from the group of f_a to that of g_b;
4. If the constructed graph has a cycle then no precedence functions exist. When there are no cycles collect the length of the longest paths from the groups of f_a and g_b respectively.

Example 4.55: Consider the above table:

	id	+	*	$
id		·>	·>	·>
+	<·	·>	<·	·>
*	<·	·>	·>	·>
$	<·	<·	<·	·>

Using the algorithm leads to the following graph:

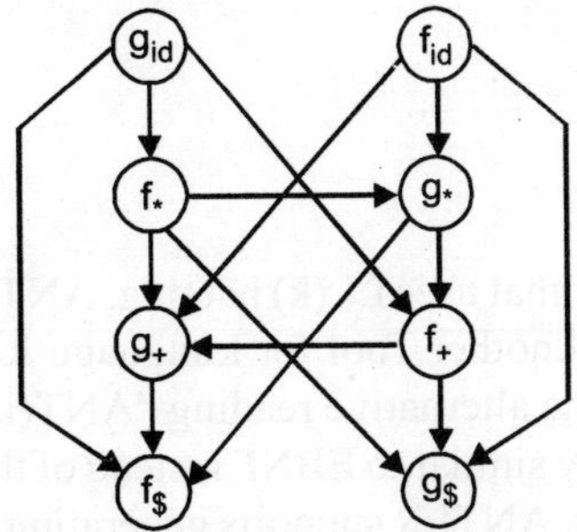

from which we extract the following precedence functions:

	id	+	*	$
f	4	2	4	0
g	5	1	3	0

4.7.3.8.7 Operator precedence parsing [Program in 'C' language is in Appendix-A (A.7)]

4.7.3.8.8 Relationship to other parsers

An operator-precedence parser is a simple shift-reduce parser capable of parsing a subset of LR (1) grammar. More precisely, the operator-precedence parser can parse all LR (1) grammar where two consecutive nonterminals never appear in the right-hand side of any rule. Operator-precedence parsers are not used often in practice; however they do have some properties that make them useful within a larger design. First, they are simple enough to write by hand, which is not generally the case with more sophisticated shift-reduce parsers. Second, they can be written to consult an operator table at runtime, which makes them suitable for languages that can add to or change their operators while parsing.

4.8 PARSER DEVELOPMENT SOFTWARE

Here some parser development software are listed as CASE tool of parser :

- ANTLR
- Bison
- Coco/R
- DMS Software Reengineering Toolkit
- GOLD
- JavaCC
- Lemon Parser
- Lex
- LRgen
- Rebol
- SableCC
- Spirit Parser Framework
- Yacc : DISCUSS IN CHAPTER .

4.8.1 ANTLR

ANTLR is the name of a parser generator that uses LL(k) parsing. ANTLR's predecessor is a parser generator known as PCCTS. ANTLR stands for "Another Tool for Language Recognition". Given that ANTLR is in competition with LR parser generators, the alternative reading "ANT(i)-LR" may not be accidental. ANTLR rules are expressed in a format deliberately similar to EBNF instead of the regular expression syntax employed by other parser generators. At the moment, ANTLR supports generating code in the following languages: C++, Java, Python, C#. ANTLR 3 is under a 3-clause BSD License.

4.8.2 Bison

The GNU equivalent of Yacc is called Bison.

4.8.3 JavaCC

JavaCC (Java Compiler Compiler) is an open source parser generator for the Java programming language. JavaCC is similar to Yacc in that it generates a parser for a grammar provided in EBNF notation, except the output is Java source code. Unlike Yacc, however, JavaCC generates top-down parsers, which limits it to the LL(k) class of grammar (in particular, left recursion cannot be used). The tree builder that accompanies it, JJTree, constructs its trees from the bottom up.

4.8.4 YACC

Yacc stands for Yet Another Compiler Compiler, first version of yacc is created by S.C. Johnson. The GNU equivalent of Yacc is called **Bison**. It is a tool that translates any grammar that describes a language into a parser for that language. It is written in Backus Naur form (BNF). By convention, a Yacc file has the suffix .y. The Yacc compiler is invoked from the compile line as:

$ yacc <options>
<filename ending with .y>

There are four steps involved in creating a compiler in Yacc:

1. Generate a parser from Yacc by running Yacc over the grammar file.
2. Specify the grammar:
   - Write the grammar in a .y file (also specify the actions here that are to be taken in C).
   - Write a lexical analyzer to process input and pass tokens to the parser. This can be done using Lex.
   - Write a function that starts parsing by calling yyparse().
   - Write error handling routines (like yyerror()).
3. Compile code produced by Yacc as well as any other relevant source files.
4. Link the object files to appropriate libraries for the executable parser.

4.8.4.1 Terminal and non-terminal symbols in YACC

Terminal Symbol: Terminal symbol represents a class of syntactically equivalent tokens. Terminal symbols are of three types:

- Named token: These are defined via the %token identifier. By convention, these are all upper case. The lexer returns named tokens.
- Character token: A character constant written in the same format as in C. For example, + is a character token.
- Literal string token: is written like a C string constant. For example, “<<” is a literal string token.

Nonterminal Symbol: Non-terminal symbol is a symbol that is a group of non-terminal and terminal symbols. By convention, these are all lower case. In the example, file is a non-terminal while NAME is a terminal symbol.

4.8.4.2 Structure of a yacc file

A *yacc* file looks much like a *lex* file:
definitions...
%%
rules
%%
code

Definitions Section

All code between %{ and %} is copied to the beginning of the resulting C file. There are three things that can go in the definitions section:

- **C Code** Any code between %{ and %} is copied to the C file. This is typically used for defining file variables, and for prototypes of routines that are defined in the code segment.
- **Definitions** The definitions section of a *lex* file was concerned with characters; in *yacc* this is tokens. These token definitions are written to a .h file when *yacc* compiles this file.
- **Associativity Rules** These handle associativity and priority of operators.

Rules Section

A number of combinations of pattern and action: if the action is more than a single command it needs to be in braces.

The rules section contains the grammar of the language you want to parse.

Code Section

This can be very elaborate, but the main ingredient is the call to yylex, the lexical analyzer. If the code segment is left out, a default main is used which only calls yylex. The minimal main program is

```
int main()
{
yyparse();
return 0;
}
```

For yacc, firstly we prepared all the specification of yacc as yacc.y. Then yacc.y is run via UNIX command as 'yacc yacc.y' to produce a 'C' compiler program as y.tab.c which is the tabular representation of LALR parse which will finally run via 'C' compiler to produce an object file as a.out.

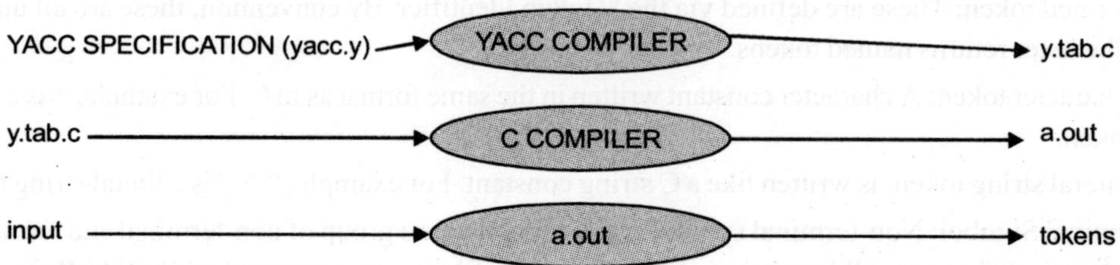

Examples in 'C' language are in **Appendix-A (A-8)**

4.8.4.3 Lex Yacc interaction

Conceptually, *lex* parses a file of characters and outputs a stream of tokens; *yacc* accepts a stream of tokens and parses it, performing actions as appropriate. In practice, they are more tightly coupled. If your *lex* program is supplying a tokenizer, the *yacc* program will repeatedly call the yylex routine. The *lex* rules will probably function by calling return everytime they have parsed a token. We will now see the way *lex* returns information in such a way that *yacc* can use it for parsing.

4.8.4.3.1 The shared header file of return codes

If *lex* is to return tokens that *yacc* will process, they have to agree on what tokens there are.
This is done as follows.
• The *yacc* file will have token definitions

```
%token NUMBER
```

in the definitions section.
• When the *yacc* file is translated with `yacc -d`, a header file `y.tab.h` is created that has definitions like

```
#define NUMBER 258
```

This file can then be included in both the *lex* and *yacc* program.
• The *lex* file can then call `return NUMBER`, and the *yacc* program can match on this token.
The return codes that are defined from `%TOKEN` definitions typically start at around 258, so that single characters can simply be returned as their integer value:

```
/* in the lex program */
[0-9]+ {return NUMBER}
[-+*/] {return *yytext}
/* in the yacc program */
sum : TERMS '+' TERM
```

4.8.4.3.2 Return values

In the above, very sketchy example, *lex* only returned the information that there was a number, not the actual number. For this we need a further mechanism. In addition to specifying the return code, the *lex* parse can return a symbol that is put on top of the stack, so that *yacc* can access it. This symbol is returned in the variable yylval. By default, this is defined as an int, so the *lex* program would have:

```
extern int llval;
%%
[0-9]+ {llval=atoi(yytext); return NUMBER;}
```

If more than just integers need to be returned, the specifications in the *yacc* code become more complicated. Suppose we want to return double values, and integer indices in a table. The following three actions are needed.

1. The possible return values need to be stated:

```
%union {int ival; double dval;}
```

2. These types need to be connected to the possible return tokens:

```
%token <ival> INDEX
%token <dval> NUMBER
```

3. The types of non-terminals need to be given:

```
%type <dval> expr
%type <dval> mulex
%type <dval> term
```

The generated .h file will now have

```
#define INDEX 258
#define NUMBER 259
typedef union {int ival; double dval;} YYSTYPE;
extern YYSTYPE yylval;
```

4.9 COMPLETE C PROGRAM FOR PARSER

Program in 'C Language is given in **Appendix-A (A.9).**

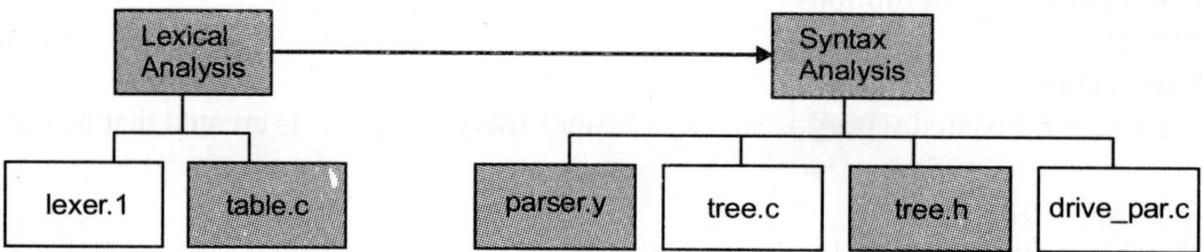

TRIBULATIONS

Syntax Tree and Attribute Grammar

4.1 Consider the following grammar:

1. G → S $$
2. S → A M
3. M → S
4. A → a E | b A A
5. E → a B | b A | ε
6. B → b E | a B B

Describe in English the language that the grammar generates.
Show the parse tree for the string "abaa".
Is the grammar LL(1). If so, show the parse table; if not, identify a prediction conflict.

4.2 Write an attribute grammar for the floating point value of a decimal number given by the following grammar.

1. Dnum → num.num
2. Num → num digit | digit
3. Digit → 0 123456789

4.3 Consider the following attributed grammar :

Production	Semantic Rule
S → ABC	B.u = S.u A.u = B.v + C.v S.v = A.v
A → a	A.v = 2 * A.u
B → b	B.v = B.u
C → c	C.v = 1

Draw the parse tree for the string abc, draw the dependency graph, describe the order of evalution, suppose S.u = 3 then what is the value of S.v when evolution finished.

4.4 Why is a tree an appropriate data structure for the internal representation of a source program by a compiler?

4.5 Draw the concrete syntax tree for the C++ version of the *while* statement used for illustration in this section.

4.6 Here is a context-free grammar for binary numbers:

1. E : N.
2. N : B / N B.
3. B : ‘0’ / ‘1’.

Write an attribute grammar based on this grammar that computes an attribute E.ones that is the number of one bits in the number represented by E.

4.7 Draw the tree that would represent the binary equivalent of the decimal number 13 if it was parsed according to the grammar in the previous question. Annotate the tree with the values of the attributes computed by your attribute grammar.

Top-down Parsing

4.8 Find FIRST and FOLLOW of following-

(i) S → aAB|bA|ε
A → aAb|ε
B → bB|C

(ii) S → v|XUW|UV|uWV
U → w|WvX|SUVW|SWX|ε
V → x|wX|ε
W → w|UXW
X → yz|SuW|SW

4.9 Test the following grammar for being LL(1)

G = { N , T , S , P }
N = { A , B }
T = { w , x , y , z }
S = A
P =
A := B (x | z) | (w | z) B
B := x B z | { y }

Write down a set of productions that describes the form that REAL literal constants may assume in Pascal, and check to see whether they satisfy the LL(1) conditions.

4.10 Can you parse following grammar using LL(1) parser.

(1) E → E + T | T
T → T * F | F
F → (E) | id

(2) $E \rightarrow E + T \mid T$

$T \rightarrow T F \mid F$

$F \rightarrow F^* \mid a \mid b$

(3) $S \rightarrow AaAb \mid BbbA$

$A \rightarrow \varepsilon$

$B \rightarrow \varepsilon$

(4) $S \rightarrow iEtSS1$

$S1 \rightarrow eS \mid E$

$E \rightarrow b$

(5) exp → atom | list

atom → **num** | **id**

list → (exp')

exp' → exp' exp | exp

(6) decl → type list

type → **int** | **float**

list → **id**,list | **id**

4.11 In Pascal there are two classes of statements that start with identifiers, namely assignment statements and procedure calls. Is it possible to find a grammar that allows this potential LL(1) conflict to be resolved? Does the problem arise in C++?

4.12 A full description of C or C++ is not possible with an LL(1) grammar. How large a subset of these languages could one describe with an LL(1) grammar?

Bottom-up Parsing

4.13 Show grammar $B \rightarrow Bb \mid a$ is SLR (1) but $B \rightarrow ABb \mid a$, $A \rightarrow \varepsilon$ is not LR (k) for any k.

4.14 Find following grammar is operator procedure or not?

$E \rightarrow ET + IT$

$T \rightarrow TF * IF$

$F \rightarrow FP \mid P \uparrow$

$P \rightarrow E \mid id$

4.15 Can you parse following grammar using LR(1) parser.

(I) $E \rightarrow E+T/T$

$T \rightarrow T^*F/F$

$F \rightarrow id$

(II) $S \rightarrow AA$

$A \rightarrow aA/b$

4.16 Construct LR(1) parse table for the following grammar :

$S \rightarrow aBD$ / AB / DAC / b

$A \rightarrow SCB$ / $SABC$ /CbD /C/ε

$B \rightarrow d$ / ε

$C \rightarrow ADC$ / c

$D \rightarrow SaC$ / SC /fg

4.17 Construct LR(0) parsers for each of the following grammar:

(a) S→cA /ccB

(b) S→aSSb /aSSS/c

(c) A→cA /a

(d) B→ccB /b

4.18 Find the canonical collection of LR(0) items for the following grammar

E→E+T / T

T→T*F / F

F→(E) /id

4.19 Construct LALR items for the grammar below :

E→E+T / T

T→T*F / F

F→(E) / id

4.20 Contruct LALR(1) parse table for the following grammar:

S→B

B→begin DA end

D→Dd; / ε

A→A;E / ε

E→B / S

FURTHER READINGS AND REFERENCES

About Top Down Parser

[1] Alfred V. Aho, Ravi Sethi, and Jeffrey D. Ullman, *The Dragon book*, in particular Section 4.4.

[2] W.H. Burge (1975), *Recursive Programming Techniques*.

[3] Charles N Fischer and Richard J LeBlanc, Jr (1991), *Crafting a Compiler with C*.

[4] Niklaus Wirth (1975), *Algorithms + Data Structures* = Programs.

[5] Niklaus Wirth (1996), *Compiler Construction*.

About LR Parser

[6] Aho, Sethi, Ullman, Addison-Wesley (1986). *Compilers: Principles, Techniques, and Tools*.

About CLR Parser

[7] Aho, Sethi, Ullman, Addison-Wesley (1986). *Compilers: Principles, Techniques, and Tools*.

About LALR Parser

[8] Alfred V. Aho, Ravi Sethi, and Jeffrey D. Ullman. *Compilers: Principles, Techniques, and Tools*. Addison-Wesley, 1986. (Describes the traditional techniques for building LALR(1) Parsers.)

[9] Frank DeRemer and Thomas Pennello. Efficient Computation of LALR(1) Look-Ahead Sets. *ACM Transactions on Programming Languages and Systems (TOPLAS)* 4:4,1982, pp. 615–649. (Describes a more efficient technique for building LALR(1) Parsers.)

[10] Richard Bornat. *Understanding and Writing Compilers, Macmillan*, 1979. (Describes the principles of automated left-to-right parsing and how to construct the parser tables, what a follow set is, etc., in English, not mathematics.)

About Operator Precedence Parser

[11] Aho, Sethi, Ullman, Addison-Wesley (1986), *Compilers: Principles, Techniques, and Tools.*

Early Parser

[12] J. Earley. An efficient context-free parsing algorithm. *Communications of the Association for Computing Machinery*, 13(2):94-102, 1970.

[13] J. Aycock and R.N. Horspool. *Practical Earley Parsing*. The Computer Journal, 45(6):620-630, 2002.

CYK Parser

[14] John Cocke and Jacob T. Schwartz (1970). *Programming languages and their compilers*: Preliminary notes. Technical report, Courant Institute of Mathematical Sciences, New York University.

[15] T. Kasami (1965). *An efficient recognition and syntax-analysis algorithm for context-free languages.* Scientific report AFCRL-65-758, Air Force Cambridge Research Lab, Bedford, MA.

[16] Daniel H. Younger (1967). *Recognition and parsing of context-free languages in time* n_3. Information and Control 10(2): 189–208.

CHAPTER 5

SEMANTIC ANALYSIS

CHAPTER HIGHLIGHTS

Semantic analysis is a pass by a compiler that adds semantical information to the parse tree and performs certain checks based on this information. The purpose of semantic analysis is to check that we have a meaningful sequence of tokens. Note that a sequence can be meaningful without being correct; in most programming languages, the phrase "x + 1" would be considered to be a meaningful arithmetic expression. However, if the programmer really meant to write "x – 1", then it is not correct. It logically follows the parsing phase or hieratical phase, in which the parse tree is generated, This is roughly the equivalent of checking that some ordinary text written in a natural language (e.g. English) actually means something (whether or not that is what it was intended to mean).Typical examples of semantical information that is added and checked is typing information (type checking) and the binding of variables and function names to their definitions (object binding). Sometimes also some early code optimization is done in this phase. For this phase the compiler usually use symbol tables in which each symbol are stored (variable names, function names, etc.) . Now in this chapter we discuss about type theory, polymorphism, overloading. Now we are standing at third phase of compiler. Input to this phase is hieratical structure of expressions from parser as given below:

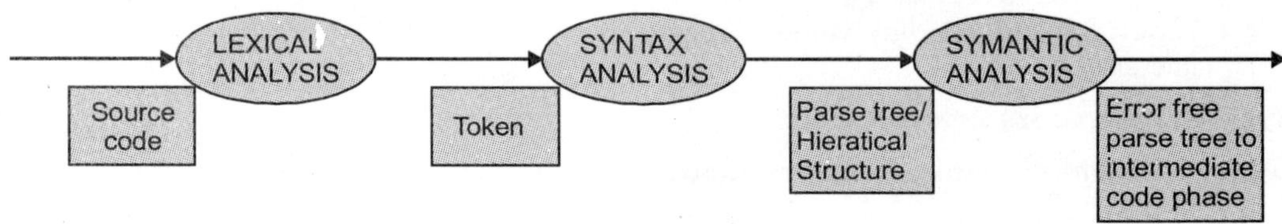

Figure 5.1

5.1 TYPE THEORY

Type theory provides the formal basis for the design, analysis and study of type systems. Indeed, many computer scientists use the term type theory to refer to the formal study of type systems for programming languages.

5.1.1 Impact of Type Theory

The most obvious application of type theory is in constructing type checking algorithms in semantic analysis phase of compilers for programming languages.

Type theory is also widely in use in theories of semantics of natural language. The most common construction takes the basic types e and t for individuals and truth-values, respectively, and defines the set of types recursively as follows:

- If a and b are types, then so is.
- Nothing except the basic types, and what can be constructed from them by means of the previous clause are types.

A complex type is the type of functions from entities of type a to entities of type b. Thus one has types like which are interpreted as elements of the set of functions from entities to truth-values, i.e. characteristic functions of sets if entities. An expression of type is a function from sets of entities to truth-values, i.e. a (characteristic function of a) set of sets.

5.2 TYPE SYSTEM

Type system defines how a programming language classifies values and expressions into types, how it can manipulate those types and how they interact. A type indicates a set of values that have the same sort of generic meaning or intended purpose. Type systems vary significantly between languages with, perhaps, the most important variations being their compile-time syntactic and run-time operational implementations. Type theory studies type systems, although the concrete type systems of programming languages originate from practical issues of computer architecture, compiler implementation and language design.

A compiler may use the static type of a value in order to optimize the storage it needs and the choice of algorithms for operations on the value. For example, in many C compilers the "float" data type is represented in 32-bits in accordance with the IEEE specification for single-precision floating point numbers or in form of double precision. Thus C uses the respective floating-point operations to add, multiply etc. those values according to hardware representation similar case arise in case of boolean value they can be represented by two way as one method store 1- bit (true /false) in a register and discard 7- bits of register and second method store only true bit in register and discard false values.

Data types refer to collections of bits or a special class of data object with set of operations used for manipulating them. Types usually have associations either with values in memory or with objects such as variables instruction code like characters, integers and floating-point numbers. Types inform programs and programmers how they should treat those bits. Major functions that type systems provide include:

- **Safety:** Use of types may allow a compiler to detect meaningless or probably invalid code. For example, we can identify an expression "Hello, World" + 3 as invalid because one cannot add (in the usual sense) a string literal to an integer. As discussed below, strong typing offers more safety, but it does not necessarily guarantee complete safety (see type-safety for more information).
- **Optimization:** Static type-checking may provide useful information to a compiler. For example, if a type says a value must align at a multiple of 4, the compiler may be able to use more efficient machine instructions.
- **Documentation:** In more expressive type systems, types can serve as a form of documentation, since they can illustrate the intent of the programmer. For instance, timestamps may be a subtype of integers — but if a programmer declares a function as returning a timestamp rather than merely an integer, this documents part of the meaning of the function.
- **Abstraction** (or **modularity**)**:** Types allow programmers to think about programs at a higher level, not bothering with low-level implementation. For example, programmers can think of strings as values instead of as a mere array of bytes. Or types can allow programmers to express the interface between two subsystems. This localizes the definitions required for interoperability of the subsystems and prevents inconsistencies when those subsystems communicate.

5.3 TYPE CHECKING

The process of verifying and enforcing the constraints of types type checking may occur either at compile-time (a static check) or run-time (a dynamic check). Static type-checking becomes a primary task of the semantic analysis carried out by a compiler. If a language enforces type rules strongly one can refer to the process as strongly typed, if not, as weakly typed. We can also classifies languages into two groups as : (I) Typed Language (II) Untyped Language:

- **Typed Languages:** A language is typed if operations defined for one data type cannot be performed on values of another data type.
- **Untyped Languages:** Untyped language, such as most assembly languages, allows any operation to be performed on any data type. High-level languages which are untyped include BCPL.

5.3.1 Static and Dynamic Typing

In some languages, the meaningless operation will be detected when the program is compiled and rejected by the compiler known as static type checking. A programming language is statically typed if type checking may be performed without testing equivalence of run-time expressions. A statically typed programming language respects the phase distinction between run-time and compile-time phases of processing. A language has a compile-time phase if separate modules of a program can be type checked separately without information about all modules that exist at run time. Static type systems for dynamic types usually need to explicitly represent the concept of an execution path, and allow types to depend on it. Static typing finds type errors reliably and at compile time. This should increase the reliability of the delivered program. Static typing advocates believe programs are more reliable when they have been type-checked. The value of static typing increases as the strength of the type system is increased. Strongly typed languages such as **ML** and **Haskell** have suggested that almost all bugs can be considered type errors, if the types used in a program are sufficiently well declared by the programmer or inferred by the compiler. Static typing allows construction of libraries which are less likely to be accidentally misused by their users. This can be used as an additional mechanism for communicating the intentions of the library developer. Static typing usually results in compiled code that executes more quickly. When the compiler knows the exact data types that are in use, it can produce optimized machine code. Further, compilers in statically typed languages can find shortcuts more easily. Statically-typed languages which lack type inference such as Java require that programmers declare the types they intend a method or function to use. This can serve as additional documentation for the program, which the compiler will not permit the programmer to ignore or drift out of synchronization. However, a language can be statically typed without requiring type declarations, so this is not a consequence of static typing.

In some languages, the meaningless operation will be detected when the program is run resulting in a runtime exception known as dynamic type checking. A programming language is dynamically typed if the language supports run-time dispatch on tagged data. In dynamic typing, type checking often takes place at runtime because variables can acquire different types depending on the execution path. A programming language is dependently typed, if the phase distinction is violated and consequently the type checking requires testing equivalence of run-time expressions. Dynamic typing often occurs in scripting languages and other rapid application development languages. Dynamic types appear more often in interpreted languages, whereas compiled languages favor static types. Dynamic typing advocates point to distributed code that has proven reliable and to small bug databases. Some dynamically-typed languages **Lisp** allow optional type declarations for optimization for this very reason , dynamic typing may allow compilers and interpreters to run more quickly, since changes to source code in dynamically-typed languages may result in less checking to perform and less code to revisit. This too may reduce the edit-compile-test-debug cycle. Dynamic typing allows constructs that some static type systems would reject as illegal. Furthermore, dynamic typing accommodates transitional code and prototyping, such as allowing a string to be used in place of a data structure. Dynamic typing typically makes metaprogramming more powerful and easier to use. For example, C++ templates are typically more cumbersome to write than the equivalent Ruby or Python code.

Example 5.1:

```
int x ; // (1)
x = 25; // (2)
x = "VIVEK" ; // (3)
```

In this example, (1) declares the name x; (2) associates the integer value 25 to the name x; and (3) associates the string value "VIVEK" to the name x. In most statically typed systems, this code fragment would be illegal, because (2) and (3) bind x to values of inconsistent type. By contrast, a purely dynamically typed system would permit the above program to execute, since types are attached to values, not variables. The implementation of a dynamically typed language will catch errors related to the misuse of values "type errors" at the time of the computation of the erroneous statement or expression.

Example 5.2:

```
int x = 25; // (1)
int y = " VIVEK" ; // (2)
int z = x + y; // (3)
```

In this code fragment, (1) binds the value 5 to x; (2) binds the value "VIVEK" to y; and (3) attempts to add x to y. In a dynamically typed language, the value bound to x might be a pair (integer, 25), and the value bound to y might be a pair (string, " VIVEK"). When the program attempts to execute line 3, the language implementation check the type tags integer and string, and if the operation + (addition) is not defined over these two types it signals an error.

Example 5.3 :

```
int x, y, z; // (1)
printf("\n ENTER THE VALUE OF X & Y %d %d" ); // (2)
scanf("%d %d", &x, &y ); // (3)
int z := x + y; // (4)
OUTPUT SCREEN :
ENTER THE VALUE OF X & Y 25 VIVEK
```

In this code fragment, (1) binds the x, y, z to storage; (2) print the statement; (3) get the values of x, y and (4) attempts to add x to y. In a dynamically typed language, the value bound to x might be a pair (integer, 25), and the value bound to y might be a pair (string, "VIVEK"). When the program attempts to execute line 4, the language implementation check the type tags integer and string, and if the operation + (addition) is not defined over these two types it signals an error.

5.3.2 Strong and Weak Typing

Programming language expert Benjamin C. Pierce, author of Types and Programming Languages and Advanced Types and Programming Languages, has said:

"I spent a few weeks... trying to sort out the terminology of "strongly typed," "statically typed," "safe," etc., and found it amazingly difficult.... The usage of these terms is so various as to render them almost useless."

Strong typing is used to describe how programming languages handle datatypes. One definition of **strongly typed** involves not allowing an operation to succeed on arguments which have the wrong type i.e. attempting to mix types raises an error. Strongly-typed languages are often termed **type-safe or safe**, but they do not make bugs impossible. EXAMPLE : Ada, Python, and ML, etc. For instance, an integer addition operation may not be used upon strings; a procedure which operates upon linked lists may not be used upon numbers or C cast gone wrong exemplifies the absence of strong typing; if a programmer casts a value in C, not only must the compiler allow the code, but the runtime should allow it as well. This allows compact and fast C code, but it can make debugging more difficult.

Weak typing means that a language will implicitly convert (or cast) types when used or Weak typing allows a value of one type to be treated as another, for example treating a string as a number. This can occasionally be useful, but it can also cause bugs; such languages are often termed **unsafe.** EXAMPLE : C, C++, and most assembly languages, etc.

Example 5.4:

```
int x = 25  ; // (1)
int y = 35 ; // (2)
z = x + y ; // (3)
```

Writing the code above in a weakly-typed language, it is not clear what kind of result one would get. Some languages such as Visual Basic, would produce runnable code which would yield the result 50, the system would convert the string "50" into the number 50 to make sense of the operation; other languages like JavaScript would produce the result "2535": the system would convert the number 25 to the string "25" and then concatenate the two. In both Visual Basic and JavaScript, the resulting type is determined by rules that take both operands (the values to the left and right of the operator) into consideration. Careful language design has also allowed languages to appear weakly-typed.

5.3.3 Attributed Grammar for Type Checking

Production	Semantic Rule
program → declaration , statements	
var_declaration → id : type-expression	Insert(id.name, type_expression.type)
type-expression → int	type-expression.type = integer
type-expression → boolean	type-expression.type = boolean
type-expression → float	type-expression.type = float
type-expression → char	type-expression.type = character
type-expression1 → array [num] of type-expression2	type-expression.type = make_type-node(array, num.size, type- expression2.type)
statement → if exp then statement	if not type-equal(exp.type, boolean) then type-error(statement)
statement → id = exp exp → exp1 op exp2	if not type-equal(look_up(id.name)exp.type) then type-error(statement) If not ((type-equal(exp1.type.integer)) and (type-equal(exp2.type.integer))) then type-error (exp)exp.type = integer
exp → exp1 op exp2	If not ((type-equal(exp1.type.float)) and (type-equal(exp2.type.float))) then type-error (exp)exp.type = float
exp → exp1 op exp2	If not ((type-equal(exp1.type.boolean)) and (type-equal(exp2.type.boolean))) then type-error (exp)exp.type = boolean

Contd....

exp → exp1 [exp2]	If is_array-type (exp1.type) and (type-equal(exp2.type.integer))) then exp.type = exp1.type.child1 Else type-error (exp)
exp → num	Exp.type = integer
exp → true	Exp.type = boolean
exp → false	Exp.type = boolean
exp → id	Exp.type = lookup(id.name)

Complete grammar for above is as

1. program → declaration , statement
2. declaration → declaration , var_declaration | var_declaration
3. var_declaration → id : type-expression
4. type-expression → int | boolean | array [num]of type-expression
5. statements → statements , statement | statements
6. statements → if exp then statement | id = exp

Here some functions are used as

- Insert(id.name, type) – which insert an identifier into symbol table with their type.
- make_type-node(array, size, type)- which construct a type node where the child of the array is the type tree given by the type parameter.

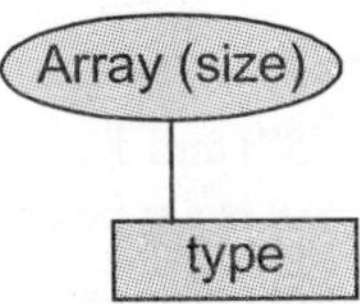

Figure 5.2

- type-equal(type, type) – which check the type of any expression.
- type-error(statement) – which show the type error.
- is_array-type (type) – check that parameter is an array type, that the tree representation of the type has a root node that represent the array type constructor.
- exp1.type.child1 indicate first child of the root node in the tree representation of an array type.
- lookup(name) – check the existing variable in the symbol table.

5.4 TYPE INFERENCE

Type inference is a feature present in some strongly statically typed programming languages. It is often characteristic of but not limited to functional programming languages in general. Some languages that include type inference are: Haskell, Cayenne, Clean, ML, OCaml, Epigram, Scala, Nemerle, D, Chrome and Boo. This feature is planned for Fortress, C# 3.0, C++0x and Perl 6.

"Type inference refers to the ability to automatically either partially or fully deduce the type of the value derived from the eventual evaluation of an expression." As this process is systematically performed at compile time, the compiler is often able to infer the type of a variable or the type signature of a function, without explicit type annotations having been given.

Example 5.5: Let us consider the Haskell function map, which may be defined as:

map f [ ] = [ ]

map f (first:rest) = f first : map f rest

From this, it is evident that the function map takes a list as its second argument, that its first argument f is a function that can be applied to the type of elements of that list, and that the result of map is constructed as a list with elements that are results of f. So we can reliably construct a type signature map :: $(a \rightarrow b) \rightarrow [a] \rightarrow [b]$

5.4.1 Algorithm 5.1: Hindley-Milner Type Inference Algorithm

The common algorithm used to perform the type inference is the one now commonly referred to as Hindley-Milner or Damas-Milner algorithm. The origin of this algorithm is the type inference algorithm for the simply typed lambda calculus, which was devised by Haskell B. Curry and Robert Feys in 1958. In 1969 Roger Hindley extended this work and proved that their algorithm always inferred the most general type. In 1978 Robin Milner, independently of Hindley's work, provided an equivalent algorithm. In 1985 Luis Damas finally proved that Milner's algorithm is complete and extended it to support systems with polymorphic references.

This algorithm proceeds in two steps. First, we need to generate a number of equations to solve, and then we need to solve them.

Generating the equations

The algorithm used for generating the equations is similar to a regular type checker, so let's consider first a regular type checker for the typed lambda calculus given by

$$e ::= E \,|v|\, (\lambda v : \tau.e) \,|\, (ee) \text{ and } \tau ::= T \,|\tau \rightarrow \tau$$

where E is a primitive expression (such as "3") and T is a primitive type (such as "Integer"). We want to construct a function f of type $\varepsilon \rightarrow t \rightarrow \tau$, where ε is a type environment and t is a term. We assume that this function is already defined on primitives. The other cases are $f\ \Gamma v = \tau$ whenever the binding $v : \tau$ is in Γ.

$f\ \Gamma\ (ge) = \tau$ Whenever $\tau_1 = \tau_2 \rightarrow \tau$ where $\tau_1 = f\ \Gamma\ g$ and $\tau_2 = f\ \Gamma e$

$f\ \Gamma(\lambda v : \tau.e) = \tau \rightarrow \tau_e$ where $\tau_e = f\ \Gamma' e$ and Γ' is Γ extended by the binding $v : \tau$

Solving the equations

Solving the equations proceeds by unification. This is - maybe surprisingly - a rather simple algorithm. The function u operates on type equations and returns a structure called a "substitution". A substitution is simply a mapping from type variables to types. Substitutions can be composed and extended in the obvious ways.

Unifying the empty set of equations is easy enough: $u\phi = i$ where i is the identity substitution. Unifying a variable with a type goes this way: $u\ ([\alpha = T] \cup C) = u\ (C).\ (\alpha \rightarrow T)$, where T is the substitution composition operator, and C' is the set of remaining constraints C with the new substitution $\alpha \rightarrow$ T applied to it. Of course, $u\ ([T = \alpha] \cup C) = u\ (\alpha = T] \cup C)$. The interesting case remains as $u\ ([S \rightarrow S' = T \rightarrow T'\ ] \cup C)] = u(\{[S = T], [S' = T']\} \cup C)$.

5.5 TYPE SYSTEM CROSS REFERENCE LIST

Programming language	Static/dynamic	Strong/weak	Safety	Nominative/structural
Ada	static	strong	safe	nominative
Assembly Language	none	strong	unsafe	structural
APL	dynamic	weak	safe	nominative
BASIC	static	weak	safe	nominative
C	static	weak	unsafe	nominative
Cayenne	dependent	strong	safe	structural
Centura	static	weak	safe	nominative
C++	static	strong	unsafe	nominative
C#	static	strong	both	nominative
Clipper	dynamic	weak	safe	duck
D	static	strong	unsafe	nominative
Delphi	static	strong	safe	nominative
E	dynamic	strong	safe	nominative + duck
Eiffel	static	strong	safe	nominative
Erlang	dynamic	strong	safe	nominative
Fortran	static	strong	safe	nominative
Groovy	dynamic	strong	safe	duck
Haskell	static	strong	safe	structural
Io	dynamic	strong	safe	duck
Java	static	strong	safe	nominative
JavaScript	dynamic	weak	safe	duck
Lisp	dynamic	strong	safe	structural
Lua	dynamic	strong	safe	structural
ML	static	strong	safe	structural
Objective-C	dynamic	weak	safe	duck
Pascal	static	strong	safe	nominative
Perl 1-5	dynamic	weak	safe	nominative
Perl 6	hybrid	hybrid	safe	duck
PHP	dynamic	weak	safe	....

Contd...

Pike	static+dynamic	strong	safe	structural
Python	dynamic	strong	safe	duck
Ruby	dynamic	strong	safe	duck
Scheme	dynamic	strong	safe	nominative
Smalltalk	dynamic	strong	safe	duck
Visual Basic	hybrid	hybrid	safe	nominative
Windows PowerShell	hybrid	hybrid	safe	duck
xHarbour	dynamic	weak	safe	duck

5.5.1 Comparison with Generics and Structural Subtyping

Very flexible static binding capabilities, called generics or templates or operator overloading, provided the same advantages, but typically not as late as run time. This static polymorphism was distinguished from runtime facilities for dynamic types.

5.5.2 Duck Typing

Duck typing is a form of dynamic typing in which a variable's value itself implicitly determines what the variable can do. This implies that an object is interchangeable with any other object that implements the same interface, regardless of whether the objects have a related inheritance hierarchy. Duck typing attempts to limit any object is interchangeable with any other at runtime, the most flexible kind of dynamic typing while eliminating a source of possible errors before runtime. Yet another approach similar to duck typing is **OCaml's structural subtyping,** where object types are compatible if their method signatures are compatible, regardless of their declared inheritance. This is all detected at compile time through OCaml's type inference system.

The term is a reference to the duck test — "If it walks like a duck and quacks like a duck, it must be a duck". This technique is called "duck typing", based on the aphorism, "If it waddles like a duck, and quacks like a duck, it's a duck!"

Duck typing is a feature of programming languages such as Python, Ruby, and ColdFusion. C++ templates implement a static form of duck typing. An iterator, for example, does not inherit its methods from an Iterator base class.

ColdFusion, a web application scripting language, also allows duck typing although the technique is still fairly new to the ColdFusion developer community. Function arguments can be specified to be of type any so that arbitrary objects can be passed in and then method calls are bound dynamically at runtime. If an object does not implement a called method, a runtime exception is thrown which can be caught and handled gracefully. An alternative argument type of WEB-INF.cftags.component restricts the passed argument to be a ColdFusion Component (CFC), which provides better error messages should a non-object be passed in.

5.5.3 Explicit or Implicit Declaration and Inference

Many static type systems, such as C's and Java's, require type declarations: the programmer must explicitly associate each variable with a particular type. Others, such as Haskell's, perform type inference: the compiler draws conclusions about the types of variables based on how programmers use those variables. For example, given a function f(x,y) which adds x and y together, the compiler can infer that x and y must be numbers since addition is only defined for numbers. Therefore, any call to f elsewhere in the program that specifies a non-numeric type (such as a string or list) as an argument would signal an error.

Numerical and string constants and expressions in code can and often do imply type in a particular context. For example, an expression 3.14 might imply a type of floating-point; while [1, 2, 3] might imply a list of integers; typically an array.

5.5.4 Structural Type System

A structural type system is a class of type system, in which type compatibility and equivalence are determined by the type's structure and not through explicit declarations. Structural systems are used to determine if types are equivalent, as well as if a type is a subtype of another. It contrasts with nominative systems, where comparisons are based on explicit declarations or the names of the types.

In structural typing, two objects or terms are considered to have compatible types if the types have identical structure. Depending on the semantics of the language, this generally means that for each feature within a type, there must be a corresponding and identical feature in the other type. Structural subtyping is arguably more flexible than nominative subtyping, as it permits the creation of adhoc types and interfaces; in particular, it permits creation of a type which is a supertype of an existing type T, without modifying the definition of T. However this may not be desirable where the programmer wishes to create closed abstractions.

5.5.5 Nominative Type System

A nominative type system is a class of type system, in which type compatibility and equivalence is determined by explicit declarations or the name of the types. Nominative systems are used to determine if types are equivalent, as well as if a type is a subtype of another. It contrasts with structural systems, where comparisons are based on the structure of the types in question and do not require explicit declarations. Nominal typing means that two variables have compatible types only if they appear in either the same declaration or in declarations that use same type name. Note that many languages provide a way of type aliasing; or declaring multiple names of the same type. The C/C++ typedef feature is an example of this capability.

5.6 TYPES OF TYPES

A type of types is a kind. Kinds appear explicitly in typeful programming, such as a type constructor in the Haskell programming language, which returns a simple type after being applied to enough simple types. However, in most programming languages type construction is implicit and hard coded in the grammar, there is no notion of kind as a first class entity.

Types fall into several broad categories:

- **Primitive types** — e.g., integer and floating-point number.
- **Integral types** —e.g., integers and natural numbers.
- **Floating point types** — types of numbers in floating-point representation
    - **Composite types** —e.g., arrays or records. Abstract data types have attributes of both composite types and interfaces, depending on whom you talk to.
- **Subtype**
- **Derived type**
- **Object types** —e.g., type variable
- **Partial type**
- **Recursive type**
- **Function types** —e.g., binary functions
- **Universally quantified types** —e.g., parameterized types

- **Existentially quantified types**—e.g., modules
- **Refinement types**, types which identify subsets of other types
- **Dependent types** types which depend on run-time values

5.7 TYPE CONVERSION

Type Conversion or Typecasting refers to changing an entity of one data type into another. This is done to take advantage of certain features of type hierarchies. For instance, values from a more limited set, such as integers, can be stored in a more compact format and later converted to a different format enabling operations not previously possible, such as division with several decimal places' worth of accuracy. In object-oriented programming languages, type conversion allows programs to treat objects of one type as one of their ancestor types to simplify interacting with them. There are two types of conversion: implicit and explicit.

5.7.1 Implicit Type Conversion

Implicit type conversion, also known as **coercion. kinds of ad hoc polymorphism** is an automatic type conversion by the compiler. Some languages allow, or even require, compilers to provide coercion. In a mixed-type expression, data of one or more subtypes can be converted to a super type as needed at runtime so that the program will run correctly.

Example 5.6:

```
double d ; // (1)
long l ; // (2)
int i ; // (3)
if ( d > i )     d = i ; // (4)
if ( i > l )     l = i ; // (5)
if ( d == l ) d *= 2 ; // (6)
```

Although d, l and i belong to different data types, they will be automatically converted to the same data type each time a comparison or assignment is executed. This behaviour should be used with caution, as unintended consequences can arise. For example, in the above comparisons, there would be a loss of information in a conversion from type double to type int if the value of d is larger than i can hold. Data can also be lost when floating-point representations are converted to integral representations as the fractional components of the floating-point values will be truncated (rounded down). Conversely, converting from an integral representation to a floating-point one can also lose precision, as floating-point representations are generally not capable of holding integer values precisely. This can lead to situations such as storing the same integer value into two variables of type int and type double which return false if compared for equality.

Example 5.7:

There's one function for adding two integers and one for adding two floating-point numbers in this hypothetical programming environment, but note that there is no function for adding an integer to a floating-point number. The reason why we can still do this is that when the compiler/interpreter finds a function call f(a1, a2, ...) that no existing function named f can handle, it starts to look for ways to convert the arguments into different types in order to make the call conform to the signature of one of the functions named f. This is coercion. In our case, since any integer can be converted into a floating-point number without loss of precision.

5.7.2 Explicit Type Conversion

Explicit type conversion, also known as **casting**. There are several kinds of explicit conversion.

- **Checked :** Before the conversion is performed, a runtime check is done to see if the destination type can hold the source value. If not, an error condition is raised.
- **Unchecked :** No check is performed. If the destination type cannot hold the source value, the result is undefined.
- **Bit Pattern :** The data is not interpreted at all, and its raw bit representation is copied verbatim. This can also be achieved via aliasing.

5.8 SIGNATURE

- **Type Signature**: Type signature defines the inputs and outputs for a function or method. A type signature includes at least the function name and the number of its parameters. In some programming languages, it may also specify the function's return type or the types of its parameters.

Example 5.8:

Java : In the Java virtual machine, internal type signatures are used to identify methods and classes at the level of the virtual machine code. For instance The method String, String.substring(int, int) is represented as java/lang/String/substring(II)Ljava/lang/String;

- **Method Signature:** A method is commonly identified by its unique method signature. This usually includes the method name, the number and type of its parameters, and its return type. A method signature is the smallest type of a method.

5.9 TYPE POLYMORPHISM

The term "polymorphism" refers to the ability of code (in particular, functions or classes) to act on values of multiple types, or to the ability of different instances of the same data-structure to contain elements of different types. **A mechanism allowing a given function to have many different specifications, depending on the types to which it is applied, or, more specifically.** Type systems that allow polymorphism generally do so in order to improve the potential for code re-use or polymorphism means allowing a single definition to be used with different types of data (specifically, different classes of objects). For instance, a polymorphic function definition can replace several type-specific ones, and a single polymorphic operator can act in expressions of various types. The concept of polymorphism applies to data types in addition to functions. A function that can evaluate to and be applied to values of different types is known as a polymorphic function. A data type that contains elements of different types is known as a polymorphic data type. There are two fundamentally different kinds of polymorphism, as first informally described by Christopher Strachey in 1967 as AD HOC POLYMORPHISM and PARAMETRIC POLYMORPHISM.

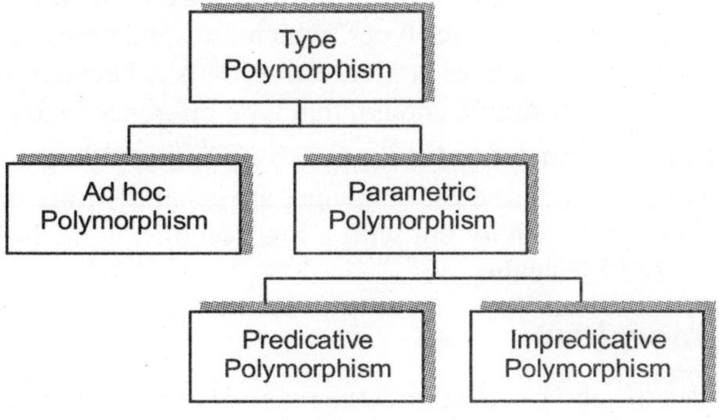

Figure 5.3

5.9.1 Ad hoc Polymorphism

If the range of actual types that can be used is finite and the combinations must be specified individually prior to use, it is called adhoc polymorphism. usually refers to overloading, but sometimes automatic type conversion, known as implicit type conversion or coercion, is also considered to be a kind of ad hoc polymorphism. The name refers to the manner in which this kind of polymorphism is typically introduced: **"Oh, hey, let's make the + operator work on strings, too!"** . Ad hoc polymorphism is a **dispatch mechanism** i.e. code moving through one named function is dispatched to various other functions without having to specify the exact function being called.

5.9.2 Parametric Polymorphism

If all code is written without mention of any specific type and thus can be used transparently with any number of new types, it is called parametric polymorphism. Programming using parametric polymorphism is called generic programming, particularly in the object-oriented community and function programming. Using parametric polymorphism, a function or a data type can be written generically so that it can deal equally well with any objects without depending on their type. For example, a function append that joins two lists can be constructed so that it does not care about the type of elements: it can append lists of integers, lists of real numbers, lists of strings, and so on. Let the type variable a denote the type of elements in the lists. Then append can be typed $[a] \times [a] \rightarrow [a]$, where [a] denotes a list of elements of type a. We say that the type of append is parameterized by a for all values of a. Parametric polymorphism was first introduced to programming languages in ML in 1976. Today it exists in Standard ML, O'Caml, Haskell, Visual Prolog and others. Parametric polymorphism is a way to make a language more expressive, while still maintaining full static type-safety. It is thus irrelevant in dynamically typed languages, since by definition they lack static type-safety. However, any dynamically typed function f that takes n arguments can be given a static type using parametric polymorphism: $f : p1 \times ... \times pn \rightarrow r$, where p1, ..., pn and r are type parameters.

Type systems with parametric polymorphism can be classified into predicative and impredicative systems. The key difference is in how parametric values may be instantiated.

For example, consider the append function described above, which has type $[a] \times [a] \rightarrow [a]$; in order to apply this function to a pair of lists, a type must be substituted for the variable a in the type of the function such that the type of the arguments matches up with the resulting function type.

In an **impredicative system,** the type being substituted may be any type whatsoever, including a type that is itself polymorphic; thus append can be applied to pairs of lists with elements of any type even to lists of polymorphic functions such as append itself. In a predicative system, type variables may not be instantiated with polymorphic types. This restriction makes the distinction between polymorphic and non-polymorphic types very important; thus in predicative systems polymorphic types are sometimes referred to as type schemas to distinguish them from ordinary (monomorphic) types, which are sometimes called monotypes. Polymorphism in the language ML and its close relatives is predicative. This is because predicativity, together with other restrictions, makes the type system simple enough that type inference is possible.

In languages where explicit type annotations are necessary when applying a polymorphic function, the predicativity restriction is less important; thus these languages are generally **impredicative.** Haskell manages to achieve type inference without predicativity but with a few complications. In type theory, the most frequently studied impredicative typed λ-calculus.

5.9.3 Subtyping Polymorphism

Some languages employ the idea of subtypes to restrict the range of types that can be used in a particular case of parametric polymorphism. In these languages, subtyping polymorphism or dynamic polymorphism or dynamic typing, allows a function to be written to take an object of a certain type T, but also work correctly if passed an object that belongs to a type S that is a subtype of T. This type relation is sometimes written S <: T. Conversely, T is said to be a supertype of S—written T :> S. Object-oriented programming languages offer subtyping polymorphism using sub classing or inheritance. In typical implementations, each class contains what is called a virtual table a table of functions that implement the polymorphic part of the class interface and each object contains a pointer to the "vtable" of its class, which is then consulted whenever a polymorphic method is called. This mechanism is an example of:

- Late Binding: because virtual function calls are not bound until the time of invocation.
- Single Dispatch: because virtual function calls are bound simply by looking through the vtable provided by the first argument (this object), so the runtime types of the other arguments are completely irrelevant.

Example 5.9:

If Number, Rational, and Integer are types such that Number :> Rational and Number :> Integer, a function written to take a Number will work equally well when passed an Integer or Rational as when passed a Number. The actual type of the object can be hidden from clients into a black box, and accessed via object identity. In fact, if the Number type is abstract, it may not even be possible to get your hands on an object whose most-derived type is Number.

Example 5.10:

This example aims to illustrate three different kinds of polymorphism described. Though overloading an originally arithmetic operator to do a wide variety of things in this way may not be the most clear-cut example, it allows some subtle points to be made. An operator + that may be used in the following ways:

1. 1 + 2 = 3
2. 3.14 + 0.0015 = 3.1415
3. 1 + 3.7 = 4.7
4. [1, 2, 3] + [4, 5, 6] = [1, 2, 3, 4, 5, 6]
5. [true, false] + [false, true] = [true, false, false, true]
6. "foo" + "bar" = "foobar"

To handle these six function calls, four different pieces of code are needed :

- In the first case, integer addition must be invoked.
- In the second and third cases, floating-point addition must be invoked because it is the case of implicit type conversion or ad hoc polymorphism. '1' is automatically converted into '1.0' and floating point addition takes place.
- In the fourth and fifth cases, list concatenation must be invoked because the reason why we can concatenate both lists of integers, lists of booleans, and lists of characters, is that the function for list concatenation was written without any regard to the type of elements stored in the lists. This is an example of **parametric polymorphism.** If you wanted to, you could make up a thousand different new types of lists, and the generic list concatenation function would happily and without requiring any augmentation accept instances of them all.
- In the last case, string concatenation must be invoked, unless this too is handled as list concatenation (as in, e.g., Haskell).

Thus, the name + actually refers to three or four completely different functions. This is also an example of overloading.

5.9.4 Advantages of Polymorphism

Polymorphism allows client programs to be written based only on the abstract interfaces of the objects which will be manipulated (interface inheritance). This means that future extension in the form of new types of objects is easy, if the new objects conform to the original interface. In particular, with object-oriented polymorphism, the original client program does not even need to be recompiled (only relinked) in order to make use of new types exhibiting new (but interface-conformant) behaviour.

(In C++, for instance, this is possible because the interface definition for a class defines a memory layout, the virtual function table describing where pointers to functions can be found. Future, new classes can work with old, precompiled code because the new classes must conform to the abstract class interface, meaning that the layout of the new class's virtual function table is the same as before; the old, precompiled code can still look at the same memory offsets relative to the start of the object's memory in order to find a pointer to the new function. It is only that the new virtual function table points to a new implementation of the functions in the table, thus allowing new, interface-compliant behaviour with old, precompiled code.)

Since program evolution very often appears in the form of adding new types of objects (i.e. classes), this ability to cope with and localize change that polymorphism allows is the key new contribution of object technology to software design.

5.10 OVERLOADING

Overloading are kinds of ad hoc polymorphism. In general, in human linguistics, the meaning of a word in a sentence is only clear by its context and usage.

EXAMPLE: They saw the wood. In this case, the word saw is an overloaded expression meaning the past tense of to see and is not intended to mean the wood cutting tool.

Overloading allows multiple functions taking different types to be defined with the same name and the compiler or interpreter automatically calls the right one. This way, functions appending lists of integers, lists of strings, lists of real numbers, and so on could be written, and all be called append and the right append function would be called based on the type of lists being appended. This differs from parametric polymorphism, in which the function would need to be written generically, to work with any kind of list. Using overloading, it is possible to have a function perform two completely different things based on the type of input passed to it; this is not possible with parametric polymorphism. Another way to look at overloading is that a routine is uniquely identified not by its name, but by the combination of its name and the number, order and types of its parameters. This type of polymorphism is common in object-oriented programming languages, many of which allow operators to be overloaded in a manner similar to functions.

Advantage

An advantage that is sometimes gained from overloading is the appearance of specialization, e.g., a function with the same name can be implemented in multiple different ways, each optimized for the particular data types that it operates on. This can provide a convenient interface for code that needs to be specialized to multiple situations for performance reasons.

5.10.1 Operator Overloading

Operator overloading or operator ad hoc polymorphism is a specific case of polymorphism in which some or all of operators like +, =, or == have different implementations depending on the types of their arguments. Sometimes the overloadings are defined by the language; sometimes the programmer can implement support for new types. It is useful because it allows the developer to program using notation closer to the target domain and allows user types to look like types built into the language. It can easily be emulated using function calls.

Example 5.11: Consider for integers a, b, c:

a + b × c

In a language that supports operator overloading this is effectively a more concise way of writing:

```
operator_add_integers (a, operator_multiply_integers (b,c))
(the × operator has higher precedence than +.)
```

However, in C++ templates or even C macros, operator overloading is needed in writing down generic, primitive operations such as summing elements when implementing a vector template. The only way to write primitive addition is a + b and this works for all types of elements only because of its overloading. Actually, in C++ one could define an overloaded function add to use instead, but not in C.

A more general variant of operator overloading, called **expression reduction**, allows expressions containing one or multiple operators to be reduced to a single function call. The expression above could be reduced to:

```
operator_add_and_multiply_integers(a, b, c)
```

Criticisms of Operator Overloading

Operator overloading has been criticized because it allows programmers to give operators completely different functionality depending on the types of their operands. The common reply to this criticism, given by programmers who favor operator overloading, is that the same argument applies to function overloading as well. Further, even in absence of overloading, a programmer can define a function to do something totally different from what would be expected from its name. An issue that remains is that languages such as C++ provide a limited set of operator symbols, thus removing from programmers the option of choosing a more suitable operator symbol for their new operation.

Example 5.12: C++'s usage of the << operator is an example of criticisms of operator overloading. The expression

`a << 1 will return twice the value of a if a is an integer variable, but if a is an output stream instead this will write "1" to it because operator overloading allows the original programmer to change the usual semantics of an operator and to catch any subsequent programmers by surprise, it is usually considered good practice to use operator overloading with care.`

Example 5.13: Certain rules from mathematics can be expected or unintentionally assumed.

`a + b`

usually (but not always) means the same as `b + a`, but `"school" + "bag"` is different from `"bag" + "school"` in languages that overload + for string concatenation. The same kind of difference exists in the world of mathematics, where some matrix operations are not commutative.

Catalog :

A classification of some common programming languages by whether their operators are overloadable by the programmer and whether the operators are limited to a predefined set.

Operators	Not overloadable	Overloadable
Limited set	• C • Java • JavaScript • Objective-C • Pascal	• Ada • C++ • C# • D • Object Pascal (Delphi, since 2005)

Contd...

	• BASIC • PHP	• Perl • Python • Visual Basic 2005
New definable	• ML • Pico	• ALGOL 68 • Fortran • Haskell • Lisp • Prolog • Ruby • Perl 6 • Smalltalk • Eiffel

5.10.2 Method Overloading

Method overloading is a feature found in various object oriented programming languages such as C++ and Java that allows the creation of several functions with the same name which differ from each other in terms of the type of the input and the type of the output of the function. An example of this would be a square function which takes a number and returns the square of that number. In this case, it is often necessary to create different functions for integer and floating point numbers.

Method overloading is usually associated with statically-typed programming languages which enforce type checking in function calls. When overloading a method, you are really just making a number of different methods that happen to have the same name. It is resolved at compile time which of these methods are used. Method overloading should not be confused with ad hoc polymorphism or virtual functions. In those, the correct method is chosen at runtime.

5.11 COMPLETE C PROGRAM FOR SEMANTIC ANALYSIS

Program in 'C' Language is given in Appendix-A (A.10)

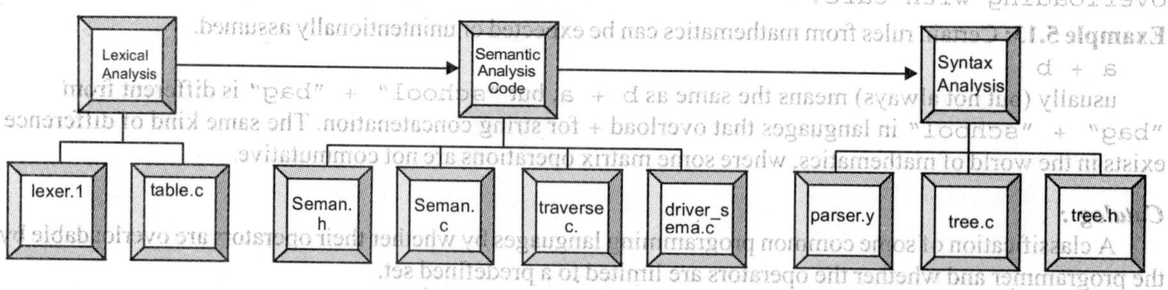

Figure 5.4

TRIBULATIONS

5.1 A *type coercion* is an automatic conversion from a value of one type to a value of another type. Some languages (Ada, for example) perform no coercions whatsoever, while others (C++, for example) not only do many by default, but can be extended by the programmer to do more. Which approach do you prefer (or would you like something in-between)? Why?

5.2 Briefly explain the difference between structural and name equivalence for types. In the following code, which of the variables will the compiler consider to have compatible types under structural equivalence? Under (strict and loose) name equivalence?

1. type T = array [1..10] of integer; S = T;
2. var A : T; B : T; C : S; D : array [1..10] of integer;

5.3 Garbage collection, which used to appear primarily in functional languages, has over time been incorporated into many imperative lanauges. Still, however, it remains a controversial feature, and is not universally available. Summarize the arguments for and against it.

FURTHER READINGS AND REFERENCES

About Type Theory and Polymorphism

[1] Ernest Nagel (1951): *"Causal Character of Modern Physical Theory"*, Freedom and Reason, The Free Press, Editors: Salo W. Baron, Ernest Nagel and Koppel B. Pinson. pp.244-268, as reprinted on page 759, The World of Physics, Editor: Jefferson Hane Weaver.

[2] Barwise, Jon and Robin Cooper (1981). *Generalized quantifiers in English. Linguistics and Philosophy* 4:159-219.

[3] Andrews, Peter B. (2002). *An Introduction to Mathematical Logic and Type Theory*: To Truth Through Proof, 2nd ed. Kluwer Academic Publishers.

[4] Cardelli, Luca (1997). "*Type Systems*," in Allen B. Tucker, ed., *The Computer Science and Engineering Handbook*. CRC Press: 2208-2236.

[5] Mendelson, Elliot (1997). *Introduction to Mathematical Logic*, 4th ed. Chapman & Hall.

[6] Montague, Richard (1973). *The proper treatment of quantification in English*. In Hintikka, K. et al., editor, Approaches to Natural Language, pages 221–242.

[7] Pierce, Benjamin (2002). *Types and Programming Languages*. MIT Press.

[8] Thompson, Simon (1991). *Type Theory and Functional Programming*. Addison-Wesley.

[9] Winskel, Glynn (1993). *The Formal Semantics of Programming Languages– An Introduction*. MIT Press.

[10] Wittgenstein, Ludwig (1922). *Tractatus Logico-Philosophicus*. New York, NY: Routledge, 2005.

Type Inference

[11] Pierce, Benjamin C. (2002). *Types and Programming Languages*. MIT Press.

About Overloading

[12] Luca Cardelli, Peter Wegner. *On Understanding Types, Data Abstraction, and Polymorphism,* from Computing Surveys, (December, 1985)

[13] Philip Wadler, Stephen Blott. *How to make ad-hoc polymorphism less ad hoc,* from Proc. 16th ACM Symposium on Principles of Programming Languages, (January, 1989)

[14] Christopher Strachey. *Fundamental Concepts in Programming Languages,* from Higher-Order and Symbolic Computation, (April, 2000)

[15] Paul Hudak, John Peterson, Joseph Fasel. *A Gentle Introduction to Haskell Version 98.*

CHAPTER 6

THREE ADDRESS CODE GENERATION

CHAPTER HIGHLIGHTS

The form of the internal representation among different compilers varies widely. If the back end is operates as a subroutine by the front end then the intermediate representation is likely to be some form of annotated parse tree, possibly with supplementary tables. If the back end operates as a separate program then the intermediate representation is likely to be some low-level pseudo assembly language or some register transfer language (it could be just numbers, but debugging is easier if it is human-readable).

Three address code (TAC) is a form of representing intermediate code used by compilers to aid in the implementation of code-improving transformations. Each TAC can be described as a quadruple (operator, operand1, operand2, result), triple (operator, operand1, operand2), indirect triple. Each statement has the general form of:

x := y op z

where *x*, *y* and *z* are variables, constants or temporary variables generated by the compiler. *op* represents any operator, *e.g.* an arithmetic operator. The term three address code is still used even if some instructions use more or less than two operands. The key features of three address code are that every instruction implements exactly one fundamental operation, and that the source and destination may refer to any available register. A refinement of three address code is static single assignment form.

Now in this chapter we discuss about ***all types of optimizations and target of optimization***. Now we are standing at fourth phase of compiler. Input to this phase is error less parse tree from symantic analysis as:

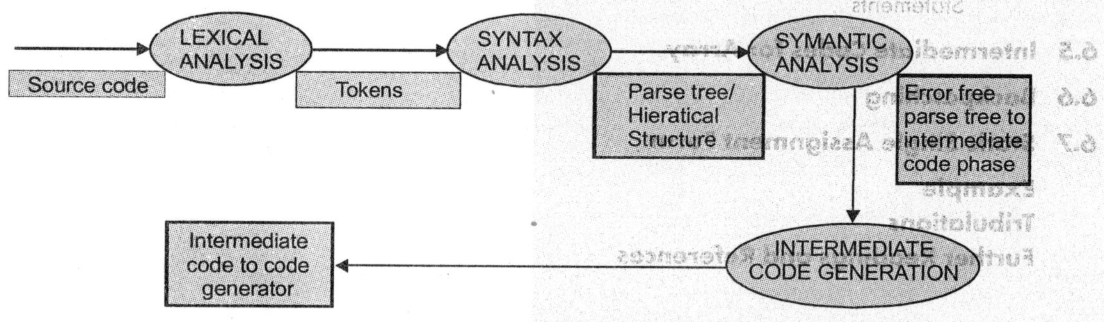

Figure 6.1: *Process of Three Address Code Generation*

The three address code table:

Table 6.1: *Forms of Intermediate Code*

Assignment Statement	x := y op z x := op y	x, y, z are names, constants, or compiler generated temporaries; op is any binary operator op is a unary operator
Indexed Assignment	x := y[i], x[i] := y	x, y, i are data objects
Copy Statement	x := y	x, y are data objects
Unconditional jump	goto L	L is the label of the next statement to be executed
Conditional jump	if x relop y goto L	x, y are data objects, relop is a binary operator that compares x to y and indicates true/false, L is the label of the next statement to be executed if relop indicates true

Contd....

Procedure calls and returns	param x call p, n return y	x is a parameter p is the procedure, n is the number of parameters y is an optional return value
Address and pointer assignments	x := & y;x := *y;*x := y	x is set to the location of y, x is set to the value at the location y, the value pointed to by x is set to the r-value of y

6.1 INTERMEDIATE LANGUAGES

An intermediate language is the language of an abstract machine designed to aid in the analysis of computer programs. The term comes from their use in compilers, where a compiler first translates the source code of a program into a form more suitable for code-improving transformations, as an intermediate step before generating object or machine code for a target machine. The design of an intermediate language typically differs from that of a practical machine language in three fundamental ways:

- Each instruction represents exactly one fundamental operation; *e.g.* "shift-add" addressing modes common in microprocessors are not present.
- Control flow information may not be included in the instruction set.
- The number of registers available may be large, even limitless.

  A popular format for intermediate languages is three address codes. All programs can be translated directly to target code but using an intermediate code allows :

  - simpler retargeting
  - machine-independent code optimization
  - can easily be done by parser

A variation in the meaning of this term is those languages used as an intermediate language by some high-level programming languages which do not output object or machine code, but output the intermediate language only, to submit to a compiler for such language, which then outputs finished object or machine code. This is usually done to gain optimization much as treated above or portability by using an intermediate language that has compilers for many processors and operating systems, such as C. Some intermediate programming languages:

- C is used as an intermediate language by numerous programming languages including Eiffel, Sather, and Esterel. Variants of C have been designed to provide C's features as a portable assembly language, including one of the numerous languages called C–, the C Intermediate Language and the Low Level Virtual Machine.
- In case of Java, Java Virtual Machine Language is the intermediate language used by all compilers targeting the Java Virtual Machine, before just-in-time compilation to machine code.
- Microsoft's Common Intermediate Language is an intermediate language designed to be shared by all compilers for the .NET Framework, before static or dynamic compilation to machine code.
- The Gnu Compiler Collection (gcc) uses internally several intermediate languages to simplify portability and cross-compilation. Among these languages are
  - Register Transfer Language (RTL)
  - SSA-based GIMPLE.

Here are three types of intermediate language as:

- High Level Intermediate Language
- Medium Level Intermediate Language
- Low Level Intermediate Language

High Level Intermediate Language : High level intermediate language are used almost entirely in the earliest stages of the compilation process before compilation. They are produced by compiler front ends and are usually transformed shortly into low level language forms and then transformed back into source code in the original language or other language. Abstract syntax tree is the form of high level intermediate language which makes explicit structure of program. EXAMPLE : Here is a code for array referencing as : t1 = a[i, J+2]

Medium Level Intermediate Language : A single tree traversal by a compiler component i.e. the knowledge about the semantic of the source language to transform the abstract syntax tree into a medium level intermediate code. Medium level intermediate language are generally designed to reflect the range of features in a set of source language are designed to be good bases for generation of efficient machine code for one or more architectures. They provide a way to represent source variable, temporaries, registers to reduce control flow to simple conditional and unconditional branches, calls and returns and to make explicit the operations necessary to support block structure and procedure.

Example 6.1:

1. t1 = j +2
2. t2 = i *20
3. t3 = t1 + t2
4. t4 = 4 * t3
5. t5 = add [a]
6. t6 = t5 + t4
7. t7 = *t6

Low Level Intermediate Language: Low level intermediate language deviate from one to one correspondence generally in case where they are alternatives for the most effective code to generate for them. Low level intermediate language may have an integer multiply operator while the target architecture may not have multiply instruction or multiply instruction may not be the best choice of code to generate for some combination of operands.

Example 6.2:

1. r1 = [bp – 4]
2. r2 = r1 + 2
3. r3 = [bp – 8]
4. r4 = r3 * 20
5. r5 = r4 + r2
6. r6 = 4 * r5
7. r7 = bp – 216
8. f1 = [r7 + r6]

6.2 INTERMEDIATE REPRESENTATION

An intermediate representation is a data structure that is constructed from input data to a program, and from which part or all of the output data of the program is constructed in turn. Use of the term usually implies that most of the information present in the input is retained by the intermediate representation, with further annotations or rapid lookup features. A canonical example is found in most modern compilers, where the linear human-readable text representing a program is transformed into an intermediate graph data structure that allows flow analysis and re-arrangements before starting to create the list of actual CPU instructions that will do the work. Genernally three addresss code are represented by three types of data structure as

1. Quadruple
2. Triples
3. Indirect Triples

Quadruple: A quadruple is a record data structure with four fields or columns for holding three address codes i.e. 'operator', 'argument1', 'argument2' and 'result'. Operator field holds the operator that are applied to operand or arguments as intermediate form of three address code, operand are hold in argument fields i.e. in 1, 2 and result field store the result of corresponding operator on correspond operand as intermediate form.

Example 6.3: We generate quadruple for expression "A = B + C * D / E + - F * -G". This expression can be written as A = ((B + (C * (D / E))) + ((- F) * (-G))). So now quadruple representation look like as:

Table 6.2: Quadruple Forms of Intermediate Code

	Operator	Argument1	Argument 2	Result
(0)	DIV	D	E	T1
(1)	MUL	T1	C	T2
(2)	MINUS	F		T3
(3)	MINUS	G		T4
(4)	MUL	T3	T4	T5
(5)	ADD	B	T2	T6
(6)	ADD	T6	T5	T7
(7)	=	T7		A

Triples: To avoid entering temporary names into symbol table, we use triples that use position instead of temporary values. In this way, a triple is a record data structure with three fields or columns for holding three address codes i.e., 'operator', 'argument1', and 'argument2'. Operator field holds the operator that are applied to operand or arguments as intermediate form of three address code, operand are hold in argument fields i.e. in 1, 2 and position field store the result of corresponding operator on correspond operand as intermediate form.

Example 6.4: We generate triple for expression "A = B + C * D / E + –F * –G". This expression can be written as A = ((B + (C * (D / E))) + ((–F) * (–G))). So now triple representation look like as:

Table 6.3: Triple Forms of Intermediate Code

	Operator	Argument 1	Argument 2
(0)	DIV	D	E
(1)	MUL	(0)	C
(2)	MINUS	F	
(3)	MINUS	G	
(4)	MUL	(2)	(3)
(5)	ADD	B	(1)
(6)	ADD	(5)	(4)
(7)	=	(6)	A

Notes: Another triple for array as

(0)	[ ]=	X	I
(1)	assign	(0)	Y

X [I] = Y

(0)	= [ ]	Y	I
(1)	assign	X	(0)

X = Y [I]

Indirect Triples:

We use another method for implementing three address code as indirect triples in which we point the triples to main memory and store triples in secondary memory or not in main memory to save space in primary memory. In this way, a indirect triple is a record data structure with two tables/records in which on point to triple table/ records and triple table/records have three fields or columns for holding three address codes i.e. 'operator', 'argument1', and 'argument2'. Operator field holds the operator that are applied to operand or arguments as intermediate form of three address code, operand are hold in argument fields i.e. in 1, 2 and position field store the result of corresponding operator on correspond operand as intermediate form.

Example 6.5 : We generate indirect triple for expression "A = B + C * D / E + –F * –G". This expression can be written as A = ((B + (C * (D / E))) + ((–F) * (–G))). So now indirect triple representation look like as:

Table 6.4: Indirect Triple Forms of Intermediate Code

	Statement
(0)	(10)
(1)	(11)
(2)	(12)
(3)	(13)
(4)	(14)
(5)	(15)
(6)	(16)
(7)	(17)

	Operator	Argument 1	Argument 2
(10)	DIV	D	E
(11)	MUL	(10)	C
(12)	MINUS	F	
(13)	MINUS	G	
(14)	MUL	(12)	(13)
(15)	ADD	B	(11)
(16)	ADD	(15)	(14)
(17)	=	(16)	A

6.3 BOOLEAN EXPRESSIONS

- Boolean expressions have two purposes as:

First to compute boolean values like:

- b: boolean := a and not c or i < k;

Second as a conditional expression for statements like :

- IF a and not c or i < k THEN
- put(i);
- END IF;

So, we saw that simple expression are boolean if and only composed of the boolean operators like AND, OR, NOT or relational operator RELOP like '>', '<', '=', '≠', '≤', '≥'or have value TRUE as '1' or FALSE as '1'. Now we produced a grammar that generates boolean expression as:

EXPR → EXPR OR EXPR
EXPR → EXPR AND EXPR
EXPR → NOT EXPR
EXPR → id RELOP id (>)
EXPR → id RELOP id (<)
EXPR → id RELOP id (=)
EXPR → id RELOP id ('≠')
EXPR → id RELOP id ("≤")
EXPR → id RELOP id ("≥")
EXPR → TRUE
EXPR → FALSE
EXPR → (EXPR)

Here we present two methods of evaluating boolean expressions:

6.3.1 Arithmetic Method

Boolean expression that are evaluated with false = 0 or true = 1. All Boolean expressions in arithmetic method are evaluated using given grammar as:

Table 6.5: Grammar for Boolean Expression as Arithematic Expression

Production	Rule
expr → $expr_1$ OR $expr_2$	expr.place : = tempo emit(expr.place := $expr_1$ .place OR $expr_2$.place)
expr → $expr_1$ AND $expr_2$	expr.place : = tempo emit(expr.place := $expr_1$ .place AND $expr_2$.place)
expr → NOT $expr_1$	expr.place : = tempo emit(expr.place := NOT $expr_1$ .place)
expr → id_1 RELOP id_2	expr.place : = tempo emit('if' id1.place RELOP id_2.place 'goto' statement + 3) emit(expr.place := 0) emit('goto' statement + 2) emit(expr .place := 1)
expr → true	expr.place : = tempo emit(expr.place := '1')
expr → false	expr.place : = tempo emit(expr.place := '0'
expr → (expr)	expr.place : = expr.place

Example 6.6: Intermediate code for 7a< b and e>d or e<7f and 7g <7h and i<j or 7k>7L using arithmetic method

```
99     t0 = 7a
100    if t0 <b then goto 103
101    t1 = 0
102    goto 104
103    t1 = 1
104    if e > d then goto 107
```

```
105    t2 = 0
106    goto 108
107    t2 = 1
108    t0 = 7f
109    if e <t0 then goto 112
110    t3 = 0
111    goto 113
112    t3 = 1
113    to″ = 7g
114    to‴ = 7h
115    if t0″ < t0‴ then goto 118
116    t4 = 0
117    goto 119
118    t4 = 1
119    if i < j then goto 122
120    t5 = 0
121    goto 123
122    t5= 1
123    to = 7k
124    to″ = 7l
125    if t0  > t0″ then goto 128
126    t6 = 0
127    goto 121
128    t6 = 1
129    t7 = t6 or t5
130    t8 = t7 and t4
131    t9 = t8 and t3
132    t10 = t9 or t2
133    t11 = t0 and t1
```

6.3.2 Control Flow

Control flow (or alternatively, flow of control) refers to the order in which the individual statements or instructions of an imperative program are performed or executed. **A control flow statement is an instruction that when executed can cause a change in the subsequent control flow to differ from the natural sequential order in which the instructions are listed.** Flow of control generate required labels at beginning of construct and by flow of control

- value is represented by reaching a position in a program
- ANDs and ORs may be short-circuited
- NOTs never add code, just switch true and false locations

The kinds of control flow statements available differ by language, but can be roughly categorized by their effect:

- continuation at a different statement (jump),
- executing a set of statements only if some condition is met (choice),
- executing a set of statements repeatedly (loop; equivalent to jumping to an earlier point in the code),
- executing a set of distant statements, after which the flow of control returns (subroutine),
- stopping the program, preventing any further execution (halt).

All boolean expressions in arithmetic method are evaluated using given grammar as:

Table 6.6: Grammar for Boolean Expression as Control Flow

Production	Rule
expr → $expr_1$ OR $expr_2$	$expr_1$.true : = expr.true $expr_1$.false := newlabel $expr_2$.true := expr.true $expr_2$.false := expr.false expr.code := $expr_1$ .code || emit($expr_1$.false) || $expr_2$.code
expr → $expr_1$ AND $expr_2$	$expr_1$.true : = newlabel $expr_1$.false := expr.false $expr_2$.true := expr.true $expr_2$.false := expr.false expr.code := $expr_1$ .code || emit($expr_1$.true) || $expr_2$.code
expr → NOT $expr_1$	$expr_1$.true : = expr.false $expr_1$.false : = expr.true expr.code : = $expr_1$ .code
expr → id_1 RELOP id_2	emit('if' id_1.place RELOP id_2.place 'goto' expr.true) emit('goto' expr.false)
expr → true	expr.goto : = emit('goto' expr.true)
expr → false	expr.goto : = emit('goto' expr.false)
expr → (expr)	$expr_1$.true : = expr.true $expr_1$.false := expr.false expr.code := $expr_1$ .code

Example 6.7:

```
        While (A<C and B>D)
              do if A=1 then
                    C=C+1
              else
        while A< = D do
                    A= A+3
L1:     If A<C then goto L2
        goto L next
L2:     If B>D then goto L3
        goto L next
L3:     if A=1 then goto L4
        goto L5
L4:     t0=C+1
```

```
        C= t0
        goto L1
L5:     If A< = D goto L6
        goto L1
L6:     t1=A+3
        A= t1
        goto L5
L next:————————————
```

Example 6.8: Generate three address code for given using flow-of-control.

```
while ((A<C and B<D) or C>E & F>G))
        if (A=1 & B=2) then
                C=C+d*e/f+g+h;
        else
                while A<D & C>B
                        if (A=5 & C=2 or B=5)
                                C=A*C*B
                        else
                                C=A–1
```

```
L1:     if A<C then goto L2
        goto L3
L2:     if B<D then goto L3
        goto L3
L3:     if C>E then goto L4
        goto L next
L4:     if F>G then goto L5
        goto L next
L5:     if A=1 then goto L6
        goto L8
L6:     if B=2 then goto L7
        goto L8
L7:     t =e / f
        t1= d * t
        t2 = C + t1
        t3 = g + t2
        t4 = h + t3
        C = t4
        goto L1
L8:     if A<=D then goto L9
        goto L1
L9:     if C>B then goto L10
        goto L1
```

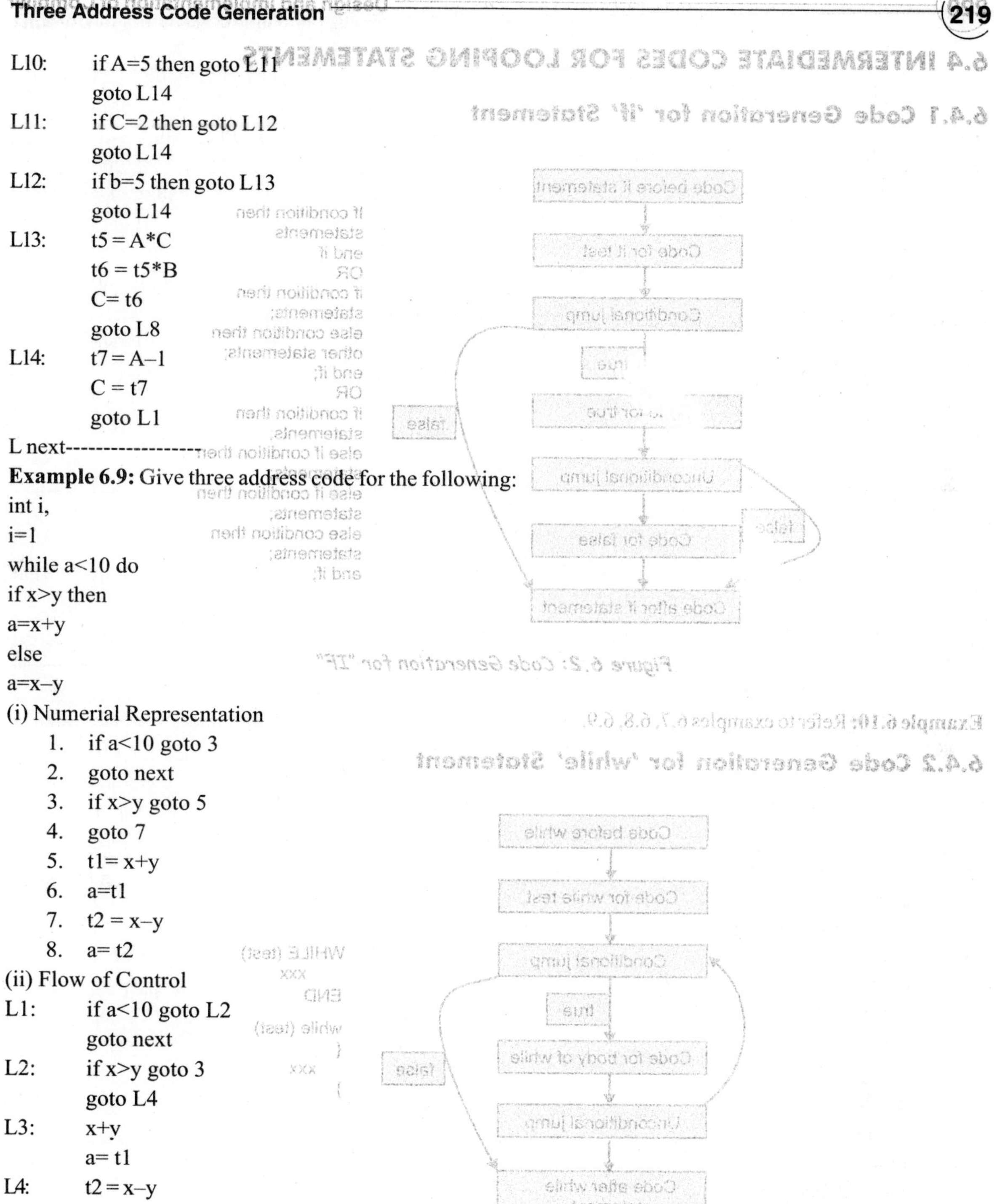

```
L10:    if A=5 then goto L11
        goto L14
L11:    if C=2 then goto L12
        goto L14
L12:    if b=5 then goto L13
        goto L14
L13:    t5 = A*C
        t6 = t5*B
        C= t6
        goto L8
L14:    t7 = A–1
        C = t7
        goto L1
L next-----------------
```

Example 6.9: Give three address code for the following:

```
int i,
i=1
while a<10 do
if x>y then
a=x+y
else
a=x–y
```

(i) Numerial Representation

```
1. if a<10 goto 3
2. goto next
3. if x>y goto 5
4. goto 7
5. t1= x+y
6. a=t1
7. t2 = x–y
8. a= t2
```

(ii) Flow of Control

```
L1:     if a<10 goto L2
        goto next
L2:     if x>y goto 3
        goto L4
L3:     x+y
        a= t1
L4:     t2 = x–y
        a=t2
```

6.4 INTERMEDIATE CODES FOR LOOPING STATEMENTS

6.4.1 Code Generation for 'if' Statement

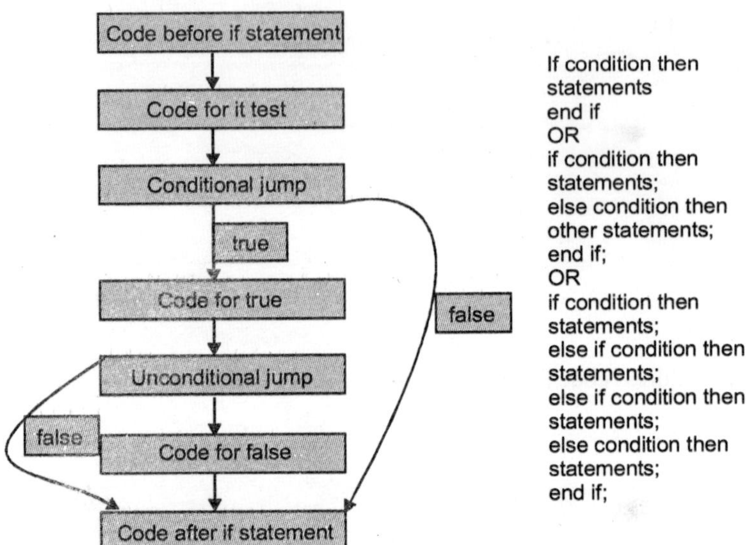

Figure 6.2: Code Generation for "IF"

Example 6.10: Refer to examples 6.7, 6.8, 6.9.

6.4.2 Code Generation for 'while' Statement

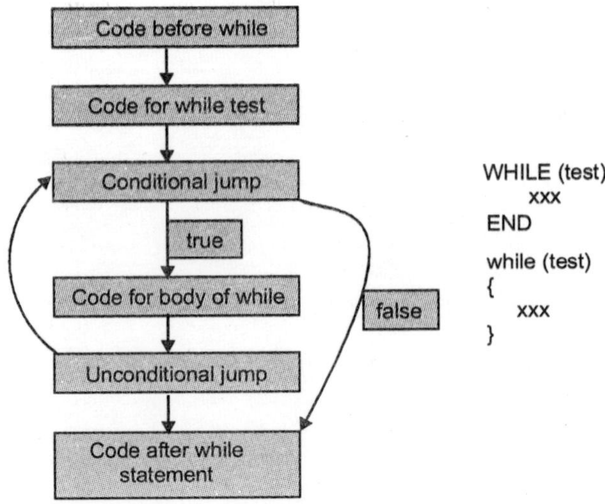

Figure 6.3: Code Generation for "WHILE"

Example 6.11: Refer to example 6.7, 6.8, 6.9.

6.4.3 Code Generation for 'do while' Statement

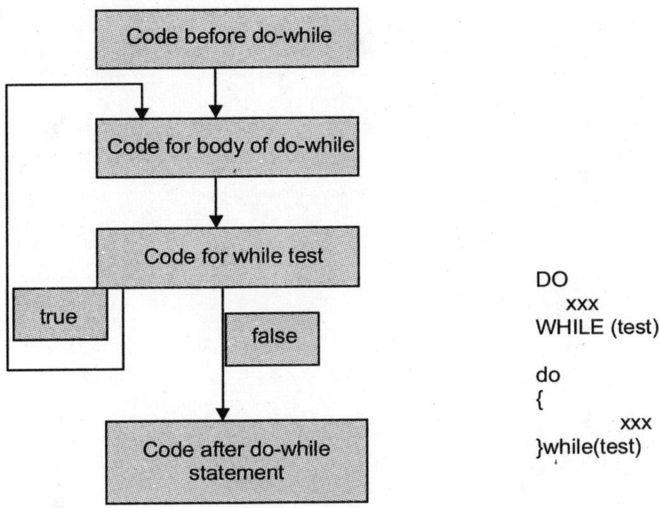

DO
    xxx
WHILE (test)

do
{
        xxx
}while(test)

Figure 6.4: Code Generation for "DO-WHILE"

Example 6.12: Refer to example 6.7

6.4.4 Code Generation for 'for' Statement

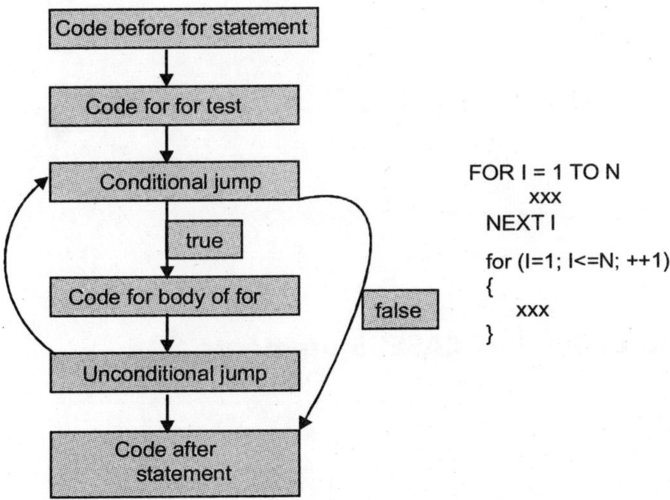

FOR I = 1 TO N
    xxx
NEXT I

for (I=1; I<=N; ++1)
{
    xxx
}

Figure 6.5: Code Generation for "FOR"

Example 6.13: Following example illustrate for and while loop.

```
for(j=2;j<=n;j++)
{
        key=A[j];
i=j–1;
while(i>0 && A[i]>key)
{
        A[i+1] *= A[i];
        i = i–1;
}
A[i+1]=key;
}
```

Three Address Code

```
(1)     j=2
(2)     if j<=n goto 4
(3)     goto next
(4)     t2=4*j
(5)     t3=a[t2]
(6)     key=t3
(7)     t4=j–1
(8)     i=t4
(9)     if i>0 goto 11
(10)    goto 21
(11)    t5=4*i
(12)    t6=A[t5]
(13)    if t6>key goto 15
(14)    goto 21
(15)    t7=i+1
(16)    t8=t7
(17)    t9=4*t8
(18)    t10=A[t9]
(19)    t10=t6
(20)    t11=i-1
(21)    i=t11
(22)    goto 9
(23)    t10=key
(24)    t12=j+1
(25)    j=t12
(26)    goto 2 (next)
```

6.4.5 Intermediate Codes for 'CASE' Statements

```
Switch ( a + b )
{
        case 2: x = y:
                break;
        case 5: {
                switch ( x )
```

```
            case 0: a = b + 1;
                    break;
            case 1:a = b + 3;
                    break;
            default: a=2;
                    break;
            }
      break;
case 9: x=y–1;
      break;
}
//code for evaluate a+b into t
        goto test
L1:      x = y                                  // code for S1
        goto next
L2:     goto test 1                             // code for evaluate x into t1
L3:     t3= b+1;
        a= t3;                                  // code for S3
        goto next
L4:     t4 = b+3;
        a=t4;                                   // code for S4
        goto next
L5:     a=2;                                    // code for S5
        goto next
test 1: if t1=0 goto L3
        if t1=1 goto L4
        goto L5
        next
L6:     t5=y–1;                                 // code for S6
        x=t5
        goto next
test:   if t=2 goto L1
        if t=5 goto L2
        if t=9 goto L6
next :
```

6.5 INTERMEDIATE CODES FOR ARRAY

The translation scheme for addressing 2-D array elements use following semantic actions grammar:

(1) S → L = E
(2) E → E + E
(3) E → (E)
(4) E → L
(5) L → Elsit]
(6) L → **id**
(7) Elist → Elsit , E
(8) Elsit → **id** [E

We generate a normal assignment if *L* is a simple name, and an indexed assignment into the location denoted by *L* otherwise:

```
(1)     S       →L=E
                {
if L.offset = null then /* L is a simple id */
                                emit(L.place ':=' E.place);
                        else
                                emit (L.place' ['L.offset']' ':=' E.place)
                }
```

The code for arithmetic expressions is exactly the same as in section 8.3.

```
(2)     E       →E+E
                {
E.place : = newtemp;
                        emit (E. place ':=' E 1 .place '+' E 2 .place)
                }
(3)     E       →(E1)
                {
                        E.place := E 1. place
                }
```

When an array reference *L* is reduced to *E*, we want the r-value of *L*. Therefore we use indexing to obtain the contents of the location *L.place [L. offset]:*

```
(4)     E       →L
                {
if L. offset = null then / * L is a simple id * /
                                E.place := L.place
                        else
                                begin
                                        E.place : = newtemp;
                                        emit(E.place ':=' L.place' ['L.offset']')
                                end
                }
(5)     L       → Elsit ]
                {
                L.place : = newtemp;
                L. offset: = newtemp;
                emit(L.place ':=' c(Elist.array»;
                emit(L.offset ':=' Elist.place '*' width (Elist.array))
                }
(6)     L       → id
                {
                L.place := id.place;
                L.offset :=Null
                }
(7)     Elist   → Elsit , E
                {
t : = newtemp;
                  m := Elistl.ndim + I;
```

```
                    emit(t' :=' Elist).place '*' limit(Elistl.array, m));
                    emit(t ':=' t '+' E.place);
                    Elist.array : = Elist I .array;
                    Elist.place : = t;
                    Elist.ndim := m
                    }
(8)     Elsit      → id [ E
                    {
                      Elist.array := id.place;
                      Elist.place : = E.place;
                      Elist.ndim := I
                    }
```

Example 6.14: Above grammar can be easily understood by following example.

```
for(i=0;i<=n;i++)
{
        for(j=0;j<n;j++)
        {
        c[i,j]=0;
        }
}
for(i=0;i<=n;i++)
{
        for(j=0;j<=n;j++)
        {
                for(k=0;k<=n;k++)
                {
                c[i,j]=c[i,j]+a[i,k]*b[k,j];
                }
        }
}
```

Three Address Code

```
(1)     i=0
(2)     if i<n goto 4 (L)          //(L) represent leader
(3)     goto 18 (L)
(4)     j=0 (L)
(5)     if j<n goto 7 (L)
(6)     goto 15 (L)
(7)     t1=i*k¹  (L)
(8)     t1=t1+j
(9)     t2=Q
(10)    t3=4*t1
(11)    t4=t2[t3]
(12)    t5=j+1
(13)    j=15
(14)    goto 5
(15)    t6=i+1 (L)
```

```
(16)    i=t6
(17)    goto 2
(18)    i=0 (L)
(19)    if i<=n goto 21 (L)
(20)    goto next (L)
(21)    j=0
(22)    if j<=n goto 24 (L)
(23)    goto 52 (L)
(24)    k=0 (L)
(25)    if k<=n goto 27 (L)
(26)    goto 49 (L)
(27)    t7 =t*k^1 (L)
(28)    t7=t7+j
(29)    t8=Q
(30)    t9=4*t7
(31)    t10=t8[t9]
(32)    t11=i*k^1
(33)    t11=t11+k
(34)    t12=Q
(35)    t13=t11*4
(36)    t14=t12[t13]
(37)    t15=k+k^1
(38)    t15=t15+j
(39)    t16=Q
(40)    t17=4*t15
(41)    t18=t16[t17]
(42)    t19=t14*t18
(43)    t20=t10+t19
(44)    t10=t20
(45)    t21=k+1
(46)    k=t21
(47)    goto 25
(48)    t22=j+1 (L)
(49)    j=t22
(50)    goto 22
(51)    t23=i+1 (L)
(52)    i=t23
(53)    goto 19
(next)
```

6.6 BACKPATCHING

The main problem with generating code for boolean expression and flow of control statements in a single pass is that during one single pass we may not know the labels that control must go to at the time the jump statements are generated. We can get around this problem by generating a series of branching statements with the targets of the jumps temporarily left unspecified.Each such statement will be put on a list of goto statements whose labels will be filled in when the proper label can be determined. We call this subsequent action filling in of labels backpatching.

Backpatching can be used to generate code for boolean expressions and flow of control statements in one pass. The translation we generate will be of the same form as those in section 6.3 except for the manner in which we generate labels. To manipulate lists of labels, we use three functions:

1. **Make_address_list(i):** creates a new list containing only i, an index into the array quadruples. Make_address_list returns a pointer to the list it has made.

2. **Merge_list (p1, p2):** concatenates the lists pointed to by P1 and P2, and return a pointer to the concatenated list.

3. **Backpatch (p, i):** inserts i as the target label for each of the statements on the list pointed to by p.

For backpatching we use the following grammar as:

- EXPR → EXPR1 or E EXPR2
- EXPR → EXPR1 and E EXPR2
- EXPR → not(EXPR1)
- EXPR → (EXPR1)
- EXPR → ID1 relop ID2
- EXPR → true
- EXPR → false
- E → ∈

Synthesized attributes 'truelist' and 'falselist' of nonterminal E are used to generate jumping code for boolean expressions. The translation schema is as:

Table 6.7: Translation schema for backpatching

Production	Rule
EXPR→EXPR1 or E EXPR2	{ Backpatch(EXPR1.falselist, E.val); EXPR.truelist : = Merger_list(EXPR1.truelist, EXPR2.truelist); EXPR.falselist := EXPR2.false}

EXPR→ EXPR1 and E EXPR2	{
	Backpatch(EXPR1.truelist, E.val);
	EXPR.truelist := EXPR2.truelist;
	EXPR.falselist := Merger_list(EXPR1.falselist, EXPR2. falselist);
	}

EXPR→ not(EXPR1)	{ EXPR.truelist := EXPR1.falselist; EXPR.falselist := EXPR1.truelist}

EXPR→ (EXPR1)	{
	EXPR.truelist : = EXPR1 .truelist;
	EXPR.falselist : = EXPR1 .falselist
	}

EXPR→ ID1 relop ID2	{

Contd....

	EXPR.truelist := Make_address_list(nextval); EXPR.falselist := Make_address_list(nextval+1); emit (' if' ID1.place relop.op ID2.place ' goto...........' emit(' goto..........') }

EXPR→ true	{
	EXPR.truelist := Make_address_list(nextval);
	emit ('goto —')
	}

EXPR→ false
 	
E→ ∈
	{
	EXPR.falselist := Make_address_list(nextval);emit('goto —')
	}
	{E.val = nextval}

Example 6.15: Consider the expression a < b or c < d and e < f. see in figure 6.6
STEP1: Reduction of a < b to EXPR by production (5), the two quadruples are generated as
100: if a < b goto ——
101: goto ——
The E in the production EXPR→EXPR1 or E EXPR2 records the value of nextval, which is 102.
STEP2: Reduction of c < d to EXPR by production (5), the two quadruples are generated as
102: if c < d goto ——
103 : goto —
Now seen EXPR1 in the production EXPR→ EXPR1 and E EXPR2. The E in this production records the current value of nextval, which is now 104.
STEP3: Reduction of e < f to EXPR by production (5), the two quadruples are generated as
104: if e < f. goto ——
105: goto ——
STEP4: We now reduce by EXPR→ EXPR1 and E EXPR2. The corresponding semantic action calls Backpatch ({102}, 104) where {102} as argument denotes a pointer to the list containing only 102, that list being the one pointed to by EXPR1.truelist. This call to back patch fills in 104 in statement 102. The six statements generated so far are thus:
100: if a < b goto ——
101: goto ——
102: if c < d goto 104
103: goto ——
104: if e < f, goto ——
105: goto ——
STEP 5: Final reduction by EXPR→ EXPR1 or E EXPR2 calls backpatch({101},102) which leaves the statements looking like:
100: if a < b goto ——
101: goto 102

102: if c < d goto 104
103: goto
104: if e < f goto ——
105: goto ——
The entire expression is true if and only if the goto's of statements 100 or
104 are reached, and is false if and only if the goto's of statements 103 or 105 are reached.

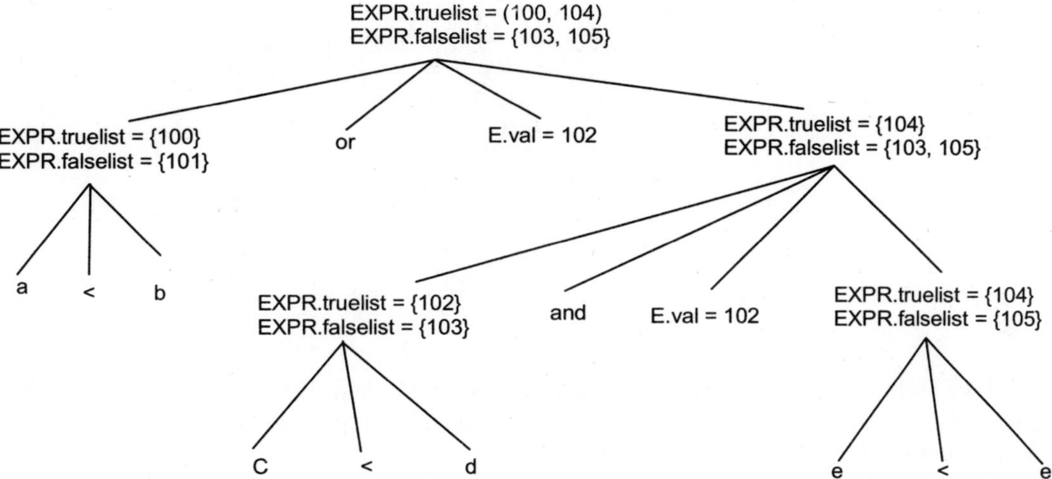

Figure 6.6: Annotated parse tree for example 6.14 using backpatching

6.7 STATIC SINGLE ASSIGNMENT FORM

Static single assignment form (often abbreviated as SSA form or SSA) is an intermediate representation (IR) in which every variable is assigned exactly once. Existing variables in the original IR are split into versions, new variables typically indicated by the original name with a subscript, so that every definition gets its own version. SSA was developed by Ron Cytron, Jeanne Ferrante, Barry Rosen, Mark Wegman, and Ken Zadeck, researchers at IBM in the 1980s.

Example 6.16:

Original code	In SSA form
y := 1 y := 2 x := y	y_1 := 1 y_2 := 2 x_1 := y_2

Converting to SSA

Converting ordinary code into SSA form is primarily a simple matter of replacing the target of each assignment with a new variable, and replacing each use of a variable with the "version" of the variable reaching that point. For example, consider the following control flow graph:

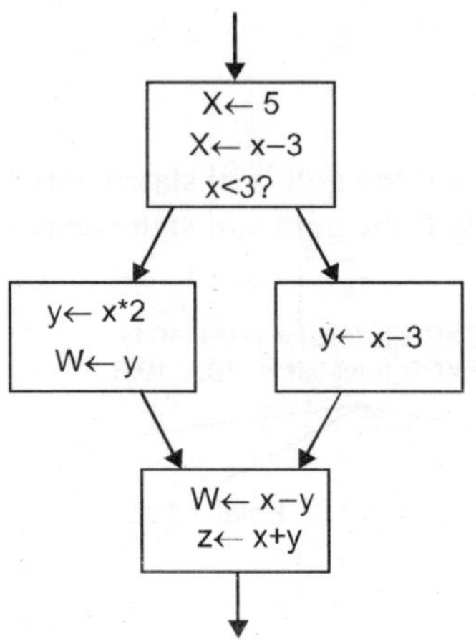

Figure 6.7: Control Flow Graph

Notice that we could change the name on the left side of "x ← x – 3", and change the following uses of x to use that new name, and the program would still do the same thing. We exploit this in SSA by creating two new variables, x1 and x2, each of which is assigned only once.

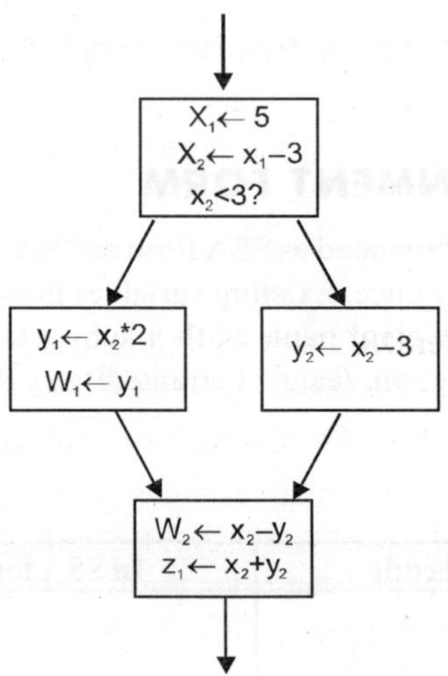

Figure 6.8: Step 1

One thing now remaining: the uses of y in the bottom block could be referring to either y1 or y2, depending on which way the control flow came from. So how do we know which one to use? The answer is that we add a special statement, called an ϕ (Phi) function, to the beginning of the last block. This statement will generate a new definition of y, y3, by "choosing" either y1 or y2, depending on which arrow control arrived from:

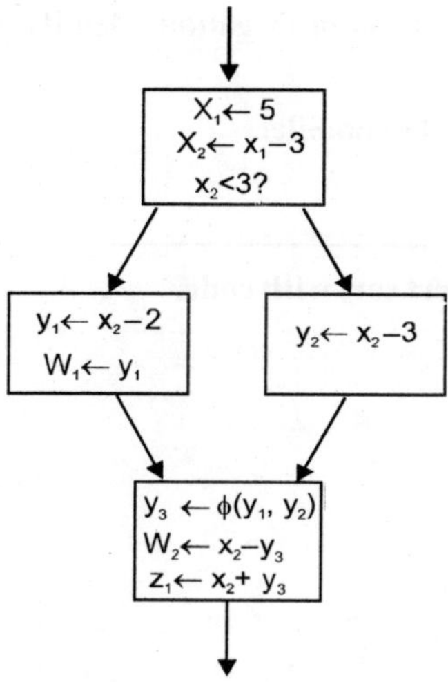

Figure 6.9: Step 2

Now, the uses of *y* in the last block can simply use y_3, and they'll obtain the correct value either way.

Compilers using SSA form

SSA form is a relatively recent development in the compiler community. As such, many older compilers only use SSA form for some part of the compilation or optimization process, but most do not rely on it. Examples of compilers that rely heavily on SSA form include:

- The LLVM Compiler Infrastructure uses SSA form for all scalar register values in its primary code representation.
- The open source SGI compiler ORC uses SSA form in its global scalar optimizer, though the code is brought into SSA form before and taken out of SSA form afterwards. ORC uses extensions to SSA form to represent memory in SSA form as well as scalar values.
- IBM's open source adaptive Java virtual machine, Jikes RVM, uses extended Array SSA, an extension of SSA that allows analysis of scalars, arrays, and object fields in a unified framework. Extended Array SSA analysis is only enabled at the maximum optimization level, which is applied to the most frequently executed portions of code.
- Sun Microsystem's Java HotSpot Virtual Machine uses an SSA-based intermediate language in its JIT compiler.
- Mono uses SSA in its JIT compiler called Mini.
- jackcc is an open-source compiler for the academic instruction set Jackal 3.0. It uses a simple 3-operand code with SSA for its intermediate representation. As an interesting variant, it replaces ϕ

functions with a so-called SAME instruction, which instructs the register allocator to place the two live ranges into the same physical register.

- Although not a compiler, the Boomerang decompiler uses SSA form in its internal representation. SSA is used to simplify expression propagation, identifying parameters and returns, preservation analysis, and more.
- Portable.NET uses SSA in its JIT compiler.

EXAMPLE

EX. : Write three address code for insert sort with code.

```
for(j=2;j<=n;j++)
{
        key=A[j];
        i=j–1;
        while(i>0 && A[i]>key)
{
        A[i+1] *= A[i];
        i = i–1;
        }
A[i+1]=key;
}
```

```
(1)     j=2
(2)     if j<=n goto 4
(3)     goto next
(4)     t2=4*j
(5)     t3=a[t2]
(6)     key=t3
(7)     t4=j–1
(8)     i=t4
(9)     if i>0 goto 11
(10)    goto 21
(11)    t5=4*i
(12)    t6=A[t5]
(13)    if t6>key goto 15
(14)    goto 21
(15)    t7=i+1
(16)    t8=t7
(17)    t9=4*t8
(18)    t10=A[t9]
(19)    t10=t6
(20)    t11=i–1
(21)    i=t11
(22)    goto 9
```

(23) t10=key
(24) t12=j+1
(25) j=t12
(26) goto 2
(next)

TRIBULATIONS

6.1 Give the sequence of three address code instruction for following in form of quadraples, triples, indirect triples

1. 2+3+4+5
2. 2+(3+(4+5))
3. a*b+a*b*c
4. a[a[i]]=b[i=2]

6.2 Give three address code for

1. read a
2. read b
3. if b =0 then
4. b=0;
5. else
6. do
   i. temp =b
   ii. v= a – a / b*b;
   iii. a= temp;
7. while (b=0)
8. write (a)

6.3 Design general target code patterns that suffice for do-while/repeat-until loops in languages like C and Pascal. If you have more than one possible implementation strategy, what criteria might you use to make the choice?

6.4 Consider new kind of programming language statement "alternate s1 with s2 and s3 end" where s1, s2, and s3 are arbitrary statements. An alternate statement executes s1 repeatedly with the executions of s1 followed first by s2, then by s3, then by s2 again, and so on. i.e., an execution trace looks like: s1, s2, s1, s3, s1, s2, s1,...Describe a general pattern of target machine code that could be used to implement an alternate statement.

6.5 Suppose that you also had to be able to implement skip statements with the following semantics. A skip statement executed within an alternate statement in s1 causes the current execution of s1 to terminate and the next execution of s1 to start *without* executing s2 or s3 first. That execution of s2 or s3 should get done the next time through. Describe how skip statements could be implemented.

6.6 Assembly for the following C code, using if-the-else-constructs:

1. switch (a)
2. {
3. case 1:

```
                    printf("a is true/n");
                    break;
        case 0:
                    printf("a is false/n");
                    break;
        dafault:
                    printf("a is not a boolean/n");
    }
```

6.7 Write a subroutine for if then else after drawing translation diagram.

6.8 Can you forecast any practical difficulties in using C as an intermediate language?

FURTHER READINGS AND REFERENCES

[1] Appel, Andrew W. (1999). *Modern Compiler Implementation in ML.* Cambridge University Press. Also available in Java and C 1998 versions.

[2] Cooper, Keith D.; & Torczon, Linda. (2003). *Engineering a Compiler.* Morgan Kaufmann.

[3] Muchnick, Steven S. (1997). *Advanced Compiler Design and Implementation.* Morgan Kaufmann.

[4] Richard A. Kelsey (March 1995). "*A Correspondence between Continuation Passing Style and Static Single Assignment Form*". ACM SIGPLAN Notices 30 (3): 13-22.

[5] Andrew W. Appel (April 1998). "*SSA is Functional Programming*". ACM SIGPLAN Notices 33 (4): 17-20.

CHAPTER 7

CODE OPTIMIZATION

CHAPTER HIGHLIGHTS

In computing, optimization is the process of modifying a system to make some aspect of it work more efficiently or use fewer resources. For instance, a computer program may be optimized so that it executes more rapidly, or is capable of operating within a reduced amount of memory storage, or draws less battery power (ie, in a portable computer). Optimization can occur at a number of levels. At the highest level the design may be optimized to make best use of the available resources. The implementation of this design will benefit from the use of efficient algorithms and the coding of these algorithms will benefit from the writing of good quality code. Use of an optimizing compiler can help ensure that the executable program is optimized. At the lowest level, it is possible to bypass the compiler completely and write assembly code by hand. With modern optimizing compilers and the greater complexity of recent CPUs, it takes great skill to write code that is better than the compiler can generate and few projects ever have to resort to this ultimate optimization step.

Optimization will generally focus on one or two of execution time, memory usage, disk space, bandwidth or some other resource. This will usually require a tradeoff— where one is optimized at the expense of others. For example, increasing the size of cache improves runtime performance, but also increases the memory consumption. Other common tradeoffs include code clarity and conciseness.

"The order in which the operations shall be performed in every particular case is a very interesting and curious question, on which our space does not permit us fully to enter. In almost every computation a great variety of arrangements for the succession of the processes is possible, and various considerations must influence the selection amongst them for the purposes of a Calculating Engine. One essential object is to choose that arrangement which shall tend to reduce to a minimum the time necessary for completing the calculation." - Ada Byron's notes on the analytical engine 1842.

"We should forget about small efficiencies, say about 97% of the time: premature optimization is the root of all evil. Yet we should not pass up our opportunities in that critical 3%." - Knuth

The optimizer (a program that does optimization) may have to be optimized as well. The compilation with the optimizer being turned on usually takes more time, though this is only a problem when the program is significantly large. In particular, for just-in-time compilers the performance of the optimizer is a key in improving execution speed. Usually spending more time can yield better code, but it is also the precious computer time that we want to save; thus in practice tuning the performance requires the trade-off between the time taken for optimization and the reduction in the execution time gained by optimizing code.

Compiler optimization is the process of tuning the output of a compiler to minimize some attribute (or maximize the efficiency) of an executable program. The most common requirement is to minimize the time taken to execute a program; a less common one is to minimise the amount of memory occupied, and the growth of portable computers has created. It has been shown that some code optimization problems are NP-complete. Now in this chapter we discuss about all types of optimizations and target of optimization. Now we are standing at fifth phase of compiler. Input to this phase is intermediate code of expressions from intermediate code generator as:

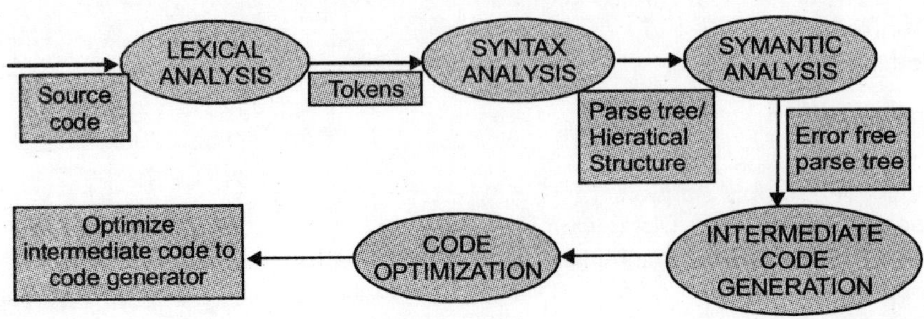

Figure 7.1

7.1 TYPES OF OPTIMIZATIONS

Techniques in optimization can be broken up among various **scopes** which affect anything from a single statement to an entire program. Some examples of scopes include:

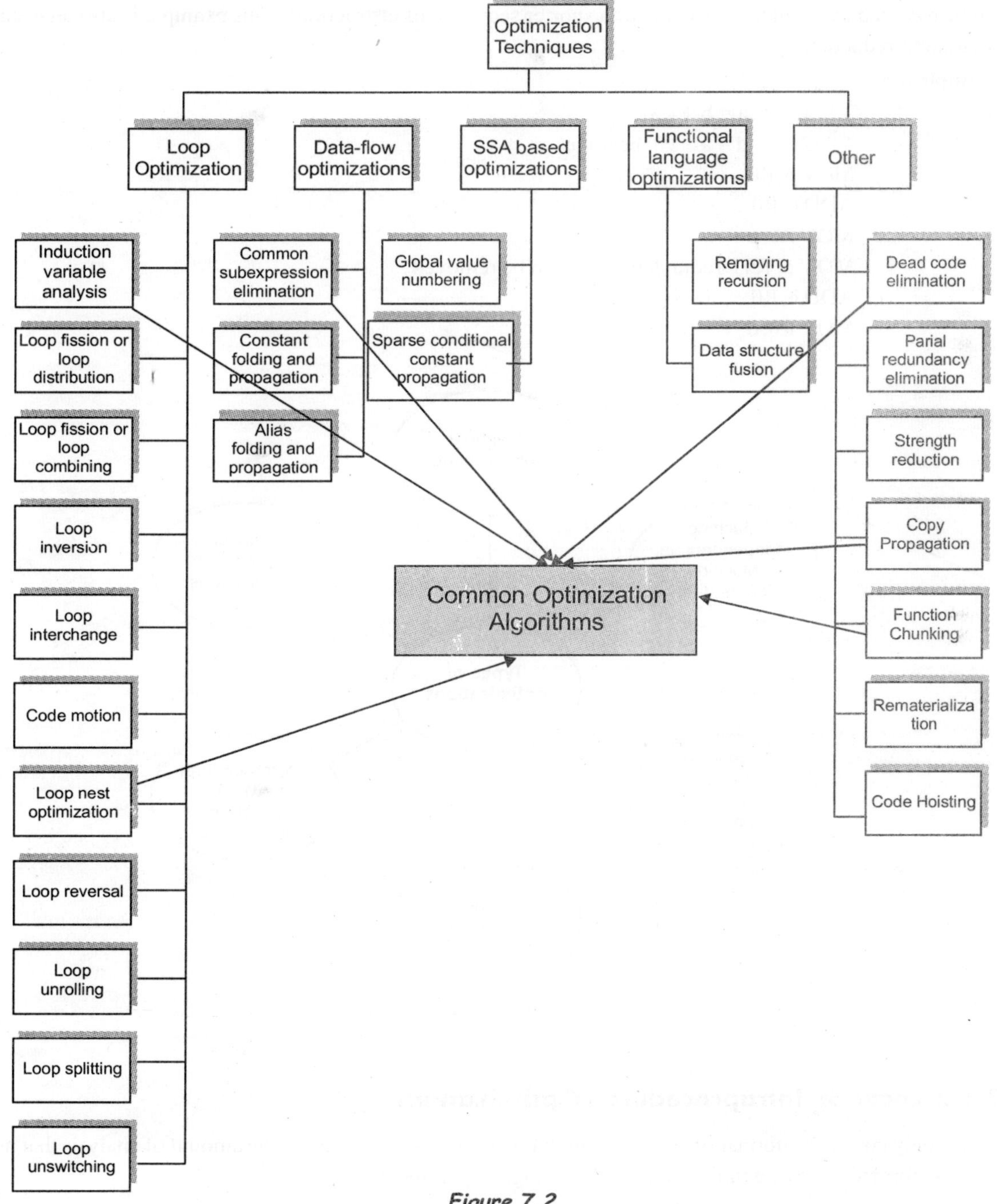

Figure 7.2

7.1.1 Peephole Optimizations

Usually performed late in the compilation process after machine code has been generated. This form of optimization examines a few adjacent instructions (like looking through a peephole at the code) to see whether they can be replaced by a single instruction or a shorter sequence of instructions. This example is also an instance of strength reduction.

Example 7.1:

1. a = b + c;
2. d = a + e ; becomes

```
MOV b, R0
ADD c, R0
MOV R0, a
MOV a, R0 # redundant load, can be removed
ADD e, R0
MOV R0, d
```

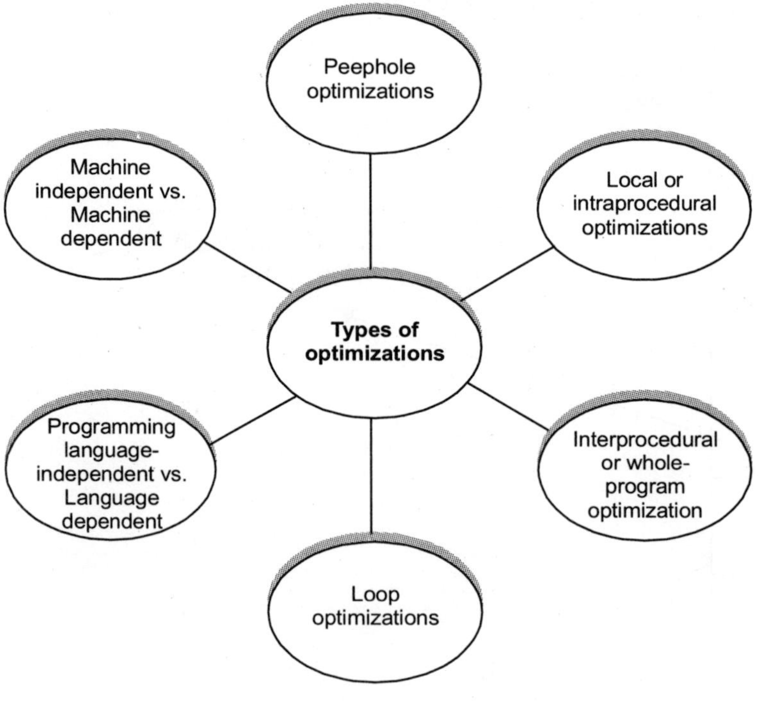

Figure 7.3

7.1.2 Local or Intraprocedural Optimizations

These only consider information local to a function definition. This reduces the amount of analysis that needs to be performed i.e.saving time and reducing storage requirements.

7.1.3 Interprocedural or Whole-Program Optimization

These analyse all of a programs source code. The greater quantity of information extracted means that optimizations can be more effective compared to when they only have access to local information (i.e., within a single function). This kind of optimization can also allow new techniques to be performed. For instance function inlining, where a call to a function is replaced by a copy of the function body.

7.1.4 Loop Optimizations

These act on the statements which make up a loop, such as a for loop. Loop optimizations can have a significant impact because many programs spend a large percentage of their time inside loops.

In addition to scoped optimizations there are two further general categories of optimization:

7.1.5 Programming Language-independent vs. Language-dependent

Most high-level languages share common programming constructs and abstractions — decision (if, switch, case), looping (for, while, repeat... until, do... while), encapsulation (structures, objects). Thus similar optimization techniques can be used across languages. However certain language features make some kinds of optimizations possible or difficult. For instance, the existence of pointers in C and C++ makes certain optimizations of array accesses difficult. Conversely, in some languages functions are not permitted to have "side effects". Therefore, if repeated calls to the same function with the same arguments are made, the compiler can immediately infer that results need only be computed once and the result referred to repeatedly.

7.1.6 Machine Independent vs. Machine Dependent

Many optimizations that operate on abstract programming concepts (loops, objects, structures) are independent of the machine targeted by the compiler. But many of the most effective optimizations are those that best exploit special features of the target platform.

7.2 AIM OF OPTIMIZATION

1. **Avoid redundancy:** If something has already been computed, it is generally better to store it and reuse it later, instead of recomputing it.
2. **Less code:** There is less work for the CPU, cache, and memory. So, likely to be faster.
3. **Straight line code/ fewer jumps:** Less complicated code. Jumps interfere with the prefetching of instructions, thus slowing down code.
4. **Code locality:** Pieces of code executed close together in time should be placed close together in memory, which increases spatial locality of reference.
5. **Extract more information from code**: The more information the compiler has, the better it can optimize.
6. **Avoid memory accesses:** Accessing memory, particularly if there is a cache miss, is much more expensive than accessing registers.
7. **Speed:** Improving the runtime performance of the generated object code. This is the most common optimisation.
8. **Space:** Reducing the size of the generated object code.
9. **Safety:** Reducing the possibility of data structures becoming corrupted (for example, ensuring that an illegal array element is not written to).

"Speed" optimizations make the code larger, and many "Space" optimizations make the code slower — this is known as the space-time tradeoff.

7.3 FACTORS AFFECTING OPTIMIZATION

7.3.1 The Machine Itself

Many of the choices about which optimizations can and should be done depend on the characteristics of the target machine. GCC is a compiler which exemplifies this approach.

7.3.2 The Architecture of the Target CPU

- ***Number of CPU registers:*** To a certain extent, the more registers, the easier it is to optimize for performance. Local variables can be allocated in the registers and not on the stack. Temporary/ intermediate results can be left in registers without writing to and reading back from memory.
- ***RISC vs CISC:*** CISC instruction sets often have variable instruction lengths, often have a larger number of possible instructions that can be used, and each instruction could take differing amounts of time. RISC instruction sets attempt to limit the variability in each of these: instruction sets are usually constant length, with few exceptions, there are usually fewer combinations of registers and memory operations, and the instruction issue rate is usually constant in cases where memory latency is not a factor. There may be several ways of carrying out a certain task, with CISC usually offering more alternatives than RISC.
- ***Pipelines:*** A pipeline is essentially an ALU broken up into an assembly line. It allows use of parts of the ALU for different instructions by breaking up the execution of instructions into various stages: instruction decode, address decode, memory fetch, register fetch, compute, register store, etc. One instruction could be in the register store stage, while another could be in the register fetch stage. Pipeline conflicts occur when an instruction in one stage of the pipeline depends on the result of another instruction ahead of it in the pipeline but not yet completed. Pipeline conflicts can lead to pipeline stalls: where the CPU wastes cycles waiting for a conflict to resolve.
- ***Number of functional units:*** Some CPUs have several ALUs and FPUs (Floating Point Units). This allows them to execute multiple instructions simultaneously. There may be restrictions on which instructions can pair with which other instructions and which functional unit can execute which instruction. They also have issues similar to pipeline conflicts.

7.3.3 The Architecture of the Machine

- **Cache Size (256 KB–4 MB) & type (direct mapped, 2-/4-/8-/16-way associative, fully associative):** Techniques like inline expansion may increase the size of the generated code and reduce code locality. The program may slow down drastically if an oft-run piece of code suddenly cannot fit in the cache. Also, caches which are not fully associative have higher chances of cache collisions even in an unfilled cache.
- **Cache/memory transfer rates:** These give the compiler an indication of the penalty for cache misses. This is used mainly in specialized applications.

7.4 BASIC BLOCK

A basic block is a straight-line piece of code without jump targets in the middle; jump targets, if any, start a block, and jumps end a block.

or

A sequence of instructions forms a basic block if the instruction in each position dominates, or always executes before, all those in later positions, and no other instruction executes between two instructions in the sequence.

Basic blocks are usually the basic unit to which compiler optimizations are applied in compiler theory. Basic blocks form the vertices or nodes in a control flow graph or they can be represented by **control flow graph.** The blocks to which control may transfer after reaching the end of a block are called that **block's successors**, while the blocks from which control may have come when entering a block are called that **block's predecessors**.

Instructions which begin a new basic block include

- Procedure and function entry points.
- Targets of jumps or branches.
- Instructions following some conditional branches.
- Instructions following ones that throw exceptions.
- Exception handlers.

Instructions that end a basic block include

- Unconditional and conditional branches, both direct and indirect.
- Returns to a calling procedure.
- Instructions which may throw an exception.
- Function calls can be at the end of a basic block if they may not return, such as functions which throw exceptions or special calls.

7.4.1 Algorithm 7.1 (Partition into Basic Block)

INPUT: A sequence of three address code

OUTPUT: A list of basic block.

FUNCTION:

1. Find out leaders as per following rules .
   - First statement of three address code is header.
   - Statement for which 'goto' statement indicate.
   - Statement next to 'goto' statement.
2. Every statement between first header to next header including first header and excluding next header form basic block.

Example 7.2: Basic Blocks are shown in example 7.1(Page 238).

7.5 CONTROL FLOW GRAPH

A **control flow graph (CFG)** is a representation, using graph notation, of all paths that might be traversed through a program during its execution. Each node in the graph represents a basic block and directed edges are used to represent jumps in the control flow. There are two specially designated blocks: the **entry block**, through which control enters into the flow graph, and the **exit block**, through which all control flow leaves.

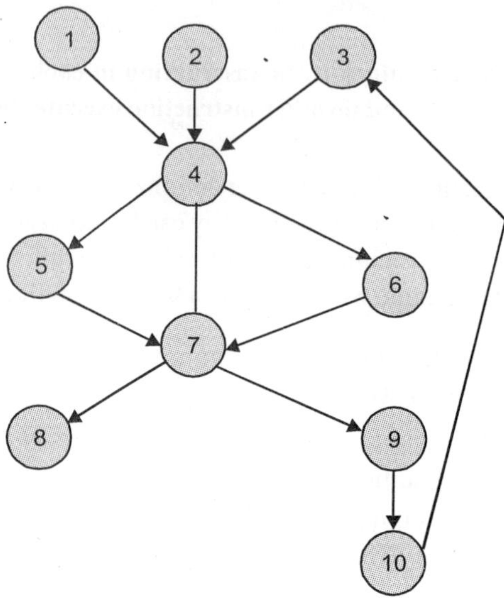

Figure 7.4

Terminology: These terms are commonly used when discussing control flow graphs

Entry block: Block through which all control flow enters the graph. (4 is entry block for 5, 6, 7, 8, 9, 0)

Exit block: Block through which all control flow leaves the graph. (8 is exit block)

Back edge: An edge that points to an ancestor in a depth-first (DFS) traversal of the graph. (edge from 0 to 3)

Critical edge: An edge which is neither the only edge leaving its source block, nor the only edge entering its destination block. These edges must be split (a new block must be created in the middle of the edge) in order to insert computations on the edge.

Abnormal edge: An edge whose destination is unknown. These edges tend to inhibit optimization. Exception handling constructs can produce them.

Impossible edge / Fake edge: An edge which has been added to the graph solely to preserve the property that the exit blocks post dominates all blocks. It cannot ever be traversed.

Dominator: Block M dominates block N written as M dom N if every path from the entry node to block N has to pass through block M or if every possible execution path from entry to N includes M. The entry block dominates all blocks. Dominator must satisfy three properties as:

(i) Reflexive: Due to every node dominates itself.

(ii) Transitive: If A dom B and B dom C then A dom C.

(iii) Antisymmetric : If A dom B and B dom A then A = B

4 dominates 7, 8, 9, 0 not 5 and 6 because there is an edge from 4 to 7 similar 5 dominates 5 also 6 dominates 6.

Post-dominator: Block M postdominates block N if every path from N to the exit has to pass through block M. The exit block postdominates all blocks. (7 is Postdominator for 8 and 9)

Immediate dominator: Block M immediately dominates block N written as M idom N if M dominates N, and there is no intervening block P such that M dominates P and P dominates N. In other words, M is the last dominator on any path from entry to N. Each block has a unique immediate dominator, if it has any at all. (7 is immediate dominator for 9 not for 0)

Immediate postdominator: Similar to immediate dominator.

Dominator tree: An ancillary data structure depicting the dominator relationships. There is an arc from Block M to Block N if M is an immediate dominator of N known as dominator tree.

Postdominator tree: Similar to dominator tree. This tree is rooted at the exit block.

Loop header: Loop header dominates all blocks in the loop body and sometimes called as the entry point of the loop.

(1, 2, 3 are loop header)

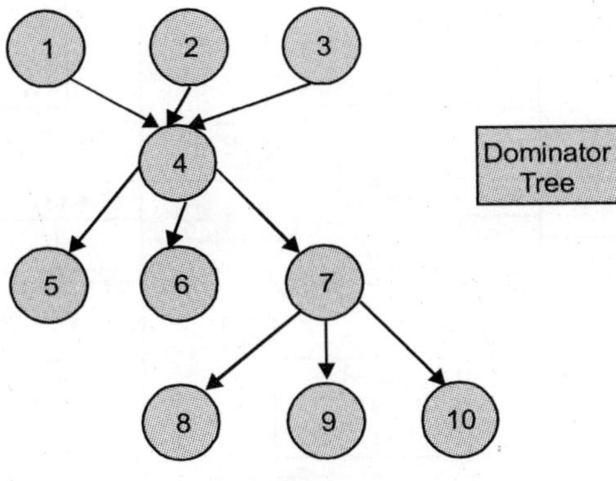

Figure 7.5

7.6 COMMON OPTIMIZATION ALGORITHMS

Common optimization algorithms deal with specific cases:

1. Common Sub-expression Elimination
2. Copy Propagation
3. Dead Code Elimination
4. Code motion
5. Induction variable Elimination
6. Reduction in strength
7. Function Chunking

Common Sub-expression elimination:

Common sub-expression elimination is a speed optimization that aims to reduce unnecessary recalculation by identifying, through code-flow, expressions (or parts of expressions) which will evaluate to the same value i.e. the recomputation of an expression can be avoided if the expression has previously been computed and the values of the operands have not changed since the previous computation.

Example 7.3: Consider the following program:

```
a = b + c
d = e + f
g = b + c
```

In the this example, the first and last statement's right hand side are identical and the value of the operands do not change between the two statements; thus this expression can be considered as having a common sub-expression.

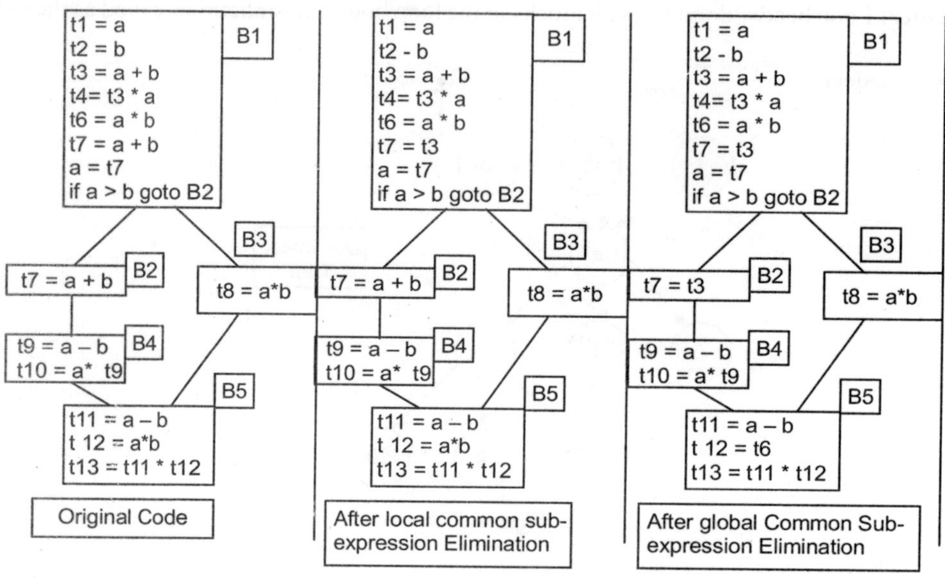

Figure 7.6

The common sub-expression can be avoided by storing its value in a temporary variable which can cache its result. After applying this Common Sub-expression Elimination technique the program becomes:

$t_0 = b + c$
$a = t_0$
$d = e + f$
$g = t_0$

Thus in the last statement the recomputation of the expression b + c is avoided. Compiler writers distinguish two kinds of CSE:

- **Local Common Subexpression Elimination** works within a single basic block and is thus a simple optimization to implement.
- **Global Common Subexpression Elimination** works on an entire procedure, and relies on dataflow analysis which expressions are available at which points in a procedure.

Copy propagation

Copy propagation is the process of replacing the occurrences of targets of direct assignments with their values. A direct assignment is an instruction of the form x = y, which simply assigns the value of y to x.

From the following code:

y=x

z=3+y

Copy propagation would yield:

z=3+x

Copy propagation often makes use of reaching definitions, use-def chains* and def-use chains+ when computing which occurrences of the target may be safely replaced. If all upwards exposed uses of the target may be safely modified, the assignment operation may be eliminated. Copy propagation is a useful "clean up" optimization frequently used after other optimizations have already been run. Some optimizations require that copy propagation be run afterward in order to achieve an increase in efficiency. Copy propagation also classified as local and global copy propagation.

- Local copy propagation is applied to an individual basic block.
- Global copy propagation is applied to all code's basic block.

Dead code elimination

Removation of instructions that will not affect the behaviour of the program, for example definitions which have no uses or code which will never execute regardless of input called dead code and this process is known as dead code elimination which is a size optimization (although it also produces some speed improvement) that aims to remove logically impossible statements from the generated object code. This technique is common in debugging to optionally activate blocks of code; using an optimizer with dead code elimination eliminates the need for using a preprocessor to perform the same task.

Example 7.4: Consider the following program:

```
a = 5
if (a != 5) {
  // Some complicated calculation
}
...
```

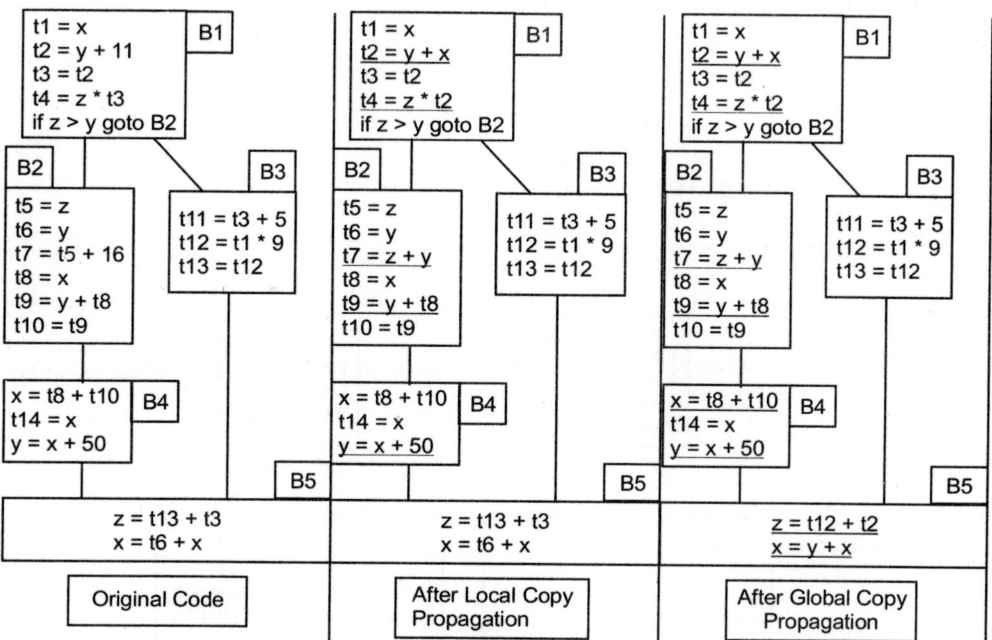

Figure 7.7

It is obvious that the complicated calculation will never be performed; since the last value assigned to **a** before the **if** statement is a constant, we can calculate the result at compile-time. Simple substitution of arguments produces if (5 != 5), which is **false**. Since the body of if(false) statement will never execute - it is dead code we can rewrite the code:

```
a = 5
// Some statements
```

Example 7.5:

```
int foo()
{
    int a = 24;
    int b = 25; # Assignment to dead variable
    int c;
    c = a << 2;
    return c;
    b = 24; # Unreachable code
}
```

The variable b is assigned a value after a return statement, which makes it impossible to get to. That is, since code execution is linear, and there is no conditional expression wrapping the return statement, any code after the return statement cannot possibly be executed. Furthermore, if we eliminate that assignment, then we can see that the variable b is never used at all, except for its declaration and initial assignment. Depending on the aggressiveness of the optimizer, the variable b might be eliminated entirely from the generated code.

Example 7.6:

```
int main() {
int a = 5;
int b = 6;
int c;
c = a * (b >> 1);
if (0) {    /* DEBUG */
  printf("%d\n", c);
}
return c;
}
```

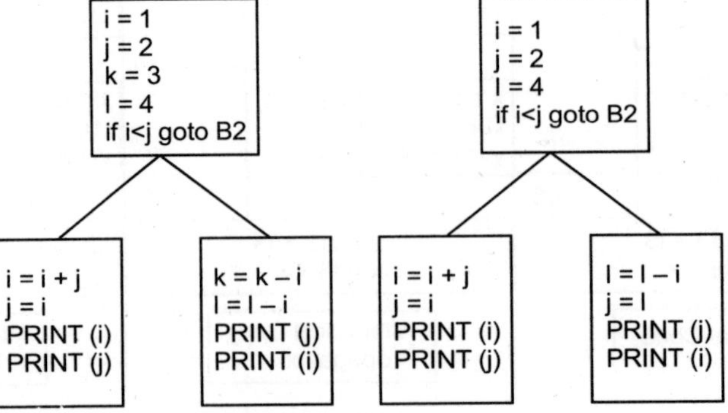

Figure 7.8

Because the expression 0 will always evaluate to false, the code inside the if statement can never be executed, and dead code elimination would remove it entirely from the optimized program.

Code motion : This optimization technique mainly deals to reduce the number of source code lines in the program, which could be moved to before the loop (if the loop always terminates), or after the loop, without affecting the semantics of the program as a result it is executed less often, providing a speedup. For correct implementation, this technique must be used with loop inversion, because not all code is safe to be hoisted outside the loop.

Example 7.7: Consider the code below

```
for(i=0;i<=10;i++)
{
  a = a + c;
}
```

In the above mentioned code, a = a + c can be moved out of the 'for' loop.

Example 7.8: If we consider the following code

Original loop	After

while (j < maximum – 1)
{ j = j + (4+array[k])*pi+5; }
	int maxval = maximum – 1;
	int calcval = (4+array[k])*pi+5;
	while (j < maxval){ j = j + calcval; }

The calculation of maximum – 1 and (4+array[k])*pi+5 can be moved outside the loop, and precalculated, resulting in something similar to:

Induction variable elimination: An induction variable is a variable that gets increased or decreased by a fixed amount on every iteration of a loop. A common compiler optimization is to recognize the existence of induction variables and replace them with simpler computations.

Example 7.9:

(i) In the following loop, i and j are induction variables:

Original loop	After

for (i=0; i < 10; ++i) {
j = 17 * i;
}
	j = 0;
	for (i=0; i < 10; ++i) {
	j = j + 17;}

(ii) In some cases, it is possible to reverse this optimization in order to remove an induction variable from the code entirely.

Original loop	After

extern int sum;
int foo(int n) {
int i, j;
j = 5;
	extern int sum;
	int foo(int n) {
	int i;
	for (i=0; i < n; ++i) {

Contd...

for (i=0; i<n; ++i) {
j += 2;
sum += j;
}
return sum;
}
	sum += (5 + 2*i);
	}
	return sum;
	}

This function's loop has two induction variables: i and j either one can be rewritten as a linear function of the other.

7.6.1 Algorithm 7.2 (Reduction in Strength)

Strength reduction is a compiler optimization where replacing a complex or difficult or expensive operations with simpler ones. In a procedural programming language this would apply to an expression involving a loop variable and in a declarative language it would apply to the argument of a recursive function. One of the most important uses of the strength reduction is computing memory addresses inside a loop. Several peephole optimizations also fall into this category, such as replacing division by a constant with multiplication by its reciprocal, converting multiplies into a series of bit-shifts and adds, and replacing large instructions with equivalent smaller ones that load more quickly.

Example 7.10: Multiplication can be replaced by addition.

Original loop	After

`void foo(int *img)`
`{`
`for(int y=0; y<320; y++)`
`for(int x=0; x<200; x++)`
`img[y * 320 + x] = 0;`
`}`
	`void foo(int *img)`
	`{`
	`for(int y=0; y<320; y++)`
	`for(int x=0; x<200; x++)`
	`img[y + 320 + x] = 0;`
	`}`

Function chunking: Function chunking is a compiler optimization for improving code locality. Profiling information is used to move rarely executed code outside of the main function body. This allows for memory pages with rarely executed code to be swapped out.

7.7 PROBLEMS OF OPTIMIZATION

As compiler technologies have improved, good compilers can often generate better code than human programmers and good post pass optimizers can improve highly hand-optimized code even further. Compiler optimization is the key for obtaining efficient code, because instruction sets are so compact that it is hard for a human to manually schedule or combine small instructions to get efficient results. However, optimizing compilers are by no means perfect. There is no way that a compiler can guarantee that, for all program source code, the fastest (or smallest) possible equivalent compiled program is output. Additionally, there are a number of other more practical issues with optimizing compiler technology:

- Usually, an optimizing compiler only performs low-level, localized changes to small sets of operations. In other words, high-level inefficiency in the source program (such as an inefficient algorithm) remains unchanged.

- Modern third-party compilers usually have to support several objectives. In so doing, these compilers are a 'jack of all trades' yet master of none.
- A compiler typically only deals with a small part of an entire program at a time, at most a module at a time and usually only a procedure; the result is that it is unable to consider at least some important contextual information.
- The overhead of compiler optimization. Any extra work takes time, whole-program optimization (interprocedural optimization) is very costly.
- The interaction of compiler optimization phases: what combination of optimization phases are optimal, in what order and how many times?

Work to improve optimization technology continues. One approach is the use of so-called **"post pass" optimizers**. These tools take the executable output by an "optimizing" compiler and optimize it even further. As opposed to compilers which optimize intermediate representations of programs, post pass optimizers work on the assembly language level.

7.8 DATA FLOW ANALYSIS

Data flow analysis is a technique for gathering information about the possible set of values calculated at various points in a computer program. A program's control flow graph is used to determine those parts of a program to which a particular value assigned to a variable might propagate. The information gathered is often used by compilers when optimizing a program. A canonical example of a data flow analysis is reaching definitions.

A simple way to perform data flow analysis of programs is to set up **data flow equations** for each node of the control flow graph and solve them by repeatedly calculating the output from the input locally at each node until the whole system stabilizes, i.e., it reaches a fixpoint. This general approach was developed by **Gary Kildall** while teaching at the **Naval Postgraduate School.** Data flow analysis analysis can be partitioned into two parts as:

- Local Data Flow Analysis : Data flow analysis that is applied to only one basic block.
- Global Data Flow Analysis : Data flow analysis that is applied to all function at a time.

7.8.1 Causes that Effect Data Flow Analysis

Data flow analysis is inherently flow-sensitive and typically path-insensitive. Some causes are :

- A flow-sensitive analysis takes into account the order of statements in a program. For example, a flow-insensitive pointer alias analysis may determine "variables x and y may refer to the same location", while a flow-sensitive analysis may determine "after statement 20, variables x and y may refer to the same location".
- A path-sensitive analysis only considers valid paths through the program. For example, if two operations at different parts of a function are guarded by equivalent predicates, the analysis must only consider paths where both operations execute or neither operation executes. Path-sensitive analyses are necessarily flow-sensitive.
- A context-sensitive analysis is an interprocedural analysis that takes the calling context into account when analyzing the target of a function call. For example, consider a function that accepts a file handle and a boolean parameter that determines whether the file handle should be closed before the function returns. A context-sensitive analysis of any callers of the function should take into account the value of the boolean parameter to determine whether the file handle will be closed when the function returns.

7.8.2 Data Flow Equation

Data flow analysis of programs is to set up **data flow equations** for each node of the control flow graph. General form of data flow equation is :

$$OUT[S] = GEN[S] \cup (IN[S] - KILL[S])$$

We define the GEN and KILL sets as follows:

$$GEN[d: y \leftarrow f(x_1, ..., x_n)] = \{d\}$$

$$KILL[d: y \leftarrow f(x_1, ..., x_n)] = \{DEFS[y] - \{d\}$$

Where DEFS[y] is the set of all definitions that assign to the variable y. Here d is a unique label attached to the assigning instruction.

7.8.3 Causes that Effect Data Flow Equations

The efficiency of iteratively solving data flow equations is influenced by the order at which local nodes are visited and whether the data flow equations are used for forward or backward data flow analysis over the CFG. In the following, a few iteration orders for solving data flow equations are discussed.

- **Random order:** This iteration order is not aware whether the data flow equations solve a forward or backward data-flow problem. Therefore, the performance is relatively poor compared to specialized iteration orders.
- **Post order:** This is a typical iteration order for backward data flow problems. In postorder iteration a node is visited after all its successor nodes have been visited. Typically, the postorder iteration is implemented with the depth-first strategy.
- **Reverse post order:** This is a typical iteration order for forward data flow problems. In reverse-postorder iteration a node is visited before all its successor nodes have been visited, except when the successor is reached by a back edge.

7.8.4 Reaching Definition

A definition of a variable 'x' is a statement that assigns or may assign a value to 'x'. The most common forms of definition are assignments to 'x' and the statements that read a value from input device and store it in 'x'. These statements certainly define value for 'x' and they are referred to as unambiguous definition of 'x'. a variable 'z' reaches to a point 'y' if there is a path from the point following z to y such that 'z' is not killed along that path. The most common forms of ambiguous definition of 'x' are :

- A call of a procedure with 'x' as a parameter or procedure that access 'x'.
- An assignment through a pointer that could refer to 'x'.

A definition of variable is said to reach a given point in a function if there is an execution path from the definition to that point. Reaching definition can be done in classic form know as an 'iterative forward bit vector problem' – 'iterative' because we construct a collection of data flow equation to represent the information flow and solve it by iteration from an appropriate set of initial values; 'forward' because information flow is in the direction of execution along the control flow edge in the program; 'bit vector' because we can represent each definition by a 1 or a 0.

7.8.5 Data Flow Analysis of Structured Program

This concept include some grammar for structured program and control flow graph for them by which we calculate the data flow equations.

1. $S \rightarrow id := E \mid S ; S \mid if\ E\ then\ S\ else\ S \mid do\ S\ while\ E$
2. $E \rightarrow \text{id} + \text{id} \mid \text{id}$

7.8.6 Reducible Flow Graph

Reducible results from several kinds of transformation that can be applied to control flow graph that collapse sub graphs into single nodes and reduce the control flow graph to simpler graph.

A control flow graph (V, E) is reducible iff E can be partitioned into disjoint sets EF (forward edge set) and back edge (EB) i.e. (V, EF) froms a DAG in which each node can be reached from entry node.

Some control flow graph pattern makes flow graph irreducible called improper graph.

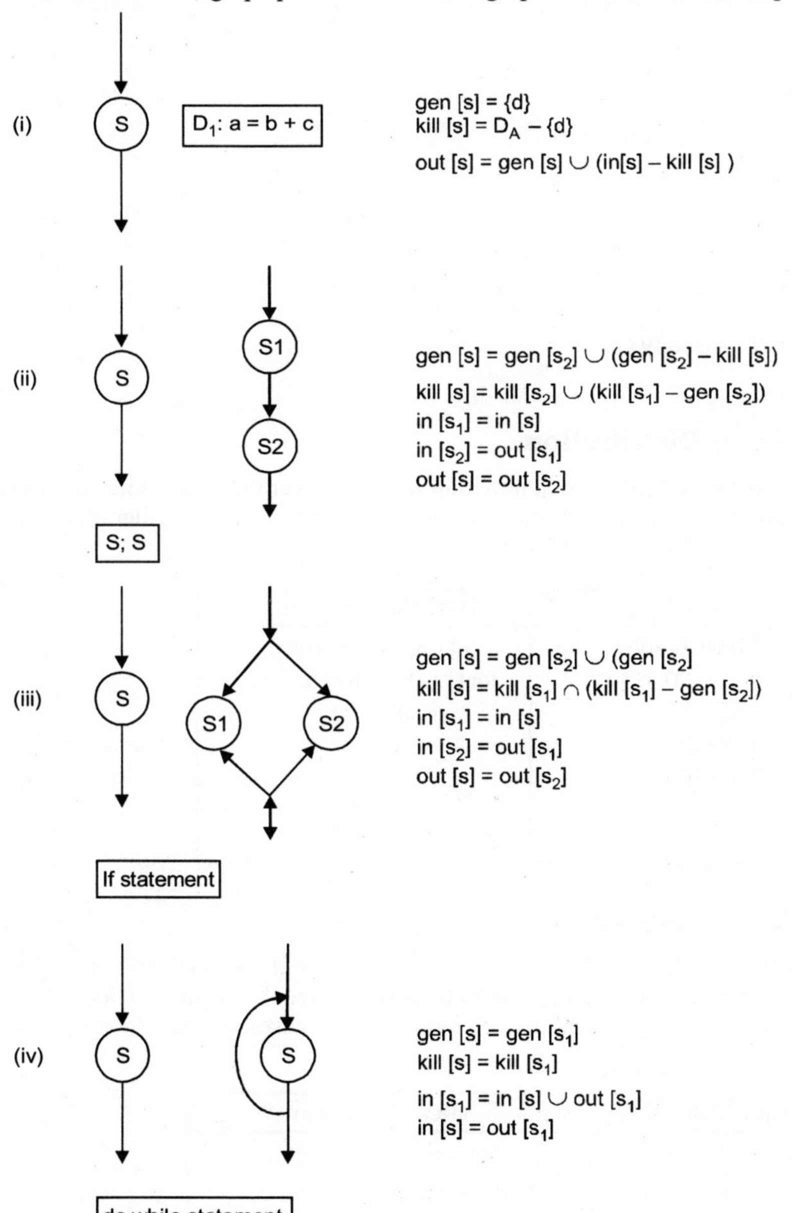

gen [s] = {d}
kill [s] = D_A – {d}
out [s] = gen [s] ∪ (in[s] – kill [s])

gen [s] = gen [s_2] ∪ (gen [s_2] – kill [s])
kill [s] = kill [s_2] ∪ (kill [s_1] – gen [s_2])
in [s_1] = in [s]
in [s_2] = out [s_1]
out [s] = out [s_2]

gen [s] = gen [s_2] ∪ (gen [s_2]
kill [s] = kill [s_1] ∩ (kill [s_1] – gen [s_2])
in [s_1] = in [s]
in [s_2] = out [s_1]
out [s] = out [s_2]

gen [s] = gen [s_1]
kill [s] = kill [s_1]
in [s_1] = in [s] ∪ out [s_1]
in [s] = out [s_1]

7.9 LOOP OPTIMIZATION

Some optimization techniques primarily designed to operate on loops include:

- Code Motion
- Induction variable analysis
- Loop fission or loop distribution
- Loop fusion or loop combining
- Loop inversion
- Loop interchange
- Loop nest optimization
- Loop unrolling
- Loop splitting
- Loop unswitching

7.9.1 Code Motion

Similar to section 7.6.

7.9.2 Induction Variable Analysis

Similar to section 7.6.

7.9.3 Loop Fission or Loop Distribution

Loop fission is a technique attempting to break a loop into multiple loops over the same index range but each taking only a part of the loop's body. The goal is to break down large loop body into smaller ones to achieve better data locality. It is the reverse action to loop fusion.

Original loop	After loop fission

int i, a[100], b[100];
for (i = 0; i < 100; i++) {
a[i] = 1;
b[i] = 2;}
for (i = 0; i < 100; i++) {
b[i] = 2;
}
	int i, a[100], b[100];
	for (i = 0; i < 100; i++) {
	a[i] = 1;
	}

7.9.4 Loop Fusion or Loop Combining

Loop fusion is a loop transformation, which replaces multiple loops with a single one but don't always improve the run-time performance, due to architectures that provide better performance if there are two loops rather than one, for example due to increased data locality within each loop. In those cases, a single loop may be transformed into two.

Original loop	After loop fusion

int i, a[100], b[100];
for (i = 0; i < 100; i++) {
a[i] = 1;
	int i, a[100], b[100];
	for (i = 0; i < 100; i++) {
	a[i] = 1;

Contd...

}
 for (i = 0; i < 100; i++) {
 b[i] = 2;}
	b[i] = 2;
	 }

7.9.5 Loop Inversion

Loop inversion is a loop transformation, which replaces a while loop by an if block containing a do...while loop.

Original loop	After loop inversion

int i, a[100];
 i = 0;
 while (i < 100) {
 a[i] = 0;
 i++;
 }
	int i, a[100];
	 i = 0;
	 if (i < 100) {
	 do {
	 a[i] = 0;
	 i++;} while (i < 100);
	 }

At a first glance, this seems like a bad idea: there's more code so it probably takes longer to execute. However, most modern CPUs use a pipeline for executing instructions. By nature, any jump in the code causes a pipeline stall. Let's watch what happens in Assembly-like Three address code version of the above code:

```
        i := 0
L1:     if i >= 100 goto L2
        a[i] := 0
        i := i + 1
        goto L1
L2:
```

If *i* had been initialized at 100, the order of instructions at runtime would have been:

```
1: if i >= 100
2: goto L2
```

On the other hand, if we looked at the order of instructions at the moment when *i* was assigned value 99, we would have seen:

```
1: goto L1
2: if i >= 100
3: a[i] := 0
4: i := i + 1
5: goto L1
6: if i >= 100
7: goto L2
8: <<at L2>>
```

Now, let's look at the optimized version:

```
        i := 0
        if i >= 100 goto L2
L1:     a[i] := 0
        i := i + 1
        if i < 100 goto L1
L2:
```

Again, let's look at the order of instructions executed for *i* equal 100

```
if i >= 100
goto L2
```

We didn't waste any cycles compared to the original version. Now again jump into when *i* was assigned value 99:

```
if i < 100
goto L1
a[i] := 0
i := i + 1
if i < 100
<<at L2>>
```

As you can see, two *gotos* (and thus, two pipeline stalls) have been eliminated in the execution.

7.9.6 Loop Interchange

Loop interchange is the process of exchanging the order of two iteration variables. When the loop variables index into an array then loop interchange can improve locality of reference, depending on the array's layout. One major purpose of loop interchange is to improve the cache performance for accessing array elements. Cache misses occur if the contiguously accessed array elements within the loop come from a different cache line. Loop interchange can help prevent this. The effectiveness of loop interchange depends on and must be considered in light of the cache model used by the underlying hardware and the array model used by the compiler. It is not always safe to exchange the iteration variables due to dependencies between statements for the order in which they must execute. In order to determine whether a compiler can safely interchange loops, dependence analysis is required.

Original loop	After loop inversion
for i from 0 to 10 for j from 0 to 20 a[i,j] = i + j	for j from 0 to 20 for i from 0 to 10 a[i,j] = i + j

Example 7.11:

```
do i = 1, 10000
  do j = 1, 1000
    a(i) = a(i) + b(i,j) * c(i)
  end do
end do
```

Loop interchange on this example can improve the cache performance of accessing b(i,j), but it will ruin the reuse of a(i) and c(i) in the inner loop, as it introduces two extra loads (for a(i) and for c(i)) and one extra store (for a(i)) during each iteration. As a result, the overall performance may be degraded after loop interchange.

7.9.7 Loop Nest Optimization

To ever-smaller processes making it possible to put very fast fully pipelined floating-point units onto commodity CPUs. But delivering that performance is also crucially dependent on compiler transformations that reduce the need for the high-bandwidth memory system.

Example 7.12: Matrix Multiply

Many large mathematical operations on computers end up spending much of their time doing matrix multiplication. Examining this loop nest can be quite instructive. The operation is:

C = A*B

where A, B, and C are NxN arrays. Subscripts, for the following description, are in the form C[row][column].

The basic loop is:

```
for( i=0; i < N; i++ )
  for( j=0; j < N; j++ ) {
    C[i][j] = 0;
    for( k=0; k < N; k++ )
      C[i][j] += A[k][j] * B[i][k];
  }
```

There are three problems to solve:

- Floating point additions take some number of cycles to complete. In order to keep an adder with multiple cycle latency busy, the code must update multiple accumulators in parallel.
- Machines can typically do just one memory operation per multiply-add, so values loaded must be reused at least twice.
- Typical PC memory systems can only sustain 18-byte doubleword per 10-30 double-precision multiply-adds, so values loaded into the cache must be reused many times.

The original loop calculates the result for one entry in the result matrix at a time. By calculating a small block of entries simultaneously, the following loop reuses each loaded value twice, so that the inner loop has four loads and four multiply-adds, thus solving problem #2. By carrying four accumulators simultaneously, this code can keep a single floating point adder with a latency of 4 busy nearly all the time (problem #1). However, the code does not address the third problem.

```
for( i=0; i < N; i += 2 )
  for( j=0; j < N; j +=2 ) {
    acc00 = acc01 = acc10 = acc11 = 0;
    for( k=0; k < N; k++ ) {
      acc00 += A[k][j+0] * B[i+0][k];
      acc01 += A[k][j+1] * B[i+0][k];
      acc10 += A[k][j+0] * B[i+1][k];
      acc11 += A[k][j+1] * B[i+1][k];
    }
    C[i+0][j+0] = acc00;
    C[i+0][j+1] = acc01;
    C[i+1][j+0] = acc10;
    C[i+1][j+1] = acc11;
  }
```

This code has had both the i and j iterations blocked by a factor of two, and had both the resulting two-iteration inner loops completely unrolled. This code would run quite acceptably on a Cray Y-MP, which can sustain 0.8 multiply-adds per memory operation to main memory. The Y-MP was built in the early 1980s. A machine like a 2.8 GHz Pentium 4, built in 2003, has slightly less memory bandwidth and vastly better floating point, so that it can sustain 16.5 multiply-adds per memory operation. As a result, the code above will run slower on the 2.8 GHz Pentium 4 than on the 166 MHz Y-MP!

7.9.8 Loop Unwinding (or Loop Unrolling)

Loop unwinding, also known as loop unrolling, is a technique for optimizing, the idea is to save time by reducing the number of overhead instructions that the computer has to execute in a loop, thus improving the cache hit rate and reducing branching. To achieve this, the instructions that are called in multiple iterations of the loop are combined into a single iteration. This will speed up the program if the overhead instructions of the loop impair performance significantly.

The major side effects of loop unrolling are:

(a) the increased register usage in a single iteration to store temporary variables, which may hurt performance.

(b) the code size expansion after the unrolling, which is undesirable for embedded applications.

Example 7.13:

A procedure in a computer program needs to delete 100 items from a collection. This is accomplished by means of a for-loop which calls the function. If this part of the program is to be optimized, and the overhead of the loop requires significant resources, loop unwinding can be used to speed it up.

Original loop	After

for (int x = 0; x < 100; x++)
{
delete(x);
}
	for (int x = 0; x < 100; x += 5)
	{
	delete(x);
	delete(x+1);
	delete(x+2);
	delete(x+3);
	delete(x+4);
	}

As a result of this optimization, the new program has to make only 20 loops, instead of 100. There are now 1/5 as many jumps and conditional branches that need to be taken, which over many iterations would be a great improvement in the loop administration time while the loop unrolling makes the code size grow from 3 lines to 7 lines and the compiler has to allocate more registers to store variables in the expanded loop iteration.

7.9.9 Loop Splitting

Loop splitting / loop peeling that attempts to simplify a loop or eliminate dependencies by breaking it into multiple loops which have the same bodies but iterate over different contiguous portions of the index range. A useful special case is loop peeling, which can simplify a loop with a problematic first iteration by performing that iteration separately before entering the loop.

Example 7.14:

Original loop	After

`for i from 1 to 100 do`
`x[i] = x[1] + y[i];`
	`x[1] = x[1] + y[1]`
	`for i from 2 to 100 do`
	`x[i] = x[1] + y[i];`

7.9.10 Loop Unswitching

Loop unswitching moves a conditional inside a loop outside of it by duplicating the loop's body, and placing a version of it inside each of the if and else clauses of the conditional. This can improve the parallelization of the loop. Since modern processors can operate fast on vectors this increases the speed.

Example 7.15:

Suppose we want to add the two arrays x and y (vectors) and also do something depending on the variable w. The conditional inside this loop makes it hard to safely parallelize this loop. After unswitching this becomes:

Original loop	After

for i to 1000 do
x[i]=x[i]+y[i];
if (w) then y[i]=0;
end_for;
	if (w) then
	for i to 1000 do
	x[i]=x[i]+y[i];
	y[i]=0;
	end_for;
	else
	for i to 1000 do
	x[i]=x[i]+y[i];
	end_for
	end_if;

Each of these new loops can be separately optimized. Note that loop unswitching will double the amount of code generated.

7.10 DATA FLOW OPTIMIZATION

Data flow optimizations, based on Data flow analysis, primarily depend on how certain properties of data are propagated by control edges in the control flow graph. Some of these include:

- Common Subexpression elimination
- Constant folding and propagation
- Aliasing.

7.10.1 Common Subexpression Elimination

Similar to section 7.6.

7.10.2 Constant Folding and Propagation

Constant folding and constant propagation are related optimization techniques used by many modern compilers. A more advanced form of constant propagation known as sparse conditional constant propagation may be utilized to simultaneously remove dead code and more accurately propagate constants.

Constant folding is the process of simplifying constant expressions at compile time. Terms in constant expressions are typically simple literals, such as the integer values and variables whose values are never modified or explicit variables. Constant folding can be done in a compiler's front end on intermediate representation, then that represents the high-level source language, before it is translated into three-address code, or in the back end. Consider the statement:

i = 320 * 200 * 32;

Most modern compilers would not actually generate two multiply instructions and a store for this statement. Instead, they identify constructs such as these, and substitute the computed values at compile time (in this case, 2,048,000), usually in the intermediate representation.

Constant propagation is the process of substituting the values of known constants in expressions at compile time. A typical compiler might apply constant folding now, to simplify the resulting expressions, before attempting further propagation.

Original loop	After constant propagation

`int x = 14;`
`int y = 7 - x / 2;`
`return y * (28 / x + 2);`
	`int x = 14;`
	`int y = 7 - 14 / 2;`
	`return y * (28 / 14 + 2);`

Example 7.16:

Original loop	After constant folding & propagation

`int a = 30;`
`int b = 9 - a / 5;`
`int c;`
`c = b * 4;`
`if (c > 10){`
`c = c - 10;`
`}`
`return c * (60 / a);`
	`int a = 30;`
	`int b = 3;`
	`int c;`
	`c = b * 4;`
	`if (c > 10){`
	`c = c - 10;`
	`}`
	`return c * 2;`

As a and b have been simplified to constants and their values substituted everywhere they occurred, the compiler now applies dead code elimination to discard them, reducing the code further:

```
int c;
c = 12;
if(12 > 10) {
  c = 2;
}
return c * 2;
```

7.10.3 Aliasing

Aliasing is a term that generally means that one variable or some reference, when changed, has an indirectly effect on some other data. For example in the presence of pointers, it is difficult to make any optimizations at all, since potentially any variable can have been changed when a memory location is assigned to.

Example 7.17:

(i) ***Array bounds checking:*** C programming language does not perform array bounds checking. If an array is created on the stack, with a variable laid out in memory directly beside that array, one could index outside that array and then directly change that variable by changing the relevant array element. For example, if we have a int array of size ten (for this example's sake, calling it vector), next to another int variable (call it i), vector [10] would be aliased to i if they are adjacent in memory.

This is possible in some implementations of C because an array is in reality a pointer to some location in memory, and array elements are merely offsets off that memory location. Since C has no bounds checking, indexing and addressing outside of the array is possible. Note that the aforementioned aliasing behaviour is implementation specific. Some implementations may leave space between arrays and variables on the stack, for instance, to minimize possible aliasing effects. C programming language specifications do not specify how data is to be laid out in memory.

(ii) ***Aliased pointers:*** Another variety of aliasing can occur in any language that can refer to one location in memory with more than one name .See the C example of the xor swap algorithm that is a function; it assumes the two pointers passed to it are distinct, but if they are in fact equal (or aliases of each other), the function fails. This is a common problem with functions that accept pointer arguments, and their tolerance (or the lack thereof) for aliasing must be carefully documented, particularly for functions that perform complex manipulations on memory areas passed to them.

Specified Aliasing

Controlled aliasing behaviour may be desirable in some cases. It is common practice in FORTRAN. The Perl programming language specifies, in some constructs, aliasing behaviour, such as in for each loops. This allows certain data structures to be modified directly with less code. For example,

```
my @array = (1, 2, 3);
foreach my $element (@array) {
    # Increment $element, thus automatically
    # modifying @array, as $element is *aliased*
    # to one of @array's elements.
    $element++;
}
print "@array\n";
```

will print out "2 3 4" as a result. If one would want to bypass aliasing effects, one could copy the contents of the index variable into another and change the copy.

Conflicts With Optimization

(i) Many times optimizers have to make conservative assumptions about variables in the presence of pointers. For example, a constant propagation process which knows that the value of variable x is 5 would not be able to keep using this information after an assignment to another variable (for example, *y = 10) because it could be that *y is an alias of x. This could be the case after an assignment like y = &x. As an effect of the assignment to *y, the value of x would be changed as well, so propagating the information that x is 5 to the statements following *y = 10 would be potentially wrong . However, if we have information about pointers, the constant propagation process could make a query like: can x be an alias of *y? Then, if the answer is no, x = 5 can be propagated safely.

(ii) Another optimisation that is impacted by aliasing is code reordering; if the compiler decides that x is not an alias of *y, then code that uses or changes the value of x can be moved before the assignment *y = 10, if this would improve scheduling or enable more loop optimizations to be carried out. In order to enable such optimisations to be carried out in a predictable manner, the C99 edition of the C programming language specifies that it is illegal (with some exceptions) for pointers of different types to reference the same memory location. This rule, known as "strict aliasing", allows impressive increases in performance, but has been known to break some legacy code.

7.11 SSA BASED OPTIMIZATIONS

These optimizations are intended to be done after transforming the program into a special form called static single assignment. Although some function without SSA, they are most effective with SSA. Compiler optimization algorithms which are either enabled or strongly enhanced by the use of SSA include:

- Constant propagation
- Sparse conditional constant propagation
- Dead code elimination
- Global value numbering
- Partial redundancy elimination
- Strength reduction

SSA based optimization includes :

- Global value numbering
- Sparse conditional constant propagation

7.11.1 Global Value Numbering

Global value numbering (GVN) is based on the SSA intermediate representation so that false variable name-value name mappings are not created. It sometimes helps eliminate redundant code that common subexpression evaluation (CSE) does not. GVN are often found in modern compilers. Global value numbering is distinct from local value numbering in that the value-number mappings hold across basic block boundaries as well, and different algorithms are used to compute the mappings.

Global value numbering works by assigning a value number to variables and expressions. To those variables and expressions which are provably equivalent, the same value number is assigned.

Example 7.18:

Original loop	After global value numbering
w := 3	w := 3
x := 3	x := w
y := x + 4	y := w + 4
z := w + 4	z := y

The reason that GVN is sometimes more powerful than CSE comes from the fact that CSE matches lexically identical expressions whereas the GVN tries to determine an underlying equivalence. For instance, in the code:

a := c × d

e := c

f := e × d

CSE would not eliminate the recomputation assigned to f, but even a poor GVN algorithm should discover and eliminate this redundancy.

7.11.2 Sparse Conditional Constant Propagation

Sparse conditional constant propagation is an optimization frequently applied after conversion to static single assignment form (SSA). It simultaneously removes dead code and propagates constants throughout a program. It must be noted, however, that it is strictly more powerful than applying dead code.

7.12 FUNCTIONAL LANGUAGE OPTIMIZATIONS

Functional language optimizations includes:

- Removing recursion
- Data structure fusion.

7.12.1 Removing Recursion

Recursion is often expensive, as a function call consumes stack space and involves some overhead related to parameter passing and flushing the instruction cache. Tail recursive algorithms can be converted to iteration, which does not have call overhead and uses a constant amount of stack space, through a process called tail recursion elimination.

7.12.2 Data Structure Fusion

Because of the high level nature by which data structures are specified in functional languages such as Haskell, it is possible to combine several recursive functions which produce and consume some temporary data structure so that the data is passed directly without wasting time constructing the data structure.

7.13 OTHER OPTIMIZATIONS TECHNIQUES

Other optimizations techniques included:

- Dead code elimination
- Partial redundancy elimination
- Strength reduction
- Copy Propagation
- Function Chunking
- Rematerialization
- Code Hoisting.

7.13.1 Dead Code Elimination

Similar to Section 7.6 (point 3)

7.13.2 Partial Redundancy Elimination

Partial redundancy elimination (PRE) eliminates expressions that are redundant on some but not necessarily all paths through a program. PRE is a form of common subexpression elimination.

An expression is called partially redundant if the value computed by the expression is already available on some but not all paths through a program to that expression. An expression is fully redundant if the value computed by the expression is available on all paths through the program to that expression. PRE can eliminate partially redundant expressions by inserting the partially redundant expression on the paths that do not already compute it, thereby making the partially redundant expression fully redundant.

Example 7.19:

Original loop	After global value numbering

`if (some_condition) {`
`// some code`
`y = x + 4;`
`}`
`else {`
`// other code`
`}`
`z = x + 4;`
	`if (some_condition) {`
	`// some code`
	`y = x + 4;`
	`t = y;`
	`}`
	`else {`
	`// other code`
	`t = x + 4;`
	`}`
	`z = t;`

The expression x+4 assigned to z is partially redundant because it is computed twice if some_condition is true. PRE would perform code motion on the expression to yield optimized code as above.

7.13.3 Strength Reduction

Similar to section 7.6.

7.13.4 Copy Propagation

Similar to section 7.6.

7.13.5 Function Chunking

Similar to section 7.6.

7.13.6 Rematerialization

Rematerialization saves time by recomputing a value instead of loading it from memory. It is typically tightly integrated with register allocation, where it is used as an alternative to *spilling* registers to memory. It was conceived by Preston Briggs, Keith D. Cooper, and Linda Torczon in 1992. Rematerialization decreases register pressure by increasing the amount of CPU computation. To avoid adding more computation time than necessary, rematerialize is done only when the compiler can be confident that it will be of benefit i.e. when a register spill to memory would otherwise occur.

Rematerialization works by keeping track of the expression used to compute each variable, using the concept of available expressions. Sometimes the variables used to compute a value are modified, and so can no longer be used to rematerialize that value. The expression is then said to no longer be available. Other criteria must also be fulfilled, for example a maximum complexity on the expression used to rematerialize the value; it would do no good to rematerialize a value using a complex computation that takes more time than a load.

7.13.7 Code Hoisting

Code Hoisting finds expressions that are always executed or evaluated following some point in a program, without meaning of execution path and moves them to the latest point beyond which they would be executed. This process must reduce the space occupied by program.

EXAMPLE

EX.: Write three address code for the following code and then perform optimization technique

```
for(i=0;i<=n;i++)
{
  for(j=0;j<n;j++)
  {
  c[i,j]=0 ;
  }
}
for(i=0;i<=n;i++)
{
  for(j=ΰ;j<=n;j++)
  {
          for(k=0;k<=n;k++)
          {
          c[i,j]=c[i,j]+a[i,k]*b[k,j] ;
          }
  }
}
```

SOL. : Here we represent three address code for the given code after that perform optimization:

Three Address Code

(1) i=0
(2) if i<n goto 4 (L)
(3) goto 18 (L)
(4) j=0 (L)
(5) if j<n goto 7 (L)
(6) goto 15 (L)
(7) t1=i*k[1] (L)
(8) t1=t1+j
(9) t2=Q
(10) t3=4*t1
(11) t4=t2[t3]
(12) t5=j+1
(13) j=15
(14) goto 5
(15) t6=i+1 (L)

```
(16)   i=t6
(17)   goto 2
(18)   i=0 (L)
(19)   if <=n goto 21 (L)
(20)   goto next (L)
(21)   j=0
(22)   if j<=n goto 24 (L)
(23)   goto 52 (L)
(24)   k=0 (L)
(25)   if k<=n goto 27 (L)
(26)   goto 49 (L)
(27)   t7 =i*k^1 (L)
(28)   t7=t7+j
(29)   t8=Q
(30)   t9=4*t7
(31)   t10=t8[t9]
(32)   t11=i*k^1
(33)   t11=t11+k
(34)   t12=Q
(35)   t13=t11*4
(36)   t14=t12[t13]
(37)   t15=k+k^1
(38)   t15=t15+j
(39)   t16=Q
(40)   t17=4*t15
(41)   t18=t16[t17]
(42)   t19=t14*t18
(43)   t20=t10+t19
(44)   t10=t20
(45)   t21=k+1
(46)   k=t21
(47)   goto 25
(48)   t22=j+1 (L)
(49)   j=t22
(50)   goto 22
(51)   t23=i+1 (L)
(52)   i=t23
(53)   goto 19
(next) ————
```

Now we constructing basic block for given code as:

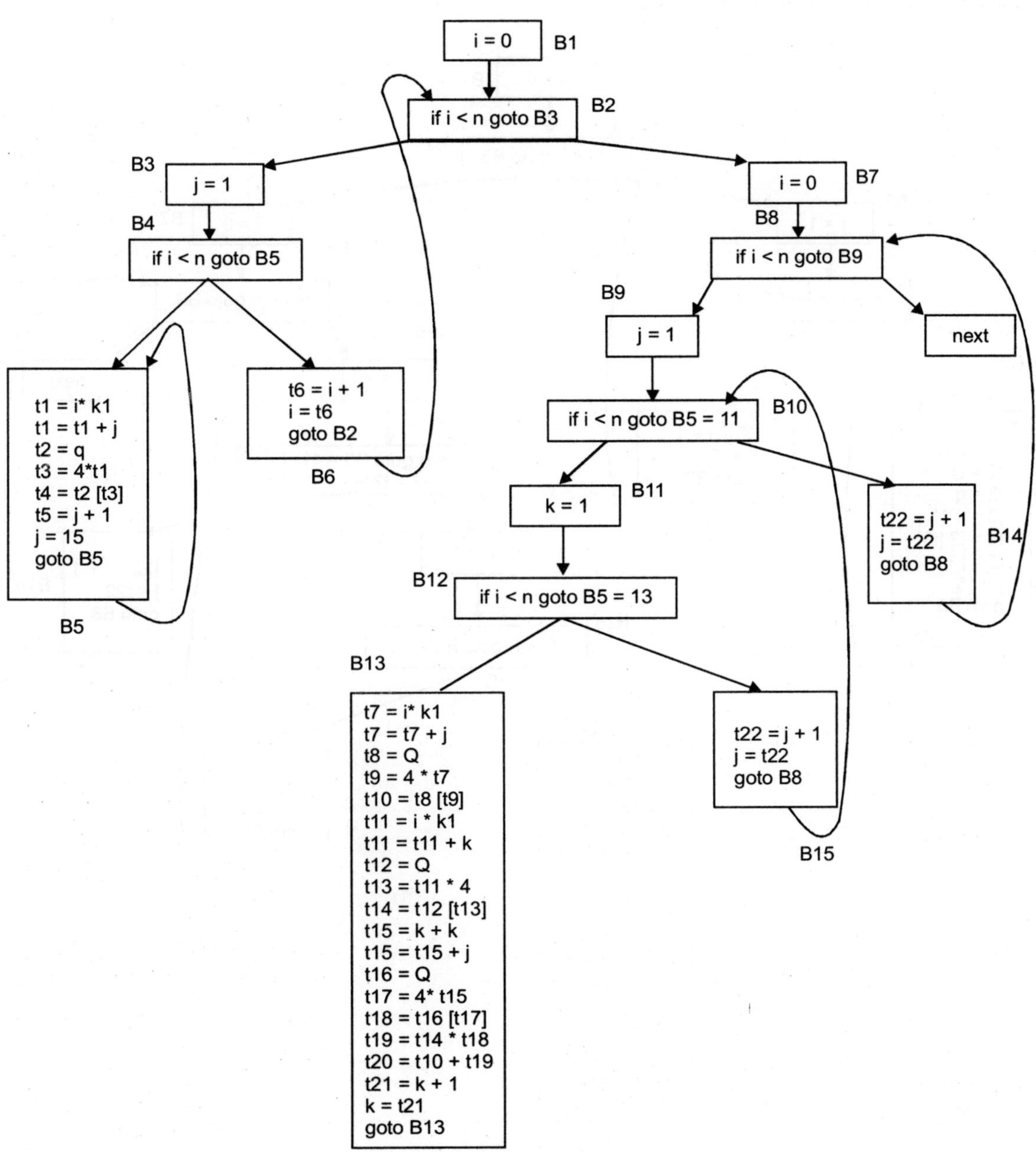

Figure 7.9

Now we apply optimization techniques by which only two blocks are change as B8, B10, B13. First statement of B13 is moved towards B8 block, other second statement is moved to B10 block and one statement is deleted, after that all blocks look like as:

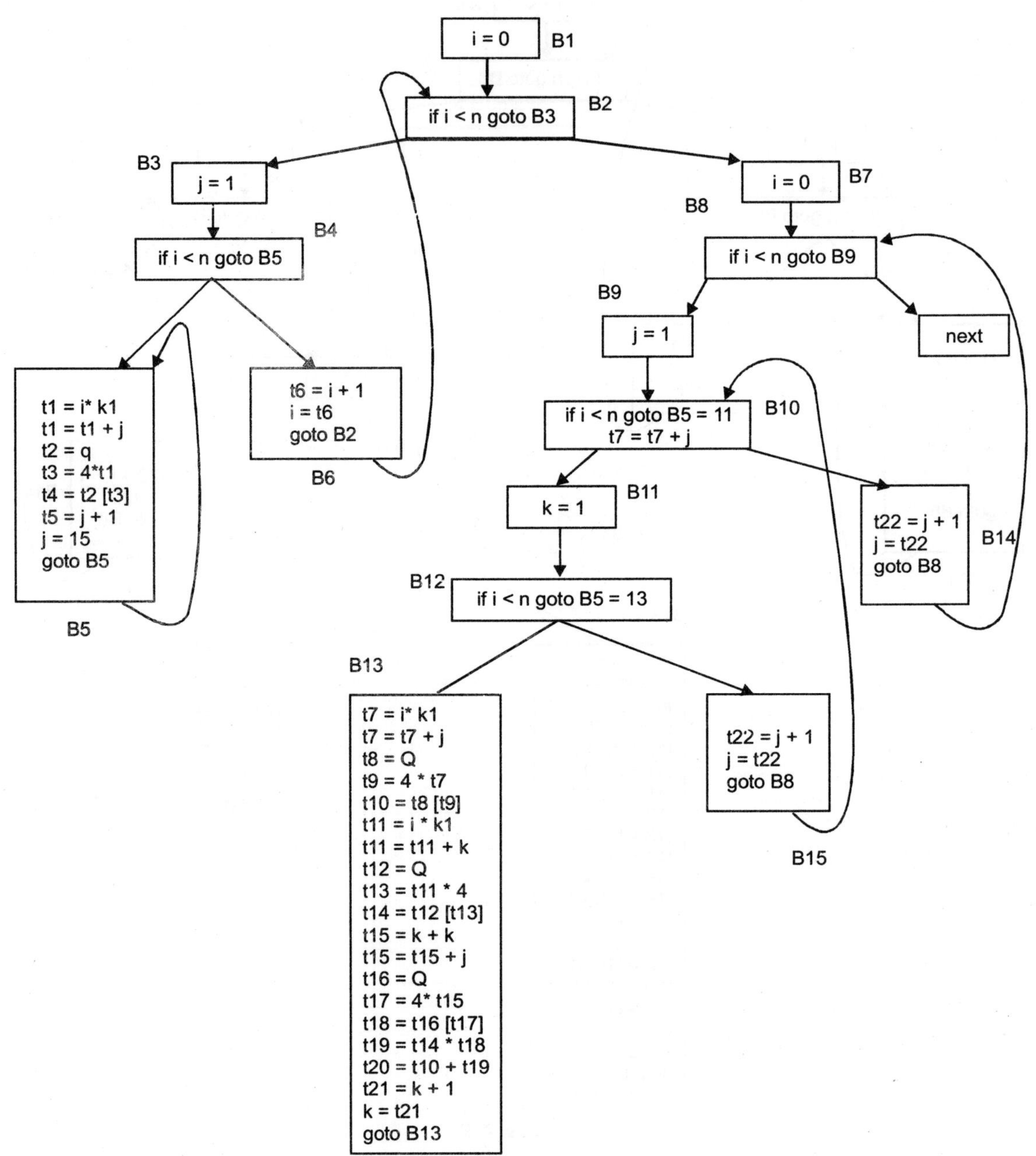

Figure 7.10

FURTHER READINGS AND REFERENCES

[1] Aho, Alfred V.; Sethi, Ravi; & Ullman, Jeffrey D. (1986). *Compilers: Principles, Techniques and Tools.* Addison Wesley.

Common Optimization Techniques

[2] Steven S. Muchnick, *Advanced Compiler Design and Implementation* (Morgan Kauffmann, 1997) pp. 378-396.

[3] John Cocke. *"Global Common Subexpression Elimination."* Proceedings of a Symposium on Compiler Construction, ACM SIGPLAN Notices 5(7), July 1970, pages 850-856.

[4] Briggs, Preston, Cooper, Keith D., and Simpson, L. Taylor. "*Value Numbering.*" Software-Practice and Experience, 27(6), June 1997, pages 701-724.

[5] Knuth, Donald: *Structured Programming with Goto Statements.* Computing Surveys 6:4 (1974), 261–301.

[6] Jon Bentley: *Writing Efficient Programs.*

[7] Donald Knuth: *The Art of Computer Programming.*

Data Flow Analysis and Loop Optimization

[8] Aho, Alfred V.; Sethi, Ravi; & Ullman, Jeffrey D. (1986). *Compilers: Principles, Techniques and Tools.* Addison Wesley.

[9] Kildall, Gary (1973). *"A Unified Approach to Global Program Optimization"*. Proceedings of the 1st Annual ACM SIGACT-SIGPLAN Symposium on Principles of Programming Languages. Retrieved on 2006-11-20.

[10] Hecht, Matthew S. *Flow Analysis of Computer Programs*. Elsevier North-Holland Inc. 1977.

[11] Appel, Andrew W. (1999). *Modern Compiler Implementation in ML.* Cambridge University Press.

[12] Cooper, Keith D.; & Torczon, Linda. (2005). *Engineering a Compiler.* Morgan Kaufmann.

[13] Muchnick, Steven S. (1997). *Advanced Compiler Design and Implementation.* Morgan Kaufmann.

[14] Kennedy, Ken; & Allen, Randy. (2001). *Optimizing Compilers for Modern Architectures: A Dependence-based Approach.* Morgan Kaufmann.

Data Flow Optimization

[15] Muchnick, Steven S. *Advanced Compiler Design and Implementation*. Morgan Kaufmann, 1997.

SSA Based Optimization

[16] Alpern, Bowen, Wegman, Mark N., and Zadeck, F. Kenneth. "*Detecting Equality of Variables in Programs.*"

[17] L. Taylor Simpson, "*Value-Driven Redundancy Elimination.*" Technical Report 96-308, Computer Science.

[18] Muchnick, Steven S. *Advanced Compiler Design and Implementation*. Morgan Kaufmann, 1997.

Dead Code Elimination And Partial Redundancy Elimination

[19] Muchnick, Steven S. *Advanced Compiler Design and Implementation*. Morgan Kaufmann, 1997.

[20] Morel, E., and Renvoise, *C. Global Optimization by Suppression of Partial Redundancies*. Communications of the acm, Vol. 22, Num. 2, Feb. 1979.

[21] Knoop, J., Ruthing, O., and Steffen, B. Lazy Code Motion. ACM SIGPLAN Notices Vol. 27, Num. 7, Jul. 1992, '92 Conference on PLDI.

[22] Kennedy, R., Chan, S., Liu, S.M., Lo, R., Peng, T., and Chow, *F. Partial Redundancy Elimination in SSA Form ACM Transactions on Programming Languages* Vol. 21, Num. 3, pp. 627-676, 1999.

[23] VanDrunen, T., and Hosking, A.L. *Value-Based Partial Redundancy Elimination*, Lecture Notes in Computer Science Vol. 2985/2004, pp. 167-184, 2004.

[24] Xue, J. and Knoop, J. A Fresh Look at PRE as a *Maximum Flow Problem. International Conference* on *Compiler Construction* (CC'06), pages 139-154, Vienna, Austria, 2006.

[25] Xue, J. and Cai Q. *A lifetime optimal algorithm for speculative PRE. ACM Transactions on Architecture and Code Optimization* Vol. 3, Num. 3, pp. 115-155, 2006.

Rematerialization

[26] P. Briggs, K. D. Cooper, and L. Torczon. Rematerialization. Proceedings of the SIGPLAN 92 Conference on Programming Language Design and Implementation, SIGPLAN Notices 27(7), pp. 311-321, July 1992. The original paper, in gzip'ed Postscript format.

CHAPTER 8

CODE GENERATION

CHAPTER HIGHLIGHTS

Code generation is the process by which a compiler's code generator converts a syntactically-correct program into a series of instructions that could be executed by a machine. Sophisticated compilers may use several cascaded code generation stages to fully compile code; this is due to the fact that algorithms for code optimization are more readily applicable in an intermediate code form, and also facilitates a single compiler that can target multiple architectures called target machines as only the final code generation stage would need to change from target to target. The input to the code generator stage typically consists of a parse tree, abstract syntax tree, intermediate three address code. Since the target machine may be a physical machine such as a microprocessor, or an abstract machine such as a virtual machine. The output of code generator could be machine code, assembly code, code for an abstract machine (like JVM), or anything between.

In a more general sense, code generation is used to produce programs in some automatic manner, reducing the need for human programmers to write code manually. Code generations can be done either at runtime, including load time, or compiler time. Just-in-time compilers are an example of a code generator that produces native or nearly native code from byte-code or the like when programs are loaded onto the compilers. On the other hand, a compiler-compiler, (yacc, for example) almost always generates code at compiler time. A preprocessor is an example of the simplest code generator, which produces target code from the source code by replacing predefined keywords.

When code generation occurs at runtime, it is important that it is efficient in space and time. For example, when regular expressions are interpreted and used to generate code at runtime, a non-determistic finite state machine instead of deterministic one is often generated because usually the former can be created more quickly and occupies less memory space than the latter. Despite it generally generating less efficient code, code generation at runtime can take the advantage of being done at runtime. Some people cite this fact to note that a JIT compiler can generate more efficient code than a compiler invoked before runtime, since it is more knowledgeable about the context and the execution path of the program than when the compiler generates code at compile time. So, code generation must do following things:

- Produce correct code
- make use of machine architecture.
- run efficiently.

Now in this chapter we discuss about code generator optimizations, major tasks in code generation, target machine and object machine. Now we are standing at sixth phase of compiler. Input to this phase is optimize intermediate codes of expressions from code optimizer as :

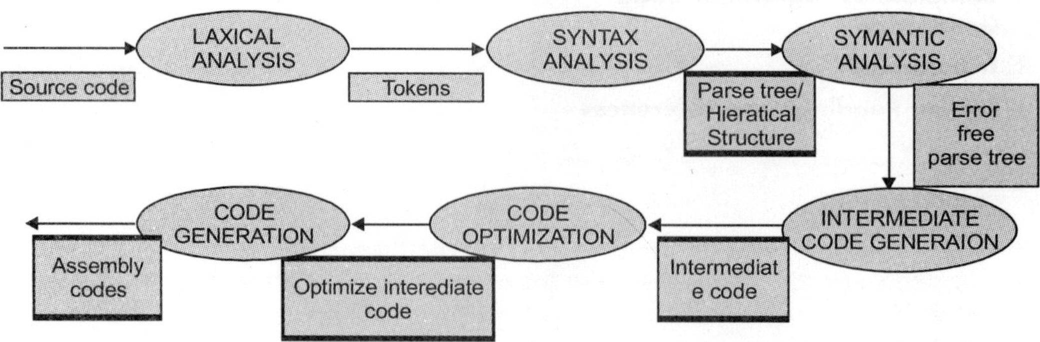

Figure 8.1

Here we present a general example of code generation by Borland C++ and Turbo Pascal for a single-accumulator machine. We list the actual code generated by various MS-DOS compilers for statement

WHILE (1 < P) AND (P < 9)
DO P := P + Q END

```
   Borland C++ 3.1 (47 bytes)           Turbo Pascal (46 bytes)
                                        (with no short circuit evaluation)

CS:A0 BBB702 MOV BX,02B7            CS:09  833E3E0009  CMP WORD PTR[003E],9
CS:A3 C746FE5100 MOV  WORD PTR      CS:0E  7C04        JL    14
                 [BP-2],0051
CS:A8 EB07       JMP  B1            CS:10  B000        MOV   AL,0
CS:AA 8BC3       MOV  AX,BX         CS:12  EB02        JMP   16
CS:AC 0346FE     ADD  AX,[BP-2]     CS:14  B001        MOV   AL,1
CS:AF 8BD8       MOV  BX,AX         CS:16  8AD0        MOV   DL,AL
CS:B1 83FB01     CMP  BX,1          CS:18  833E3E0001  CMP   WORD
PTR[003E],1
CS:B4 7E05       JLE  BB            CS:1D  7F04        JG    23
CS:B6 B80100     MOV  AX,1          CS:1F  B000        MOV   AL,0
CS:B9 EB02       JMP  BD            CS:21  EB02        JMP   25
CS:BB 33C0       XOR  AX,AX         CS:23  B001        MOV   AL,01
CS:BD 50         PUSH AX            CS:25  22C2        AND   AL,DL
CS:BE 83FB09     CMP  BX,9          CS:27  08C0        OR    AL,AL
CS:C1 7D05       JGE  C8            CS:29  740C        JZ    37
CS:C3 B80100     MOV  AX,1          CS:2B  A13E00      MOV   AX,[003E]
CS:C6 EB02       JMP  CA            CS:2E  03064000    ADD   AX,[0040]
CS:C8 33C0       XOR  AX,AX         CS:32  A33E00      MOV   [003E],AX
CS:CA 5A         POP  DX            CS:35  EBD2        JMP   9
CS:CB 85D0       TEST DX,AX
CS:CD 75DB       JNZ  AA
```

8.1 CODE GENERATOR OPTIMIZATIONS

Register Allocation

The most frequently used variables should be kept in processor registers for fastest access. To find which variables to put in registers an interference-graph is created. Each variable is a vertex and when two variables are used at the same time (have an intersecting liverange) they have an edge between them. This graph is coloured using for example Chaitin's algorithm using the same number of colours as there are registers. If the colouring fails one variable is "spilled" to memory and the colouring is retried.

Instruction Selection

Most architectures, particularly CISC architectures and those with many addressing modes, offer several different ways of performing a particular operation, using entirely different sequences of instructions. The job of the instruction selector is to do a good job overall of choosing which instructions to implement which operators in the low-level intermediate representation with. For example, on many processors in the 68000 family, complex addressing modes can be used in statements like "lea 25(a1,d5*4), a0", allowing a single instruction to perform a significant amount of arithmetic with less storage.

Instruction Scheduling

Instruction scheduling is an important optimization for modern pipelined processors, which avoids stalls or bubbles in the pipeline by clustering instructions with no dependencies together, while being careful to preserve the original semantics.

Rematerialization

Rematerialization recalculates a value instead of loading it from memory, preventing a memory access. This is performed in tandem with register allocation to avoid spills.

Example 8.1: Code generation in Borland 3.0 C Compiler

We can understand this problem by an example as : (x = x + 3) + 4. the assembly code for this expression is as :

```
1.  mov ax, word ptr [ bp-2 ]          // moves the value of x to ax
2.  add ax, 3                          // add constant 3 to this register.
3.  mov word ptr [ bp -2 ], ax         // move added value to location of x
4.  add ax, 4                          // add 4 to ax
```

In this code the accumulator register 'ax' is used as the main temporary location for the computation. The location for local variable x is bp-2, reflecting the use of the register bp(base pointer) as the frame pointer and the fact that integer variables occupy two bytes on this machine.

Int i,j;
int a[10];

```
 1. mov  bx , word ptr [ bp -2 ]     //move value of i into bx
 2. shl bx , 1                       //multiply value of i by 2 (left shift 1 bit)
 3. lea ax, word ptr[bp-22]          //load base address of a to ax ( lea =load effective address )
 4. add bx, ax                       //computing base address of a[i+1] to bx
 5. mov ax, 2                        //move constant 2 to ax
 6. mov word ptr[bx], ax             //stores result of instruction 5 to address of a[i+1]
 7. mov bx, word ptr [bp-4]          //move value of j to bx
 8. shl bx, 1                        //multiply value of j by 2
 9. lea dx, word ptr [bp-24]         //load base address of a into register dx
10. add bx,  dx                      //computes address of a[j] to bx
11. add ax, word ptr [bx]            //add value stored at this address to ax
```

- bp-2 is the location of i
- bp-4 is location of j
- bp -24 is base address of a (24 = array index size 10 * integer size 2 bytes + 4 byte space for i & j)

8.2 USE OF GENERATED CODE

Debugging: When a programmer is still writing an application, they will recompile and test often, and so compilation must be fast. This is one reason most optimizations are avoided while debugging. Also, debugging code is usually stepped through in a symbolic debugger, and optimizing transformations, particularly those that reorder code, can make it difficult to identify the output code with the line numbers in the source code from which the code was generated. This can confuse the debugging tools and the programmer using them.

General purpose: Prepackaged software is very often expected to be executed on a variety of machines and CPUs that may share the same instruction set, but have different timing, cache or memory characteristics. So, the code may not be tuned to any particular CPU, or may be tuned to work well on the most popular CPU and work reasonably on other CPUs.

Special purpose: If the software is compiled to be used on one or a few very similar machines, with known characteristics, then the compiler can heavily tune the generated code to those machines alone. Important special cases include code designed for parallel and vector processors, for which we have parallelizing compilers.

8.3 MAJOR TASKS IN CODE GENERATION

In addition to basic conversion from optimize intermediate representation into machine instructions, code generator also tries to use faster instructions, use fewer instructions, exploit available fast registers and avoid redundant computations.

- ***Instruction selection***: With the diverse instructions supported in a target machine, instruction selection deal with the problem of which instructions to use.
- ***Memory management***
- ***Instruction scheduling:*** In what order to run the instructions.
- ***Register allocation:*** The speed gap between processors and memory is partially bridged by the registers in processors. How to put useful variables into registers has a great impact of the final performance.

The usual method is a state machine, or weak artificial intelligence scheme that selects and combines templates for computations.

8.4 INSTRUCTION SELECTION

Instruction selection is a compiler optimization that transforms an intermediate representation of a program into the final compiled code, either in binary or assembly format. A basic approach in instruction selection is to use some templates for translation of each instruction in an intermediate representation. But naive use of templates leads to inefficient code in general. Additional attention need to be paid to avoid duplicated memory access by reordering and merging instructions and promote the usage of registers.

For example, the address code is:

$$a := b + c$$

$$d := a + e$$

Inefficient assembly code is:

1. MOV b, R_0 $\quad R_0 \leftarrow b$
2. ADD c, R_0 $\quad R_0 \leftarrow c + R_0$
3. MOV R_0, a $\quad a \leftarrow R_0$
4. MOV a, R_0 $\quad R_0 \leftarrow a$
5. ADD e, R_0 $\quad R_0 \leftarrow e + R_0$
6. MOV R_0, d $\quad d \leftarrow R_0$

Here the fourth statement is redundant, and so is the third statement if 'a' is not subsequently used.

Typically, instruction selection is implemented with a backwards dynamic programming algorithm which computes the "optimal" tiling for each point starting from the end of the program and based from there. Instruction selection can also be implemented with a greedy algorithm that chooses a local optimum at each step.The code that performs instruction selection is usually automatically generated from a list of valid patterns.

Some machine operations are described by a single byte instruction set and others require two bytes, and have the format

Byte 1 Opcode

Byte 2 Address field

Mnemonic Hex Decimal Function opcode

The following are single-byte instructions.

NOP	00h	0	No operation (this might be used to set a break point in an emulator)
CLA	01h	1	Clear accumulator A
CLC	02h	2	Clear carry bit C
CLX	03h	3	Clear index register X
CMC	04h	4	Complement carry bit C
INC	05h	5	Increment accumulator A by 1
DEC	06h	6	Decrement accumulator A by 1
INX	07h	7	Increment index register X by 1
DEX	08h	8	Decrement index register X by 1
TAX	09h	9	Transfer accumulator A to index register X
INI	0Ah	10	Load accumulator A with integer read from input in decimal
INH	0Bh	11	Load accumulator A with integer read from input in hexadecimal
INB	0Ch	12	Load accumulator A with integer read from input in binary
INA	0Dh	13	Load accumulator A with ASCII value read from input (a single character)
OTI	0Eh	14	Write value of accumulator A to output as a signed decimal number
OTC	0Fh	15	Write value of accumulator A to output as an unsigned decimal number
OTH	10h	16	Write value of accumulator A to output as an unsigned hexadecimal number
OTB	11h	17	Write value of accumulator A to output as an unsigned binary number
OTA	12h	18	Write value of accumulator A to output as a single character
PSH	13h	19	Decrement SP and push value of accumulator A ontc stack
POP	14h	20	Pop stack into accumulator A and increment SP
SHL	15h	21	Shift accumulator A one bit left
SHR	16h	22	Shift accumulator A one bit right
RET	17h	23	Return from subroutine (return address popped from stack)
HLT	18h	24	Halt program execution

The following are all double-byte instructions.

LDA	B	19h	25	Load accumulator A directly with contents of location whose address is given as B

LDX	B	1Ah	26	Load accumulator A with contents of location whose address is given as B, indexed by the value of X (that is, an address computed as the value of B + X)
LDI	B	1Bh	27	Load accumulator A with the immediate value B
LSP	B	1Ch	28	Load stack pointer SP with contents of location whose address is given as B
LSI	B	1Dh	29	Load stack pointer SP immediately with the value B
STA	B	1Eh	30	Store accumulator A on the location whose address is given as B
STX	B	1Fh	31	Store accumulator A on the location whose address is given as B, indexed by the value of X
ADD	B	20h	32	Add to accumulator A the contents of the location whose address is given as B
ADX	B	21h	33	Add to accumulator A the contents of the location whose address is given as B,indexed by the value of X
ADI	B	22h	34	Add the immediate value B to accumulator A
ADC	B	23h	35	Add to accumulator A the value of the carry bit C plus the contents of the location whose address is given as B
ACX	B	24h	36	Add to accumulator A the value of the carry bit C plus the contents of the location whose address is given as B, indexed by the value of X
ACI	B	25h	37	Add the immediate value B plus the value of the carry bit C to accumulator A
SUB	B	26h	38	Subtract from accumulator A the contents of the location whose address is given as B
SBX	B	27h	39	Subtract from accumulator A the contents of the location whose address is given as B, indexed by the value of X
SBI	B	28h	40	Subtract the immediate value B from accumulator A
SBC	B	29h	41	Subtract from accumulator A the value of the carry bit C plus the contents of the location whose address is given as B
SCX	B	2Ah	42	Subtract from accumulator A the value of the carry bit C plus the contents of the location whose address is given as B, indexed by the value of X
SCI	B	2Bh	43	Subtract the immediate value B plus the value of the carry bit C from accumulator A
CMP	B	2Ch	44	Compare accumulator A with the contents of the location whose address is given as B
CPX	B	2Dh	45	Compare accumulator A with the contents of the location whose address is given as B, indexed by the value of X
CPI	B	2Eh	46	Compare accumulator A directly with the value B

8.5 INSTRUCTION SCHEDULING

Instruction scheduling is a compiler optimization used to improve instruction-level parallelism, which improves performance on machines with instruction pipelines. Put more simply, without changing the meaning of the code, it tries to

- Avoid pipeline stalls by rearranging the order of instructions.
- Avoid illegal or semantically ambiguous operations (typically involving subtle instruction pipeline timing issues or non-interlocked resources.)

The pipeline stalls can be caused by structural hazards (processor resource limit), data hazards (output of one instruction needed by another instruction) and control hazards (branching).

8.5.1 Data Hazards

Instruction scheduling is typically done on a single basic block. In order to determine whether rearranging the block's instructions in a certain way preserves the behaviour of that block, we need the concept of a data dependency. There are three types of dependencies, which also happen to be the three data hazards:

1. **Read after Write (RAW or "True"):** Instruction 1 writes a value used later by Instruction 2. Instruction 1 must come first, or Instruction 2 will read the old value instead of the new.
2. **Write after Read (WAR or "Anti"):** Instruction 1 reads a location that is later overwritten by Instruction 2. Instruction 1 must come first, or it will read the new value instead of the old.
3. **Write after Write (WAW or "Output"):** Two instructions both write the same location. They must occur in their original order.

To make sure we respect these three types of dependencies, we construct a dependency graph, which is a directed graph where each vertex is an instruction and there is an edge from I_1 to I_2 if I_1 must come before I_2 due to a dependency. Then, any topological sort of this graph is a valid instruction schedule.

8.5.2 Order of Instruction Scheduling

Instruction scheduling may be done either before or after register allocation or both before and after it. The advantage of doing it before register allocation is that this results in maximum parallelism. The disadvantage of doing it before register allocation is that this can result in the register allocator needing to use a number of register exceeding those available and then there will be false dependencies introduced by the register allocation that will limit the amount of instruction motion possible by the scheduler. This will cause spill/fill code to be introduced which will reduce the performance of the section of code in question.

List Scheduling

The basic idea of list scheduling is to make an ordered list of processes by assigning them some priorities, and then repeatedly execute the following two steps until a valid schedule is obtained :

·Select from the list, the process with the highest priority for scheduling.

·Select a resource to accommodate this process.

The priorities are determined statically before scheduling process begins. The first step choose the process with highest priority, the second step select the best possible resource. Some known list scheduling strategies are:

- Highest Level First algorithm or HLF
- Longest Path algorithm or LP
- Longest Processing Time
- Critical Path

8.5.3 Types of Instruction Scheduling

The are several varieties of scheduling they are:

1. **Global scheduling:** In global scheduling instructions can move across the basic block boundary.
2. **Basic block scheduling:** is where the instructions can't move across the basic block boundaries.
3. **Modulo scheduling:** Another name for software pipelining which, in actuality, is a form of instruction scheduling, if properly implemented.

8.6 REGISTER ALLOCATION

Register allocation is the process of multiplexing a large number of target program variables onto a small number of CPU registers. The goal is to keep as many operands as possible in registers to maximize the execution speed of software programs. Register allocation can happen over a basic block **(local register allocation)** or a whole function/procedure (**global register allocation**). Most computer programs need to process large numbers of different data items. However, most CPUs can only perform operations on a small fixed number of "slots" called registers. Even on machines that support memory operands, register access is considerably faster than memory access. Therefore the data items to be processed have to be loaded into and out of the registers from RAM at the moments they are needed.

Register allocation is an NP-complete problem. The number of variables in a typical program is much larger than the number of available registers in a processor, so the contents of some variables have to be saved into memory locations. The cost of such saving is minimized by saving the least frequently used variables first; however it is not easy to know which variables will be used the least. In addition to this the hardware and operating system may impose restrictions on the usage of some registers.

8.6.1 Global Register Allocation

Like most other compiler optimizations, register allocation is based on the result of some compiler analysis, mostly the result data flow analysis. Formally, there are two steps in register allocation:

1. **Register allocation (what register?):** This is a register selection process in which we select the set of variables that will reside in register.
2. **Register assignment (what variable?):** Here we pick the register that contain variable. Note that this is a NP-Complete problem.

In phase two, a graph is constructed where nodes are symbolic registers and an edge connects two nodes if one is live when the other is defined, which means two variables will be live together some time during the execution. The problem then equals to colour the graph using k colours, where k is the number of actual available physical registers. To do so, the graph is reduced in size in repeating steps until no further simplification is possible

- **Removing action:** Repeatedly remove a node in graph if it has fewer than k neighbours connected by edges. Also remove related edges. This step eliminates all variables with less than k other concurrently. living variables.
- **Stop:** If the result simplified graph has no nodes left, all removed nodes will be coloured in the reverse order in which they were removed, ensuring a different colour is used compared to its neighbours.
- **Saving action:** If the result graph have nodes left and each of them has more than k neighbours, choose one node to be spilled. Remove the spilled node and its edges and repeat the removing and spilling actions until the graph is empty.

Major attention has been paid to choose the right nodes to be spilled. The less frequently used variables are often the victims.

8.6.2 Register Allocation by Interference Graph

The interference graph is used for assigning registers to temporary variables. If two variables do not interfere ie, there is no edge between these two variables in the interference graph then we can use the same register for both of them, thus reducing the number of registers needed. On the other hand, if there is a graph edge between two variables, then we should not assign the same register to them since this register needs to hold the values of both variables at one point of time.

Suppose that we have n available registers: $r_1, r_2, ..., r_n$. If we view each register as a different colour, then the register allocation problem for the interference graph is equivalent to the graph colouring problem where we try to assign one of the 'n' different colours to graph nodes so that no two adjacent nodes have the same colour. This algorithm is used in map drawing where we have countries or states on the map and we want to colour them using a small fixed number of colours so that states that have a common border are not painted with the same colour.

The register allocation algorithm uses various operation as:

- Simplification
- Spilling
- Selection
- Coalescing
- Freezing

The register allocation algorithm uses a stack of graph nodes to insert all nodes of the interference graph one at a time. Each time it selects a node that has fewer than n neighbours. The idea is that if we can colour the graph after we remove this node, then of course we can colour the original graph because the neighbours of this node can have n – 1 different colours in the worst case; so we can just assign the available nth colour to the node. This is called ***simplification*** of the graph. Each selected node is pushed in the stack.

Sometimes though we cannot simplify any further because all nodes have n or more neighbours. In that case we select one node to be spilled into memory instead of assigning a register to it. This is called ***spilling*** and the spilled victim can be selected based on priorities. The spilled node is also pushed on the stack.

When the graph is completely reduced and all nodes have been pushed in the stack, we pop the stack one node at a time, we rebuild the interference graph and at the same time we assign a colour to the popped-out node so that its colour is different from the colours of its neighbours. This is called the ***selection* phase**.

If there is a move instruction in a program (i.e., an assignment of the form a: = b) and there is no conflict between a and b, then it is a good idea to use the same register for both a and b so that you can remove the move instruction entirely from the program. In fact you can just merge the graph nodes for a and b in the graph into one node. Those way nodes are now labeled by sets of variables, instead of just one variable. This is called ***coalescing***. A common criterion for coalescing is that we coalesce two nodes if the merged node has fewer than n neighbours of degree greater than or equal to 'n' (where n is the number of available registers). This is called the Briggs criterion. A slight variation of this is the George criterion where we coalesce nodes if all the neighbours of one of the nodes with degree greater than or equal to n already interfere with the other node.

If we derive an irreducible graph at some point of time, there is another phase, called ***freezing*** that de-coalesces one node (into two nodes) and continues the simplification.

Consider the following interference graph from the previous section:

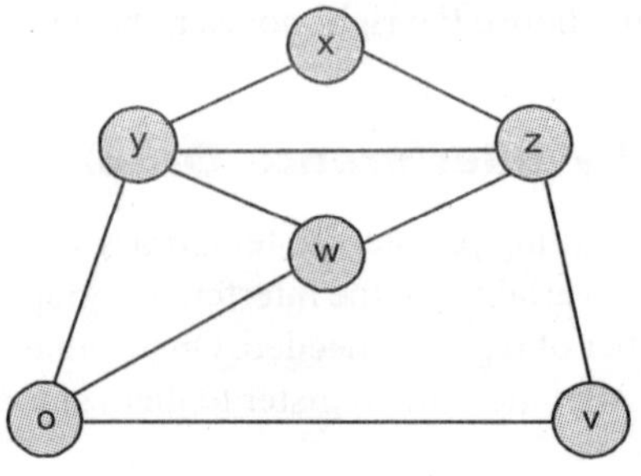

Figure 8.2

The nodes are pushed in the stack in the order of xvuzyw. Then, at the selection phase, xyzwuv variables are assigned the registers $R_0R_2R_1R_0R_1R_0$.

8.6.3 Problem of Register Allocation

1. Special use of hardware for example, some instructions require specific register.
2. Convention for Software:

For example,

- Register R6 (say) always return address.
- Register R5 (say) for stack pointer.
- Similarly, we assigned registers for branch and link, frames, heaps, etc.,

3. Choice of Evaluation order

Changing the order of evaluation may produce more efficient code.

This is NP-complete problem but we can bypass this hindrance by generating code for quadruples in the order in which they have been produced by intermediate code generator.

```
ADD x, Y, T1
ADD a, b, T2
```

is legal because X, Y and a, b are different (not dependent).

8.7 CODE GENERATION FOR TREES

Suppose that you want generate assembly code for the expression (A – B) + ((C + D) + (E*F)), which corresponds to the syntax tree:

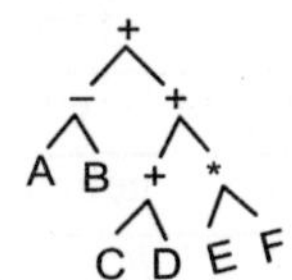

We want to generate the following assembly code:

```
load R2, C
add  R2, D
load R1, E
mult R1, F
add  R2, R1
load R1, A
sub  R1, B
add  R1, R2
```

That is, we used only two register.

There is an algorithm that generates code with the least number of registers. It is called the ***Sethi-Ullman*** algorithm. It consists of two phases: ***numbering*** and ***code generation***.

The **numbering** phase assigns a number to each tree node that indicates how many registers are needed to evaluate the subtree of this node. Suppose that for a tree node *T*, we need *l* registers to evaluate its left subtree and r registers to evaluate its right subtree. Then if one of these numbers is larger, say $l > r$, then we can evaluate the left subtree first and store its result into one of the registers, say R_k. Now we can evaluate the right subtree using the same registers we used for the left subtree, except of course R_k since we want to remember the result of the left subtree. But this is always possible since $l > r$. This means that we need l registers to evaluate T too. The same happens if $r > l$ but now we need to evaluate the right subtree first and store the result to a register. If $l = r$ we need an extra register R_{l+1} to remember the result of the left subtree. If T is a tree leaf, then the number of registers to evaluate T is either 1 or 0 depending whether T is a left or a right subtree. So the numbering algorithm starts from the tree leaves and assigns 1 or 0 as explained. Then for each node whose children are labelled l and r, if $l = r$ then the node number is $l + 1$ otherwise it is $max(l, r)$. For example, we have the following numbering for the previous example:

```
        2
       / \
      /   \
     1     2
    /\    / \
   1  0  1   1
         /\  /\
         1 0 1 0
```

The **code generation** phase is as follows. We assume that for each node T has numbering $regs(T)$. We use a stack of available registers which initially contains all the registers in order (with the lower register at the top).

generate(T) =	
	if T is a leaf write "load top(), T"
	if T is an internal node with children l and r then
	if $regs(r) = 0$ then { generate(l); write "op top(), r" }
	if $regs(l) >= regs(r)$
	then { generate(l)
	R := pop()
	generate(r)
	write "op R, top()"
	push(R) }
if $regs(l) < regs(r)$	
then {	swap the top two elements of the stack
	generate(r)
	R := pop()
	generate(l)
	write "op top(), R"
	push(R)
	swap the top two elements of the stack }

This assumes that the number of registers needed is no greater than the number of available registers. Otherwise, we need to spill the intermediate result of a node to memory.

8.8 THE TARGET MACHINE

Target machine is:

1. Byte addressable (factor of 4).
2. 4 byte per word.
3. 16 to 32 (or n) general purpose register.
4. Two addressable instruction of form:

Op source, destination.

e.g., move A, B

add A, D

- Byte-addressable memory with 4 bytes per word and n general-purpose registers, $R_0, R_1, \ldots, R_{n-1}$. Each integer requires 2 bytes (16-bits).
- Two address instruction of the form mnemonic source, destination

Mode	Form	Address	Example	Added-Cost
Absolute	M	M	ADD R_0, R_1	1
register R	R	ADD temp,	R_1	0
Index c (R)	c + contents (R)	ADD 100(R_2),	R_1	1
Indirect register	*R	contents (R)	ADD * R_2, R_1	0
Indirect Index	*c (R)	contents (c + contents (R)	ADD * 100 1 (R_2), R_1	
Literal # c	constant c	ADD # 3, R_1	1	

Instruction costs :

Each instruction has a cost of 1 plus added costs for the source and destination.

⇒ cost of instruction = 1 + cost associated the source and destination address mode.

This cost corresponds to the length (in words) of instruction.

Example 8.2:

1. Move register to memory $R_0 \rightarrow M$.
   MOV R_0, M cost = 1+1 = 2.
2. Indirect indexed mode:
   MOV * 4 (R_0), M
   cost = 1 plus indirect index plus instruction word
   = 1 + 1 + 1 = 3
3. Indexed mode:
   MOV 4(R_0), M
   cost = 1 + 1 + 1 = 3

4. Litetral mode:
MOV #1, R_0
cost = 1 + 1 = 2

Move memory to memory
MOV m, m   cost = 1 + 1 + 1 = 3

8.9 ABSTRACT MACHINE

An abstract machine, also called an abstract computer, is a theoretical model of a computer hardware or software system used in Automata theory. Abstraction of computing processes is used in both the computer science and computer engineering disciplines and usually assumes discrete time paradigm.

In the theory of computation, abstract machines are often used in thought experiments regarding computability or to analyze the complexity of algorithms (see computational complexity theory). A typical abstract machine consists of a definition in terms of input, output, and the set of allowable operations used to turn the former into the latter. The best-known example is the Turing machine.

More complex definitions create abstract machines with full instruction sets, registers and models of memory. One popular model more similar to real modern machines is the RAM model, which allows random access to indexed memory locations. As the performance difference between different levels of cache memory grows, cache-sensitive models such as the external-memory model and cache-oblivious model are growing in importance.

Diagrammatically we might represent this machine as

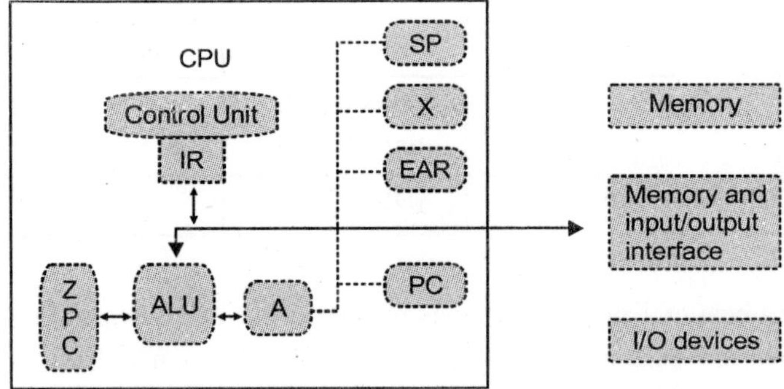

An abstract machine can also refer to a microprocessor design which has yet to be (or is not intended to be) implemented as hardware. An abstract machine implemented as a software simulation, or for which an interpreter exists, is called a virtual machine. Through the use of abstract machines it is possible to compute the amount of resources (time, memory, etc.) necessary to perform a particular operation without having to construct an actual system to do it.

8.9.1 Simple Machine Architecture

Many CPU chips used in modern computers have one or more internal **registers** which may be regarded as highly local memory where simple arithmetic and logical operations may be performed and between which local data transfers may take place. These registers may be restricted to the capacity of a single byte (8 bits).

8.9.2 Categories of Registers

Registers are normally measured by the number of bits they can hold, for example, an "8-bit register" or a "32-bit register". Registers are now usually implemented as a register file, but they have also been implemented using individual flip-flops. There are several classes of registers according to the content:

- **Address registers** hold memory addresses and are used to access memory. In some CPUs, a special address register is an index register, although often these hold numbers used to modify addresses rather than holding addresses.
- **Conditional registers** hold truth values often used to determine whether some instruction should or should not be executed.
- **Constant registers** hold read-only values (e.g., zero, one, pi, ...).
- **Data registers** are used to store integer numbers. In some older and simple current CPUs, a special data register is the accumulator, used implicitly for many operations.
- **Floating point registers** (FPRs) are used to store floating point numbers in many architectures.
- **General purpose registers** (GPRs) can store both data and addresses, i.e., they are combined Data/ Address registers.
- **Index registers** are used for modifying operand addresses during the run of a program.
- **Instruction register** is the part of a CPU's control unit that stores the instruction currently being executed. In simple processors each instruction to be executed is loaded into the instruction register which holds it while it is decoded, prepared and ultimately executed, which can take several steps. More complicated processors use a pipeline of instruction registers where each stage of the pipeline does part of the decoding, preparation or execution and then passes it to the next stage for its step.
- **Special purpose registers** hold program state; they usually include the program counter, stack pointer, and status register.
- **Vector registers** hold data for vector processing done by SIMD instructions (Single Instruction, Multiple Data).
- **Processor register** is a small amount of very fast computer memory used to speed the execution of computer programs by providing quick access to commonly used values. Processor registers are the top of the memory hierarchy, and provide the fastest way for the system to access data.

8.9.3 Addressing Mode

Addressing modes are an aspect of the instruction set architecture in most central processing unit (CPU) designs. The various addressing modes that are defined in a given instruction set architecture define how machine language instructions in that architecture identify the operand (or operands) of each instruction. An addressing mode specifies how to calculate the effective memory address of an operand by using information held in registers and/or constants contained within a machine instruction or elsewhere.

8.9.4 Types of Addressing Mode

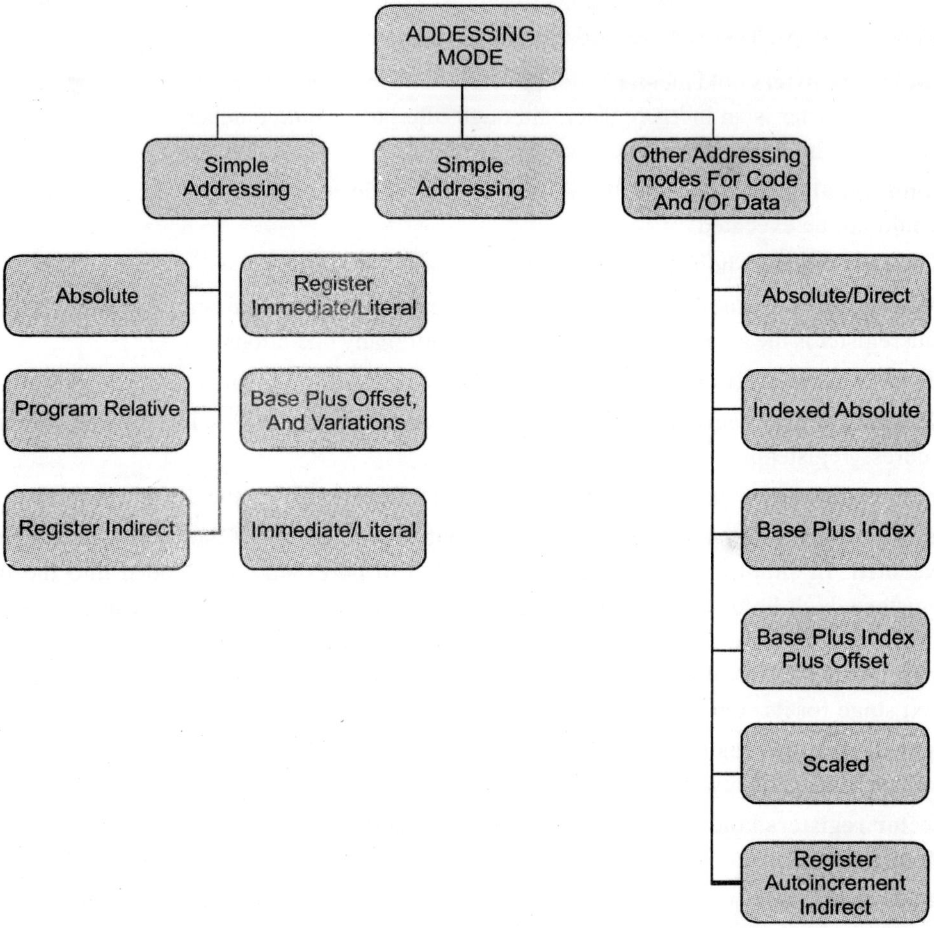

ADDESSING MODE

- Simple Addressing
  - Absolute
  - Program Relative
  - Register Indirect
  - Register Immediate/Literal
  - Base Plus Offset, And Variations
  - Immediate/Literal
- Simple Addressing
- Other Addressing modes For Code And /Or Data
  - Absolute/Direct
  - Indexed Absolute
  - Base Plus Index
  - Base Plus Index Plus Offset
  - Scaled
  - Register Autoincrement Indirect

Figure 8.3

Simple Addressing Modes for Code

Absolute

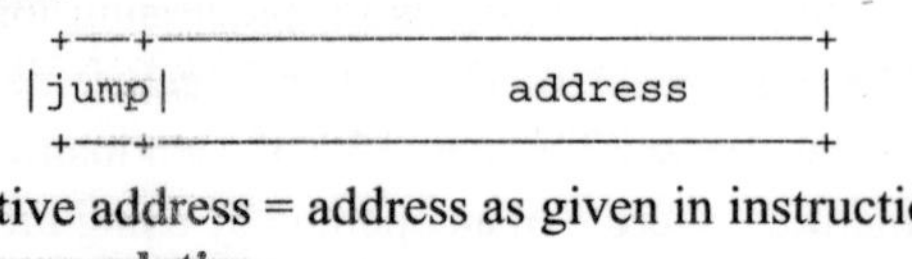

Effective address = address as given in instruction

Program relative

```
+------+-----+-----+--------------------------+
|jumpEQ| reg1| reg2|              offset      |     jump relative if reg1=reg2
+------+-----+-----+--------------------------+
```

Effective address = offset plus address of next instruction. The offset is usually signed, in the range –32768 to +32767. This is particularly useful in connection with conditional jumps, if or while statements.

Register indirect

```
+--------+-------+
|jumpVia| reg    |
+--------+-------+
```

Effective address = contents of specified register. The effect is to transfer control to the instruction whose address is in the specified register. Such an instruction is often used for returning from a subroutine call, since the actual call would usually have placed the return address in a register.

Simple Addressing Modes for Data

Register

```
+------+-----+-----+-----+
| mul  | reg1| reg2| reg3|          reg1 := reg2 * reg3;
+------+-----+-----+-----+
```

This 'addressing mode' does not have an effective address and is not considered to be an addressing mode on some computers.

Base Plus Offset, and Variations

```
+------+-----+-----+----------------+
| load | reg | base|          offset|
+------+-----+-----+----------------+
```

Effective address = offset plus contents of specified base register. The offset is usually a signed 16-bit value (though the 80386 is famous for expanding it to 32-bit, though x64 didn't). If the offset is zero, this becomes an example of register indirect addressing; the effective address is just that in the base register.

Immediate/literal

```
+------+-----+-----+----------------+
| add  | reg1| reg2|    constant    |      reg1 := reg2 + constant;
+------+-----+-----+----------------+
```

This 'addressing mode' does not have an effective address, and is not considered to be an addressing mode on some computers. The constant might be signed or unsigned.

Other Addressing Modes for Code and/or Data

Absolute/Direct

```
+----+----+---------------------------+
| load | reg |        address         |
+----+----+---------------------------+
```

Effective address = address as given in instruction.

Indexed Absolute

```
+----+----+----+----------------------------+
| load | reg |index|  32-bit address        |
+----+----+----+----------------------------+
```

Effective address = address plus contents of specified index register. This also requires space in an instruction for quite a large address. The address could be the start of an array or vector, and the index could select the particular array element required. The index register may need to have been scaled to allow for the size of each array element.

Base Plus Index

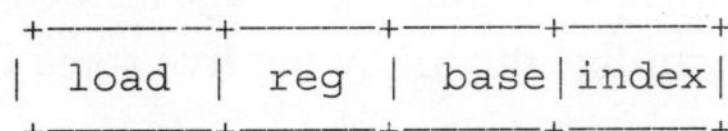

```
+------+-----+-----+-----+
| load | reg | base|index|
+------+-----+-----+-----+
```

Effective address = contents of specified base register plus contents of specified index register.The base register could contain the start address of an array or vector, and the index could select the particular array element required. The index register may need to have been scaled to allow for the size of each array element. This could be used for accessing elements of an array passed as a parameter.

Base Plus Index Plus Offset

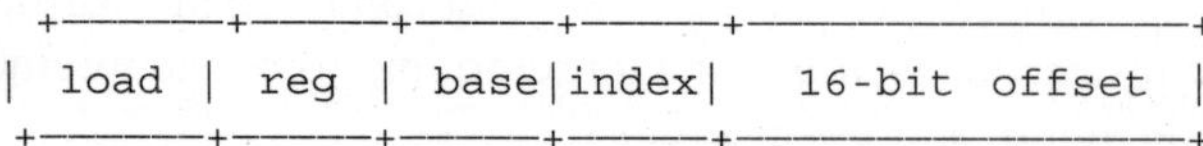

Effective address = offset plus contents of specified base register plus contents of specified index register. The base register could contain the start address of an array or vector of records, the index could select the particular record required, and the offset could select a field within that record. The index register may need to have been scaled to allow for the size of each record.

Scaled

```
+------+------+------+------+
| load | reg  | base|index|
+------+------+------+------+
```

Effective address = contents of specified base register plus scaled contents of specified index register. The base register could contain the start address of an array or vector, and the index could contain the number of the particular array element required.

Register Indirect

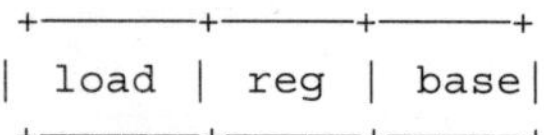

Effective address = contents of base register. A few computers have this as a distinct addressing mode. Many computers just use base plus offset with an offset value of 0.

Register Autoincrement Indirect

```
+------+------+------+
| load | reg  | base|
+------+------+------+
```

Effective address = contents of base register. After determining the effective address, the value in the base register is incremented by the size of the data item that is to be accessed.

Autodecrement Register Indirect

```
+------+------+------+
| load | reg  | base|
+------+------+------+
```

Before determining the effective address, the value in the base register is decremented by the size of the data item which is to be accessed. Effective address = new contents of base register.

8.9.5 The Instruction Cycle

There are different cycles with complex instruction sets that typically utilize five stages: Each CPU have different cycles based on different instruction sets. Typically they utilize the following five stage Cycle.

- **Fetch the Instruction from main memory :** The CPU presents the value of the program counter (PC) on the address bus. The CPU then fetches the instruction from main memory via the data bus into the Current Instruction Register (CIR), a circuit that holds the instruction so that it can be decoded and executed.

- **Decode the instruction :** The instruction decoder (ID) interprets and implements the instruction
- **Fetch data from main memory:** Read the effective address from main memory if the instruction has an indirect address. Fetch required data from main memory to be processed and place into registers.
- **Execute the instruction :** From the instruction register, the data forming the instruction is decoded by the control unit. It then passes the decoded information as a sequence of control signals to the relevant function units of the CPU to perform the actions required by the instruction such as reading values from registers, passing them to the Arithmetic logic unit (ALU) to add them together and writing the result back to a register. A condition signal is sent back to the control unit by the ALU if it is involved.
- **Store results :** The result generated by the operation is stored in the main memory, or sent to an output device. Based on the condition feedback from the ALU, the PC is either incremented to address the next instruction or updated to a different address where the next instruction will be fetched. The cycle is then repeated.

Fetch cycle: Steps 1 and 2 of the Instruction Cycle are called the Fetch Cycle. These steps are the same for each instruction.

Execute cycle : Steps 3 and 4 of the Instruction Cycle are part of the Execute Cycle. These steps will change with each instruction.

8.10 OBJECT FILE

Object Code / Object File, is the representation of code that a compiler generates by processing a source code file. Object files contain compact code, often called "binaries". A linker is used to generate an executable or library by linking object files together. An object file consists of machine code (code directly executed by a computer's CPU), together with relocation information, program symbols (names of variables and functions), and possibly debugging information.

8.10.1 Object File Formats

An **object file format** is a computer file format used for the storage of object code and related data typically produced by a compiler or assembler.

There are many different object file formats; originally each type of computer had its own unique format, but with the advent of UNIX and other portable operating systems, some formats, such as COFF and ELF, have been defined and used on different kinds of systems. It is common for the same file format to be used both as linker input and output, and thus as the library and **executable file format**.

The design and/or choice of an object file format is a key part of overall system design; it affects the performance of the linker and thus programmer turnaround while developing, and if the format is used for executables, the design also affects the time programs take to begin running, and thus the responsiveness for users. Most object file formats are structured as blocks of data all of the same sort; these blocks can be paged in as needed by the virtual memory system, needing no further processing to be ready to use.

The simplest object file format is the DOS COM format, which is simply a file of raw bytes that is always loaded at a fixed location. Other formats are an elaborate array of structures and substructures whose specification runs to many pages.

Debugging information may either be an integral part of the object file format, as in COFF, or a semi-independent format which may be used with several object formats, such as stabs or DWARF. See debugging format.

Types of data supported by typical object file formats:

- BSS (Block Started by Symbol)
- Text Segment
- Data Segment

8.10.2 Notable Object File Formats

- DOS
  - COM
  - DOS executable (MZ)
  - Relocatable Object Module Format (commonly known as "OBJ file" or "OMF"; also used in Microsoft Windows by some tool vendors)
- Embedded
  - IEEE-695
  - S-records
- Macintosh
  - PEF/CFM
  - Mach-O (NEXTSTEP, Mac OS X)
- Unix
  - a.out
  - COFF (System V)
    - ECOFF (Mips)
    - XCOFF (AIX)
  - ELF (SVR4; used in most modern systems)
  - Mach-O (NeXT, Mac OS X)
- Microsoft Windows
  - 16-bit New Executable
  - Portable Executable (PE)
- Others
  - IBM 360 object format
  - NLM
  - OMF (VME)
  - SOM (HP)
  - XBE - Xbox executable
  - APP - Symbian OS executable file format.
  - RDOFF

8.11 COMPLETE C PROGRAM FOR CODE GENERATION

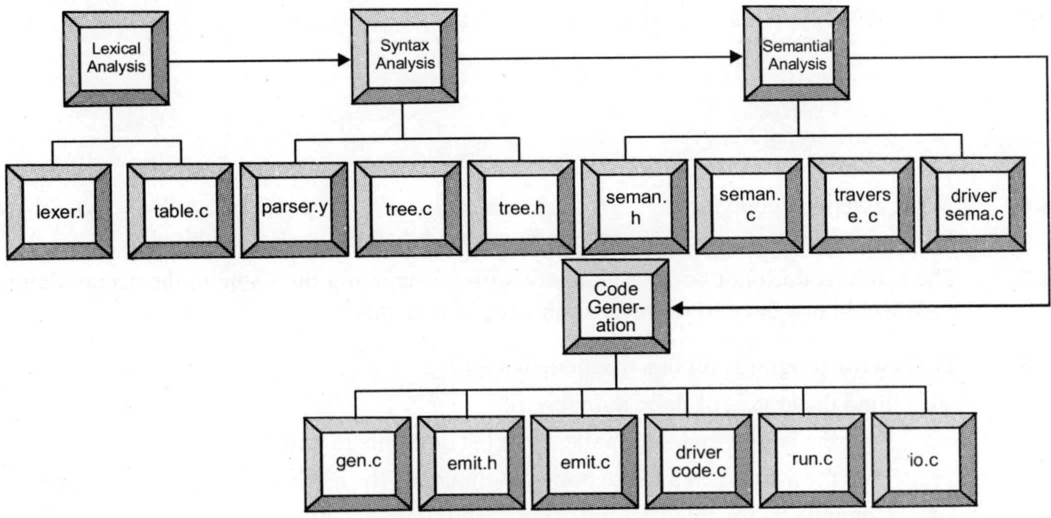

Figure 8.4

TRIBULATIONS

8.1 Using the given instruction set generate assembly code

```
int a=1;
int b=100;
while (a)  {
    b--;
    if b==0
        a=0;
}
```

8.2 Outline the general form of the target code for switch statements in C

1. *Using if-then-else constructs.*
2. *Using a jump table.*

8.3 Give assembly code for the following C code for:

```
switch(a)
{
case 1:
printf("a is true/n");
break;
case 0:
printf("a is false/n");
break;
default:
printf("a is not a boolean/n");
}
```

8.4 Write assembly code for 10 * 20-5+100/5.

8.5 What does following code do?

```
LOAD  A
ADD   B
MUL   C
STR   D
```

8.6 Write assembly code for.- *(i) If statement (ii) For loop (iii) while loop (iv) Do-while(v)* `IF ... THEN ... ELSE` statement, with the "dangling else" ambiguity.

8.7 The machine does not possess an instruction for negating the value in the accumulator. What code would one have to write to be able to achieve this?

8.8 Try to write programs for this machine that will

1. Find the largest of three numbers.
2. Find the largest and the smallest of a list of numbers terminated by a zero
3. Find the average of a list of non-zero numbers, the list being terminated by a zero.
4. Compute N! for small N. Try using an iterative as well as a recursive approach.
5. Read a word and then write it backwards.
6. Determine the prime numbers between 0 and 255.
7. Determine the longest repeated sequence in a sequence of digits.
8. Sort an array of integers or characters using insert, bubble and quick sort.

FURTHER READINGS AND REFERENCES

[1] Alfred V. Aho, Ravi Sethi, and Jeffrey D. Ullman. *Compilers: Principles, Techniques, and Tools.* Addison-Wesley, 1986.

[2] John R. Levine, *Linkers and Loaders* (Morgan Kaufmann Publishers, 2000)

[3] Kenneth C. Louden. *Compiler Construction Principles and Practice.*

[4] *Compilers and Compiler Generators an introduction with C++* by P.D. Terry, Rhodes University, 1996.

CHAPTER 9

SYMBOL TABLE

CHAPTER HIGHLIGHTS

After syntax tree have been constructed, the compiler must check whether the input program is type-correct (called *type checking* and part of the semantic analysis). During type checking, a compiler checks whether the use of names (such as variables, functions, type names) is consistent with their definition in the program. Consequently, it is necessary to remember declarations so that we can detect inconsistencies and misuses during type checking. This is the task of **a *symbol table***. Note that a symbol table is a compile-time data structure. It's not used during run time by statically typed languages. Formally, a symbol table maps names into declarations (called attributes), such as mapping the variable name `x` to its type `int`. More specifically, a symbol table stores:

- For each type name, its type definition.
- For each variable name, its type. If the variable is an array, it also stores dimension information. It may also store storage class, offset in activation record etc.
- For each constant name, its type and value.
- For each function and procedure, its formal parameter list and its output type. Each formal parameter must have name, type, type of passing (by-reference or by-value), etc.

9.1 OPERATION ON SYMBOL TABLE

We need to implement the following operations for a symbol table:

1. insert (String key, Object binding)
2. object_lookup (String key)
3. begin_scope () and end_scope ()

(1) insert (s,t)- return index of new entry for string 's' and token 't'

(2) lookup (s)- return index of new entry for string 's' or o if 's' is not found.

(3) begin_scope () and end_scope () : When we have a new block (ie, when we encounter the token {), we begin a new scope. When we exit a block (i.e. when we encounter the token }) we remove the scope (this is the end_scope). When we remove a scope, we remove all declarations inside this scope. So basically, scopes behave like stacks. One way to implement these functions is to use a stack. When we begin a new scope we push a special marker to the stack (e.g., 1). When we insert a new declaration in the hash table using insert, we also push the bucket number to the stack. When we end a scope, we pop the stack until and including the first –1 marker.

Example 9.1: Consider the following program:

```
1) {
2)  int a;
3)  {
4)    int a;
5)    a = 1;
6)  };
7)  a = 2;
8) };
```

we have the following sequence of commands for each line in the source program (we assume that the hash key for a is 12):

1) push(–1)
2) insert the binding from a to int into the beginning of the list table[12]
   push(12)
3) push(–1)
4) insert the binding from a to int into the beginning of the list table[12]

Contd...

push(12)
6) pop()
remove the head of table[12]
pop()
7) pop()
remove the head of table[12]
pop()

Recall that when we search for a declaration using lookup, we search the bucket list from the beginning to the end, so that if we have multiple declarations with the same name, the declaration in the innermost scope overrides the declaration in the outer scope.

(4) Handling Reserve Keywords: Symbol table also handle reserve keywords like 'PLUS', MINUS', 'MUL' etc. This can be done in following manner.

insert ("PLUS", PLUS);

insert ("MINUS", MINUS);

In this case first 'PLUS' and 'MINUS' indicate lexeme and other one indicate token.

9.2 SYMBOL TABLE IMPLEMENTATION

The data structure for a particular implementation of a symbol table is sketched in **figure 9.1**. In **figure 9.1**, a separate array 'arr_lexemes' holds the character string forming an identifier. The string is terminated by an end-of-string character, denoted by EOS, that may not appear in identifiers. Each entry in symbol-table array 'arr_symbol_table' is a record consisting of two fields, as *"lexeme_pointer"*, pointing to the beginning of a lexeme, and token. Additional fields can hold attribute values. In **figure 9.1**, the 0th entry is left empty, because lookup return 0 to indicate that there is no entry for a string. The 1st, 2nd, 3rd, 4th, 5th, 6th, and 7th entries are for the 'a', 'plus' 'b' 'and', 'c', 'minus', and 'd' where 2nd, 4th and 6th entries are for reserve keyword.

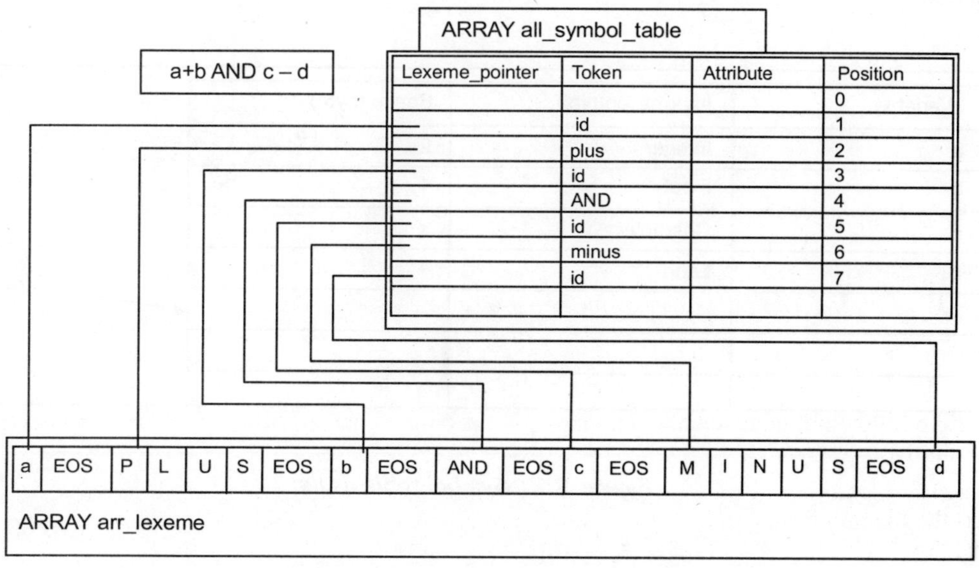

Figure 9.1: Implemented symbol table

When lexical analyzer reads a letter, it starts saving letters, digits in a buffer 'lex_buffffer'. The string collected in lex_bufffer is then looked in the symbol table, using the lookup operation. Since the symbol table initialized with entries for the keywords plus, minus, AND operator and some identifiers as shown in **figure 9.1** the lookup operation will find these entries if lex_buffer contains either div or mod. If there is no entry for the string in lex_buffer, i.e., lookup return 0, then lex_buffer contains a lexeme for a new identifier. An entry for the identifier is created using insert( ). After the insertion is made; 'n' is the index of the symbol-table entry for the string in lex_buffer. This index is communicated to the parser by setting tokenval to n, and the token in the token field of the entry is returned.

9.3 DATA STRUCTURE FOR SYMBOL TABLE

9.3.1 List

The simplest and easiest to implement data structure for symbol table is a linear list of records. We use single array or collection of several arrays for this purpose to store name and their associated information. Now names are added to end of array. End of array always marks by a point known as space. When we insert any name in this list then searching is done in whole array from 'space' to beginning of array. If word is not found in array then we create an entry at 'space' and increment 'space' by one or value of data type. At this time insert ( ), object look up ( ) operation are performed as major operation while begin_scope ( ) and end_scope( ) are used in simple table as minor operation field as 'token type' attribute etc. In implementation of symbol table first field always empty because when 'object-lookup' work then it will return '0' to indicate no string in symbol table.

Complexity: If any symbol table has 'n' names then for inserting any new name we must search list 'n' times in worst case. So cost of searching is O(n) and if we want to insert 'n' name then cost of this insert is O(n^2) in worst case.

Variable	Information(type	Space (byte)
a	Integer	2
b	Float	4
c	Character	1
d	Long	4

SPACE

Figure 9.2: Symbol table as list

9.3.2 Self Organizing List

To reduce the time of searching we can add an addition field 'linker' to each record field or each array index. When a name is inserted then it will insert at 'space' and manage all linkers to other existing name.

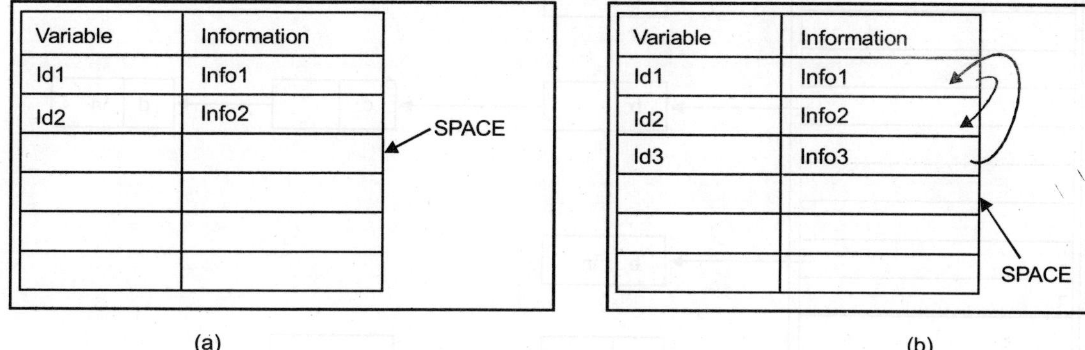

Figure 9.3: Symbol table as self organizing list

In above figure (a) represent the simple list and (b) represent self organzing list in which Id1 is related to Id2 and Id3 is related to Id1.

9.3.3 Hash Table

A **hash table**, or a **hash map**, is a data structure that associates keys with values 'Open hashing' is a key that is applied to hash table. In hashing –open, there is a property that no limit on number of entries that can be made in table. Hash table consist an array 'HESH' and several buckets attached to array HESH according to hash function. Main advantage of hash table is that we can insert or delete any number or name in O (n) time if data are search linearly and there are 'n' memory location where data is stored. Using hash function any name can be search in O(1) time. However, the rare worst-case lookup time can be as bad as O(n). A good hash function is essential for good hash table performance. A poor choice of a hash function is likely to lead to clustering, in which probability of keys mapping to the same hash bucket (i.e. a collision) occur. One organization of a hash table that resolves conflicts is chaining. The idea is that we have list elements of type:

```
class Symbol {
    public String key;
    public Object binding;
    public Symbol next;
     public Symbol  ( String k, Object v, Symbol r ) { key=k; binding=v;
next=r; }
}
```

Structure of hash table look like as

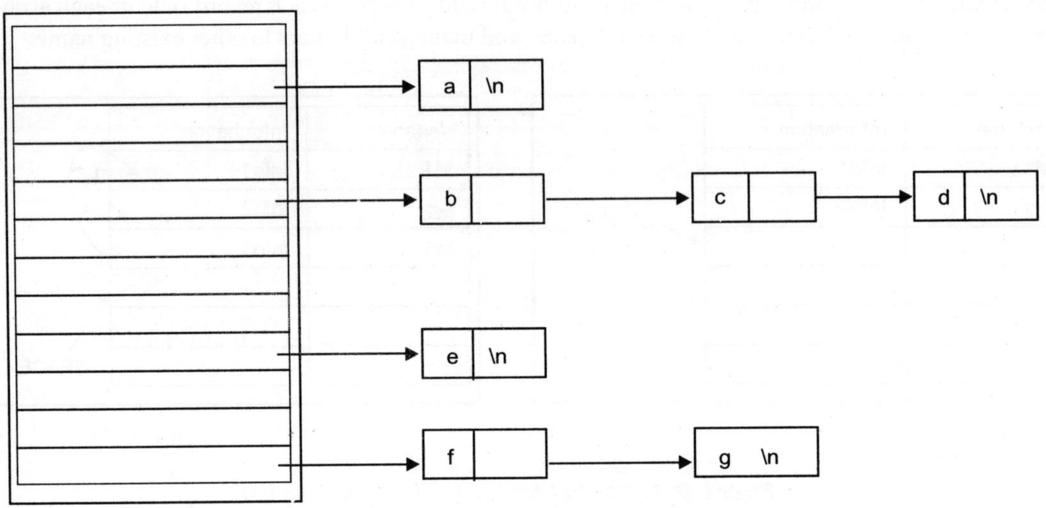

Figure 9.4: Symbol table as hash table (\n represent NULL)

9.3.4 Search Tree

Another approach to organize symbol table is that we add two link fields i.e. left and right child, we use these field as binary search tree. All names are created as child of root node that always follow the property of binary tree i.e. name <name ie and Namej <name. These two statements show that all smaller name than Namei must be left child of name otherwise right child of namej. For inserting any name it always follow binary search tree insert algorithm.

Example 9.2: Create list, search tree and hash table for given program for given program

```
int a,b,c;
int sum (int x, int y)
{
        a = x+y
        return (a)
}
main ()
{
        int u,
        u=sum (5,6);
}
```

(i) List

Variable	Information	Space(byte)
u	Integer	2 byte
a	Integer	2 byte
b	Integer	2 byte
c	Integer	2 byte
x	Integer	2 byte
y	Integer	2 byte
sum	Integer	2 byte

Space

Figure 9.5: Symbol table as list for example 9.2

(ii) Hash Table

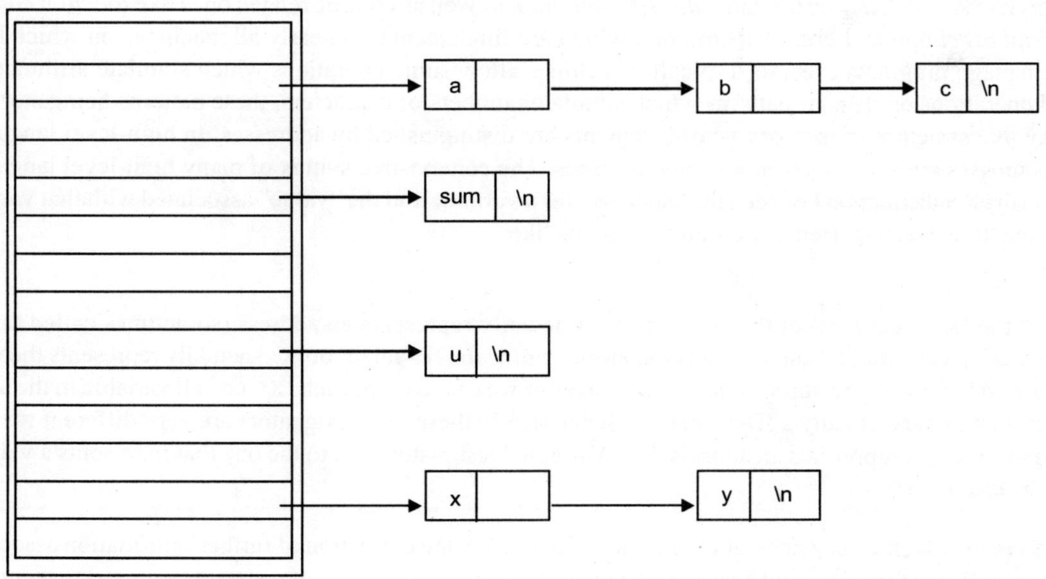

Figure 9.6: Symbol table as hash table for example 9.2

(iii) Search Tree

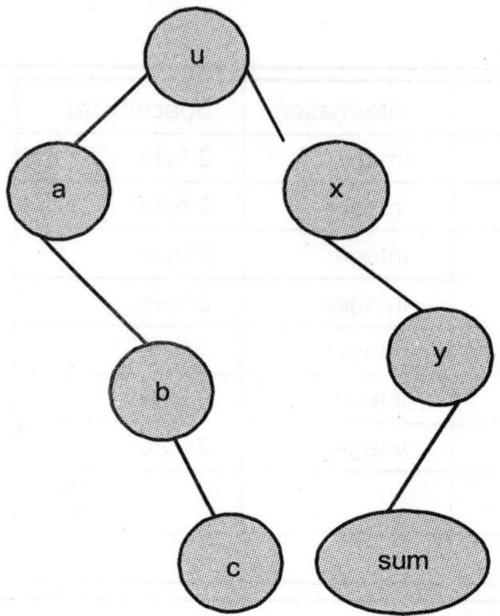

Figure 9.7: Symbol table as search tree for example 9.2

9.4 SYMBOL TABLE HANDLER

Any interface i.e. symbol table between source and object code must take recognisance of data-related concepts like *storage*, *addresses* and *data representation* as well as control-related ones like *location counter, sequential execution* and *branch instruction* which are fundamental to nearly all machines on which high-level language programs execute. Typically machines allow some operations which simulate arithmetic or logical operations on data bit patterns which simulate numbers or characters, these patterns being stored in an array like structure of memory whose elements are distinguished by addresses. In high-level languages these addresses are usually given mnemonic names. The context-free syntax of many high-level languages seems to draw a distinction between the "address" for a variable and the "value" associated with that variable and stored at its address. Hence we find statements like

$$X := X + 4$$

in which the 'X' on the left of the ':=' operator actually represents an address (sometimes called the 'L-value' of 'X') while the 'X' on the right (sometimes called the 'R-value' of 'X') actually represents the value of the quantity currently residing at the same address or we can say that each 'X' i.e., all variable in the above assignment was syntactically a 'Designator'. Semantically these two designators are very different we shall refer to the one that represents an address as a 'Variable Designator' and to the one that represents a value as a 'Value Designator'.

To perform its task, the code generation interface will require the extraction of further information associated with user-defined identifiers and best kept in the symbol table. In the case of constants we need to record the associated values and in the case of variables we need to record the associated addresses and storage demands (the elements of array variables will occupy a contiguous block of memory).

Handling the different manners of entries that need to be stored in a symbol table can be done in various ways (described in section 9.4). One different method from 9.4 is object-oriented class based implementation one might define an abstract base class to represent a generic type of entry and then derive classes from this to represent entries for variables or constants. The traditional way, still required if one is hosting a compiler in a language that does not support inheritance as a concept, is to make use of union (in C++ terminology). Since the class-based implementation gives so much scope for exercises, we have chosen to illustrate the variant record approach which is very efficient and quite adequate for such a simple language. We extend the declaration of the 'TABLE_entries' type to be

```
struct TABLE_entries {
  TABLE_alfa name;          // identifier
  TABLE_idclasses idclass;  // class
  union {
    struct {
      int value;
    } c;                    // constants
    struct {
      int size, offset;     // number of words, relative address
      bool scalar;          // distinguish arrays
    } v;                    // variables
  };
};
```

TRIBULATIONS

9.1 How would you check that no identifier is declared more than once?

9.2 How do real compilers deal with symbol tables?

9.3 How do real compilers keep track of type checking via symbol table? Why should name equivalence be easier to handle than structural equivalence?

9.4 Why do some languages simply prohibit the use of "anonymous types" and why don't more languages forbid them?

9.5 How do you suppose compilers keep track of storage allocation for struct or RECORD types, and for union or variant record types?

9.6 Find out how storage is managed for dynamically allocated variables in language like C++.

9.7 How does one cope with arrays of variable (dynamic) length in subprograms?

9.8 Identifiers that are undeclared by virtue of mistyped declarations tend to be trying for they result in many subsequent errors being reported. Perhaps in languages as simple as ours one could assume that all undeclared identifiers should be treated as variables and entered as such in the symbol table at the point of first reference. Is this a good idea? Can it easily be implemented? What happens if arrays are undeclared?

9.9 C language array declaration is different from a C++ one the bracketed number in C language specifies the highest permitted index value, rather than the array length. This has been done so that one can declare variables like

```
VAR Scalar, List[10], VeryShortList[0];
```

How would you modify C language and Topsy to use C++ semantics, where the declaration of VeryShortList would have to be forbidden?

9.10 Yet another approach is to construct the symbol table using a hash table which probably yields the shortest times for retrievals. Develop a hash table implementation for your C compiler.

9.11 We might consider letting the scanner interact with the symbol table. Develop a scanner that stores the strings for identifiers and string literals in a string table.

9.12 Develop a symbol table handler that utilizes a simple class hierarchy for the possible types of entries inheriting appropriately from a suitable base class. Once again construction of such a table should prove to be straightforward regardless of whether you use a linear array, tree or hash table as the underlying storage structure. Retrieval might call for more initiative since C++ does not provide syntactic support for determining the exact class of an object that has been statically declared to be of a base class type.

9.13 Why can we easily allow the declaration of a pointer type to precede the definition of the type it points to even in a one-pass system?

9.14 One might accuse the designers of Pascal and C of making a serious error of judgement they do not introduce a string type as standard but rely on programmers to manipulate arrays of characters and to use error level ways of recognizing the end or the length of a string. Do you agree? Discuss whether what they offer in return is adequate and if not why not. Suggest why they might deliberately not have introduced a string type.

9.15 Many authors dislike pointer types because they allow insecure programming. What is meant by this? How could the security be improved? If you do not like pointer types, can you think of any alternative feature that would be more secure?

FURTHER READINGS AND REFERENCES

[1] Alfred V. Aho, Ravi Sethi, and Jeffrey D. Ullman. *Compilers: Principles, Techniques and Tools.*

[2] Holub, Allen. *Compiler Design in C Extensive examples in "C".*

[3] Appel, Andrew. *Modern Compiler Implementation in C/Java/ML* is a set of cleanly written texts on compiler design, studied from various different methodological perspectives.

[4] Brown, P.J. *Writing Interactive Compilers and Interpreters.* Useful practical advice, not much theory.

[5] Fischer, Charles & LeBlanc, Richard. *Crafting A Compiler.* Uses an ADA like pseudo-code.

[6] Weinberg, G.M. *The Psychology of Computer Programming: Silver Anniversary.* Interesting insights and anecdotes.

[7] Wirth, Niklaus. *Compiler Construction.* From the inventor of Pascal, Modula-2 and Oberon-2, examples in Oberon.

[8] Compiler textbook references *A collection of references to mainstream Compiler Construction Textbook.*

[9] Wirth, Niklaus *Compiler Construction,* Addison-Wesley 1996, pp.176.

[10] Cifuentes, C. *Reverse Compilation Techniques.* PhD thesis, Queensland University of Technology, 1994. (available as compressed postscript).

[11] Czarnota, B. and Hart R.J. *Legal protection of computer programs in Europe*: a guide to the EC directive. 1991, London: Butterworths.

[12] Terry, P.D. *Compilers and Compiler Generators an introduction with C++,* Rhodes University, 1996.

CHAPTER 10

RUN TIME MANAGEMENT

CHAPTER HIGHLIGHTS

10.1 PROGRAM, SUBPROGRAM, SUBROUTINE, COROUTINE, PROCEDURE, FUNCTION

Program: Program is a sequence of statements written in any language to get desired result. It contain subprogram, procedure, function, subroutine, coroution.

Subprogram: A program is composed of a single main program which call other subprogram during its execution. Subprogram must follow following properties as :

- Subprogram may not be recursive.
- Explicit call statements are required.
- Subprogram must execute completely at each time.
- Immediate transfer of control at point of call.
- Single execution sequence.

Subroutine: Subroutine is a portion of code within a larger program, which performs a specific task and is relatively independent of the remaining code. There are many advantages to breaking a program up into subroutines, including:

- reducing the redundancy in a program
- enabling reuse of code across multiple programs,
- decomposing complex problems into simpler pieces
- improving readability of a program,
- Hiding or regulating part of the program

The components of a subroutine may include:

- A body of code to be executed when the subroutine is called
- Parameters that are passed to the subroutine from the point where it is called
- A value that is returned to the point where the call occurs

Coroutine: Coroutines are program components that generalize subroutines to allow multiple entry points and suspending and resuming of execution at certain locations. Coroutines are simple subprogram that violate one property of subprogram i.e., subprogram must execute completely at each time.Coroutines are more generic and flexible than subroutines, but are less widely used in practice. Here's a simple example of how coroutines can be useful. Suppose you have a consumer-producer relationship where one routine creates items and adds them to a queue and another removes items from the queue and uses them. For reasons of efficiency, you want to add and remove several items at once. The code might look like this:

```
var q := new queue

coroutine produce
    loop
        while q is not full
            create some new items
            add the items to q
        yield to consume

coroutine consume
    loop
        while q is not empty
```

Contd....

```
        remove some items from q
        use the items
    yield to produce
```

Each coroutine does as much work as it can before yielding control to the other using the '*yield*' command. The '*yield*' causes control in the other coroutine to pick up where it left off, but now with the queue modified so that it can do more work.

Procedure: A procedure is a specification of the series of actions, acts or operations which have to be executed in the same manner in order to obtain always the same result in the same circumstances and it will never return value to callee.

Function: Function is a procedure that always returns a value to callee.

10.2 ACTIVATION TREE

Any program is made of several subprogram, procedure, function and coroutines. When any function call other then they form tree for this situation. At this time tree is created using following four rules as:

(i) Each node represents an activation of a procedure.

(ii) The root represents the activation of main program.

(iii) The node for 'a' is the parent of the node for 'b' if and only if control flows from activation 'a' to 'b'.

(iv) The node for 'a' is the left of the node for 'b' if only if the lifetime of 'a' occur before the lifetime of 'b'.

Example 10.1

```
void sum (int x, int y)
{
        z = x + y ;
}
void sub ( int x,int y)
{
        z = x − y ;
}
void main()
{
        int x = 5 ;
        int y = 5 ;
        sum ( x, y ) ;
        sub ( x, y ) ;
}
```

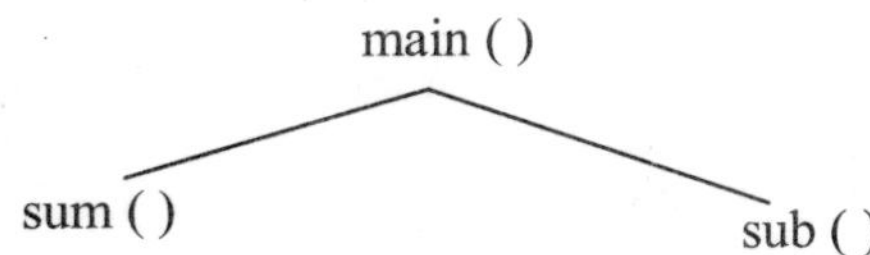

Figure 10.1: Activation tree of example 10.1

(according to rule (iii) and (iv))

Example 10.2:

```
void partition (int *a, int p, int r)
{
    ____________
    ____________
    ____________
    ____________

}
void quicksort (int *a, int p, int r)
{
    int q;
    q = partition (a, p, q);
    quick sort (a, p, q–1);
    quick sort (a, q+1, r);
}
void main ( )
{
    int a[10];
    p=0;
    r=9;
    quick sort (a, p, r);
}
```

For above program activation tree look like as:

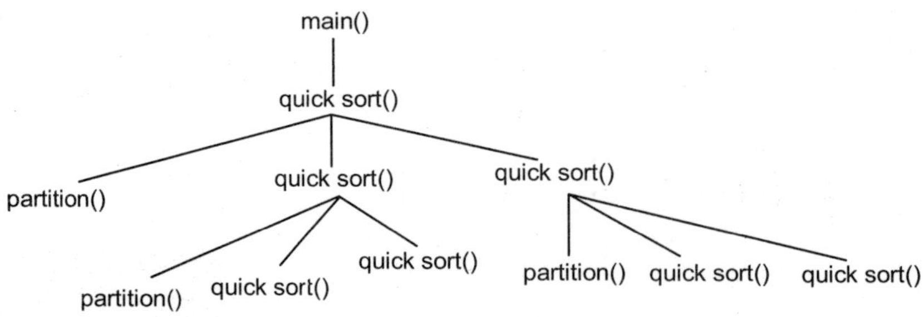

Figure 10.2: Activation Tree of example 10.2

Referencing environment and state: Referencing environment refer to a function that maps a name to a storage location. When we assign any value to any variable then they never change its referencing environment. State refers to a function that maps a storage location to value held there. Each assignment statement change state of variable.

10.3 ACTIVATION RECORD

When we call a function **f**, we push a new ***activation record*** on the run-time stack, which is particular to the function **f.** Each activation record can occupy many consecutive bytes in the stack and may not be of a fixed size. When the callee function returns to the caller, the activation record of the callee is popped out. For example, if the main program calls function **P**, P calls **E**, and **E** calls P, then at the time of the second call to P, there will be **4** activation records in the stack in the following *order: main, P, E, P.*

There two things that we need to do though when executing a function: the first is that we should be able to pop-out the current activation record of the callee and restore the caller activation record . This can be done with the help of a pointer in the current activation record, called the ***dynamic link***, that points to the previous activation record. Thus all activation records are linked together in the stack using dynamic links. This is called the ***dynamic chain***. The second thing that we need to do, is if we allow nested functions, we need to be able to access the variables stored in previous activation records in the stack. This is done with the help of the ***static link***. Activation records linked together with static links form a ***static chain***. The static link of a function **f** points to the latest activation record in the stack of the function that statically contains **f**. If **f** is not lexically contained in any other function, its static link is null. For example, if **P** called **Q** then the static link of **Q** will point to the latest activation record of **P** in the stack.

A typical organization of an activation record as following in figure 10.3:

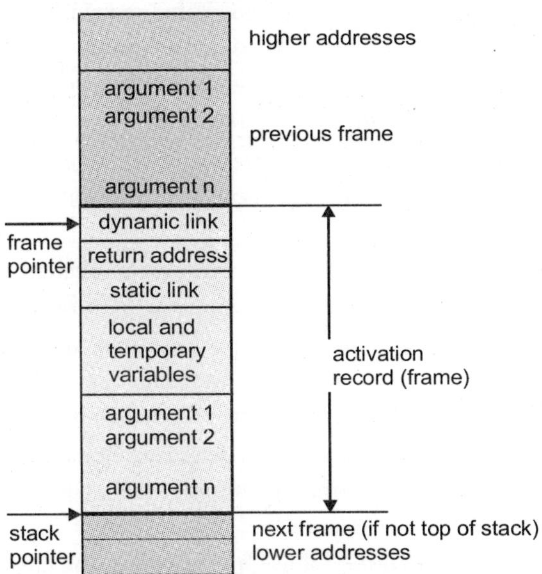

Figure 10.3: Activation record

We can classify the variables in a program into four categories:

- **Statically allocated data** that reside in the static data part of the program; these are the global variables.
- **Dynamically allocated data** that reside in the heap; these are the data created by malloc in C.
- **Register allocated variables** that reside in the CPU registers; these can be function arguments, function return values, or local variables.
- **Activation record-resident variables** that reside in the run-time stack; these can be function arguments, function return values, or local variables.

Every activation record-resident variable (i.e., a local variable) can be viewed as a pair of (level, offset). Activation record can also have following fields as:·

- **Code Segment for Translated User Programs:** A major block of storage in any system must be allocated to store the code segments representing the translated form of user program, regardless of whether program are hardware or software interpreted.
- **System Run-Time Programs:** Another substantial block of storage during exaction must be allocated to system programs that support the execution of the user programs. These may range from simple library routines, such as sine, cosine or print-string function, to software interpreters or translators present during execution.
- **User-Defined Data Structure and Constant:** Space for user data must be allocated for all data structures declared in or created by user programs including constants.
- **Subprogram Return Points:** Subprograms have the property that they may be invoked from different points in a program. Therefore, internally generated sequence control information, such as subprogram return point, or event notices for scheduled subprogram, must be allocated storage.
- **Referencing Environment:** Storage of Referencing Environment during execution may require substantial space, as, for example, the LISP A-list.
- **Temporaries in Expression Evaluation:** Expression evaluation requires the use of system-defined temporary storage for the intermediate results of the evaluation. For example, in evaluation of the expression like in example 6.6, 6.7 etc.
- **Temporaries in Parameter Passing:** When a subprogram is called, a list of actual parameter must be evaluated and the resulting values stored in temporaries storage.
- **Input-Output Buffer:** Ordinarily input and output operations work through buffers, which serve as temporary storage areas where data are stored between the time of the actual physical transfer of the data to or from external storage and the program-initiated input and output operation.
- **Miscellaneous System Data:** In almost every language implementation, storage is required for various system data tables, status information for input-output, and various miscellaneous pieces of state information.
- **Data Structure Creation and Destruction Operations:** If the language provides operations that allow new data structure to be created at arbitrary points during program execution (rather than only on subprogram entry) then those operations ordinarily require storage allocation that is separate from that allocated on subprogram entry.

10.4 STORAGE ALLOCATION STRATEGIES

10.4.1 Run Time Storage Organization

An executable program generated by a compiler will have the following organization in memory:

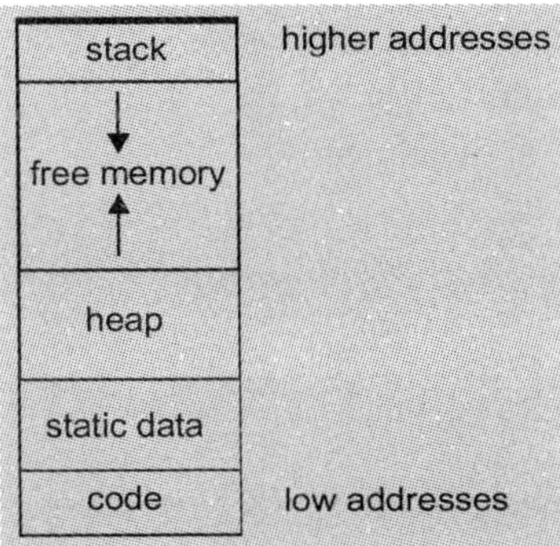

Figure 10.4: Run-time storage organizations

This is the layout in memory of an executable program. Note that in virtual memory architecture, some parts of the memory layout may in fact be located on disk blocks and they are retrieved in memory by demand. The machine code of the program is typically located at the lowest part of the layout.

After the code, there is a section to keep all the fixed size static data in the program. The dynamically allocated data i.e., the data created using *malloc* in C are kept in the heap. The heap grows from low to high addresses. When you call *malloc* in C to create a dynamically allocated structure, the program tries to find an empty place in the heap with sufficient space to insert the new data; if it can't do that, it puts the data at the end of the heap and increases the heap size.

The focus of this section is the stack in the memory layout. It is called the *run-time stack*. The stack grows in the opposite direction upside-down: from high to low addresses, which is a bit counterintuitive. The stack is not only used to push the return address when a function is called, but it is also used for allocating some of the local variables of a function during the function call.

Storage Management Phases: It is convenient to identify three basic aspects of storage management as:

- **Initial Allocation:** At the start of execution each piece of storage may be either allocated for some use or free. If free initially, it is available for allocation dynamically as execution proceeds. Any storage management system requires some technique for keeping track of free storage as well as mechanisms for allocation of free storage as the need arises during execution.
- **Recovery:** Storage that has been allocated and used and that subsequently becomes available must be recovered by the storage manager for reuse. Recovery may be very simple, as in the repositioning of a stack pointer, or very complex, as in garbage collection.
- **Compaction and Reuse:** Storage recovered may be immediately ready for reuse, or compaction may be necessary to construct large blocks of free storage from small pieces. Reuse of storage ordinarily involves the same mechanisms as initial allocation.

10.4.2 Static Allocation

In static allocation, names are bound to storage as program is compiled, so there is no need for run time support package. Since binding do not change at run time whenever every time procedure is activated. Every time when procedure is actives, it always bound to same storage location This property allow that value of local names to be retained across activation of procedure i.e., value of locals are same as they were before activation. Fortran is a language that support for static allocation.

Main problems of static allocation are:

(i) Size of data object must be known at compile time.

(ii) Recursive procedure are not allowed

(iii) Data structure can be created at dynamically.

Example 10.3:

```
PROGRAM SUM
    INTEGER a
    INTEGER b
    INTEGER c
        a = 5
        b = 5
        c = a + b
```

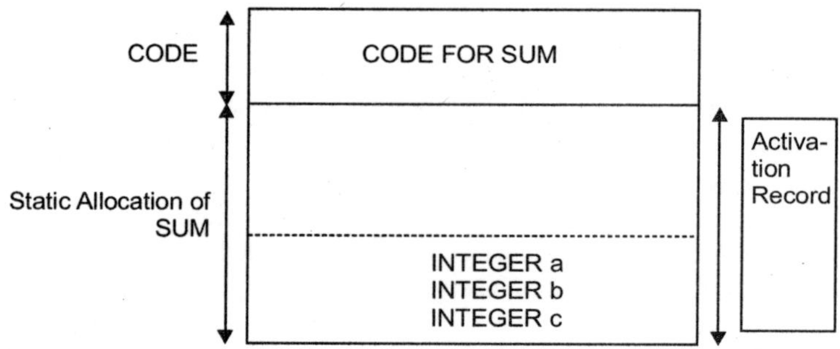

Figure 10.5: Static allocation of example 10.3

10.4.3 Stack Allocation

Stack allocation use stack for storing variables. In stack all variables are pushed when they are activated and pop when they are deactivated. In this case, stack top is incremented or decremented by the size of variable. Stack allocation may be dived into two parts as:

(i) **Stack allocation for fix size variable:** This method is simple for storing fix size data object. In this case, only stack pointer is incremented by the size of data object when they are activated and decremented when they are deactivated.

(ii) **Stack allocation for variable length size variable:** This method is not so simple as previous one. Main example of category is array. In this case storage for array is not a part of activation record. Activation record contain only a pointer to array's base address.

Example 10.4: Following example is complete example of stack allocation for fix size variable and stack allocation for variable length size variable.

```
void function
{
    int a,b,c
    int x[10], y [10]
    c= a+b;
}
```

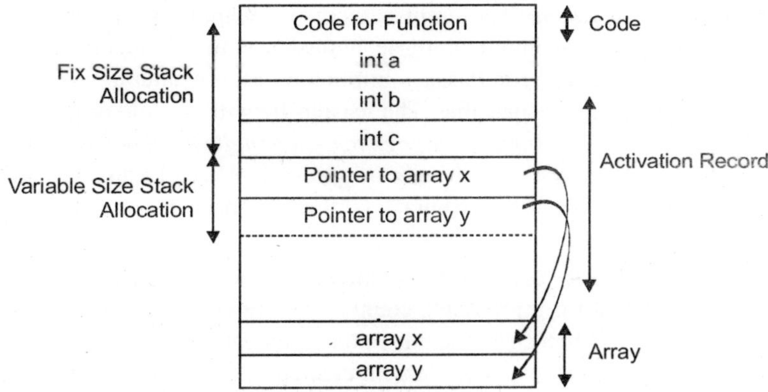

Figure 10.6: Stack allocation of example 10.3

Problem of stack allocation

(i) Value of local name must be retained when activation end.

(ii) A called activation outlines the caller

10.4.4 Heap Allocation

Problem of Stack Allocation: The problems of storage allocation, recovery compaction and reuse may be strict in stack allocation. There is no single heap storage management technique, but rather a collection of techniques for handing various aspects or managing this memory.

Need of Heap Storage Allocation: The need for heap storage arises when a language permits storage to be allocated and freed at arbitrary points during program execution, as when a language allows creation, destruction or examination of program points. It is convenient to divide heap storage management techniques into two categories, depending on whether the elements allocated are always of the same fixed size or of variable size as

- Fix Size Heap and
- Variable Size Heap

10.4.4.1 Fix Size Heap

Fix Size Heap is where fixed-size elements are used, management techniques may be considerably simplified. Compaction, in particular, is not problem since all available elements are the same size.

Assume that each fixed-size element that is allocated from the heap and later recovered occupies N words of memory. Typically N might be 1 or 2. Assuming the heap occupies a contiguous block of memory, we conceptually divide the heap block into a sequence of K elements, each N words long, such that $K \times N$ is the size of the heap. Whenever an element is needed, one of these is allocated from the heap. Whenever an element is freed, it must be one of these original heap elements.

Initially the K elements are linked together to form a free-space list (i.e., the first word of each item on the free list points to the first word of the next item on the free list). To allocate an element, the first element on the free-space list is removed from the list and a pointer to it is returned to the operation requesting the storage. When an element is freed, it is simply linked back in at the head of the free-space list.

Recovery: Reference Counts and Garbage Collection

Explicit return by programmer or system: The simplest recovery technique is that of explicit return. When an element that has been in use becomes available for reuse, it must be explicitly identified as "free" and returned to the free-space list (e.g., a call to dispose in Pascal). Explicit return is a natural recovery technique for heap storage, but unfortunately it is not always feasible. The reasons lie with two old problems: *garbage and dangling references*. In the context of *heap storage management, a dangling reference* is a pointer to an element that has been returned to free space list (which may have also been reallocated for another purpose) and *garbage element* is one that is available for reuse but not on the free-space list, and thus it has become inaccessible.

Reference counts: The use of reference counts is the simpler of the two techniques. Within each element in the heap some extra space is provided for a reference counter. The reference counter indicates the number of pointer to that element that exists. When an element is initially allocated from the free space list, its reference count is set to 1. Each time a new pointer to the element created, its reference count is increased by 1. Each time a pointer is destroyed, the reference count is decreased by 1. When the reference count of an element reaches zero; the element is free and may be returned to the free-space list.

10.4.4.2 Variable Size Heap

Heap storage management is use as variable size where variable-size elements are allocated and recovered is more difficult than with fixed-size elements. Variable-size elements arise in many situations. For example, if space is being used for programmer defined data structures stored sequentially, such as arrays, then variable-size blocks of space will be required, or activation records for tasks might be allocated in a heap in sequential blocks of varying sizes.

The major difficulties with variable size elements concern reuse of recovered space.

- **Initial Allocation and Reuse**

  With fix size elements it was appropriate to split the heap immediately into a sets and then base initial allocation on a free-space list containing these elements. Such a technique is not acceptable with variable-size elements. Initially consider the heap as simply one large block of free storage. A heap pointer is appropriate for initial allocation. When a block of N words is requested, the heap pointer is advanced by N and the original heap pointer value returned as a pointer to newly allocated element. Two possibilities for reuse present because of the variable size of the elements:

  1. Use the free space list for allocation, searching the list for an appropriate size block and returning any leftover space to the free list after the allocation.
  2. Compact the free space by moving all the active elements to one end of the heap, leaving the free space as a single block at the end and resetting the heap pointer to begging of this block.

- **Recovery**

  Explicit return of freed space to a free-space list is the simplest technique, but the problems of garbage and dangling references are again present. Reference counts may be used in the ordinary manner. Garbage collection is also a feasible technique. Some additional problems arise with variable-size blocks, however.

- **Compaction and the Memory Fragmentation Problem**

  The problem that any heap storage management system using variable-size elements faces is that of memory fragmentation. One begins with a single large block of free space. As computation proceeds, this block is progressively fragmented into smaller pieces through allocation, recovery, and reuse. If only the simple first-fit or best-fit allocation technique is used, it is apparent that free-space blocks continue to split into ever smaller pieces. Ultimately one reaches a point where a storage allocator cannot honour a request for a block of N words because no sufficiently large block exists, even though the free-space list contains in total far more than N word. Without some compaction of free blocks into larger blocks, execution will be hanging by a lack of free storage faster than necessary.

10.5 PARAMETER PASSING

10.5.1 Parameters and Arguments

A parameter is a variable which can be accepted by a subroutine. The subroutine uses the values assigned to its parameters to alter its behaviour at runtime. Most programming languages can define subroutines that accept zero or more parameters. Parameters are also commonly referred to as arguments, though arguments are more properly thought of as the actual values or references assigned to the parameter variables when the subroutine is called at runtime. When discussing code that is calling into a subroutine, any values or references passed into the subroutine are the arguments, and the place in the code where these values or references are given is the parameter list.

Many programmers use parameter and argument interchangeably, depending on context to distinguish the meaning. In practice, distinguishing between the two terms is usually unnecessary in order to use them correctly or communicate their use to other programmers. Alternatively, the equivalent terms formal parameter and actual parameter may be used.

To better understand the difference, consider the following subroutine written in C:

```
int sum(int addend1, int addend2)
{
   return addend1 + addend2;
}
```

The subroutine sum accepts two parameters, named addend1 and addend2. It adds the values passed into the parameters, and returns the result to the subroutine's caller (using a technique automatically supplied by the C compiler).

The code which calls the sum subroutine might look like this:

```
int sumValue;
int value1 = 40;
int value2 = 2;
sumValue = sum(value1, value2);
```

The variables value1 and value2 are initialized with values. The variables are not arguments or parameters.

At runtime, the values assigned to these variables are passed to the subroutine sum. In the sum subroutine, the parameters addend1 and addend2 are evaluated, yielding the arguments 40 and 2, respectively. The values of the arguments are added, and the result is returned to the caller, where it is assigned to the variable sumValue.

10.5.2 Default Argument

A default argument is an argument to a function that a programmer is not required to specify. In most programming languages, functions may take one or more arguments.

Later languages (for example, in C++) allow the programmer to specify default arguments that always have some value, even if the calling program do not write them. For example, in the following function definition:

```
int MyFunc(int a, int b, int c=12);
```

This function takes three arguments, of which the last one has a default of twelve. The programmer may call this function in two ways:

result = MyFunc(1, 2, 3);

result = MyFunc(1, 2);

In the first case the value for the argument called c is specified as normal. In the second one, the argument is omitted, and the default 12 value will be used instead.

The called function has no way of knowing if the argument has been specified by the caller or using the default value.

10.5.3 Variable-length Parameter Lists

Some languages allow subroutines to be defined with a variable number of arguments. For such languages, the subroutines must iterate through the list of arguments.

10.5.4 Named Parameters

Some programming languages allow subroutines to have named parameters. Naming of parameters (or named parameters) means that the method signature clearly states the name (meaning) of each parameter. This allows the calling code to be more self-documenting. It also provides more flexibility to the caller, often allowing the order of the arguments to be changed, or for arguments to be omitted as needed. This is not used in languages like Java and C++. It is supported in languages like Ada, PL/SQL, Smalltalk and Objective C; in Objective Caml, named parameters are called labels.

10.5.5 Parameter Evaluation Strategy

An evaluation strategy is a set of (usually deterministic) rules for determining the evaluation of expressions in a programming language. Emphasis is typically placed on functions or operators — an evaluation strategy defines when and in what order the arguments to a function are evaluated, when they are substituted into the function, and what form that substitution takes. The lambda calculus, a formal system for the study of functions, has often been used to model evaluation strategies, where they are usually called reduction strategies.

Evaluation strategies divide into two basic groups, strict and non-strict, based on how arguments to a function are handled. A language may combine several evaluation strategies; for example, C++ combines call-by-value with call-by-reference. Most languages that are predominantly strict use some form of non-strict evaluation for boolean expressions and if-statements.

10.5.5.1 Strict evaluation

In strict evaluation, the arguments to a function are always evaluated completely before the function is applied.

Under Church encoding, eager evaluation of operators maps to strict evaluation of functions; for this reason, strict evaluation is sometimes called "eager". Most existing programming languages use strict evaluation for functions.

Applicative order: Applicative order (or leftmost innermost) evaluation refers to an evaluation strategy in which the arguments of a function are evaluated from left to right in a post-order traversal of reducible expressions (radixes). Unlike call-by-value, applicative order evaluation reduces terms within a function body as much as possible before the function is applied.

10.5.5.1.1 Call by value

Call by value evaluation is the most common evaluation strategy, used in languages as far-ranging as C. In call-by-value, the argument expression is evaluated, and the resulting value is bound to the corresponding variable in the function (usually by capture-avoiding substitution or by copying the value into a new memory region). If the function or procedure is able to assign values to its parameters, only the local copy is assigned — that is, anything passed into a function call is unchanged in the caller's scope when the function returns.

Call by value is not a single evaluation strategy, but rather the family of evaluation strategies in which a function's argument is evaluated before being passed to the function. While many programming languages that use call by value evaluate function arguments left to right, some (such as O'Caml) evaluate functions and their arguments right to left.

Example 10.5:

```
#include<stdio.h>
#include<conio.h>
int sum (int , int );
void main()
{
    int a = 10;
    int b = 5;
    int c = sum(a,b);
    clrscr();
    printf("The Sum is::::%d",c);   // 15
    getch();
}
int sum (int x, int y)
{
    int z = x + y;
    return (z);
}
```

10.5.5.1.2 Call by reference

In call by reference evaluation, a function is passed an implicit reference to its argument rather than the argument value itself. If the function is able to modify such a parameter, then any changes it makes will be visible to the caller as well. If the argument expression is an L-value, its address is used. Otherwise, a temporary object is constructed by the caller and a reference to this object is passed; the object is then discarded when the function returns.

Some languages contain a notion of references as first class values. ML, for example, has the "ref" constructor; references in C++ may also be created explicitly. In these languages, "call by reference" may be used to mean passing a reference value as an argument to a function.

In languages (such as C) that contain unrestricted pointers instead of or in addition to references, call by address is a variant of call by reference where the reference is an unrestricted pointer.

Example 10.6:

```
#include<stdio.h>
#include<conio.h>
```

```
void sum (int , int );
void main()
{
    int a = 10;
    int b = 5;
    sum(&a,&b);
    clrscr();
    getch();
}
void  sum (int x, int y)
{
    int z = x + y;
    printf("The Sum is::::%d",z);   // 15
}
```

10.5.5.1.3 Call by copy-restore

Call by copy-restore, call by value-result or call by value-return (as termed in the Fortran community) is a special case of call by reference where the provided reference is unique to the caller. If a parameter to a function call is a reference that might be accessible by another thread of execution, its contents are copied to a new reference that is not; when the function call returns, the updated contents of this new reference are copied back to the original reference ("restored").

The semantics of call by value-return also differ from those of call by reference where two or more function arguments alias one another; that is, point to the same variable in the caller's environment. Under call by reference, writing to one will affect the other; call by value-return avoids this by giving the function distinct copies, but leaves the result in the caller's environment undefined (depending on which of the aliased arguments is copied back first).

When the reference is passed to the callee uninitialized, this evaluation strategy may be called call by result.

Example 10.7:

```
Program copyrestore (input, output);
    var a : integer;
    procedure copy (var x : integer);
        Begin
                x = 20;
a = 10;
        end
    begin
        a = 1;
        copy(a);
println(a);                            // output is 20 not 10 due to copy restore
    end
```

10.5.5.1.4 Partial evaluation

In partial evaluation, evaluation may continue into the body of a function that has not been applied. Any sub-expressions that do not contain unbound variables are evaluated, and function applications whose argument values are known may be reduced. In the presence of side-effects, complete partial evaluation may produce unintended results; for this reason, systems that support partial evaluation tend to do so only for "pure" expressions (expressions without side-effects) within functions.

10.5.5.2 Non-strict evaluation

In non-strict evaluation, arguments to a function are not evaluated unless they are actually used in the evaluation of the function body.

Under Church encoding, lazy evaluation of operators maps to non-strict evaluation of functions; for this reason, non-strict evaluation is sometimes referred to as "lazy". Boolean expressions in many languages use lazy evaluation; in this context it is often called short circuiting. Conditional expressions also usually use lazy evaluation, albe it for different reasons.

Normal order: Normal-order (or leftmost outermost) evaluation is the evaluation strategy where the outermost **redex** is always reduced, applying functions before evaluating function arguments. It differs from call-by-name in that call by name does not evaluate inside the body of an unapplied function.

10.5.5.2.1 Call-by-name

Call-by-name evaluation is rarely implemented directly, but frequently used in considering theoretical properties of programs and programming languages. In call-by-name evaluation, the arguments to functions are not evaluated at all — rather, function arguments are substituted directly into the function body using capture-avoiding substitution. If the argument is not used in the evaluation of the function, it is never evaluated; if the argument is used several times, it is re-evaluated each time. For this reason, real-world languages with call-by-name semantics tend to be implemented using call by need.

It can be preferable because call-by-name evaluation always yields a value when a value exists, whereas call by value may not terminate if the function's argument is a non-terminating computation that is not needed to evaluate the function. Opponents of call-by-name claim that it is significantly slower when the function argument is used, and that in practice this is almost always the case.

Note that because evaluation of expressions may happen arbitrarily far into a computation, languages using call-by-need generally do not support computational effects (such as mutation) except through the use of monads. This eliminates any unexpected behaviour from variables whose values change prior to their delayed evaluation.

Example 10.8: all in-line function are example of call by name.

10.5.5.2.2 Call-by-need

Call-by-need is a memorized version of call-by-name where, if the function argument is evaluated, that value is stored for subsequent uses. In a "pure" (effect-free) setting, this produces the same results as call-by-name; when the function argument is used two or more times, call-by-need is almost always faster.

Haskell is perhaps the most well-known language that uses call-by-need evaluation.

10.5.5.2.3 Call-by-macro-expansion

Call-by-macro expansion is similar to call-by-name, but uses textual substitution rather than capture-avoiding substitution. Macros are generally best used for very small tasks where this difference can be easily taken into account by the programmer. With incautious use, however, macro substitution may result in variable capture; this effect is put to appropriate use in the writing of obfuscated code, but may lead to undesired behaviour elsewhere.

10.5.5.3 Non-deterministic strategies

10.5.5.3.1 Full β-reduction

Under full β-reduction, any function application may be reduced (substituting the function's argument into the function using capture avoiding substitution) at any time. This may be done even within the body of an unapplied function.

10.5.5.3.2 Call-by-future

Call-by-future (or parallel call-by-name) is like call-by-need, except that the function's argument may be evaluated in parallel with the function body (rather than only if used). The two threads of execution synchronize when the argument is needed in the evaluation of the function body; if the argument is never used, the argument thread may be killed.

10.5.5.3.3 Optimistic evaluation

Optimistic evaluation is another variant of call-by-need in which the function's argument is partially evaluated for some amount of time (which may be adjusted at runtime), after which evaluation is aborted and the function is applied using call-by-need. This approach avoids some of the runtime expense of call-by-need, while still retaining the desired termination characteristics.

10.6 SCOPE INFORMATION

In general, a scope is an enclosing context. Scopes have contents which are associated with them. Various programming languages have various types of scopes. The type of scope determines what kind of entities it can contain and how it affects them. Depending on its type, a scope can:

- contain declarations or definitions of identifiers;
- contain statements and/or expressions which define an executable algorithm or part thereof;
- nest or be nested.

10.6.1 Variables

- **Local variable:** A local variable is a variable that is given local scope. Such variables are accessible only from the function or block in which it is declared. Local variables are contrasted with global variables. Local variables are special because in most languages they are automatic variables stored on the call stack directly.
- **Static local variables:** A special type of local variable, called a static local, is available in many mainstream languages, including C/C++, Java and VB.NET, which allows a value to be retained from one call of the function to another. In this case, recursive calls to the function also have access to the variable. In all of the above languages, variables are declared as such with the static keyword.
- Static locals in global functions can be thought of as global variables, because their value remains in memory for the life of the program. The only difference is that they are only accessible through one function.
- **Global variable:** A global variable is a variable that does not belong to any subroutine or class and can be accessed from anywhere in a program. They are contrasted with local variables. A global variable can potentially be modified from anywhere, and any part of the program may depend on it.

A global variable therefore has an unlimited potential for creating mutual dependencies, and adding mutual dependencies increases complexity. Global variables are used extensively to pass in formations between sections of code that don't share a caller/callee relation like concurrent threads and signal handlers.

Example 10.9: Following example show local, static local, global variable.

```
int a;                          // Global Variable
static int b;                   // Static Global Variable
void fun()
{
    int x;                      // Local Variable
    static int y;               // Static Local Variable
}
void main()
{
    int c = 5, b=10;
    a = b + c;
}
```

In above, example 'x' is a local variable that can never be used in 'main' function and 'a' is global variable that can be used in 'fun' or in 'main'.

Extern variable: As an alternative to local variables, it is possible to define variables that are external to all functions i.e. variables that can be accessed by name by any function. An external variable must be defined, exactly once, outside of any function; this sets aside storage for it. The variable must also be declared in each function that wants to access it; this states the type of the variable. The declaration may be an explicit extern statement or may be implicit from context.

10.6.2 Lexical/Static *vs.* Dynamic Scoping

One of the basic reasons for scoping is to keep variables in different parts of the program distinct from one another. Since there are only a small number of short variable names, and programmers share habits about the naming of variables (e.g., i for an array index), in any program of moderate size the same variable name will be used in multiple different scopes. The question of how to match various variable occurrences to the appropriate binding sites is generally answered in one of two ways: static scoping or lexical scoping and dynamic scoping.

Lexical scoping was first introduced in Lisp 1.5 (via the FUNARG device developed by Steve Russell, working under John McCarthy) and added later into Algol 60 (also by Steve Russell), and has been picked up in other languages since then. Descendants of dynamically scoped languages often adopt lexical scoping. In Lisp, for example, Emacs Lisp uses dynamic scoping. Common Lisp has both dynamic and lexical scoping, and Scheme uses lexical scoping exclusively. The original Lisp used dynamic scoping. In other cases, languages which already had dynamic scoping have added lexical scoping afterwards, such as Perl, C and Pascal have always had lexical scoping, since they are both influenced by the ideas that went into Algol.

Static scoping

With static scoping, a variable always refers to its nearest enclosing binding. This is a property of the program text and unrelated to the runtime call stack. Because matching a variable to its binding only requires analysis of the program text, this type of scoping is sometimes also called lexical scoping. Static scope is standard in modern functional languages such as ML and Haskell because it allows the programmer to reason as if variable bindings are carried out by substitution. Static scoping also makes it much easier to make modular code and reason about it, since its binding structure can be understood in isolation.

Correct implementation of static scope in languages with first-class nested functions can be subtle, as it requires each function value to carry with it a record of the values of the variables that it depends on (the pair of the function and this environment is called a closure). When first-class nested functions are not used or not available (such as in C), this overhead is of course not incurred. Variable lookup is always very efficient with static scope, as the location of each value is known at compile time.

Dynamic scoping

In dynamic scoping, each identifier has a global stack of bindings. Introducing a local variable with name x pushes a binding onto the global x stack which is popped off when the control flow leaves the scope. Evaluating x in any context always yields the top binding. In other words, a global identifier refers to the identifier associated with the most recent environment. Note that this cannot be done at compile time because the binding stack only exists at runtime, which is why this type of scoping is called dynamic scoping. Some languages, like Perl and Common Lisp, allow the programmer to choose lexical or dynamic scoping when (re)defining a variable.

Dynamic scoping is very simple to implement. To find an identifier's value, the program traverses the runtime stack, checking each activation record (each function's stack frame) for a value for the identifier. This is known as **deep binding**. An alternate strategy that is usually more efficient is to maintain a stack of bindings for each identifier; the stack is modified whenever the variable is bound or unbound, and a variable's value is simply that of the top binding on the stack. This is called **shallow binding**.

Example10.10: Static scope v/s Dynamic scope

```
int x = 0;
int f()
{
        return x;
}
int g ()
{
        int x = 1;
        return f();
}
```

With static scoping, calling g will return 0 since it has been determined at compile time that the expression 'x' in any invocation of f will yield the global x binding which is unaffected by the introduction of a local variable of the same name in 'g'.

With dynamic scoping, the binding stack for the x identifier will contain two items when f is invoked: the global binding to 0, and the binding to 1 introduced in g (which is still present on the stack since the control flow hasn't left g yet). Since evaluating the identifier expression by definition always yields the top binding, the result is 1.

TRIBULATIONS

10.1 Consider the following fragment of code in C:

```
1.  { int a, b, c;
2.    ...
3.      { int d, e;
4.        ...
5.          { int f;
```

```
        ...
    }
    ...
  }
  ...
  { int g, h, i;
    ...
  }
  ...
}
```

Assuming that an integer takes four bytes of storage, how much memory is needed if we allocate all of the variables in static memory without sharing any locations? If we allocate statically but share memory between variables where possible, what is the minimum amount of memory we can get away with?

10.2 Consider the following program in a C like language.

```
int x;
void set_x (int n)
{
x = n;
}
void print_x ()
{
printf ("%d ", x);
}
void first ()
{
set_x (1);
print_x ();
}
void second ()
{
int x;
set_x (2);
print_x ();
}
void start ()
{
set_x (0);
first ();
print_x ();
second ();
print_x ();
}
```

What does this program print when the start function is called and the language uses static scoping? What does it print with dynamic scoping? Why?

10.3 Explain why the presence of recursion in a language makes it impossible for a compiler to use static allocation for all variables. What is usually done to get around this problem?

10.4 Consider the following Pascal program.

```
program foo (input, output);
type
   a = array [1..10] of integer;
var
   b : a;

procedure bar (var a : integer);
var
   b : boolean;
begin
   a := 99 + d;
   b := true;
end;

function bletch (b : boolean; c : real) : integer;

procedure blerk;
const
   a = false;
begin
   b := a;
end;

begin
   blerk;
   if b then
      bletch := trunc (c),
   else
      bletch := -1;
end;

begin
   b[3] := 42;
   bar (b[5], a + 1);
   b[5] := bletch (true, 8.8);
   writeln (b[5]);
end.
```

Find all of the defining and applied occurrences of identifiers in this program. Identify the various scopes in this program and construct the environments that might be used by a compiler during name analysis of this program. Show how the environments are related to each other.

10.5 In some implementations of Fortran IV, the following code would print a 3. Can you suggest an explanation? How do you suppose more recent Fortran implementations get round this problem?

```
c main program
 call foo (2)
 print* 2
 stop
 end
 subroutine foo (x)
    x = x + 1
    return
    end
```

Write a procedure or function that will have four different effects, depending on whether arguments are passed by value, by reference, by value/result or by name.

10.6 A variable is said to have *unlimited extent* if its lifetime may continue after control has returned from the scope in which the variable was declared. Explain the rationale for unlimited extent in functional programming languages.

10.7 Consider the following program in C:

```
void foo ()
{
  int i;
  printf ("%d", i++);
}

int main ()
{
  int j;
  for (j = 1; j <= 10; j++) foo ();
}
```

Which is incorrect because the local variable i in subroutine foo is never initialized. On many systems however, the program will show repeatable behaviour, printing 0 1 2 3 4 5 6 7 8 9. Suggest an explanation. Also explain why the behaviour on other systems might be different or non-deterministic.

10.8 For each of the variables a, b, c, d, e in the following C program, say whether the variable should be kept in memory or a register, and why:

```
int f(int a, int b)
{
int c[3], d, e;
d = a + 1;
```

5. e = g(c, &b);
6. return e + c[1] + b;
7. }

10. 9 What is the output of program when we use
(i) Call by value
(ii) Call by reference

```
Procedure SUM (x,y,z)
    begin
        y=y+1;
        z=z+x;
    End
    Main
        Begin
            A=2
            B=2;
            SUM (A+B, A, A);
            print A,
        End.
```

10.10 Write a subroutine for if then else after drawing translation diagram.

FURTHER READINGS AND REFERENCES

[1] Wilkes, M. V.; Wheeler, D. J., Gill, S. (1951). *Preparation of Programs for an Electronic Digital Computer.* Addison-Wesley.

[2] Donald Knuth. *Fundamental Algorithms*, Third Edition. Addison-Wesley, 1997. Section 1.4.1: Subroutines, pp.186–193.

[3] Terrence, W. Pratt and Marvin, V. Zelkowitz. *Programming Languages design and implementation.*

[4] M.E. Conway, *Design of a separable transition-diagram compiler*, Communications of the ACM, Vol. 6, No. 7, July 1963

About Parameter Passing and Scope

[5] Harold Abelson and Gerald Jay Sussman. *Structure and Interpretation of Computer Programs*, Second Edition. MIT Press, 1996.

[6] Henry G. Baker, Jr. *"The Incremental Garbage Collection of Processes"*, with Carl Hewitt, ACM Sigplan Notices 12, August 8, 1977, pp.55–59.

[7] Robert Ennals and Simon Peyton Jones. *"Optimistic Evaluation: a fast evaluation strategy for non-strict programs"*, in ICFP'03. ACM Press, 2003.

[8] Jocelyn Frechot. "*Partial Evaluation*", documentation for the Compose project. Online, Sept. 25, 2003.

[9] Bertram Ludäscher. CSE 130 lecture notes. January 24, 2001.

[10] Benjamin C. Pierce. *Types and Programming Languages*. MIT Press, 2002.

[11] P. Sestoft. "*Demonstrating Lambda Calculus Reduction*", in T. Mogensen, D. Schmidt, I. H. Sudburough (editors): The Essence of Computation: Complexity, Analysis, Transformation. Essays Dedicated to Neil D. Jones. Lecture Notes in Computer Science 2566. Springer-Verlag, 2002. pp. 420–435.

CHAPTER 11

ERROR DETECTION AND RECOVERY

CHAPTER HIGHLIGHTS

As it is well known, users of high-level languages are appropriate to make many errors in the development of even quite simple programs. Thus the various phases of a compiler, especially the earlier ones, also communicate with an **error handler** and **error reporter** which are invoked when errors are detected. It is desirable that compilation of erroneous programs be continued, if possible, so that the user can clean several errors out of the source before recompiling. This raises very interesting issues regarding the design of **error recovery** and **error correction** techniques. (We speak of error recovery when the translation process attempts to carry on after detecting an error and of error correction or error repair when it attempts to correct the error from context - usually a contentious subject, as the correction may be nothing like what the programmer originally had in mind.)

Error detection at compile-time in the source code must not be confused with error detection at run-time when executing the object code. Many code generators are responsible for adding error-checking code to the object program (to check that subscripts for arrays stay in bounds, for example). This may be quite rudimentary, or it may involve adding considerable code and data structures for use with sophisticated debugging systems. Such ancillary code can drastically reduce the efficiency of a program, and some compilers allow it to be suppressed.

Sometimes mistakes in a program that are detected at compile time are known as ***errors***, and errors that show up at run time are known as ***exceptions***, but there is no universally agreed terminology for this.

11.1 ERROR REPRESENTATION

The manner in which a compiler reports errors can greatly affect how pleasant and economical it is to use its' language on a given machine. Good error diagnostics should possess a number of properties:

- The messages should pinpoint the errors in terms of the original source program, rather than in terms of some internal representation that is totally mysterious to the user.
- The error messages should be tasteful and understandable by the user. (e.g., "missing right parenthesis in line 5" rather than a cryptic error code such as "OH 17".)
- The messages should be specific and should localize the problem (e.g., "ZAP not declared In procedure BLAH" rather than "missing declaration").
- The messages should not be redundant. If a variable ZAP is undeclared, that should be said once, not every time ZAP appears in the program.Most components of a compiler have to be prepared to signal that something has gone away in the compilation process. To allow all of this to take place in a uniform way, we have chosen to introduce a base class with a very small interface:

```
class REPORT {
 public:
  REPORT();
  // Initializes error reporter
  virtual void error(int errorcode);
  // Reports on error designated by suitable errorcode number
  bool anyerrors(void);
  // Returns true if any errors have been reported
 protected:
  bool errors;
};
```

Error reporting is then standardized by calling on the **error** member of this class whenever an error is detected, passing it a unique number to distinguish the error.

The base class can choose simply to abort compilation altogether. Although at least one highly successful microcomputer Pascal compiler uses this strategy (Turbo Pascal, from Borland International), it tends to become very tiring when one is developing large systems. Since the **error** member is virtual, it is an easy matter to derive a more suitable class from this one, without, of course, having to amend any other part of the system. For our hand-crafted system we can do this as follows:

```
class clangReport : public REPORT {
  public:
    clangReport(SRCE *S)   { Srce = S; }
    virtual void error(int errorcode)
      { Srce->reporterror(errorcode); errors = true; }
  private:
    SRCE *Srce;
};
```

and the same technique can be used to enhance Coco/R generated systems. The Modula-2 and Pascal implementations achieve the same functionality through the use of procedure variables.

11.2 SOURCES OF ERRORS

It is difficult to give a precise classification scheme for programming errors. One way to classify errors is according to how they are introduced. If we look at the entire process of designing and implementing a program, we see that errors can arise at every stage of the process.

At the very onset, the design specifications for the program may be inconsistent or faulty.

- The algorithms used to meet the design may be inadequate or incorrect 'algorithmic errors'.
- The programmer may introduce errors in implementing the algorithms, either by introducing logical errors or by using the programming-language constructs improperly 'coding errors'.
- Keypunching or transcription errors can occur when the program is typed onto cards or into a file.
- The program may exceed a compiler or machine limit not implied by the definition of the programming language. For example, an array may be declared with too many dimensions to fit in the symbol table.
- A compiler can insert errors as it translates the source program into an object program 'compiler errors'.

11.3 LEXICAL-PHASE ERRORS

The function of the lexical analyzer is to carve the stream of characters constituting the source program into a sequence of tokens. Each token class has a specification which is typically a regular set. If, after some processing, the lexical analyzer discovers that no prefix of the remaining input fits the specification of any token class, it can invoke an error-recovery routine that can take a variety of remedial actions.

Unfortunately, there is no one remedial action that will ideally suit all situations. The problem of recovering from lexical errors is further hampered by the lack of redundancy at the lexical level of a language. The simplest expedient is to skip erroneous characters until the lexical analyzer can find another token. This action will likely cause the parser to see a deletion error.

11.4 SYNTAX ERROR DETECTION AND RECOVERY

Up to this point our *parsers have been satisfied just* to stop when a syntactic error is detected. In the case of a real compiler this is probably unacceptable. However, if we modify the parser as given above so as simply not to stop after detecting an error, the result is likely to be chaotic. The analysis process will quickly get out of step with the sequence of symbols being scanned, and in all likelihood will then report a plethora of spurious errors.

One useful feature of the compilation technique we are using is that the parser can detect a syntactically incorrect structure after being presented with its first "unexpected" terminal. This will not necessarily be at the point where the error really occurred. For example, in parsing the sequence

```
BEGIN
    IF A > 6
        DO B := 2;
        C := 5
    END
END
```

We could hope for a sensible error message when **DO** is found where **THEN** is expected. Even if parsing does not get out of step, we would get a less helpful message when the second **END** is found - the compiler can have little idea where the missing **BEGIN** should have been. Some other examples of syntax errors are as:

- Missing right parenthesis: MIN(X, 5 + 3* (Y /2)
- Extraneous comma: if (x > y) ,
- Colon in place of semicolon: int i = 2;
  - int j = 5:
  - int k = 6;
- Missing semicolon: int i = 2;
  - int j = 5
- Misspelled keyword: flaot z = 3.5;
  - logn y ;

A production quality compiler should aim to issue appropriate diagnostic messages for all the "genuine" errors, and for as few "spurious" errors as possible. This is only possible if it can make some likely assumption about the nature of each error and the probable intention of the author, or if it skips over some part of the malformed text, or both. Various approaches may be made to handle the problem. Some compilers go so far as to try to correct the error, and continue to produce object code for the program. Error correction is a little dangerous, except in some trivial cases. Many systems confine themselves to attempting **error recovery,** which is the term used to describe the process of simply trying to get the parser back into step with the source code presented to it. The art of doing this for hand-crafted compilers is rather intricate, and relies on a mixture of fairly well defined methods and intuitive experience, both with the language being compiled, and with the class of user of the same.

Since recursive descent parsers are constructed as a set of routines, each of which tackles a sub-goal on behalf of its caller, a fairly obvious place to try to regain lost synchronization is at the entry to and exit from these routines, where the effects of getting out of step can be confined to examining a small range of known FIRST and FOLLOW symbols. To enforce synchronization at the entry to the routine for a non-terminal *S* we might try to employ a strategy like:

```
IF Sym ∈ FIRST(S) THEN
 ReportError; SkipTo(FIRST(S))
END
```

where *SkipTo* is an operation which simply calls on the scanner until it returns a value for *Sym* that is a member of FIRST(*S*). Unfortunately this is not quite adequate - if the leading terminal has been omitted we might then skip over symbols that should be processed later, by the routine which called *S*.

At the exit from *S*, we have postulated that *Sym* should be a member of FOLLOW(*S*). This set may not be known to *S*, but it should be known to the routine which calls *S*, so that it may conveniently be passed to *S* as a parameter. This suggests that we might employ a strategy like:

```
IF Sym ∈ FOLLOW(S) THEN
 ReportError; SkipTo(FOLLOW(S))
END
```

The use of FOLLOW(*S*) also allows us to avoid the danger mentioned earlier of skipping too far at routine entry, by employing a strategy like

```
IF Sym ∈ FIRST(S) THEN
 ReportError; SkipTo(FIRST(S) | FOLLOW(S))
END;
IF SYM.Sym ∈ FIRST(S) THEN
  Parse(S);
 IF SYM.Sym ∈ FOLLOW(S) THEN
  ReportError; SkipTo(FOLLOW(S))
  END
END
```

Although the FOLLOW set for a non-terminal is quite easy to determine, the legitimate follower may itself have been omitted, and this may lead to too many symbols being skipped at routine exit. To prevent this, a parser using this approach usually passes to each sub-parser a *Followers* parameter, which is constructed so as to include:

- The minimally correct set FOLLOW(*S*), augmented by
- Symbols that have already been passed as *Followers* to the calling routine (that is, later followers), and also so-called **beacon symbols**, which are on no account to be passed over, even though their presence would be quite out of context. In this way the parser can often avoid skipping large sections of possibly important code.

We can also use another method for error correction as **minimum distance correction of syntactic error.** This one theoretical way of defining errors and their location is the minimum **'Hamming distance method'.** We define a collection of error transformations. We then say that a program P has k errors if the shortest sequence of error transformations that will map any valid program into P has length k.

For example, if we let our error transformations be the insertion of a single character or the deletion of a single character, then the program fragment is at distance one from error.

The following code has error in first line:

```
For(i=0i<10;i++)
    SUM = SUM + A;
```

The error is missing of semicolon i.e., at one distance from error correction as:

For(i=0i<10;i++)

SUM = SUM + A;

Although minimum-distance error correction is a convenient theoretical, it is not generally used in practice because it is too costly to implement.

11.5 SEMANTIC ERRORS

Semantic errors can be detected both at compile time and run time. The most common semantic errors that can be detected at compile time are errors of declaration and scope. Typical examples are undeclared or multiply-declared identifiers. Leaving out the declaration of one identifier can spawn multiply of undeclared identifier error messages unless some provision is made to enter a special "error flag" for that identifier in the symbol table. Type incompatibilities between operators and operands, and between formal and actual parameter are another common source of semantic errors that can be detected in many languages at compile time. The amounts of type checking that can be done, however, depend on the languages at hand. Some languages (such as BLISS) have only one data type, so no type disagreements can arise. Other languages (such as PASCAL) have many types, but the type of every name and expression must be calculable at compile time. Such language are said to be strongly typed. Consequently, a PASCAL compiler can do vigorous type checking at compile time and so catch many potential errors. Languages such as PL/I define type conversions which automatically occur between operators and operands of disparate types. In such languages automatic type conversion eliminates the possibility of general semantic error detection.

TRIBULATIONS

11.1 Do you suppose interpreters might find it difficult to handle I/O errors in user programs?

11.2 Investigate the efficacy of the scheme suggested for parsing variable declarations, by tracing the way in which parsing would proceed for incorrect source code such as the following:

VAR A, B C , , D; E, F;

11.3 Trace out the behaviour of the operator-precedence, LR, and LL error-correcting parsers

(a) (id + (* id)

(b) * + id) + (id *

11.4 The following grammar is operator-precedence and SLR(l).

S → if *e* then S else

S → while *e* do S

S → begin Lend

s → *s*

L → S ;L | S

Construct error-correcting parsers of the operator-precedence and LR type for this grammar.

11.5 The grammar in Exercise 11.2 can be made LL by left-factoring the productions for L as:

L → SL′

L → ;S | ∈

Construct for the revised grammar an error-correcting LL parser.

FURTHER READINGS AND REFERENCES

[1] Alfred V. Aho and Jeffrey D. Ullman. *Principles of Compile Design.*

[2] Alfred V. Aho Ravi Sethi and Jeffrey D. Ullman.*Compiler Design Principle, technique and tools.*

[3] Good treatments of the material of this section may be found in the books by Welsh and McKeag (1980), Wirth (1976b), Gough (1988) and Elder (1994). A much higher level treatment is given by Backhouse (1979), while a rather simplified version is given by Brinch Hansen (1983, 1985). Papers by Pemberton (1980) and by Topor (1982), Stirling (1985)

CHAPTER 12

COMPILER PROJECTS

CHAPTER HIGHLIGHTS

12.1 PROJECT 1: 'C' COMPILER CONSTRUCTION

PROJECT: A Translator that generates "THREE ADDRESS CODE" from a source file that contains subset of "C" source code.

Objective: We have to implement the 'C' compiler in C programming language.

Introduction: It is 'C' Compiler completely written in C. It is used to compile the C source code file and its output is three address codes (which can be easily converted into any target language).

Details: Phases of project.

1. **Feasibility study:** In this phase we discuss whether Compiler Construction is feasible for us. It takes approximately one week.
2. **Requirement analysis:** In this phase we gather all the requirements of Compiler Construction. It takes approximately one week.
3. **Designing:** This phase comprises breaking of problem into small parts and different modules(These modules are divided according to phases). It takes approximately four week's.
4. **Coding:** In this phase the actual codes are written for modules designed above. This coding is done in 'C' language. It takes approximately three week's.
5. **Integration and Testing:** In this phase different modules are combined together and thoroughly tested for errors and boundary conditions. It takes approximately three week's.

12.1.1 The Project

The "C" statements covered are as follows

1. Arithmetic Expression with operator precedence.
2. Relation Expression with && and || operator.
3. Assignment statements.
4. if else ladder that can contain "else if" blocks.
5. while LOOPS.
6. do..while LOOPS.
7. for LOOPS.
8. data types declarations of char, int, long data types.

The program makes only one pass over the input file to generate it's equivalant "THREE ADDRESS CODE" if the source code is error free. It uses the "PANIC MODE ERROR RECOVERY" to recover from the error and continue parsing and spot further errors. It also prints the LINE NO and some useful description of the error to help the user spot the error.

12.1.1.1 Files

The main file is "compiler.c". The input is given in "input.c", and the output is in the file "output.txt" which will contain three address code of the input file if the input is error free. The error notifications if any are shown on the screen that is CRT.

12.1.1.2 To run

To run the program write the input that you want to give to the "input.c" file and then run the "compiler.c" file.

Or

The other way you may give the command line arguments as the file name you may want to compile.

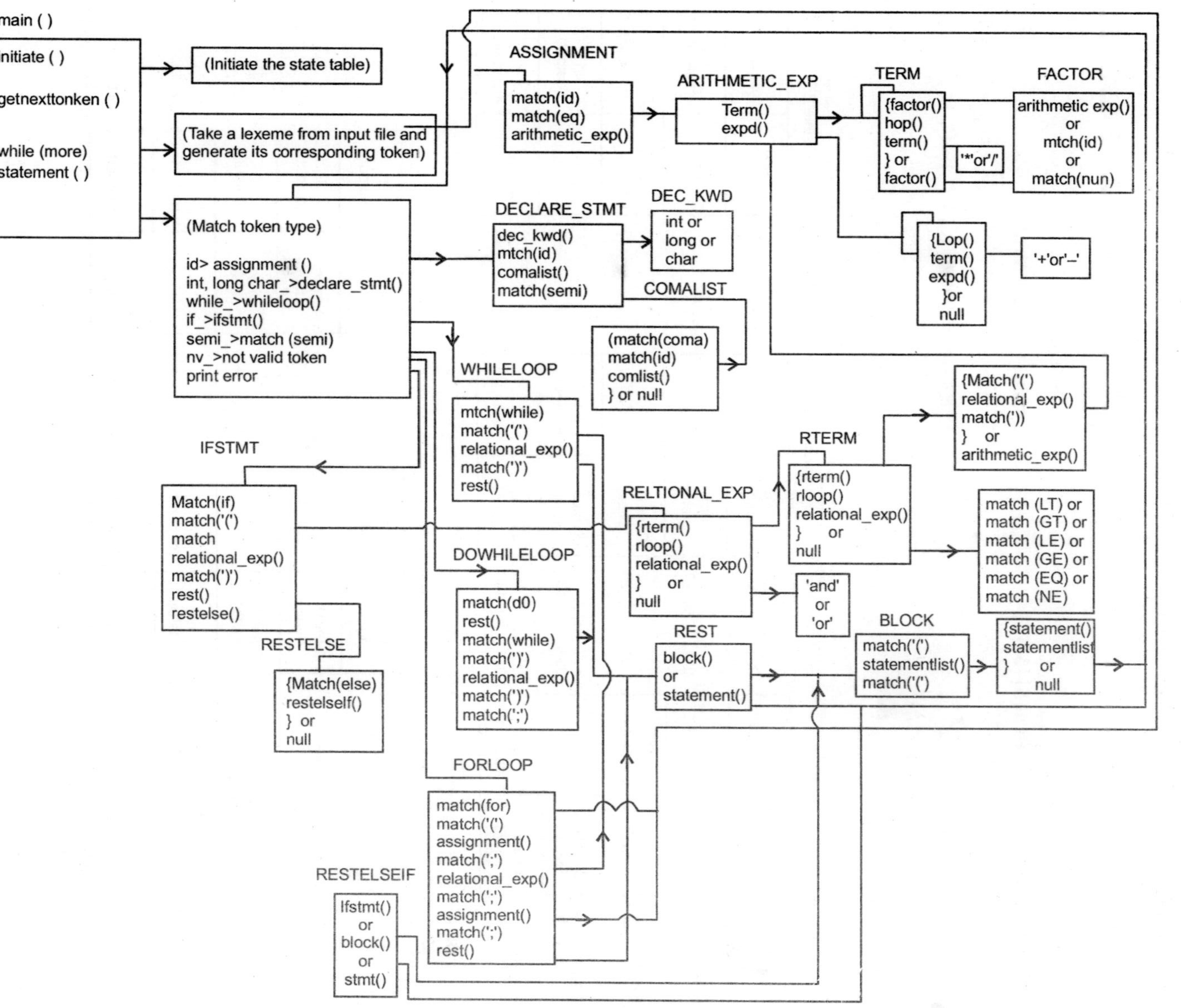

Figure 12.1: Class Diagram

Array representation of State table

a[state] [input] [action] = a [5] [5] [2]

INPUT->

0 = space, null, tab.

1 = digit (0-9)

2 = char ('a'-'z', 'A'-'Z').

3 = operator ('+', '–', '*', /',>,<,<=,>=,'.,&&,II)

4= special operator ('[,']',' {',}',' (',')',',')

state 0

SPACE	000	0 (next state)	0 (no action)	001
DIGIT	010	1 (next state)	2 (append)	011
CHAR	020	2 (next state)	2 (append)	021
OPE	030	3 (next state)	2 (append)	031
SPOPE	040	4 (next state)	2 (append)	041

state 1

100	0 (next state)	1 (output)	101
110	1 (next state)	2 (append)	111
120	2 (next state)	1 (output)	121
130	3 (next state)	1 (output)	131
140	4 (next state)	1 (output)	141

state 2

200	0 (next state)	1 (output)
210	1 (next state)	1 (output)
220	2 (next state)	2 (append)
230	3 (next state)	1 (output)
240	4 (next state)	1 (output)

state 3

SPACE	300	0 (next state)	1 (output)	301
DIGIT	310	1 (next state)	1 (output)	311
CHAR	320	2 (next state)	1 (output)	321
OPE	330	3 (next state)	2 (append)	331
SPOPE	340	4 (next state)	1 (output)	341

state 4

400	0 (next state)	1 (output)	401
410	1 (next state)	1 (output)	411
420	2 (next state)	1 (output)	421
430	3 (next state)	1 (output)	431
440	4 (next state)	1 (output)	441

Figure 12.2: *State Diagram*

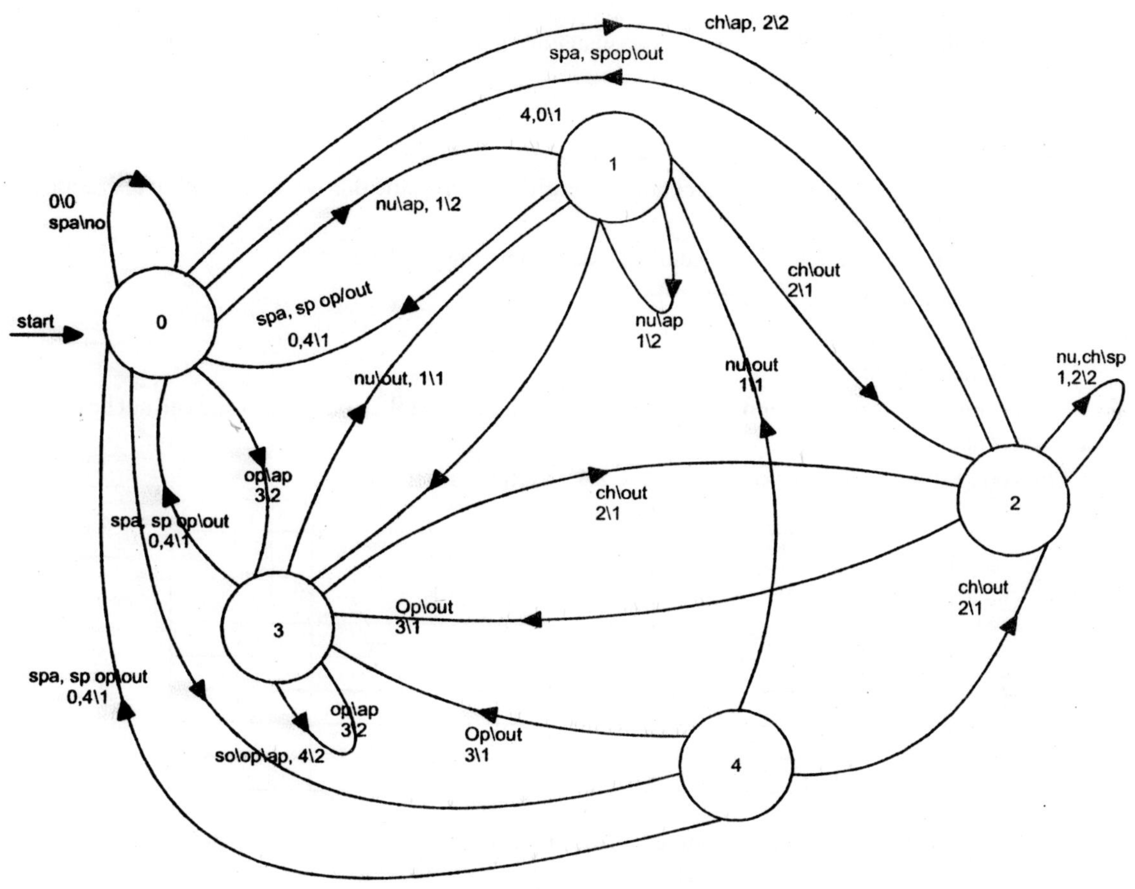

***Figure 12.3:** Mealy machine for lexical analysis*

input → 0 = space, null, tab
1 = digit (0-9)
2 = char ('a'–'z', 'A'–'Z')
3 = operators(/,*,+,–,>,<=, <=, II, &&!)
4= special operators ('{','}','[',']','(',')', '"',',') - Mealy machine for lexical analysis

action→ 0=no/action
1=output the token
2=append token

12.1.1.3 Related compiler files

1. The lexical analyzer: The lexical analyzer in the project is called by the parser to get the next token. That is when the parser wants a token it gives the next token from the input stream to the parser. The tokens returned to parser on the call of getnexttoken( ) are self-explanatory and can be seen in the file "compiler.c", they are enumerated as token_type.

The Actions: 0= No Action

1= Output the Token because the Token complete

2= Append — append the current char in the current token value this is a intermediate operation when the token is not fully formed.

The States :0= In between the tokens, scanning spaces, new lines, tabs etc.

1= Scanning a word

2= Scanning a Number

3= Scanning a Operator

4= Scanning a Special Operator like (,),[,],{,} which forms a token of it's own and can not be combined with any other operator.

2. The state table: Each entry contains: next_state/Action pair in it as:

ip states	space	char	num	operator	sp.op.
0	0/0	1/2	2/2	3/2	4/2
1	0/1	1/2	2/1	3/1	0/1
2	0/1	2/2	2/2	3/1	0/1
3	0/1	1/1	2/1	3/2	0/1
4	0/1	1/1	2/1	3/1	0/1

The keywords of the language are resolved using simple comparison as the other operators. Please consult the file "compiler's" for more the comments specify the programmer working.

3. The syntax directed definition: The syntax directed definition contains the context free grammar along with the semantic rules. Here we have specified only the "Context Free Grammar" the semantic rules are implemented in the file "compiler.c" that generates the three address code. The Context Free Grammar for the compile as:

start —> statement

statement —> ifstmt | whileloop | dowhileloop | declarestmt | forloop | assignment | ;

assignment —> id = arithmetic_exp

whileloop —> while (relational_exp restwhile

restwhile —> block | statement

dowhileloop —> do restdo while (relational_exp) ;

restdo —> block | statement

forloop —> for(assignment ; relational_exp ; assignment) restfor

restfor —> block | statement

ifstmt —> if (relational_exp) restif restelse
restif —> block | statement
restelse —> else restelseif | NULL
restelseif —> ifstmt | block | statement
declarestmt —> dec_kwd id commalist ;
dec_kwd —> INT | LONG | CHAR
commalist —> , id commalist | NULL
arithmetic_exp —> term expd
expd —> lop term expd | NULL
lop —> + | -
term —>factor hop term | factor
hop —> * | /
factor —> (arithmetic_exp) | id | NUM
relational_exp —> rterm rlop relational_exp | rterm
rlop —> AND | OR
rterm —> rfactor rhop rterm | rfactor
rhom —> LT | GT | LE | GE | EQ | NE
rfactor —> (relational_exp) | arithmatic_exp
block —> {stmt_list}
stmt_list —> statement stmt_list | NULL

12.1.2 The Code

This code is copyrighted. Do not copy and sell it.

12.1.2.1 C File (Compiler.c)

```
/*********************************** C COMPILER*************************/
/*********THIS COMPILER COUSTRUCT THREE ADDRESS CODE OF C SOURCE
CODE***********/

/**************INCLUDING HEADER FILES*******/
#include<conio.h>
#include<stdio.h>
#include<process.h>
#include<string.h>
#include<alloc.h>

/*************Defining macros*****************/
#define STATES 5
#define INPUTS 5
```

```
#define ACTIONS 2
#define TEMP 1
#define LABLE 0

/*************defining enum's*******************/
enum actions {NOACTION ,OUTPUT , APPEND};
enum boolean {false,true};
enum token_type
{NV,KWD,OP,SOP,ID,NUM,IF,ELSE,DEC,ASGN,LT,EQ,LE,GE,NE,GT,AND,OR,FOR,WHILE,DO,LP,RP,LB,RB,
LBK,RBK,SEMI,COMA,INT,INT_ARRAY,LONG,LONG_ARRAY,CHAR,CHAR_ARRAY,PLMIN,MULDIV};

/***************** defining variables*****************/
int a[STATES][INPUTS][ACTIONS];         /*3-D array for dfa*/
int cur_state;
int index;
FILE* fin;                          /*file pointer for input file*/
enum token_type ttype;              /*variable for type of token*/
int op;                            /*used as flag with value 0 | 1*/
char* token;
int lineno;                        /*it stores the line no*/
int more;                         /*used as flag with value 0 | 1*/
char* lookahead;
enum token_type dtype;
int nooferr;
int errflag; /*boolean*/
int  codegeneration; /*boolean*/
char* newtemp;
int tempvalue ;
int lablevalue;
FILE* fout;
char* str;
char* lexem;
int declered; /*boolean*/

/**********function prototype******************/
void int_co(char*);
void initiate(char*);
char* getnexttoken(enum token_type*);
int indexof(char);
void take_input(char);
```

```
void perform_action(int, char);
void resolvekeywords( );
void add(char*);
int isintable(char*);
struct node* find(char*);
void resolveops( );
void_ini( );
int statement( );
void assignment( );
char * match(enum token_type);
void sementicactions(enum token_type);
void show_error( );
void movetonextstmt( );
void declare_statement( );
void gencode(char*, char*, char*, char*, char*, int, int);
int isdeclared(char*);
void declare(char *, enum token_type);
int get_lineno( );
void commalist( );
void whileloop( );
char* gentemp(int);
char* rexpression( );
char* rterm( );
char* rfactor( );
char* aexpression( );
char* term( );
char* factor( );
void forloop( );
void block( );
void stmt_list( );
void dowhileloop( );
void ifstatement( );
void restif(char*);
void summary( );

/*****************main( ) function***************/
void main(int argc,char* argv[])
{
 clrscr( );
 initiate("input.c");      /*to initialize the dfa & open the input file*/
```

```
lookahead =(char*) getnexttoken(& ttype); /*to get the next token*/
ini( );          /*to initialize*/
while(more)
    statement( );
summary( );
printf("press any key to exit....");
getch( );
}

void int_co(char* str1)
{
str = str1;
}

void initiate(char* filename)
{
int i, j;
cur_state = 0;
lineno = 1;
op =0;
index = 0;
int_co("({[]});\'\",.");
for(i=0;i<STATES;i++)
{
    for(j=0;j<INPUTS;j++)
    {
        if(j!=4||i==0)
                a[i][j][0] = j;
        else
                a[i][j][0] = 0;
        if(i==0&&j==0)
                a[i][j][1]=NOACTION;
        else if(i==0&&j==4)
                a[i][j][1]=APPEND;
        else if(i==4||j==4)
                a[i][j][1]=OUTPUT;
        else if(i==0||i==j)
                a[i][j][1]=APPEND;
        else
```

```
                a[i][j][1]=OUTPUT;
    }
}
a[2][1][0]=2;
a[2][1][1]=APPEND;
fin=fopen(filename,"r");
if(!fin)
{
    printf("File not found : ");
    exit(1);
}
more=1;
}
```

char* getnexttoken(enum token_type* t)

```
{
char ch;
while(op!=1)
{
    ch=fgetc(fin);
    if(ch==EOF)
    {
        take_input(' ');
        more=0;
        break;
    }
    if(ch!='\n')
        take_input(ch);
    else
    {
        take_input(' ');
        lineno++;
    }
}
op= 0;
t = (enum token_type*) ttype;
return token;
}
```

```
int indexof(char c)
{
 char ch = str[0];
 int i=0,set=0;
 while(ch!=NULL)
 {
      if(ch==c)
      {
           set = 1;
           break;
      }
      ch = str[++i];
 }
 if(set==1)
      return i;
 else
      return –1;
}

void take_input(char ch)
{
 int input,action ;
 if(ch==' '||ch==NULL)
       input = 0;
 else if(ch>='0'&&ch<='9')
       input = 1;
 else if((ch>='a'&&ch<='z')||(ch>= 'A'&&ch<='Z')||ch=='_')
       input = 2;
 else if(indexof(ch)!=–1)
       input = 4;
 else
       input = 3;
 action = a[cur_state][input][1];
 perform_action(action,ch);
cur_state = a[cur_state][input][0];
}

/*perform the specified action*/
/*it can be either output the token or append when the token is not fully formed*/
void perform_action(int action,char ip)
```

```
{
switch(action)
{
      case NOACTION :
            ttype = NV;
            break;

      case OUTPUT :
         token[index] = NULL;
          switch(cur_state)
          {
                     case 2:
                                 resolvekeywords( );
                                 break;
                     case 1:
                                 ttype = NUM;
                                 break;
                     case 3:
                                 resolveops( );
                                 break;
                     case 4:
                                 resolvesops( );
                                 break;
          }
          op = true;
          if(ip!=' ')
          {
                     ungetc(ip,fin);
                     index = 0;
          }
          else
                     index = 0;
          break;
   case APPEND :
         token[index] = ip;
         index++;
         break;
}
}
```

/*resolving the keywords and converting them to tokens*/
void resolvekeywords( )

```
{
if(strcmp(token,"int")==0)
      ttype = INT;
else if(strcmp(token,"long")==0)
      ttype = LONG;
else if(strcmp(token,"char")==0)
      ttype = CHAR;
else if(strcmp(token,"if")==0)
      ttype = IF;
else if(strcmp(token,"else")==0)
      ttype = ELSE;
else if(strcmp(token,"while")==0)
      ttype = WHILE;
else if(strcmp(token,"for")==0)
      ttype = FOR;
else if(strcmp(token,"do")==0)
      ttype = DO;
else
{
      ttype = ID;
      if(!isintable(token))
           add(token);
}
}

struct node
{
 char *lexem;
 int  declared; /*boolean*/
 enum token_type type;
 /****************type  type************/
 struct node* next;
};
struct node* first=NULL;

void add(char* str)
{
 struct node *p=(struct node*)malloc(sizeof(struct node));
```

```
p->lexem=(char*)malloc(1+strlen(str));
strcpy(p->lexem,str);
p->declared = 0;
p->type = –1;
p->next = first;
first = p;
}
```

int isintable(char* str)

```
{
 struct node* p =(struct node*)find(str);
 if(p!=NULL)
 return 1;
 return 0;
}
```

struct node* find(char* str)

```
{
 struct node* q=first;
 while(q)
 {
      if(strcmp(q->lexem,str)==0)
           return q;
      q = q->next;
 }
 return NULL;
}
```

void resolveops( )

```
{
 if(strcmp(token,"<")==0)
      ttype = LT;
 else if(strcmp(token,">")==0)
      ttype = GT;
 else if(strcmp(token,">=")==0)
      ttype = GE;
 else if(strcmp(token,"<=")==0)
      ttype = LE;
```

```
else if(strcmp(token,"==")==0)
      ttype = EQ;
else if(strcmp(token,"=")==0)
      ttype = ASGN;
else if(strcmp(token,"!=")==0)
      ttype = NE;
else if(strcmp(token,"&&")==0)
      ttype = AND;
else if(strcmp(token,"||")==0)
      ttype = OR;
else if(strcmp(token,"+")==0||strcmp(token,"–")==0)
      ttype = PLMIN;
else if(strcmp(token,"*")==0||strcmp(token,"/")==0)
      ttype = MULDIV;
else
      ttype = NV;
}

void resolvesops( )
{
if(strcmp(token,"(")==0)
      ttype = LP;
else if(strcmp(token,")")==0)
      ttype = RP;
else if(strcmp(token,"{")==0)
      ttype = LB;
else if(strcmp(token,"}")==0)
      ttype = RB;
else if(strcmp(token,"[")==0)
      ttype = LBK;
else if(strcmp(token,"]")==0)
      ttype = RBK;
else if(strcmp(token,",")==0)
      ttype = COMA;
else if(strcmp(token,";")==0)
      ttype = SEMI;
else
      ttype = NV;
}
```

```
void ini()
{
nooferr = 0;
errflag=false;
tempvalue = 1;
lablevalue = 1;
codegeneration = true;
fout=fopen("output.txt","w+");
}

int statement()
{
errflag = 0;
switch(ttype)
{
    case ID:
        assignment( );
        break;

    case INT:

    case LONG:

    case CHAR:
        dtype = ttype;
        declare_statement( );
        break;
    case WHILE:
        whileloop( );
        break;

    case FOR:
        forloop( );
        break;

    case DO:
        dowhileloop( );
        break;
```

```
    case IF:
        ifstatement( );
        break;

    case SEMI :
        match(SEMI);
        break;

    case NV:
        printf("This is a Not-Valid token\n");
        return errflag=1;

    default :
        printf("Not in the language still....%s %d\n",lookahead,ttype);
        match(ttype);
}
return errflag;
}
```

void assignment( )

```
{
char* idplace,* expplace;
if(errflag)
    return;
idplace = match(ID);
match(ASGN);
expplace = aexpression( );
match(SEMI);
gencode(idplace,"=",expplace,"","",1,1);
}
```

char* match(enum token_type t)

```
{
char* temp;
if(errflag)
    return "";
if(ttype==t)
{
```

```
sementicactions(t);
switch(t)
{
    case SEMI :
            temp="";
            break;

    case ID :

    case PLMIN :

    case MULDIV :

    case NUM :
            temp=(char*)malloc(strlen(lookahead)+1);
            strcpy(temp,lookahead);
            break;

    case AND :
            temp = "AND";
            break;

    case OR :
            temp = "OR";
            break;

    case LT :
            temp = "LT";
            break;

    case GT :
            temp = "GT";
            break;

    case LE :
            temp = "LE";
            break;
```

```
        case GE :
                temp = "GE";
                break;

        case EQ :
                temp = "EQ";
                break;

        case NE :
                temp = "NE";
                break;

        case CHAR :
                temp = "BYTE";
                break;

        case INT :
                temp = "WORD";
                break;

        case LONG :
                temp = "DWORD";
                break;

        default :
                temp = "";
    }
    if(more)
        lookahead = getnexttoken( & ttype);
}
else
    show_error( );
    return temp;
}
```

/*Some semantic actions like adding the indentifier in the symbol table...*/
void sementicactions(enum token_type t)

```
{
```

```
switch(t)
{
    case ID :
        if(!isdeclared(lookahead))
        {
            codegeneration = 0;
            printf("\n");
            printf("##### Error in lineno : %d : %s -> not declared",get_lineno( ),lexem);
/* lookahead*************************/
            nooferr++;
        }
        break;
}
}

void show_error( )
{
 codegeneration = 0 ;
 printf("\n");
 nooferr++;
 printf("!!!!! Error in lineno : %d",get_lineno( ));
 printf("Token mismatch : %s",lookahead);
 errflag = 1;
 movetonextstmt( );
}
```

/*This function skips all the token until a synchronizing token semicolon is found*/
/*(PANIC MODE ERROR RECOVERY) (PANIC MODE ERROR RECOVERY)*/
void movetonextstmt( )

```
{
 while(ttype!=SEMI)
 {
    if(more)
        lookahead = getnexttoken( & ttype);
    else
        return;
 }
if(more)
```

```
    lookahead = getnexttoken( & ttype);
else
    return;
}

/*declaration of variable only int, char and long also generates intermediate code for that maps int to WORD
char to BYTE
long to DWORD (double word)*/
void declare_statement( )
{
 char* typeplace;
 typeplace = match(ttype);
 gencode(typeplace,"","","","",0,0);
 commalist( );
 gencode("","","","","",1,1);
 match(SEMI);
}

/*Function that generates Intermediate Code ...*/
void gencode(char* t1,char* t2,char* t3,char* t4,char* t5,int semi,int nline)/* boolean semi ,nline*/
{
 if(!codegeneration)
     return;
 if(t1[0]!=NULL)
     fprintf(fout, "%s ",t1);
 if(t2[0]!=NULL)
     fprintf(fout,"%s ",t2);
 if(t3[0]!=NULL)
     fprintf(fout,"%s ",t3);
 if(t4[0]!=NULL)
     fprintf(fout,"%s ",t4);
 if(t5[0]!=NULL)
     fprintf(fout,"%s ",t5);
 if(semi)
     fprintf(fout,"%c",';');
 if(nline)
     fputc('\n',fout);
}
```

```
/*the commalist when we declare an identifier*/
/*int a,b,c; in this a,b,c is a comma list...*/
int isdeclared(char* str)
{
 struct node* p;
 p = find(str);
 return p->declared;
}

void declare(char* str,enum token_type t)
{
 struct node* p;
 p = find(str);
 p->declared = 1;
 p->type = t;
}

int get_lineno( )
{
 return lineno;
}

void commalist( )
{
 char* idplace;
 if(errflag)
      return;
 if(ttype==ID)
 {
      if(!isdeclared(lookahead)) /*this is the sementic action*/
            declare(lookahead,dtype);
      else
      {
            codegeneration = 0 ;
            printf("\n");
            printf("##### Error in lineno : %d : %s -> Already declared",get_lineno( ),lookahead);
            nooferr++;
      }
```

```
}
idplace = match(ID);
gencode(idplace,"","","","",0,0);
if(ttype==COMA)
{
    match(COMA);
    gencode(",","","","","",0,0);
    commalist( );
}
/*this was originally meant for array support but the time didn't permit that*/
}
```

/*While loop parsing and generation of intermediate code for that...*/
void whileloop( )

```
{
char* rexpplace,*out,*in;
match(WHILE);
match(LP);
in = gentemp(LABLE);
out = gentemp(LABLE);
gencode("LABLE",in,":","","",0,1);
rexpplace = rexpression( );
match(RP);
gencode("CMP",rexpplace,",","FALSE","",1,1);
gencode("JMEQ",out,"","","",1,1);
if(ttype==LB) /*strcmp(lookahead,"{")==0)*/
    block( );
else
    statement( );
gencode("JMP",in,"","","",1,1);
gencode("LABLE",out,":","","",0,1);
}
```

/*generate a temporary variable when wanted ...*/
char* gentemp(int lort)

```
{
if(codegeneration)
{
```

```
    newtemp =(char*)malloc(4);
    if(lort==TEMP)
    {
        sprintf(newtemp,"t%d",tempvalue);
        tempvalue++;
    }
    else
    {
        sprintf(newtemp,"L%d",lablevalue);
        lablevalue++;
    }
return newtemp;
}
return "";
}
```

/*Relational expression and it's supportive functions...*/

char* rexpression( )

```
{
char* rtermplace,*ropplace,*temp,*curresult;
curresult = rterm( );
while(ttype==AND||ttype==OR)
{
    ropplace = match(ttype);
    rtermplace = rterm( );
    temp = gentemp(1);
    gencode(temp,"=",curresult,ropplace,rtermplace,1,1);
    curresult = temp;
}
return curresult;
}
```

char* rterm( )

```
{
char* rfactorplace,*rtermplace,*ropplace,*temp;
rfactorplace = rfactor( );
if( (ttype>=LT) && (ttype<=GT) )
{
```

```
    ropplace = match(ttype);
    rtermplace = rterm( );
 }
 else
    return rfactorplace ;
 temp = gentemp(1);
 gencode(temp,"=",rfactorplace,ropplace,rtermplace,1,1);
 return temp;
}

char* rfactor( )
{
 char* place;
 switch(ttype)
 {
    case LP:
         match(LP);
         place = rexpression( );
         match(RP);
         break;

    case ID:

    case NUM:
         place = aexpression( );
         break;

    default:
         place = "";
         show_error( );
 }
 return place;
}
```

/*Arithmetic expression and it's supportiong functions ...*/
char* aexpression( )

```
{
 char* termplace,*opplace,*temp,*curresult;
```

```
curresult = term( );
while(ttype==PLMIN)
{
     opplace = match(PLMIN);
     termplace = term( );
     temp = gentemp(1);
     gencode(temp,"=",curresult,opplace,termplace,1,1);
     curresult = temp;
}
return curresult;
}

char* term( )
{
char* factorplace,*termplace,*opplace,*temp;
factorplace = factor( );
if(ttype==MULDIV)
{
     opplace = match(MULDIV);
     termplace = term( );
}
else
     return factorplace ;
temp = gentemp(1);
gencode(temp,"=",factorplace,opplace,termplace,1,1);
return temp;
}

char* factor( )
{
char* place;
switch(ttype)
{
     case LP:
          match(LP);
          place = aexpression( );
          match(RP);
          break;
```

```
    case ID:
        place = match(ID);
        break;

    case NUM:
        place = match(NUM);
        break;

    default:
        place = "";
        show_error( );
}
return place;
}
```

/*for loop parsing and generating intermediate code..*/
/*This is a slightly modified for loop than it is in C
for example in for(i=0;i<5;i=i+1)
i=i+1 will be executed after the first iteration of loop means at the end. But as this parser is built using non back tracking recursive decent because i=i+1 comes lexically before the statements in the loop it will be executed before the statements in the loop means at the beginning of each iteration with contrast to C in which it is executed at the end of each iteration.*/
void forloop()

```
{
char *expplace,*in,*out,*idplace;
in = gentemp(LABLE);
out = gentemp(LABLE);
match(FOR);
match(LP);
assignment( );
gencode("LABLE",in,":","","",0,1);
expplace = rexpression( );
match(SEMI);
gencode("CMP",expplace,",","FALSE","",1,1);
gencode("JMEQ",out,"","","",1,1);
idplace = match(ID);
match(ASGN);
expplace = aexpression( );
```

```
gencode(idplace,"=",expplace,"","",1,1);/****** error might be possible**********/
match(RP);
if(ttype==LB)
     block( );
else
     statement( );
gencode("JMP",in,"","","",1,1);
gencode("LABLE",out,":","","",0,1);
}

void block( )
{
match(LB);
stmt_list( );
match(RB);
}

void stmt_list( )
{
while(1)
{
     statement( );
     if(ttype==RB || ttype==NV)
          break;
}
}
/*parse and generate intermediate code for do..while loop*/
void dowhileloop( )
{
char* in,*out,*rexpplace;
match(DO);
in = gentemp(LABLE);
out = gentemp(LABLE);
gencode("LABLE",in,":","","",0,1);
if(ttype==LB)
     block( );
else
     statement( );
```

```
match(WHILE);
match(LP);
rexpplace = rexpression( );
match(RP);
match(SEMI);
gencode("CMP",rexpplace,",","FALSE","",1,1);
gencode("JMEQ",out,"","","",1,1);
gencode("JMP",in,"","","",1,1);
gencode("LABLE",out,":","","",0,1);
}
```

/*IF STATEMENT parsing and gernerate intermediate code for that..
it includes if
else if
else if
else ladder
*/

```
void ifstatement( )
{
 char* lastlable;
 if(errflag)
     return;
 lastlable = gentemp(LABLE);
 restif(lastlable);
 gencode("LABLE",lastlable,":","","",0,1);
}
void restif(char* lastlable)
{
 char* out,*expplace;
 match(IF);
 match(LP);
 out = gentemp(LABLE);
 expplace = rexpression( );
 match(RP);
 gencode("CMP",expplace,",","FALSE","",1,1);
 gencode("JMPEQ",out,"","","",1,1);
 if(ttype==LB)
     block( );
```

```
else
    statement( );
gencode("JMP",lastlable,"","","",1,1);
gencode("LABLE",out,":","","",0,1);
if(ttype==ELSE)
{
    match(ELSE);
    if(ttype==IF)
        restif(lastlable);
    else if(ttype==LB)
        block( );
    else
        statement( );
}
}

void summary( )
{
textmode(1);
printf("\n\t ***** C COMPILER *****");
printf("\n\n THIS COMPILER CONSTRUCT THREE ADDRESS");
printf("\n\t CODE OF C SOURCE CODE");
 printf("\n\n\n\n\n");
printf("————————————————————————————————\n");
printf("\nThere were %d errors in the program : \n",nooferr);
printf("\n————————————————————————————————\n");
}
```

12.1.2.2 Input file (Input.c)

```
int sum,a,b,i;
i=0;
a=3;
b=4;
sum=0;
sum=sum+a+b+i;
```

12.1.2.3 Output file

```
WORD  sum , a , b , i ;
```

```
i = 0 ;
a = 3 ;
b = 4 ;
sum = 0 ;
t1 = sum + a ;
t2 = t1 + b ;
t3 = t2 + i ;
sum = t3 ;
```

12.2 PROJECT 2: LEXICAL ANALYZER PROGRAM IN 'C' LANGUAGE ON 'UNIX' PLATFORM

In this project, there are total five files:

1. globals.cpp
2. globals.h
3. lex.cpp
4. lex.h
5. lextest.cpp

12.2.1 global.cpp

```
// globals.cpp
#include "globals.h"
TokenStream ctoken;
```

12.2.2 globals.h

```
// globals.h
#ifndef GLOBALS_H
#define GLOBALS_H
#include "lex.h"
extern TokenStream ctoken;
#endif
```

12.2.3 lex.cpp

```
//lex.cpp
// Lexical Analyzer: For a description of the tokens, see "lex.h".
#include <assert.h>
#include <ctype.h>
#include <iostream.h>
#include <stdlib.h>
#include "lex.h"
```

```
// Token::kind()
TokenKind Token::kind() const
{
return the_kind;
}

// Token::value()
// Return the value of a NUMBER token.
unsigned Token::value() const
{
        assert (the_kind == NUMBER);
        return the_value;
}

// Token::op_char()
// Return the character corresponding to the OP token.
char Token::op_char() const
{
        assert (the_kind == OP);
        return the_op_char;
}

// Token::print()
// Output the value of this token followed by a new line.
void Token::print() const
{
        switch (the_kind)
{
            case QUIT: cout << "QUIT"; break;
            case END: cout << "END"; break;
            case NUMBER: cout << "NUMBER:" << the_value; break;
            case OP: cout << "OP: " << the_op_char; break;
            case LPAREN: cout << "LPAREN"; break;
            case RPAREN: cout << "RPAREN"; break;
}
cout << endl;
}
```

```
// TokenStream::get( )
// Return the next input token and remove it from the stream.
Token TokenStream::get( )
{
Token tok; // return value
if (the_stack.empty( ))
{
tok = input( );
}
else
 {
tok = the_stack.top( );
the_stack.pop( );
}
return tok;
}

// TokenStream::peek( )
// Return the next input token but do not remove it from the stream.
// The next call to peek( ) or get( ) should return the same token as this call.
Token TokenStream::peek( )
{
if (the_stack.empty( ))
{
the_stack.push(input( ));
}
return the_stack.top( );
}

Token TokenStream::input( )
{
Token tok;
// Otherwise, get the next token from the input
while (true)
{ // loop until we can return a token
int c = cin.peek( );
if (c == EOF)
{
```

```
cerr << “Unexpected end of file” << ;
exit(EXIT_FAILURE);
}
else if(c == ‘q’)
{
tok.the_kind = QUIT;
cin.get( );
return tok;
}
else if(c == ‘=’)
{
tok.the_kind = END;
cin.get( );
return tok;
}
else if(c == ‘(‘)
{
cin.get( );
tok.the_kind = LPAREN;
return tok;
}
else if(c == ‘)’)
{
cin.get( );
tok.the_kind = RPAREN;
return tok;
}
else if(c == ‘+’ || c == ‘–’ || c == ‘*’ || c == ‘/’)
{
cin.get( ); // scan past operator
tok.the_kind = OP;
tok.the_op_char = c;
return tok;
}
else if(isdigit(c))
{
```

```
tok.the_kind = NUMBER;
tok.the_value = cin.get( ) - '0'; // read a 1–digit number
return tok;
}
else if (isspace(c))
{
// skip past token and keep looping
cin.get( );
}
else
{
// read past char; warn user; keep looping
cin.get( ); // read past character
cerr << "WARNING: Unexpected character ignored: "<< (char) c << endl;
                    }
            }
}
```

12.2.4 lex.h

```
// lex.h
#ifndef LEX_H
#define LEX_H
#include <iostream.h>
#include <stack.h>

// TokenKind defines the legal tokens in the language
enum TokenKind
 {
QUIT, // the letter 'q'
END, // equals sign is end of expression
NUMBER, // a single digit
OP, // arithmetic operator
LPAREN, RPAREN // parentheses
};

class Token
```

```
{
friend class TokenStream;
public:
TokenKind kind( ) const;
unsigned value( ) const; // return the value of a NUMBER token
char op_char( ) const; // return the character of an OP token
void print( ) const; // output the kind (and other relevant info)
private:
TokenKind the_kind;
unsigned  the_value;
char  the_op_char;
};

class TokenStream
{
public:
Token peek( ); // Return the value of the next input token without removing
// it from the stream.
Token get( ); // Return the next input token; remove it from the stream.
private:
Token input( ); // Return the next token from standard input
Token input_string ( ); // Input an ID or a keyword token.
Token input_number ( ); // Input a NUMBER token.
stack<Token> the_stack; // Used by get and peek to save tokens.
};
endif
```

12.2.5 lextest.cpp

```
// lextest.cpp
#include <iostream.h>
#include <stdlib.h>
#include "globals.h"
#include "lex.h"

// Test the lexical analyzer by reading a sequence of tokens from the
// input and outputting the value of each token, one per line
```

```
// until the QUIT token is returned.
int main ()
{
Token tok1, tok2;
cout << "\nTesting lexical analyzer...\n" << endl;
do
{
tok1 = ctoken.peek( );
tok2 = ctoken.get( );
assert (tok1.kind ( ) == tok2.kind( ));
tok2.print( );
} while (tok2.kind( ) != QUIT);
return 0;
}
```

Appendix-A
Code

EX A.1 Write a program to reorganize data type as 'integer', 'float' and 'exponent' (Chapter 1)

```
#include<stdio.h>
#include<conio.h>
#include<stdlib.h>
#include<conio.h>
#include<math.h>
#include<string.h>
void call_for_int(int,int,int);
void call_for_float(int,int,int);
void call_for_exp(int,int,int);
int flag=0,flag1=0,flag2=0;
char s[100];
int pos,j,k,len;
int a,b;

void main()
{
 clrscr();
 printf("\n ENTER THE STRING::::");
 gets(s);
 len=strlen(s);
 if(len>=1)
 {
		pos=0;
		while(s[j]!=NULL && j<=len)
		{
				if((s[pos]=='0') || (s[pos]=='1') || (s[pos]=='2') || (s[pos]=='3') || (s[pos]=='4') || (s[pos]=='5')
|| (s[pos]=='6') || (s[pos]=='7') || (s[pos]=='8') || (s[pos]=='9'))
				{
						call_for_int(pos,j,len);
						break;
				}
				else if(s[pos]=='.')
```

```
                {
                        pos++;
                        j++;
                        call_for_float(pos,j,len);
                        break;
                }
        j++;
        }
}
else
printf("\n NOT ACCEPTED");
 getch();

}

void call_for_int(int pos,int j,int len)
{

while(s[j]!=NULL && j<=len)
{
        if((s[pos]=='0') || (s[pos]=='1') || (s[pos]=='2') || (s[pos]=='3') || (s[pos]=='4') || (s[pos]=='5') ||
(s[pos]=='6') || (s[pos]=='7') || (s[pos]=='8') || (s[pos]=='9'))
        {
                pos++;
                j++;
                flag=1;
                call_for_int(pos,j,len);
                break;
        }
        else if(s[pos]=='.')
        {
                flag1=2;
                pos++;
                j++;
                call_for_float(pos,j,len);
                break;
        }
        else if(s[pos]= ='e')
        {
                pos++;
                j++;
                flag2=1;
                call_for_exp(pos,j,len);
                break;
        }
}
```

```
	if(flag==1 && flag1==0 && flag2==0)
	{
	printf("\n NUMBER IS INTEGER");
	getch();
	exit(0);
	}
}

void call_for_float(int pos,int j,int len)
{
while(s[j]!=NULL && j<=len)
{
	if((s[pos]=='0') || (s[pos]=='1') || (s[pos]=='2') || (s[pos]=='3') || (s[pos]=='4') || (s[pos]=='5') ||
(s[pos]=='6') || (s[pos]=='7') || (s[pos]=='8') || (s[pos]=='9'))
	{
		pos++;
		j++;
		flag=100;
		call_for_float(pos,j,len);
		break;
	}
	else if(s[pos]=='.')
	{
		printf("\n INVALID STATEMENT");
		break;
	}
	else if(s[pos]=='e')
	{
		pos++;
		j++;
		flag1=2;
		call_for_exp(pos,j,len);
		break;
	}
}
	if(flag==100 && flag1==2)
	{
	printf("\n NUMBER IS FLOAT");
	getch();
	exit(0);
	}

}
```

```
void call_for_exp(int pos,int j,int len)
{
while(s[j]!=NULL && j<=len)
{
        if((s[pos]=='0') || (s[pos]=='1') || (s[pos]=='2') || (s[pos]=='3') || (s[pos]=='4') || (s[pos]=='5') ||
(s[pos]=='6') || (s[pos]=='7') || (s[pos]=='8') || (s[pos]=='9'))
        {
                pos++;
                j++;
                flag=1;
                call_for_exp(pos,j,len);
                break;
        }
        else if(s[pos]=='.')
        {
                printf("\n INVALID STATEMENT");
                break;
        }
        else if(s[pos]=='e')
        {
                printf("\n INVALID STATEMENT");
                break;
        }
}
        if(flag==1 )
        {
        printf("\n NUMBER IS EXPONENT");
        getch();
        exit(0);
        }

}
```

EX A.2 Write a program to reorganize a D.F.A. as b*abb. (Chapter 1)

```
#include<stdio.h>
#include<conio.h>
int a,b;
#include<math.h>
#include<string.h>
void call(int,int,int);
 char s[100];
 int i,j,k,l;
void call1(int,int,int);
void call2(int,int,int);
```

```
void main()
{
clrscr();
printf("\n ENTER THE STRING::::");
 gets(s);
l=strlen(s);
if(l>=3)
{
        i=0;
        while(s[j]!=NULL && j<=l)
        {
                if(s[i]== 'b')
                {
                        printf("\n THIS IS FIRST STATE");
                        i++;
                }
                else if(s[i]=='a')
                {
                        call(i,j,l);
                        break;
                }
        j++;
        }
}
else
printf("\n NOT ACCEPTED");
printf("\n\n\t ****IF LAST STAGE IS FOURTH THEN STRING IS ACCEPTED****");
getch();
}

void call(int i,int j,int l)
{
while(s[j]!=NULL && j<=l)
{
if(s[i]=='a')
 {
        printf("\n THIS IS SECOND STATE");
        i++;
        j++;
        call(i,j,l);
        break;
}
else if(s[i]=='b' && s[i]!=NULL)
{
        printf("\n THIS IS THIRD STATE");
```

```
        j++;
        i++;
        call1(i,j,l);
        break;
        }
}
}

void call1(int i,int j,int l)
{
while(s[j]!=NULL && j<=l)
{
        if(s[i]=='b')
        {
                //goto call();
                printf("\n THIS IS FOURTH STATE");
        //      i++;
        //      j++;
                if(s[j]=='\0') {
                printf(" FINAL STATE ALSO");
                break;       }
                i++;
                j++;
                call2(i,j,l);
                break;
        //      i++;
        //      j++;

        }

        else if(s[i]=='a')
        {
                call(i,j,l);
                break;
        }
}
}

void call2(int i,int j,int l)
{
while(s[j]!=NULL && j<=l)
{
        if(s[i]=='b')
        {
                printf("\n THIS IS FIRST STATE");
```

```
                i++;
                j++;
                call2(i,j,l);
                break;
        }
        else if(s[i]=='a')
        {
                call(i,j,l);
                break;
}
}
}
```

Ex. A.3 A Simple Compiler Example(C Language) (Chapter 2)

The following program represents a very simple one-pass compiler, written in C. This compiler compiles an expression defined in infix notation to postfix notation and also into an assembly-like machine language.

COMPILER.C

```
#include <stdlib.h>
#include <stdio.h>
#include <string.h>

#define MODE_POSTFIX   0
#define MODE_ASSEMBLY  1

char   lookahead;
int    pos;
int    compile_mode;
char   expression[20+1];

void error()
{
    printf("Syntax error!\n");
}

void match( char t )
{
   if( lookahead == t )
   {
      pos++;
      lookahead = expression[pos];
   }
   else
      error();
}
```

```
void digit()
{
    switch( lookahead )
   {
      case '0':
      case '1':
      case '2':
      case '3':
      case '4':
      case '5':
      case '6':
      case '7':
      case '8':
      case '9':
        if( compile_mode == MODE_POSTFIX )
            printf("%c", lookahead);
          else
            printf("\tPUSH %c\n", lookahead);

            match( lookahead );
            break;
      default:
            error();
            break;
   }
}

void term()
{
    digit();
    while(1)
     {
     switch( lookahead )
     {
     case '*':
     match('*');
    digit();

    printf( "%s", compile_mode == MODE_POSTFIX ? "*" :
                  "\tPOP B\n\tPOP A\n\tMUL A, B\n\tPUSH A\n");
    break;
     case '/':
     match('/');
     digit();
```

```
        printf( "%s", compile_mode == MODE_POSTFIX ? "/": "\tPOP B\n\tPOP A\n\tDIV A,
                                                                    B\n\tPUSH A\n");
          break;

                default:
                    return;
            }
        }
}

void expr()
{
    term();
    while(1)
    {
        switch( lookahead )
        {
            case '+':
                match('+');
                term();

        printf( "%s", compile_mode == MODE_POSTFIX ? "+" : "\tPOP B\n\tPOP A\n\tADD A,
                                                                    B\n\tPUSH A\n");
                break;

            case '–':
                match('–');
                term();

        printf( "%s", compile_mode == MODE_POSTFIX ? "–": "\tPOP B\n\tPOP A\n\tSUB A,
                                                                    B\n\tPUSH A\n");
                break;

            default:
                return;
        }
    }
}
void main ( int argc, char** argv )
{
    printf("Please enter an infix-notated expression with single digits:\n\n\t");
    scanf("%20s", expression);

    printf("\nCompiling to postfix-notated expression:\n\n\t");
    compile_mode = MODE_POSTFIX;
    pos = 0;
```

```
    lookahead = *expression;
    expr();

    printf("\n\nCompiling to assembly-notated machine code:\n\n");
    compile_mode = MODE_ASSEMBLY;
    pos = 0;
    lookahead = *expression;
    expr();

    return 0;
}
```

A possible execution of this simple compiler results in the following output:

```
Please enter an infix-notated expression with single digits:
    3-4*2+2
Compiling to postfix-notated expression:
    342*-2+
Compiling to assembly-notated machine code:
    PUSH 3
    PUSH 4
    PUSH 2
    POP B
    POP A
    MUL A, B
    PUSH A
    POP B
    POP A
    SUB A, B
    PUSH A
    PUSH 2
    POP B
    POP A
    ADD A, B
    PUSH A
```

Ex A.4 Example in C Language (Chapter 4)

The following grammar is in LL(1) form (for simplicity, ident and number are assumed to be terminals):

```
program = block "." .

    block =
      ["const" ident "=" number {"," ident "=" number} ";"]
      ["var" ident {"," ident} ";"]
      {"procedure" ident ";" block ";"} statement .
```

```
statement =
  [ident ":=" expression
  | "call" ident
  | "begin" statement {";" statement} "end"

  | "if" condition "then" statement
  | "while" condition "do" statement
  ].

condition =
   "odd" expression
  | expression ("="|"#"|"<"|"<="|">"|">=") expression
  .

expression = ["+"|"–"] term {("+"|"–") term} .

term = factor {("*"|"/") factor} .

factor = ident | number | "(" expression ")" .
```

Terminals are expressed in quotes (except for ident and number). Each nonterminal is defined by a rule in the grammar.

There is a procedure for each nonterminal in the grammar. Parsing descends in a top-down manner, until the final nonterminal has been processed. The program fragment depends on a global variable, **sym**, which contains the next symbol from the input, and the global function **getsym**, which updates sym when called.

```
typedef enum {ident, number, lparen, rparen, times, slash, plus,

  minus, eql, neq, lss, leq, gtr, geq, callsym, beginsym, semicolon,
  endsym, ifsym, whilesym, becomes, thensym, dosym, constsym, comma,
  varsym, procsym, period, oddsym} Symbol;

Symbol sym; void getsym(void); void error(const char msg[]); void expression(void);

int accept(Symbol s) {

  if (sym == s) {
     getsym();
     return 1;
  }
  return 0;

}

int expect(Symbol s) {

  if (accept(s))
     return 1;
  error("expect: unexpected symbol");
  return 0;

}
```

```
void factor(void) {
  if (accept(ident)) {
      ;
  } else if (accept(number)) {
      ;
  } else if (accept(lparen)) {
      expression();
      expect(rparen);
  } else {
      error("factor: syntax error");
      getsym();
  }
}

void term(void) {
  factor();
  while (sym == times || sym == slash) {
      getsym();
      factor();
  }
}

void expression(void) {
  if (sym == plus || sym == minus)
      getsym();
  term();
  while (sym == plus || sym == minus) {
      getsym();
      term();
  }
}

void condition(void) {
  if (accept(oddsym)) {
      expression();
  } else {
      expression();
      if (sym == eql || sym == neq || sym == lss ||
          sym == leq || sym == gtr || sym == geq) {
          getsym();
          expression();
      } else {
          error("condition: invalid operator");
```

```
        getsym();
      }
    }
}

void statement(void) {
  if (accept(ident)) {
     expect(becomes);
     expression();
  } else if (accept(callsym)) {
     expect(ident);
  } else if (accept(beginsym)) {
     do {
        statement();
    } while (accept(semicolon));
    expect(endsym);
  } else if (accept(ifsym)) {
     condition();
     expect(thensym);
     statement();
  } else if (accept(whilesym)) {
     condition();
     expect(dosym);
     statement();
  }
}

void block(void) {
  if (accept(constsym)) {
     do {
        expect(ident);
        expect(eql);
        expect(number);
    } while (accept(comma));
    expect(semicolon);
  }
  if (accept(varsym)) {
     do {
        expect(ident);
    } while (accept(comma));
    expect(semicolon);
  }
  while (accept(procsym)) {
    expect(ident);
```

```
    expect(semicolon);
    block();
    expect(semicolon);
  }
  statement();
}

void program(void) {
  getsym();
  block();
  expect(period);
}
```

Ex A.5 Example in C Language (Chapter 4)

```
typedef struct _exptree exptree;
struct _exptree {
   char token;
   exptree *left;
   exptree *right;
};

exptree *parse_e(void)
{
   return parse_t();
}

exptree *parse_t(void)
{
   exptree *first_f = parse_f();

   while(cur_token() == '+') {
      exptree *replace_tree = alloc_tree();
      replace_tree->token = cur_token();
      replace_tree->left = first_f;
      next_token();
      replace_tree->right = parse_f();
      first_f = replace_token;
   }

   return first_f;
}

exptree *parse_f(void)
```

```
{
  exptree *first_i = parse_i();

  while(cur_token() == '*') {
    exptree *replace_tree = alloc_tree();
    replace_tree->token = cur_token();
    replace_tree->left = first_i;
    next_token();
    replace_tree->right = parse_i();
    first_i = replace_tree;
  }

  return first_i;
}

exptree *parse_i(void)
{
  exptree *i = alloc_tree();
  exptree->left = exptree->right = NULL;
  exptree->token = cur_token();
  next_token();
}
```

Ex A.6 Operator Precedence Parsing (*Chapter 4*)

```
#include <stdio.h>
#include <stdlib.h>
#include <string.h>
#include <math.h>
typedef enum { false , true } bool;
/* actions */
typedef enum {
  S,          /* shift */
  R,          /* reduce */
  A,          /* accept */
  E1,         /* error: missing right parenthesis */
  E2,         /* error: missing operator */
  E3,         /* error: unbalanced right parenthesis */
  R           /* error: invalid function argument */
} actEnum;
/* tokens */
typedef enum {
  /* operators */
  tAdd,         /* + */
  tSub,         /* – */
  tMul,         /* * */
```

```
  tDiv,        /* / */
  tPow,        /* ^ (power) */
  tUmi,        /* – (unary minus) */
  tFact,       /* f(x): factorial */
  tPerm,       /* p(n,r): permutations, n objects, r at a time */
  tComb,       /* c(n,r): combinations, n objects, r at a time */
  tComa,       /* comma */
  tLpr,        /* ( */
  tRpr,        /* ) */
  tEof,        /* end of string */
  tMaxOp,      /* maximum number of operators */
  /* non-operators */
  tVal         /* value */
} tokEnum;
tokEnum tok;         /* token */
double tokval;       /* token value */
#define MAX_OPR      50
#define MAX_VAL      50
char opr[MAX_OPR];     /* operator stack */
double val[MAX_VAL];   /* value stack */
int oprTop, valTop;    /* top of operator, value stack */
bool firsttok;         /* true if first token */
char parseTbl[tMaxOp][tMaxOp] = {
  /* stk    ——————————— input ———————————— */
  /*        +  –  *  /  ^  M  f  p  c  ,  (  )  $  */
  /*        —  —  —  —  —  —  —  —  —  —  —  —  — */
  /* + */ { R, R, S, S, S, S, S, S, S, R, S, R, R },
  /* – */ { R, R, S, S, S, S, S, S, S, R, S, R, R },
  /* * */ { R, R, R, R, S, S, S, S, S, R, S, R, R },
  /* / */ { R, R, R, R, S, S, S, S, S, R, S, R, R },
  /* ^ */ { R, R, R, R, S, S, S, S, S, R, S, R, R },
  /* M */ { R, R, R, R, R, S, S, S, S, R, S, R, R },
  /* f */ { R, R, R, R, R, R, R, R, R, R, S, R, R },
  /* p */ { R, R, R, R, R, R, R, R, R, R, S, R, R },
  /* c */ { R, R, R, R, R, R, R, R, R, R, S, R, R },
  /* , */ { R, R, R, R, R, R, R, R, R, R, R, R, E4},
  /* ( */ { S, S, S, S, S, S, S, S, S, S, S, S, E1},
  /* ) */ { R, R, R, R, R, R, E3, E3, E3, R, E2, R, R },
  /* $ */ { S, S, S, S, S, S, S, S, S, E4, S, E3, A }
};
int error(char *msg) {
  printf("error: %s\n", msg);
  return 1;
}
int gettok(void) {
```

```
    static char str[82];
    static tokEnum prevtok;
    char *s;
    /* scan for next symbol */
    if (firsttok) {
        firsttok = false;
        prevtok = tEof;
        gets(str);
        if (*str == 'q') exit(0);
        s = strtok(str, " ");
    } else {
        s = strtok(NULL, " ");
    }
    /* convert symbol to token */
    if (s) {
        switch(*s) {
        case '+': tok = tAdd; break;
        case '–': tok = tSub; break;
        case '*': tok = tMul; break;
        case '/': tok = tDiv; break;
        case '^': tok = tPow; break;
        case '(': tok = tLpr; break;
        case ')': tok = tRpr; break;
        case ',': tok = tComa; break;
        case 'f': tok = tFact; break;
        case 'p': tok = tPerm; break;
        case 'c': tok = tComb; break;
        default:
            tokval = atof(s);
            tok = tVal;
            break;
        }
    } else {
        tok = tEof;
    }
    /* check for unary minus */
    if (tok == tSub) {
        if (prevtok != tVal && prevtok != tRpr) {
            tok = tUmi;
        }
    }
    prevtok = tok;
    return 0;
}
int shift(void) {
```

```
if (tok == tVal) {
  if (++valTop >= MAX_VAL)
     return error("val stack exhausted");
   val[valTop] = tokval;
} else {
  if (++oprTop >= MAX_OPR)
     return error("opr stack exhausted");
   opr[oprTop] = (char)tok;
}
if (gettok()) return 1;
return 0;
}
double fact(double n) {
  double i, t;
  for (t = 1, i = 1; i <= n; i++)
     t *= i;
  return t;
}
int reduce(void) {
  switch(opr[oprTop]) {
  case tAdd:
    /* apply E := E + E */
    if (valTop < 1) return error("syntax error");
    val[valTop – – 1] = val[valTop – – 1] + val[valTop];
     valTop – –;
     break;
  case tSub:
    /* apply E := E – E */
    if (valTop < 1) return error("syntax error");
    val[valTop – –1] = val[valTop – –1] – – val[valTop];
     valTop – –;
     break;
  case tMul:
    /* apply E := E * E */
    if (valTop < 1) return error("syntax error");
    val[valTop – –1] = val[valTop – –1] * val[valTop];
     valTop –;
     break;
  case tDiv:
    /* apply E := E / E */
    if (valTop < 1) return error("syntax error");
    val[valTop – –1] = val[valTop – –1] / val[valTop];
     valTop –;
     break;
  case tUmi:
```

```
    /* apply E := – –E */
    if (valTop < 0) return error("syntax error");
    val[valTop] = – –val[valTop];
    break;
  case tPow:
    /* apply E := E ^ E */
    if (valTop < 1) return error("syntax error");
    val[valTop – –1] = pow(val[valTop – –1], val[valTop]);
    valTop – –;
    break;
  case tFact:
    /* apply E := f(E) */
    if (valTop < 0) return error("syntax error");
    val[valTop] = fact(val[valTop]);
    break;
  case tPerm:
    /* apply E := p(N,R) */
    if (valTop < 1) return error("syntax error");
    val[valTop – –1] = fact(val[valTop – –1])/fact(val[valTop – –1]– –val[valTop]);
    valTop – –;
    break;
  case tComb:
    /* apply E := c(N,R) */
    if (valTop < 1) return error("syntax error");
    val[valTop – –1] = fact(val[valTop – –1])/
      (fact(val[valTop]) * fact(val[valTop– –1]– –val[valTop]));
    valTop – ;
    break;
  case tRpr:
    /* pop () off stack */
    oprTop – –;
    break;
  }
  oprTop – –;
  return 0;
}
int parse(void) {
  printf("\nenter expression (q to quit):\n");
  /* initialize for next expression */
  oprTop = 0; valTop = –1;
  opr[oprTop] = tEof;
  firsttok = true;
  if (gettok()) return 1;
  while(1) {
    /* input is value */
```

```
        if (tok == tVal) {
            /* shift token to value stack */
            if (shift()) return 1;
            continue;
        }
        /* input is operator */
        switch(parseTbl[opr[oprTop]][tok]) {
        case R:
            if (reduce()) return 1;
            break;
        case S:
            if (shift()) return 1;
            break;
        case A:
            /* accept */
            if (valTop != 0) return error("syntax error");
            printf("value = %f\n", val[valTop]);
            return 0;
        case E1:
            return error("missing right parenthesis");
        case E2:
            return error("missing operator");
        case E3:
            return error("unbalanced right parenthesis");
        case E4:
            return error("invalid function argument");
        }
    }
}
int main(void) {
    while(1) parse();
    return 0;
}
```

Ex-A.7 (Chapter 4)

(I) Simple calculator :

This calculator evaluates simple arithmetic expressions. The *lex* program matches numbers and operators and returns them; it ignores white space, returns newlines, and gives an error message on anything else.

```
%{
#include <stdlib.h>
#include <stdio.h>
#include "calc1.h"
void yyerror(char*);
extern int yylval;
```

```
%}
%%
[ \t]+ ;
[0-9]+ {yylval = atoi(yytext);
return INTEGER;}
[–+*/] {return *yytext;}
“(“ {return *yytext;}
“)” {return *yytext;}
\n {return *yytext;}
. {char msg[25];
sprintf(msg,”%s <%s>”,”invalid character”,yytext);
yyerror(msg);}
```

Accepting the *lex* output, this *yacc* program has rules that parse the stream of numbers and operators, and perform the corresponding calculations.

```
%{
#include <stdlib.h>
#include <stdio.h>
int yylex(void);
#include “calc1.h”
%}
%token INTEGER
%%
program:
line program
| line
line: expr ’\n’ { printf(“%d\n”,$1); }
          | ’n’
expr: expr ’+’ mulex { $$ = $1 + $3; }
          | expr ’–’ mulex { $$ = $1 – $3; }
          | mulex { $$ = $1; }
mulex: mulex ’*’ term { $$ = $1 * $3; }
          | mulex ’/’ term { $$ = $1 / $3; }
          | term { $$ = $1; }
term: ’(’ expr ’)’ { $$ = $2; }
          | INTEGER { $$ = $1; }
%%
void yyerror(char *s)
{
          fprintf(stderr,”%s\n”,s);
          return;
}
int main(void)
{
          yyparse();
```

```
        return 0;
}
```

Here we have realized operator precedence by having separate rules for the different priorities. The rule for plus/minus comes first, which means that its terms, the mulex expressions involving multiplication, are evaluated first.

(II) Calculator with simple variables :

In this example the return variables have been declared of type double. Furthermore, there can now be single-character variables that can be assigned and used. There now are two different return tokens: double values and integer variable indices. This necessitates the %union statement, as well as %token statements for the various return tokens and %type statements for the non-terminals. This is all in the *yacc* file:

```
%{
#include <stdlib.h>
#include <stdio.h>
int yylex(void);
double var[26];
%}
%union { double dval; int ivar; }
%token <dval> DOUBLE
%token <ivar> NAME
%type <dval> expr
%type <dval> mulex
%type <dval> term
%%
program: line program
                | line
line: expr '\n' { printf("%g\n",$1); }
                | NAME '=' expr '\n' { var[$1] = $3; }
expr:     expr '+' mulex { $$ = $1 + $3; }
                | expr '–' mulex { $$ = $1– $3; }
                | mulex { $$ = $1; }
mulex: mulex '*' term { $$ = $1 * $3; }
                | mulex '/' term { $$ = $1 / $3; }
                | term { $$ = $1; }
term: '(' expr ')' { $$ = $2; }
                | NAME { $$ = var[$1]; }
                | DOUBLE { $$ = $1; }
%%
void yyerror(char *s)
{
        fprintf(stderr,"%s\n",s);
        return;
}
```

```
int main(void)
{
        yyparse();
        return 0;
}
```

The *lex* file is not all that different; note how return values are now assigned to a component of yylval rather than yyerror(msg);} itself.

```
%{
#include <stdlib.h>
#include <stdio.h>
#include "calc2.h"
void yyerror(char*);
%}
%%
[ \t]+ ;
(([0-9]+(\.[0-9]*)?)|([0-9]*\.[0-9]+)) {
yylval.dval = atof(yytext);
return DOUBLE;}
[-+*/=] {return *yytext;}
"(" {return *yytext;}
")" {return *yytext;}
[a-z] {yylval.ivar = *yytext;
return NAME;}
\n {return *yytext;}
. {char msg[25];
sprintf(msg,"%s <%s>","invalid character",yytext);
```

(III) Calculator with dynamic variables :

Basically the same as the previous example, but now variable names can have regular names, and they are inserted into a names table dynamically. The *yacc* file defines a routine for getting a variable index:

```
%{
#include <stdlib.h>
#include <stdio.h>
#include <string.h>
int yylex(void);
#define NVARS 100
char *vars[NVARS]; double vals[NVARS]; int nvars=0;
%}
%union { double dval; int ivar; }
%token <dval> DOUBLE
%token <ivar> NAME
%type <dval> expr
%type <dval> mulex
%type <dval> term
```

```
%%
program: line program
        | line
line: expr '\n' { printf("%g\n",$1); }
        | NAME '=' expr '\n' { vals[$1] = $3; }
expr: expr '+' mulex { $$ = $1 + $3; }
        | expr '–' mulex { $$ = $1 – $3; }
        | mulex { $$ = $1; }
mulex: mulex '*' term { $$ = $1 * $3; }
        | mulex '/' term { $$ = $1 / $3; }
        | term { $$ = $1; }
term: '(' expr ')' { $$ = $2; }
        | NAME { $$ = vals[$1]; }
        | DOUBLE { $$ = $1; }
%%
int varindex(char *var)
{
        int i;
        for (i=0; i<nvars; i++)
        if (strcmp(var,vars[i])==0) return i;
        vars[nvars] = strdup(var);
        return nvars++;
}
int main(void)
{
        yyparse();
        return 0;
}
```

The *lex* file is largely unchanged, except for the rule that recognises variable names:

```
%{
#include <stdlib.h>
#include <stdio.h>
#include "calc3.h"
void yyerror(char*);
int varindex(char *var);
%}
%%
[ \t]+ ;
(([0–9]+(\.[0–9]*)?)|([0–9]*\.[0–9]+)) {
yylval.dval = atof(yytext);
return DOUBLE;}
[–+*/=] {return *yytext;}
"(" {return *yytext;}
")" {return *yytext;}
```

```
[a-z][a-z0-9]* {
yylval.ivar = varindex(yytext);
return NAME;}
\n {return *yytext;}
. {char msg[25];
sprintf(msg,"%s <%s>","invalid character",yytext);
yyerror(msg);}
```

Ex A.8 Complete 'C' program for parser (Chapter 4)

(i) C File (driver_par.c) : contain main of parser and driving program to check command line options and invoke yypase().

(ii) parser.y: contain grammar definitions and semantic actions to build a syntax tree. It also include "lex.yy.c".

(iii) header file (tree.h): routines to build and test the syntax tree; some functions are updated and new functions are added for convenience. It use structure like typedef struct treenode

```
{    /* syntax tree node struct */
   int NodeKind, NodeOpType, IntVal;
   struct treenode *LeftC, *RightC;
} ILTree, *tree;
```

C File (tree.c): This file consists of 4 parts:

a. the data structure of a tree node

b. the tree operation functions, from "CopyTree" to "SetRightChild"

c. the tree printing function

d. the tree checker

this file include various functions like

1. tree NullExp():This function return a DUMMYNode to the caller. Note: All the dummy nodes are corresponding to the save memory location. So any attampt to use it for the other purposes will cause trouble.
2. tree MakeLeaf(Kind, N): This function will create a leafnode with it.
3. tree MakeTree(NodeOp, Left, Right): This function create a interior node of NodeOptype with children to be Left and Right, respectively.
4. tree LeftChild(T): This function returns leftchild of the tree node.
5. tree RightChild(T): This function returns rightchild of the tree node.
6. tree MkLeftC(T1, T2): This function makes subtree T1 to be the leftmost child of the tree T2, return T2.
7. tree MkRightC(T1, T2): This function makes subtree T1 to be the rightmost child of the tree T2, return T2.
8. int NodeOp(T): This function returns NodeOpType of a node.
9. int NodeKind(T): This function returns NodeKind of a node.
10. int IntVal(T): This function returns IntVal of a leafnode.
11. int IsNull(T): This function return true if the node is DUMMYNode, false otherwise.
12. tree SetNode(Target, Source): This function sets the Target Node to be source Node (only for Non Dummy Target Node).
13. tree SetNodeOp(T, Op): This function sets the NodeOpType to be to be NewOp (only for Interior EXPRNode).

14. tree SetLeftTreeOp(T, Op): This function sets the tree root and all its left subtree root to be a NewOp node, used only in construct a Record Component subtree.
15. tree T;
16. tree SetRightTreeOp(T, Op): This function sets the tree root and all its right subtree root to be a NewOp node, used only in construct a Procedure or function call subtree with arguments.
17. tree SetLeftChild(T, NewC): This function sets the LeftChild of T to be NewC.
18. tree SetRightChild(T, NewC): This function sets the RightChild of T to be NewC.
19. tree AssignTypeL(L, T): This function will assign a type T to a variable list L with left recursion, and the updated list gets returned with each variable having type T.
20. tree AssignTypeR(L, T): This function will assign a type T to a variable list L with right recursion, and the updated list gets returned with each variable having type T.
21. others modules also exits.

(iv) lexer.l: lex file from lexical analysis. It generates tokens and maintain a string buffer containing all lexemes.

(v) C File (table.c) : from lexical analysis implementation of a hash table and string buffer used to store lexemes (identifiers and string constants).

Ex A.9 Complete C Program for Semantic Analysis (Chapter 5)

(i) C File (driver_sem.c) : driving program to check command line options and invoke the parser and semantic analyzer and driver program for testing the PASC parser with semantic analysis.

(ii) File (seman.c) : routines used to augment the syntax tree generated by the parser and create the symbol table for the source code. It contain two structures as

```
/* struct of symbol table stack              */
struct
{
 bool marker;      /* mark the beginning of a block */
 int name;         /* point to the lexeme of the id */
 int st_ptr;       /* point to the id's symbol table entry */
 bool dummy;       /* dummy element to indicate a undeclared id */
 bool used;        /* this id is used? */
} stack[STACK_SIZE]; /* stack array */

/* struct of element of attribute list        */
typedef struct
{
 char attr_num;    /* attribute number ( < 256 ) */
 int attr_val;     /* attribute value */
 int next_attr;
} attr_type;       /* define the struct type and the pointer type */
```

It also include several functions as:

1. void STInit(): initialize the symbol table put predefined names into it and build trees for those names.
2. int InsertEntry(id): builds a symbol table entry for id. The current block is searched for redeclaration error. The id's name and nesting level attributes are set by this function.
3. int IsAttr(st_ptr, attr_num): return the index to the searched attribute in attrarray if it is in (nonzero).Otherwise, return false.

4. void SetAttr(st_ptr, attr_num, attr_val): set attribute. If the attribute is already there, print debugging message. Attributes for a symbol table entry are sorted by their attr_num.
5. void Push(marker, name, st_ptr, dummy): push an element onto the stack.
6. OpenBlock(): build a mark on the stack to indicate the beginning of a new block. Increment nesting level counter. It is called when reserved words "program", "procedure", "function" or "record" is encountered. Note: procedure or function name should be inserted into symbol table before calling this routine.
7. CloseBlock(): decrement nesting level counter and remove the current block from the stack called when exiting from a program, procedure, function or a record definition. Each element is checked to see if it is
8. used in the block.
9. GetAttr(): return the specified attribute value for a symbol table entry if found otherwise, report error. Note, this error is not the fault of source program but of the compiler writer. It is printed for testing and debugging.
10. LookUp(): search an id in the stack and return the symbol table entry pointer, if found. If the id is not in the stack, report error and push a dummy item on the stack so that the same error will not be reported repeatedly.
11. LookUpHere():search an id in the stack for the current block. It returns the symbol table pointer if the id is found otherwise, return 0. This routine can be used to check if there is a forward declaration for a procedure/function.
12. void error_msg(message,action,id): error handling routine.
13. void STPrint(): print symbol table.

(iii) Header File (seman.h): routines used to augment the syntax tree generated by the parser and create the symbol table for the source code and included in seman.c to manipulate the symbol table and conduct static semantic checking. Also included in traverse.c and tree.c .

(iv) C File (traverse.c) : routines used to traverse the original parse tree, build the symbol table for all identifiers, and conduct semantic analyses. The original parse tree is traversed by ValProgramOp() in preorder using codes similar to those in checktree(). A symbol table is built for all identifiers and static semantics are checked while traversing. All IDNodes in the parse tree are changed to either type nodes (integer, char, boolean) or STNodes. It include following modules:

1. void ValProgramOp(T): Start to process the syntax tree from the root. Tree will be checked on a top down fashion, looking for IDNode leaves to do the appropriate symbol table insertions.
2. ValBodyOp(T): Recursively inorder traverses a BodyOp node.
3. ValDef(T): Traverses in order a definition subtree.
4. ValTypeIdOp(T): Process a type declaration subtree. IDNode is to the child of T. The IDNode type is to the right of T.
5. ValDeclOp(T): Inorder traverses a variable declaration subtree.
6. ValCommaOp(T,kind, dup):A new entry is created in the symbol table for the variable stored as the left child of the CommaOp node. 'kind' is used to differenciate among variables, record fields, and formal parameters.
7. tree ValType(T,dimension): Process a type subtree and add the appropriate information to the symbol table. If the caller request setAttr, caller's. TYPE_ATTR is set to the type tree.
8. int ValArrayTypeOp(T,typeTree): Process an array type subtree and return the number of dimensions of the array.
9. int ValBoundOp(T): Identifiers used as array bounds must be already in the symbol table.
10. ValRecompOp(T, typeTree): Process a record type subtree.
11. ValSubrangeOp(T): Process a subrange type subtree.

12. ValConstantIdOp(T): Creates a new symbol table entry for the constant.
13. ValRoutineOp(T): Process a function or procedure declaration subtree.
14. ValHeadOp(T,root,forward): Inserts the function in the symbol table and process the formal parameter list.
15. ValArgs(T): Processes the formal parameter list for a procedure or function.
16. ValStmtOp(T): Process a sequence of statements subtree.
17. ValStmt(T):Process a statement subtree which can be either an IfStmtOp. Statement subtrees can be ifStmtOP,LoopStmtOP, AssignStmtOp, StmtOp, ExitOp, ReturnOp.
18. ValIfElseOp(T): Process an ifelse statement subtree.
19. ValIfElse(T): Process an ifelse statement subtree.
20. ValIterOp(T):Processes an iteractor subtree.
21. ValReturnOp(T): Process a return subtree.
22. ValAssignOp(T): Process an assignment subtree.
23. ValAssign(T): Process an assignment subtree; left var shouldn't be a constant.
24. ValRoutineCallOp(T):Process a routine call subtree.
25. ValCommaInCall(T, paraT, id, check):Process the list of actual parameters in a function or procedure. Semantic Check: Formal and actual number of parameters should be the same; variables are expected for reference parameters. If check is false, no check is done.
26. ValExp(T): Process an expression subtree tree T.
27. int ValVarOp(T): Process a variable reference subtree, change it to routine call and process it as a routine call if it is the case.
28. ValSelectOp(T,entry, currentType): Process indexing and field operations.
29. tree ValFieldOp(T,recType): Process a record accesing operation.
30. varOpToRoutineCallOp(T): Change a varOp to RoutineCallOp.

(v) **parser.y:** Grammar definitions and semantic actions to build a syntax tree from syntax analysis.

(vi) **C File (tree.c):** Routines to build and test the syntax tree; some functions are updated and new functions are added for convenience from syntax analysis.

(vii) **Header File (tree.h):** Tree node definitions from syntax analysis.

(viii) **lexer.l:** lex file from project 1; It generates tokens and maintains a string buffer containing all lexemes from lexical analysis.

(ix) **table.c :** implementation of a hash table and string buffer used to store lexemes (identifiers and string constants) from lexical analysis..

A.10 Complete C Program for Code Generation (Chapter 8)

(i) **Driver_code.c:** contain main of code generator.

(ii) **C File(emit.c):** Here mainly three things are implemented as:

Data definitions implemented:
—data block definition (name, type, size)
—string constant definition

Instructions implemented:
add, sub, mul, div, and, or, mov, mova, push, pusha, cmp, tst
beql, bgeq, bgtr, bleq, blss, bneq, jmp, calls

Addressing modes implemented:
relative(identifier), number constant, char constant, register

register deferred, register display

emiting functions: emit_call, _label, _goto, _most, _data, _str

emit.c contain following functions:

1. emit_call(func_name, num_arg): emit a calls instruction.
2. emit_label(l_num): emit a definition of label.
3. emit_goto(operator, l_num): emit unconditional and conditional jump instructions.
4. emit_data(name, type, size): emit one data line, name = data object name.
5. emit_most(operator, type, num_op, op1, op2, op3):operator: one of the instructions in the general group.
   i. type = L/l, W/w or B/b
   ii. num_op = 1, 2 or 3
   iii. op1..op3: operands, op2 and/or op3 can be omitted according to num_op.
6. int print_op(op): print an operand.
7. new_code(): start a new line of code.
8. new_data(): start a new line of data.
9. str_data(s): copy a string into data line.
10. str_code(s): copy a string into code line.
11. char_data(c): copy a string into data line.
12. char_code(ch): copy a string into code line.
13. tab_code(n_tab, n_char): feed proper number of tabs to justify the line
    i. n_tab = expected width
    ii. n_char = actual # of chars already there.
14. tab_data(n_tab, n_char): feed proper number of tabs to justify the line
    i. n_tab = expected width
    ii. n_char = actual # of chars already there.
15. comment_data(s): put comment into data def array.
16. char *s;
17. comment_code(s): put comment into code.

(iii) Header File(emit.h) : It contain data structures, structure, operand mode, register definition, instruction definition, general group, branch and jump group.

(iv) C File(gen.c): main functions are

1. PushLabel(label):label stack management.
2. UpperBound(T): calculate array upper bound.
3. LowerBound(T): calculate array lower bound.
4. TypeSize(T): address calculation.
5. TypeOffset(T): type offset used for record type; use in doubt.
6. ArgVarOffset(T): argument and local variable offset.
7. DataOffset(): calculate variable offset.
8. tree GetVarType(T) :code generation.
9. int GetType(T): int out type for the parameter.
10. int GetLowerBound(T, index): get the lower bound for bound checking and code generated.
11. int GetUpperBound(T, index): get upper bound for a certain index.
12. int GenIfStmt(T): generated if statement.
13. GenLoopStmt(T): generated code for loop statement.

(v) C File(io.c)

(vi) C File(run.c)

Appendix-B
Directed Acyclic Graphs (DAGs)

B.1 The DAG Representation of Basic Blocks

Directed acyclic graphs (DAGs) are useful data structure for implementing transformation on basic blocks. A DAG gives a picture of how the value computed by each statement in a basic block (section 7.4). A DAG for a basic block is a directed acyclic graph with the following labels on nodes:

1. Leaves are labeled by unique identifiers, either variable names or constants.
2. Interior nodes are labeled by an operator symbol.
3. Interior nodes represent computed values.

Dag Construction:

To construct a DAG for a basic block, we process each statement of the block in turn. When we see a statement of the form A : = B + C, we look for the following algorithm:

Input: A basic block.

Output: A DAG for the basic block containing the following information:

1. A label for each node. For leaves the label is an identifier (constants permitted), and for interior nodes, an operator symbol.
2. For each node a (possibly empty) list of attached identifiers (constants not permitted' here).

Rules: Suppose the three-address statement is either_(i) A = B+C (ii) A = op B (iii) A = B. We refer to these as cases (i), (ii), and (iii).

1. If node(B) is undefined, create a leaf labeled B, and let node(B) be this node. In case (i), if node (C) is undefined, create a leaf labeled z and let that leaf be node(C).
2. In case (I), determine if there is a node labeled 'op' whose left child is node(B) and whose right child is node(C). If not, create such a node. In case (ii), determine whether there is a node labeled 'op', whose one child is node (B). If not,create such a node.
3. Append A to the list of attached identifiers for the node found in (2) and set node (A)

Algorithm:

```
TYPE expr_kind IS (is_identifier, is_constant, is_operator, is_call);
TYPE expr_block(kind: expr_kind);
TYPE expr_tree IS ACCESS expr_block;
TYPE expr_block(kind: expr_kind) IS
 RECORD
```

```
CASE kind IS
 WHEN is_identifier =>
  entry: symbol;
 WHEN is_constant =>
  value: integer;
 WHEN is_operator =>
  op: operator;
  left, right: expr_tree;
 WHEN is_call =>
  subprogram: symbol;
  arguments: expr_tree_list;
END CASE;
END RECORD;
```

Example B1: DAG for expression t2 = a [t1]

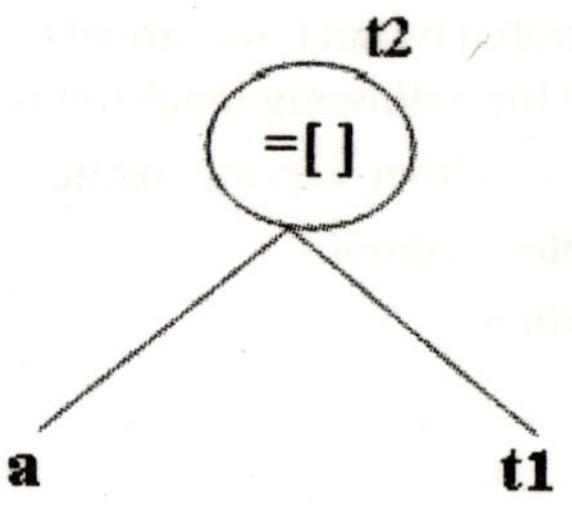

Figure B.1

Example B2: DAG for expression a [t2] = t1

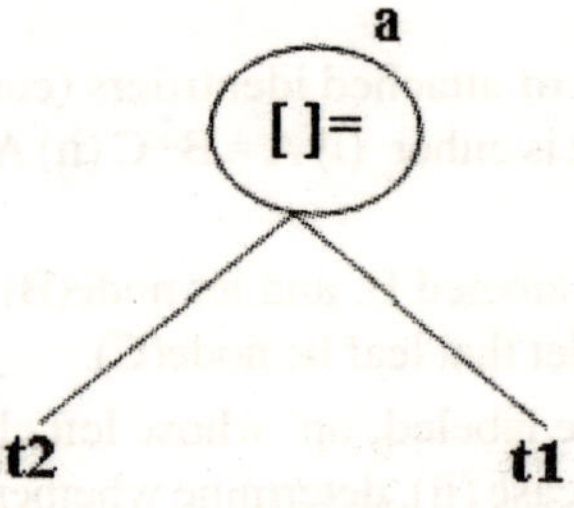

Figure B.2

Example B3: DAG for expressions

A [I] = B
*P = C
Z = A [J]
E = * P
*P = A [I]

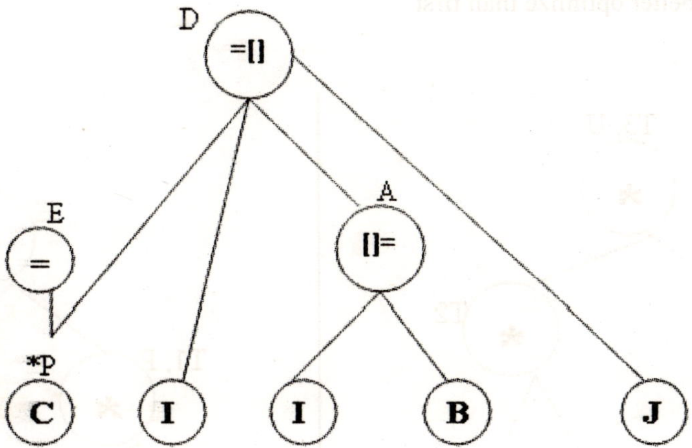

Figure B.3

B.2 Value Number:

In DAG, we check whether a node with specified node and a specified operator existed. It might appear that in order to implement this step the entire list of created nodes needs to be searched. For example, hash table can be used to enable us to make this determination almost instantaneous and the idea was termed the value number method. A node of the DAG is really just a pointer into an array i.e. a node is a number, either an absolute address or an index into an array whichever implementation is chosen by compiler writer.

Use of Hash Table as follow:

1. Given two nodes 'n' and 'm' we can hash the numbers representing 'n' and 'm' to obtain a pointer into a hash table where a list of nodes having 'n' and 'm' as children can be found immediately.
2. We could also involve the operator in the hash address, but it is unlikely that one basic block computes a collection of expression.
3. Group nodes with the same children but distinct operator.

B.3 The Use of Algebraic Identities:

Certain optimization are done on the basic of algebraic laws. For example, if we wish to create a node with left child 'x' and right child 'y' and with operator '+', we should check whether such a node already exists. But on most manipulation, some operator are commutative as '+', '*', '<', '>', '=', '≠', '≤', and '≥'. So we could also check a node with left child 'y' and right child 'x' and with operator '+' because of similar result.

Example:

We are constructing DAG for expression
P = Q * R

U = R * S * Q
In which second is better optimize than first.

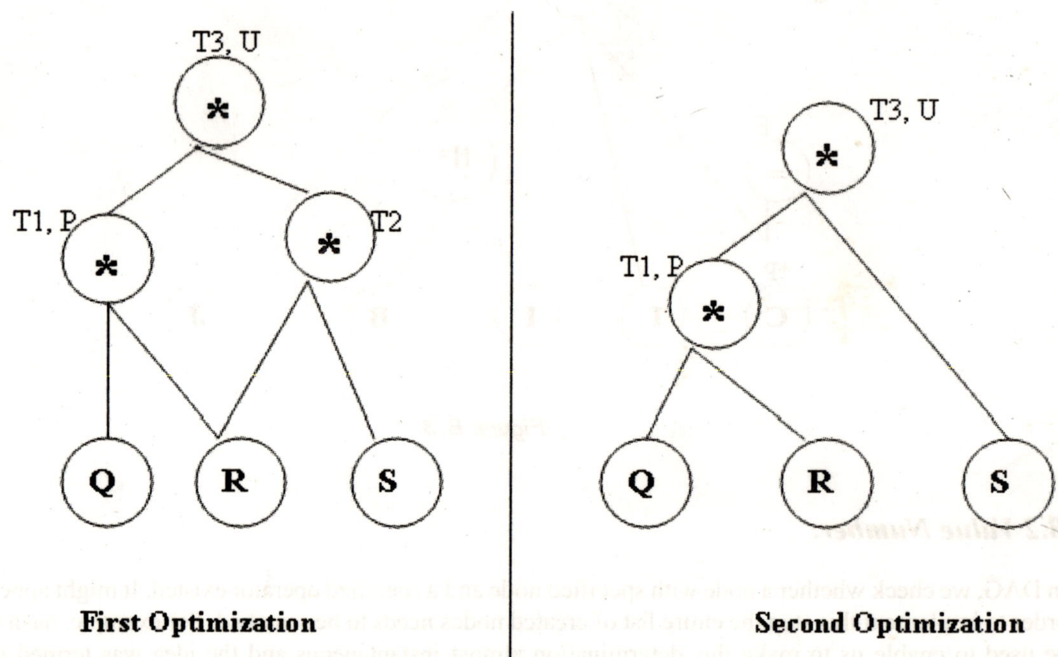

Figure B.4 Optimization using Algebraic Identities